The East Midlands from AD 1000

Regional History of England

General Editors: Barry Cunliffe and David Hey
For full details of the series, see pp. xviii–xix

The East Midlands
from AD 1000

J. V. Beckett

Longman
London and New York

Longman Group UK Limited
Longman House, Burnt Mill, Harlow,
Essex CM20 2JE, England
and Associated Companies throughout the world.

Published in the United States of America
by Longman Inc., New York

First published 1988

British Library Cataloguing in Publication Data

Beckett, J. V.
  The East Midlands from AD 1000. – (A
  Regional history of England)
  1. Midlands (England) – History
  I. Title   II. Series
  942.5   DA670.M64

ISBN 0-582-49269-6   CSD
ISBN 0-582-49270-X   PPR

Library of Congress Cataloging-in-Publication Data

Beckett, J. V.
  The East Midlands from AD 1000.

  (A Regional history of England)
  Bibliography: p.
  Includes index.
  1. Midlands (England) – History.   I. Title.
II. Series
DA670.M64B43   1988   942.3   87–2985
ISBN–0–582–49269–6
ISBN–0–582–49270–X (pbk.)

Set in Linotron 202 10/12 Sabon Roman
Produced by Longman Singapore Publishers (Pte) Ltd.
Printed in Singapore.

Contents

List of plates   ix
List of figures   xi
List of tables   xii
Preface   xiii
Acknowledgements   xv
General Preface   xvi
A Regional History of England series   xviii

Introduction   1

Part one:
The East Midlands, 1000–1500   11

Chapter 1
The Medieval Community   13
Population and Settlement   16
The Land and the People   22
The Lay Landlords   25
The Ecclesiastical Landlords   29
The People   33
Law and Order   42
Farming   46

Chapter 2
Prosperity and Decline, 1086–1348   52
Towns   53
Communications and Trade   67
Industry   71

Chapter 3
The Black Death and its Aftermath, 1348–1500   77
Population and Settlement   78

Landlords and Tenants   82
The Transition to Pasture   88
Urban Decay and Trade Depression   89
Industry   94

Part two:

The East Midlands in the Early Modern Period, 1500–1750   99

Chapter 4
The Land and the People   101
Population   103
The Church, the Dissolution of the Monasteries, and Local Society   105
The Landed Estates   108
The Homes of the Lower Orders   111
Local Government and Society   115
Farming   121

Chapter 5
Towns, Trade and Industry   131
Transport and Trade   145
Industry   154

Chapter 6
The East Midlands and the Nation   165
Reformation and Dissension   166
The Civil Wars   169
The Interregnum and Beyond   175

Part three:

The East Midlands in the Industrial Revolution, 1750–1900   187

Chapter 7
The Growth of a Regional Economy   189
Population   191
Land and People   195
Farming   200
Labour in the Countryside   208
Local Government in the Countryside   215
Education   219

Chapter 8
Towns   223
Urban Growth   223
The County Towns   225
Other Towns   232
The Market Towns   237
The Reform of the Corporations   239
The Corporations and the Drive for Improvement   244
Municipal Socialism   249
The Relief of Poverty   250
Education   253
Religion   256

Chapter 9
Communications, Trade and Industry   260
Transport   260
The Movement of People   267
The Movement of Goods   270
Industry   274
Coal   276
Iron and Steel   280
Lead and other Extractive Industries   282
Hosiery   284
Silk and Cotton   286
Lace and Elastic Web   290
Footwear and Engineering   291
Industrial Relations   293

Part four:
The East Midlands in the Twentieth Century   299

Chapter 10
Town and Country   301
Population   301
Towns   304
The County Capitals   307
Other Towns   311
Local Government   315
The Countryside   320
Farming   324

Chapter 11
Transport and Industry   327
Transport   327
Industry   331

Coal   335
Iron, Steel and Lead   341
Other Heavy Industries   343
Textiles   344
Footwear and Engineering   348

Epilogue
The East Midlands Today   350

Appendix: Population in the East Midlands, 1086–1981   354
Bibliography   357
Index   381

List of plates

1.1 Barton-upon-Humber Church, Lincolnshire   14
1.2 Oakham Castle, Rutland   23
1.3 The Castle of the Peak, Derbyshire   27
1.4 Steetley Chapel, Derbyshire   36
1.5 Laxton, Nottinghamshire, the South Field   48
2.1 Lincoln Cathedral   55
2.2 Boston, Lincolnshire   65
2.3 Heckington Church, Lincolnshire   74
3.1 Kirby Muxloe Castle, Leicestershire   84
3.2 St Mary's, Nottingham   91
3.3 Derbyshire Alabaster   97
4.1 Wollaton Hall, Nottingham   110
4.2 Cob and brick housing, Melbourne, Derbyshire   113
4.3 Excerpt from the Town Book, Ashby-de-la-Zouch, Leicestershire   120
4.4 Fen drainage, Crowland, Lincolnshire   126
5.1 The Bull Running, Stamford   138
5.2 Newark Market Place, c. 1778   142
5.3 Thomas Sandby's prospect of Nottingham, 1751   152
5.4 Derby, the Silk Mill   159
6.1 The Queen's Sconce, Newark   173
6.2 Field Row Chapel, Belper, Derbyshire   178
6.3 Ashbourne, Derbyshire   183
7.1 Thoresby Hall, Nottinghamshire   196
7.2 The impact of enclosure, Taddington, Derbyshire   202
7.3 Grimsthorpe, Lincolnshire, 1905   206
7.4 Harlaxton, Lincolnshire   211
7.5 Lincoln Prison: the chapel   216
8.1 Sketch of the interior of John Barker's bath, Buxton   236
8.2 Mansfield Town Hall   242
8.3 Victoria Dwellings, Nottingham   248
8.4 Derby, the Porcelain Factory   251

9.1 Detail from the Earl of Scarbrough's development plan for
      Skegness 269
9.2 A Stilton cheese fair, Melton Mowbray, Leicestershire 273
9.3 Cromford Mill, *c.* 1783 287
9.4 Chartism, an editorial from the *Nottingham Review*, 1838 294
10.1 The Boots site, Beeston, Nottingham 308
10.2 Grimsby, the docks 312
10.3 Loading blooms at Spalding Station just before the First World
      War 326
11.1 Ratcliffe-on-Soar power station 332
11.2 The coal strike, Nottinghamshire, 1984 340
11.3 Nottingham Forest F.C. 352

List of figures

1.1 Relief, principal towns and roads in the East Midlands 4
1.2 The distribution of population in the East Midlands in 1086 17
2.1 Medieval Lincoln, c. 1300 57
2.2 Medieval markets in the East Midlands 60
3.1 Ingarsby: a deserted village site 80
5.1 Leicester in 1722 136–7
6.1 Civil War sites in the East Midlands 170
7.1 Population growth in the East Midlands, 1801–1971 192
8.1 The growth of Nottingham, 1771–1980 226
8.2 Urban expansion in the East Midlands, 1771–1980 (selected towns) 230–1
9.1 Turnpikes in the East Midlands, c. 1700–1830 261
9.2 The principal waterways in the East Midlands, c. 1830 264
9.3 Railways in the East Midlands in the nineteenth century 266
9.4 Mineral deposits in the East Midlands 278
10.1 The growth of Derby, 1877–1934 310

List of tables

1 Recorded settlements in Domesday   18
2 Rural population at Domesday   34
3 Medieval boroughs in the East Midlands   59
4 Markets founded in the East Midlands, c. 1200–1349   62
5 Deserted medieval villages in the East Midlands   81
6 Municipal corporations in the East Midlands by 1835   133
7 Specialities of market towns in the East Midlands, 1500–1640   144
8 Principal destinations of road carrying services from London to the East Midlands, 1715   148
9 Conformists and nonconformists in the East Midlands, 1676   179
10 Population and physical size of the East Midlands counties   193
11 Migration into Nottinghamshire mining villages, 1881   194
12 Estate sizes as a proportion of total area, 1873   198
13 Parliamentary enclosure in the East Midlands (total enclosure in specific time periods as a proportion of parliamentary enclosure)   201
14 Land utilization in the East Midlands, 1870–1900   207
15 Numbers of (male) rural craftsmen in Rutland, 1851–1931   209
16 Local government in 1900   219
17 Proportion of population living in the five largest towns of each county   224
18 East Midlands fairs   238
19 The structure of population in the East Midlands in the twentieth century   302
20 The proportion of the occupied population engaged in agriculture, 1951–61   322
21 The fate of a sample of East Midlands country houses, 1880–1980   323
22 Cotton manufacturers in the East Midlands   347

Preface

Anyone brought up in Nottingham, as I was, is well aware that it is part of the East Midlands. However, it was only in 1981 when I began to teach an undergraduate course on the history of the East Midlands that I became aware of how vague is most peoples' notion of the geographical location of the area. Since 1981 generations of undergraduates, and postgraduates reading the M.A. in Local and Regional History at Nottingham, have had to put up with my efforts to persuade them that the region exists and that it has a history of its own. For the many questions that they have raised, and for the contribution that they have made to my knowledge of the region through their essays and dissertations, I should like to thank them, and to add that I hope I have not misrepresented their findings. I should like to express a similar sentiment towards the multitude of local historians whose contributions have helped to round out my view of the region, and the fruits of whose labours are recorded in the bibliography. Without their efforts this book would have been very much more difficult to write.

My task of tracking down the relevant material has been greatly aided by close proximity to the University of Nottingham's local studies library. The 'East Midlands Collection' of books, articles and pamphlets relating to the historic counties of Derbyshire, Leicestershire, Lincolnshire, Nottinghamshire and Rutland was started in 1930 as the result of a gift from Mr B. B. Granger of 242 volumes of local history books. Since that time it has been expanded into a major resource, and I should like to take this opportunity of thanking the University Librarian Mr Peter Hoare for his decision to maintain funding of the collection despite the financial constraints under which the Library has operated in recent years. Mr Michael Brook, the East Midlands Collection librarian, has been immensely helpful in drawing my attention to some of the more obscurely placed items, and I am thankful to him for his patience with my exhausting requests, and also for checking the bibliography of this volume.

Various people have helped me during the writing of this book by providing information or reading draft chapters of my manuscript. I should particularly like to thank Sheila Cook, Alan Griffin, Danuta Januszonok and

Kate Thompson for providing information, and Rita Holt for preparing the graphs. Colleagues and friends who were kind enough to read and comment on the text included Alan Cameron (Part one), Peter Seddon (Part two) and Professor R. H. Osborne (Part four). Professor Maurice Barley kindly provided me with a number of references, and read the whole manuscript. John Heath was enormously helpful, preparing material for two of the maps, providing plates, and commenting on the whole manuscript. The General Editor, Dr David Hey, willingly read all of the manuscript (some parts more than once) – and kept me up to the mark by some discreet entertaining when we met at conferences. Writing a book like this, which draws so heavily on other peoples' works, leaves me open to the obvious accusation of misrepresentation. I am, however, wholly responsible for any errors of fact or omission which may have crept into the text.

Acknowledgements

The publishers would like to acknowledge the following for their permission to use plates in the text: Aerofilms (4.4); Associated Press (11.3); The Boots Company PLC (10.1); BBC Hulton Picture Library (1.4); Camera Press and T. Marshall (photographer) (11.2); CEGB (11.1); Crown Copyright Reserved (1.3, 1.5, 6.1 and 7.2); Derbyshire Museum Service (1.4 and 8.1); M. J. Elsden, Chameleon International (10.3); John Heath (2.1, 4.2, 8.2, 8.4 and 9.4); A. F. Kersting (1.1, 1.2, 2.3, 3.1 and 7.5); Leicestershire Museums, Art Galleries and Records Service (4.3 and 9.2); Lord Scarbrough and John Heath (photographer) (9.1); Manuscripts Department, University of Nottingham (5.3, 5.4, 6.3 and 8.4); Mary Evans Picture Library (2.2); National Buildings Record (7.4); Nottingham County Museums (4.1); Nottinghamshire County Library Service (3.2, 5.2, 7.1 and 8.3); D. N. Robinson Collection, Louth, Lincolnshire (10.2); Royal Commission on the Historical Monuments of England (6.2); Stamford Museum, Lincolnshire (5.1); the Willoughby Memorial Trust and John Armstrong (7.3).

The publishers would also like to thank Methuen, London, for permission to reproduce figure 5.1.

General Preface

England cannot be divided satisfactorily into recognizable regions based on former kingdoms or principalities in the manner of France, Germany or Italy. Few of the Anglo-Saxon tribal divisions had much meaning in later times and from the eleventh century onwards England was a united country. English regional identities are imprecise and no firm boundaries can be drawn. In planning this series we have recognized that any attempt to define a region must be somewhat arbitrary, particularly in the Midlands, and that boundaries must be flexible. Even the South-West, which is surrounded on three sides by the sea, has no agreed border on the remaining side and in many ways, historically and culturally, the River Tamar divides the area into two. Likewise, the Pennines present a formidable barrier between the eastern and western counties on the Northern Borders; contrasts as much as similarities need to be emphasized here.

The concept of a region does not imply that the inhabitants had a similar experience of life, nor that they were all inward-looking. A Hull merchant might have more in common with his Dutch trading partner than with his fellow Yorkshireman who farmed a Pennine smallholding: a Roman soldier stationed for years on Hadrian's Wall probably had very different ethnic origins from a native farmer living on the Durham boulder clay. To differing degrees, everyone moved in an international climate of belief and opinion with common working practices and standards of living.

Yet regional differences were nonetheless real; even today a Yorkshireman may be readily distinguished from someone from the South East. Life in Lancashire and Cheshire has always been different from life in the Thames Valley. Even the East Midlands has a character that is subtly different from that of the West Midlands. People still feel that they belong to a particular region within England as a whole.

In writing these histories we have become aware how much regional identities may vary over time; moreover how a farming region, say, may not coincide with a region defined by its building styles or its dialect. We have dwelt upon the diversity that can be found within a region as well as upon common characteristics in order to illustrate the local peculiarities of provincial life. Yet despite all these problems of definition, we feel that the time is ripe to attempt an ambitious scheme outlining the history of England's regions in twenty-one volumes. London has not been included – except for demonstrating the many ways in which it has influenced the provinces – for its history has been very different from that of the towns and rural parishes that are our principal concern.

In recent years an enormous amount of local research, both historical and archaeological, has deepened our understanding of the former concerns of ordinary men and women and has altered our perception of everyday life in the past in many significant ways, yet the results of this work are not widely known even within the regions themselves.

This series offers a synthesis of this new work from authors who have themselves been actively involved in local research and who are present in or former residents of the regions they describe.

Each region will be covered in two linked but independent volumes, the first covering the period up to AD 1000 and necessarily relying heavily on archaeological data, and the second bringing the story up to the present day. Only by taking a wide time-span and by studying continuity and change over many centuries do distinctive regional characteristics become clear.

This series portrays life as it was experienced by the great majority of the people of South Britain or England as it was to become. The twenty-one volumes will – it is hoped – substantially enrich our understanding of English history.

Barry Cunliffe
David Hey

A Regional History of England

General Editors: Barry Cunliffe (to AD 1000) and David Hey (from AD 1000)

The regionalisation used in this series is illustrated on the map opposite.

*The Northern Counties to AD 1000   *Nick Higham*
The Northern Counties from AD 1000   *Norman McCord & Richard Thompson*

The Lancashire/Cheshire Region to AD 1550   *G. D. B. Jones with Denise Kenyon & Nick Higham*
The Lancashire/Cheshire Region from AD 1550   *John Smith & Colin Phillips*

Yorkshire to AD 1000   *T. G. Manby*
*Yorkshire from AD 1000   *David Hey*

The Severn Valley and West Midlands to AD 1000   *R. T. Rowley*
*The West Midlands from AD 1000   *Marie B. Rowlands*
The Welsh Borders from AD 1000   *R. T. Rowley*

The East Midlands to AD 1000   *Jeffrey May*
*The East Midlands from AD 1000   *J. V. Beckett*

The South Midlands and Upper Thames to AD 1000   *David Miles*
The South Midlands and Upper Thames from AD 1000   *John Broad*

The Eastern Counties to AD 1000   *W. J. Rodwell*
The Eastern Counties from AD 1000   *B. A. Holderness*

*The South West to AD 1000   *Malcolm Todd*
The South West from AD 1000   *Bruce Coleman & R. A. Higham*

Wessex to AD 1000   *Barry Cunliffe*
*Wessex from AD 1000   *J. H. Bettey*

*The South East to AD 1000   *Peter Drewett, David Rudling & Mark Gardiner*
The South East from AD 1000   *Peter Brandon & Brian Short*

*already published

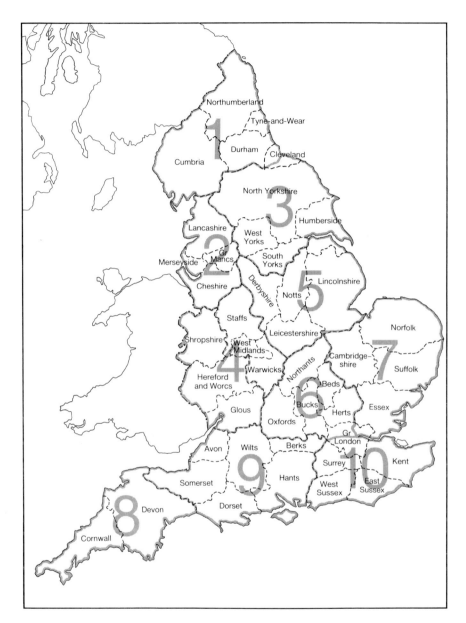

1. The Northern Counties
2. The Lancashire/Cheshire Region
3. Yorkshire
4. The Severn Valley and West Midlands
5. The East Midlands
6. The South Midlands and the Upper Thames
7. The Eastern Counties
8. The South West
9. Wessex
10. The South East

For Alison and Paul

and for Irene

Introduction

Traditionally, regions have not been particularly significant in an English context. Phrases such as Tyneside, Merseyside, or even East Midlands, do not have a lengthy heritage; rather, they are modern creations of varying historical value. In part this reflects the lack of government interest before the twentieth century in administrative units larger than the county, except occasionally for military purposes: Oliver Cromwell, for example, divided the country up regionally during the rule of the major-generals in the 1650s; regional units were used during the Napoleonic invasion scare of 1803; and Civil Defence regions were established shortly after the Second World War. After 1945 regional areas began to take preference over counties for a number of public services including gas, electricity and health; and for administrative purposes 'standard regions' have existed since 1946 (Gilbert 1960: 169–70). However, regional planning has largely been abandoned since 1979.

Under these circumstances the historical study of regions raises far more problems than a similar undertaking in France. Identifying the region is the first difficulty. Some years ago the geographer G. W. S. Robinson argued that the concept of the region was 'fatally difficult to define with precision and comprehension', with the result that geographers had divided the world into an infinite number of regions based upon a long list of different criteria (Robinson 1953: 49, 51). It is a problem with which historians also have to grapple. As Alan Everitt has warned, the use of modern regional terms may be imposing

> the wrong kind of regional pattern upon the landscape of history . . . the basic regional pattern in this country has in many ways not remained constant; it has been an evolutionary pattern. Not only have regional boundaries changed; at a more fundamental level, new kinds or types of region have from time to time come into existence and overlaid or transformed the old.
>
> (Everitt 1979: 80–1)

As he has written elsewhere, this process of overlay has included the rise of regional capitals exercising a widespread influence over a surrounding hinter-

1

land, which have tended to blot out the more clear-cut natural regions of the past (Everitt 1977: 19). In these circumstances the subject-matter of regional history has been easier to define than the boundaries of study. In the words of J. D. Marshall, 'an historic region relates to some kind of large, extended community of interest and people. It is the community side of it which should interest us.' Thus the physical boundary of a region can be a shifting phenomenon since the historian 'has to be prepared to study whole patterns of historical development across large tracts of the English countryside' (Marshall 1978a: 5–6).

In the light of these strictures the historical study of regions has to embrace a dual approach; on the one hand it is the study of a community or groups of communities in terms of their intra-dependence, and on the other hand it is the study of events and issues within a regional context. With these boundaries in mind three types of historical region have been studied. *Formal* regions have been the most attractive to historians, since they are based on areas delineated by recognizable boundaries such as the parish or the county. Studies of the latter were once the most popular form of local history, reaching their apogee in the volumes of the *Victoria County History*. *Natural* regions can be based on soil, geological structure, topography, landownership and the traditional concept of the countryside or *pays*, as well as the more nebulous idea of consciousness. Such regions seldom conformed to county boundaries; indeed, according to Everitt they formed 'a pattern of sharply-localized contrasts . . . more closely resembling the geological map than that of our modern regions or our ancient counties and kingdoms' (Everitt 1979: 83). Both formal and natural regions relate to geographically definable areas, but the third type of region, the *functional* region, can vary in shape and size. Whether it is politics, economics, trade, industry or agriculture, the spatial context can change to fit the issue under consideration. Whichever type of region is studied the historian's task is first to demonstrate a distinctive intra-dependence within the region; and second to set it in a wider comparative context, much as national history has to be written with reference to the international arena.

Of the existence of the East Midlands in the 1980s there can be little doubt. Apart from an airport, it has a series of organizations and services which proclaim themselves to be 'East Midlands' in one way or another. However, it is neither a formal nor a natural region, and this makes a clear spatial definition problematical. Professor K. C. Edwards, founder and first editor of the *East Midlands Geographer*, chose to incorporate within the region the historic counties of Derbyshire, Leicestershire, Lincolnshire, Northamptonshire, Nottinghamshire and Rutland, on the grounds that since this was the 1939 administrative unit for Civil Defence it was 'functionally coherent' (Edwards 1954). Others have been less fastidious in their definition. East Midlands has been used as a shorthand term 'for the sake of convenience' (Holderness 1979: 27), it has been extended beyond Edwards's definition to include Bedfordshire, Huntingdonshire, Buckinghamshire and Oxfordshire (Dury 1963: 1), or even to include the whole area from the Trent to the Thames (Hadfield 1966); and it has been contracted by omitting the Lincolnshire fenlands (Hoskins 1951; Thirsk 1985: I, 89), or by concentrating merely on Derbyshire, Leicestershire and Nottinghamshire (Anderson 1985).

Any definition which incorporates spatially definable limits is bound to be controversial, but for the purpose of this study the East Midlands is taken to be a loosely constructed area within the boundaries of the historic counties of Derbyshire, Leicestershire, Lincolnshire, Nottinghamshire and Rutland. It is an area bounded by the Peak District hills to the north-west, by the Yorkshire border and the river Humber to the north, by the sea to the east, and by an imaginary line through the fen and forest to the south, drawn roughly along the river Welland and the Leicestershire–Northamptonshire border. The omission of Northamptonshire partly reflects the requirements of the series in which this book appears, but also the weakness of the historical links which have sometimes given it a place within the East Midlands. In any case these boundaries are merely guideposts; areas within them which historically looked to other regions for their identity, such as north-west Derbyshire, are hardly touched upon, while issues which demand a broader spectrum will inevitably overlap these lines of demarcation.

In what, if any, senses can this area be regarded as a *formal* region? The earliest example of an east midlands region came towards the end of the ninth century when Danish invaders enforced the partition of Mercia in order to set up the Danelaw, an area where Danish laws and customs predominated. This area was roughly contiguous with the East Midlands counties, and was administered through the five boroughs of Nottingham, Derby, Lincoln, Leicester and Stamford. Place-name evidence points to the impressive strength of Danish influence, for example, in the naming of the basic administrative features of the shires, and in the overall number of names which include Scandinavian compounds and inflexions. It suggests that in the wake of the invading army considerable immigration into the area took place, particularly in the Lincolnshire wolds, and more generally in the eastern part of the region (Cameron 1965). However, the Danelaw was destined to last for only a brief period, and early in the tenth century the East Midland counties were incorporated into the kingdom of the English, ruled by the kings of Wessex. The area was then divided for administrative purposes into shires, similar to those of Saxon Wessex, based on the Danish boroughs. The counties of Derbyshire, Leicestershire and Nottinghamshire probably evolved during the tenth century. Nottinghamshire was a county by 1016 and Derbyshire by 1049, although both may have been founded anything up to a century earlier.

The formation of Lincolnshire and Rutland came later. By 1086 the names Lincolnshire and Lindsey were still used interchangeably. This was

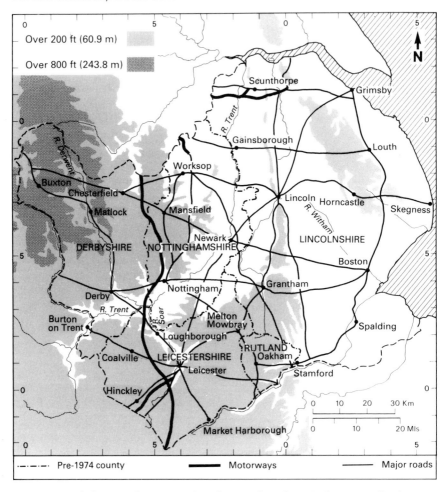

Figure 1.1   Relief, principal towns, roads and county bounderies in the East Midlands

probably a result of the position of Stamford. Alone among the Danelaw boroughs Stamford today is not a county town, but at one time it almost certainly had a shire of its own, containing part of what was later to be Rutland. As a separate county Rutland came into being by the twelfth century, but at Domesday it was still territorially divided. The northern section, *Roteland*, was fiscally accountable to Nottinghamshire, while the southern area known as Witchley formed the northern part of Northamptonshire. It is at least conceivable that Rutland's origin as a county ought not to be sought in the administrative reorganization of the tenth century which was important for the other East Midlands counties, but much earlier. However, its independent status when Kesteven and Holland were added to Lindsey to form Lincolnshire produced the peculiar situation which lasted until 1974 whereby the second largest English county lay contiguous with the smallest (Stafford 1985: 122–7, 141–2; Phythian-Adams 1977: 63–84).

The counties themselves, however, had few formal links, and those which have been established from time to time have usually included North-amptonshire. This was true, for example, of both the old Civil Defence region, and the Treasury's post-1946 standard region. Moreover, the definition of the East Midlands employed here does not coincide with either the redefinition of the standard region drawn up in 1966, or with the post-1974 region, since in both cases a dividing line drawn across Lincolnshire and Northamptonshire is included. But these variable lines show how misleading an arbitrary cluster of counties can be, and since current definitions mean little for the past there is no reason why they should be followed.

What the historic East Midlands obviously lacks, which is an essential component of the modern region, is a capital city. Nottingham can probably sustain the best claim to filling this role in the twentieth century, and in the past since its influence spread well beyond its physical boundaries. By the 1950s Nottingham's morning newspapers circulated through almost the entire re-gion, except for parts of north Lincolnshire, western Derbyshire, and western and southern Leicestershire (Edwards 1954: 4). However, Nottingham is clearly not in the same relationship to the East Midlands as Birmingham is to the West Midlands. The close proximity of Nottingham to two other major urban centres, Derby and Leicester, whose growth patterns have been similar, has ensured that no single town has been able to play a particularly dominant regional role.

If the East Midlands is not a formal region, what claim does it have to be regarded as a *natural* one? Physically it includes a variety of types of country-side, ranging from the Derbyshire uplands in the north-west with a mean altitude of 1,000 ft, to the featureless levels of the Lincolnshire fens in the east, large areas of which are below 20 ft above sea-level. Even so, much of the area has a physiographic unity rooted in its geological history. The region has a diverse variety of mineral resources. Coal is found in the Erewash valley, which stretches from the west side of Nottingham along the line of the river Erewash into Yorkshire, and in the area south-east of Burton on Trent straddling the Derbyshire–Leicestershire border around Ashby de la Zouch. The Notting-hamshire and south Yorkshire coal measures dip eastwards under Lincoln-shire, but despite a number of trial borings no workable seams have been found at economic depths (Wright 1982: 59). Iron has been mined both on the Derbyshire coalfield and, since the nineteenth century, between north Lincoln-shire and Northamptonshire (including workings around Scunthorpe, in east Leicestershire, in Kesteven and in Rutland). In Derbyshire lead has been worked in an area roughly bounded by Castleton to the north, Buxton to the west, Wirksworth to the south, and by the river Derwent to the east. In addition, limestone, gypsum, and brick, pottery and pipemaking clays have all been worked in the region at different periods (Swinnerton 1929; Edwards 1954: 8).

Geologically, much of the East Midlands lies on the great Jurassic limestone belt running from the south-west to the north-east across the country. It enters the region from Northamptonshire, and runs through Rutland and much of eastern Leicestershire, and in a somewhat narrower belt northwards to the west of Lincoln, eventually crossing the Humber into Yorkshire. This belt of limestone had a significant impact on local building practices, accounting, for example, for the marvellous collection of richly coloured medieval churches in southern Lincolnshire. Marlstone has been worked in parts of eastern Leicestershire and western Rutland, while a belt of magnesian limestone runs from just north of Nottingham along the border with Derbyshire between Mansfield, Bolsover and Worksop to enter Yorkshire. Sandstone, which is found in south Derbyshire and the western half of Leicestershire, dominates Nottinghamshire. If Lincoln Cathedral is a tribute to limestone, Southwell Minster reflects the sandstone quarries in the Mansfield area, particularly, in this instance, White Mansfield, even though the majority of Nottinghamshire's churches are built of New Red sandstone from the same areas. Finally, granite has been worked in north-west Leicestershire, and alabaster in the Trent valley (Clifton-Taylor 1972).

Soil conditions vary considerably within the region, although they fall generally into the broad zonal type known as Brown Forest soils. Edwards has classified the region into nine major soil groups (Edwards 1948: 1, 10), and this variety, coupled with the fact that since there is little rugged or unsuitable countryside agriculture has occupied a high proportion of the total surface area (Edwards 1954: 8), has led to many different types of farming being practised in the region. Boulder clay is found in much of east and north Leicestershire and south Nottinghamshire, while both Charnwood and Sherwood Forests are located on poorer soils. Fertile keuper marls are found in parts of Leicestershire. East of Nottingham rich alluvial soils are found in the flat Vale of Trent, while chalky boulder clay characterizes both the cliff area north of Lincoln, and the heath south of the city. Further east are the Lincolnshire wolds, roughly eight miles in width and forty-five miles in length, with a generally thin and chalky surface. Between the wolds and the coast is a narrow strip of marshland, low-lying and covered with boulder clay, with patches of sand and gravel, and with rich alluvial silts near to the shore. Further south, towards the Wash, are the fenlands, with their distinctive dark-coloured peats and silts (Thirsk 1985: I, 92–3).

As a region of mixed soils and varied relief the East Midlands supported a wide range of farming practice, usually combining crops with livestock. In terms of land use most important were the clayland vales and alluvial river valley bottoms, the home of the classical midlands open-field system. The lowland mixed arable and pasture area covered much of Leicestershire, eastern Nottinghamshire, and Lincolnshire west of the cliff and heath, as well as other parts of Lincolnshire. Mixed farming also took place in north-east Derbyshire bordering on Sherwood Forest, and in the south in the Trent valley adjacent to north-west Leicestershire. Anything up to three-quarters of the region was in open-field mixed farming down to the mid-eighteenth century, with a rough conformity of field systems. However, farming practices have varied from the most primitive to the most advanced at various times (Thirsk 1973a). In Derbyshire sheep farming has been a major activity on the limestone pastures of the county's uplands, and on the red marls and alluvium of the lowland areas between the Derwent and the Dove. Nottinghamshire farming has varied: convertible husbandry, based on a breck system, was found on the Bunter sandstone in the Sherwood Forest area; rich alluvial dairy and mixed farms were found on the clays and loams of the Trent valley; grain farming pre-dominated on the keuper marls in the centre of the county; and permanent pastures for sheep and cattle were to be found on the deep heavy clays straddling the Leicestershire border (Chambers 1957: 38). The relatively heavy soils of the Vale of Belvoir in east Leicestershire and the adjoining parts of Rutland have acquired a reputation for their fattening pastures, and the whole area constitutes part of the 'Midland grass counties' (Edwards 1954: 8). The chalk wolds of north-east Lincolnshire have traditionally been dominated by a sheep and barley economy, while a substantial area to the east of the Trent more or less surrounding the cliff and heath has traditionally been mixed farming country. The coastal marshlands provided excellent grazing lands, while the fens have gradually become intensively worked arable with over 75 per cent of the acreage under the plough. However, this has been possible only since improved drainage was introduced into the area late in the nineteenth century (Beastall 1978: 1–4).

The diversity of soil types and farming practices suggests that the East Midlands is physically too broad and amorphous to be regarded as a *natural* region, so can it therefore be seen as having a *functional* identity? Answering this question raises the two fundamental issues which underlie what follows. First, the question arises of the sense of region involved in dealing with these five counties, and whether writing about them as a region is a viable exercise. Are they coherent in any sense and at any time, or is the identity of the region a fiction? Unlike more obvious regions such as Tyneside and Yorkshire, the East Midlands today lacks a positive cultural identity (although negatively it is clearly different from Yorkshire and from the West Midlands), and few local people appear to have much conception of how far the area extends. It is, however, a generic term of some significance both in the twentieth century for identification purposes, and in the past for trading and to a lesser extent cultural reasons. As will become clear in the course of this book, the road and water communications of the area always exercised an influence on trade and on local connections. While it has no political or administrative unity, the region has enjoyed economic interaction. From the eleventh century when lead, wool and other commodities were carried east from the Peak District to

Boston in return for grain and other commodities, the central artery of the river Trent has continued to play an important role in fostering intra-regional activity. Thereafter down to the nineteenth century the Trent played a major communications role, facilitating the exchange of goods within the region. As urban areas grew, agricultural goods from Lincolnshire and eastern Leicestershire were exchanged for coal and iron, and economic opportunities opened up for those people prepared to migrate towards Nottingham, Leicester and Derby. How far the region became intra-dependent as a result of these opportunities is a question this book will seek to answer. Only since the coming of the railway, and, in the twentieth century, the internal combustion engine, have these connections weakened.

The second question links with this first one but not always in a clear-cut fashion, and it concerns the shift of emphasis in the region between east and west. In the first two centuries of our period Lincolnshire was by far the most advanced, populous and wealthy part of the region. Although the calculations are inevitably based on less than ideal data, it is possible that nearly two-thirds of the total regional population lived in Lincolnshire at Domesday, and this may have risen to 70 per cent by 1340. In 1086 the main towns, with the exception of Leicester, were situated in Lincolnshire, while the county town itself stood second or third to London. The decision to move the see of Dorchester to Lincoln in 1092–93 is evidence of the town's regional importance. By contrast, today fewer people live in Lincolnshire than in Derbyshire, Leicestershire, or Nottinghamshire, and even in 1971, before the radical boundary changes of 1974, just 23 per cent of the region's population lived in the county. Lincoln is no longer the largest town in its own county let alone the region, and it is far smaller than the county towns of Derby, Leicester and Nottingham. Population figures are not the only way of assessing the extent of change, but they do show a trend which has to be explained, since they largely reflect what has become the local bias of industry to settle in the urban area roughly extending from Leicester, Hinckley and Coalville in the south to Mansfield and Chesterfield in the north. Thus, as the region has developed from its medieval rural base, industrial growth has tended to alter the distribution of people within the area. But this is to anticipate, and first an attempt must be made to outline the framework of the following chapters.

Part One examines the region in what might loosely be termed the period of the manor and the local market. Although the extent of parochialism in this period must not be overplayed, since there is at least the hint of geographical and cultural unity, in medieval England even the concept of the county was sometimes of dubious value. Lincolnshire was formed by the last Saxon kings sometime between 1016 and 1086 when the two areas north and south of the river Witham were merged for administrative purposes. Even in the fourteenth century, however, there is evidence to suggest that the people of Kesteven looked to Stamford rather than to Lincoln as the focus of their region, and the sense of county community developed generally only during the fourteenth and

fifteenth centuries (Platts 1985: 1, 6). Perhaps the most interesting development in this period was in the exchange of goods. If subsistence farming was
still the major concern of the great majority of people the growth of market
towns suggests a dynamism in the local economy, particularly in Lincolnshire,
which was not necessarily limited to the major commercial concerns. On the
other hand, the dynamism was largely a product of the twelfth and thirteenth
centuries. The regional economy was already in trouble before the Black Death
arrived in 1348 and ushered in one hundred and fifty years of stagnation.

A second stage was reached about 1500 when the manor came to be
superseded by the local market with a hinterland of fifty to a hundred square
miles. This stage of development is the subject matter of Part Two. It involved
the invention of more sophisticated marketing procedures, as well as efforts to
tap resources and to increase the agricultural surplus, something which was
partly achieved by a reorganization of farming (Kerridge 1967). The town
acted both to exploit the hinterland, and also to stimulate economic development. Through its role as a market for rural produce, and as a focal point for
the communications network it allowed specialization to take place within the
rural economy, and this helped to promote efficiency and improvement. Even
in this parasitic role the town may have been performing a useful service, since
it consumed and redistributed the surplus products of the countryside which
might otherwise have sustained a higher rural population and have put pressure on agricultural resources (Abrams and Wrigley 1978).

Part Three moves the account forward into the classic industrial revolution period, although major developments of this nature reached the East
Midlands relatively late. Improved road and water communications facilitated
intra-regional communication and economic specialization. However, transport costs remained a crucial variable, particularly for those industries dealing
with one or two bulky raw materials. As a result, the degree of regional
specialization remained high, although improved technology brought about a
change in the relationship between town and country. Pre-industrialized
manufacturing relied heavily upon the products of the land for raw materials,
but this dependence gradually weakened. In addition, improved agricultural
technology pushed up productivity, thereby breaking the traditionally low
levels of achievement which had restricted town growth. No longer was it
necessary for urban populations to be a minority of the population. From the
1840s the railway began to undermine the distinctive regionalism of the canal
era between 1760 and 1830, although initially the highly fragmented nature of
the system and the differential freight pricing policies tended to strengthen
intra-regional trade (Aldcroft and Freeman 1983).

Finally, Part Four of the book is roughly coterminous with the twentieth
century. Restraints on location have gradually fallen away as a result of the
increasing use of electricity and oil (thereby reducing dependence on coal), and
lower transport costs (through road haulage). Industries have broken free from
the constraints which shackled their predecessors, hence the partial movement

of hosiery production away from its traditional base in the East Midlands during the 1960s. As towns have become the dominant centres of population and industry in the region the focus of local activities has changed. Rather than each area having an important settlement upon which its activities have centred, each town has come to have a satellite region around it; hence the titles of recent books prepared in advance of British Association meetings, *Nottingham and its Region*, and *Leicester and its Region*.

This four-stage process depicts the origin, growth, heyday and in some senses the demise of the region as, in the latter case, national specialization has been able to supersede regionalism. The *uniform* regions of the pre-industrial period, with their dependence on the county town, gradually gave way to a series of *functional* units. Initially the restrictions of transport produced separate, highly distinctive, regional units, usually based on an important urban settlement (although this did not need to be a county town). As communications improved, these traditional regions were replaced by functional areas with perhaps one or two major towns or cities dominating a whole regional unit. The chief consequence was that a high level of inter-dependence replaced the lower levels of pre-industrial society. What has arisen since the Second World War is the question of why, when locational constraints have largely been eroded, some regions of the country have prospered but others have declined. This has been attributed to inherited industrial structures, the role of corporate change in the economy, and the effect of government policy (Law 1980). Arguably, as will become clear in the pages which follow, the idea of the East Midlands has become more consciously accepted at just the time when the constraints which had dictated local and regional interlinking are falling away.

Part one

The East Midlands, 1000–1500

Chapter 1

The Medieval Community

In the year AD 1000 the face of England bore little physical resemblance to its twentieth-century counterpart. Late Saxon and Norman England was a backward and underdeveloped land, where a considerable acreage had to be cultivated, and labour expended, in order to sustain what from this distance in time seems to have been a tiny population. The great majority of people satisfied their needs from the land, and in relative terms the country enjoyed little trade or industry. Even the government was scarcely recognizable by comparison with a modern state, although pre-Conquest kings were able to exert their authority over most local magnates. This was true, for example, of the Danelaw, the area recognizable today as the East Midlands. It had been brought into the kingdom of the English early in the tenth century, but it still retained a cultural identity dating from the intensive settlement of the Danelaw period, which marked it off from Yorkshire, the West Midlands and the south. The Anglo-Danish-Norman mix produced a linguistic affinity which continued into the twelfth century, and which points towards the existence of a regional identity from the beginning of our period.

When William the Conqueror swept into England in 1066 he found a country sparsely populated but relatively wealthy by comparison with other parts of Europe. Just how sparse and how wealthy would still be a mystery but for the new monarch's wish to find out more about his kingdom. The practical outcome of this desire was the great Domesday survey of the land undertaken twenty years after he came to the throne. The survey offers a unique picture, a pen-portrait of the region at the end of the Anglo-Saxon centuries and on the threshold of Norman England. Parts of the region had certainly felt the Conqueror's wrath since 1066. Although the 'catastrophic' view of the Norman conquest no longer has many supporters, both Derbyshire and Nottinghamshire suffered during King William's harrying of the north to the extent that about one-fifth of all villages were wholly or partly waste by the time of Domesday (Darby 1977: 251).

The picture must not be overdrawn since there is evidence to suggest that in the East Midlands the king's surveyors found a relatively well-developed

region. Since the later ninth century the Scandinavian settlers had intensively colonized much of the region, often occupying new sites. While the political power of the Scandinavians had gone by the eleventh century, their physical presence remained (Darby 1976: 21–6). Lincoln and Stamford were thriving centres in the early eleventh century, while lead mining, iron smelting and pottery manufacture were all sources of income to the region's inhabitants. The number of Anglo-Saxon church survivals – mainly towers, the body of the church having later been rebuilt – also points to prosperity. Fifty-nine have been positively identified for the region as a whole, with the majority, forty-seven, in Lincolnshire. More than one-tenth of all Anglo-Saxon churches in England and Wales are to be found in Lincolnshire, including such excellent examples of the genre as those at Barton-upon-Humber and Stow. Survivals are rarer elsewhere in the region, but they include the tower at Carlton-in-Lindrick (Nottinghamshire) and the complex church of St Wystan at Repton in Derbyshire which incorporated the mausoleum of a Mercian King (Taylor and Taylor 1965; Pevsner and Williamson 1978: 303).

The agricultural landscape of the East Midlands was already widely exploited, even if it was sparsely populated. Most people produced for themselves and their families, and the isolation of the average community is highlighted by the scarcity of market towns. Some areas were not easy to penetrate. Sherwood Forest, for example, stretched north from Nottingham beyond Mansfield, and few settlements were recorded in the area at Domesday. The picture was not dissimilar to Charnwood Forest in north-west Leicestershire, Leicester Forest – just to the west of the county town – and Leighfield Forest straddling Rutland and south-east Leicestershire. By contrast no woodlands survived as distinct forest areas in Lincolnshire (Thirsk 1973a: 236–8).

In the two centuries after Domesday Book the East Midlands passed through a period of considerable prosperity (Chapter 2). The majority of people, however, primarily concerned with their everyday livelihood, can have known relatively little of the great trade in wool which passed from all over the region through the port of Boston. Most peoples' horizons stretched little further than the shadow of the manor court and the lords' dues, and even the

---

Plate 1.1 Barton-upon-Humber Church, Lincolnshire. The late-tenth-century church tower at Barton-upon-Humber in north Lincolnshire is one of many Anglo-Saxon church survivals in the county, but it is also unique because the Normans modernized it by building round rather than removing the Saxon work.

The tower, which is largely of undressed rubble stone and decorated with pilaster strips, is approximately 22 ft square on the outside, and 70 ft high. The upper belfry is late-eleventh-century and surmounts a complete tower of late-tenth-century date with another belfry. However, since bell towers were not introduced into England until the tenth century there is a possibility that the bell-stage of this tower may be post-1086. The windows, doorways and internal arches of the lower stages of the tower are among the finest examples of their type in the country.

The base of the tower formed the nave of the Saxon church. A small chancel was destroyed prior to the construction of the existing large medieval aisled nave. A fifteen-foot annexe to the west, of similar date to the tower, survives.

concept of the county was of doubtful value. Moreover, for the majority life consisted of unremitting toil designed to wring a favourable income from the soil. To this end the field systems which emerged were largely designed as risk-sharing ventures to enable everyone to make some sort of a living. Probably the most significant feature of the period which would have impinged on everyday life was the growth of population. Although crop yields were comparatively high in a national context, the evidence of population pressure outrunning available resources is not difficult to find. Leicestershire and Rutland were heavily settled in the eleventh century, Lincolnshire, South Nottinghamshire and South Derbyshire relatively so. Scope for further settlement existed in Axholme, the Witham fens and the Lincolnshire fenland; in Sherwood Forest, on the Wolds, and on the alluvium of the northern Trent lowlands in Nottinghamshire; in western Leicestershire and Charnwood Forest; and on the northern moors of Derbyshire. In Lincolnshire population pressure stimulated a drive to win land from the county's marsh and fen (Platts 1985: 84).

Population and Settlement

How many people lived in the East Midlands in the early Middle Ages? Population figures derived from Domesday Book are notoriously suspect, although a figure of 2.5–3 million for England is now widely accepted. The survey was not a census as such, and there were many omissions. Stainby in Lincolnshire, for example, had plough teams, meadow, underwood and two mills, but no mention of anyone working in the village. Where figures were given their accuracy is sometimes in doubt. An account of five Lincolnshire sokelands includes summaries for each group of villages, but when the details of each village are collated the totals do not always match. Despite these drawbacks estimates for the population of the region at Domesday suggest an overall figure of around 180,000 of which perhaps two-thirds lived in Lincolnshire. In the two centuries or so after 1086 England enjoyed a population boom, to reach something like 5 or 6 million on the eve of the Black Death (Miller and Hatcher 1978: 29). Population in the East Midlands increased steadily down to the early fourteenth century (appendix).

Within this global estimate there was great local variation. In Derbyshire population may have grown threefold between Domesday and the early thirteenth century, but this was less impressive than the picture in parts of Lincolnshire. On the county's siltlands population grew between six and tenfold in the two centuries after 1086, while something similar was happening on the fens and marshlands; Spalding, for example, grew from 91 households in 1086 to 587 in 1287, and Pinchbeck from 57 to 646 over the same period (Hallam

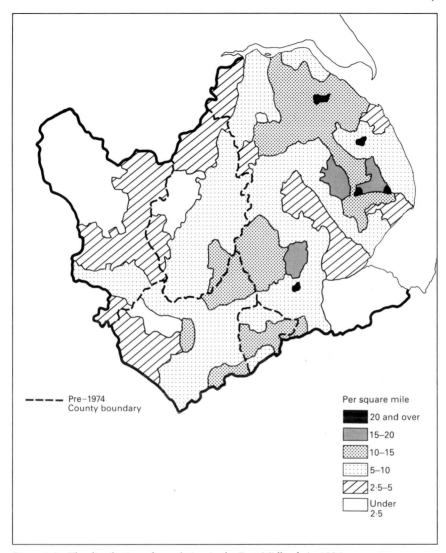

Figure 1.2   The distribution of population in the East Midlands in 1086
(after Darby 1977: 90).

1958: 340; 1981: 102; Blanchard 1967: 458). These cases were not necessarily typical, for there is also evidence of population stagnation or even decline in the region. In the forty years after Domesday a decrease in numbers seems to have taken place on the Lincolnshire estates of Peterborough Abbey; population increase was below the national average on the Nottinghamshire estates of the Bishop of Lincoln; three Leicestershire manors are known to have grown by only one-half between 1086 and 1321; and on one Rutland manor the increase in population between 1086 and 1314 was just 33 per cent. There is evidence of stagnation and falling numbers on the estates of Burton and Evesham Abbeys in Derbyshire, and decline prior to the Black Death seems to have occurred in both Nottinghamshire and Rutland. Although the evidence is fragmentary, two conclusions appear to be justified: the overall increase in population was substantial during this period, and was greatest by far in the east of the region.

Something like two-thirds of all East Midlanders lived in Lincolnshire at the time of Domesday. On the basis of modern estimates this proportion probably remained steady or even increased until the 1340s when Lincolnshire was badly affected by the Black Death. Thereafter the balance of population in the region gradually began to swing westwards (Hallam 1981: 39, 102–3; Cox 1908: 35). Even within these broad trends the spread of population was by no means consistent. In Lincolnshire it was concentrated at the southern end of the wolds, and in central Kesteven around Grantham and Sleaford. By contrast the clay basins of the rivers Trent, Witham, and Ancholme, and the marshland, had fewer inhabitants.

In Nottinghamshire the valleys of Trent and Soar were the most heavily populated while relatively few people lived in Derbyshire; indeed, the north-west (the high moorland) had a density of less than 2.5 per square mile. The county had extensive tracts of uncultivated land, of which about one-third was woodland and one-tenth was waste or unused land. King William designated this area the Forest of the High Peak. Leicestershire was heavily populated; indeed, the relative absence of new place names since 1086 suggests that few new settlements were founded after that. Even so settlement and population alike were much more thinly scattered in the county's forest area in the west than elsewhere, and the valley of the river Soar seems to have formed a significant boundary. West Leicestershire manors in 1086 averaged fewer than two plough teams per 1,000 acres, whereas in the east, on the light soils of the middle lias rocks and in the Vale of Belvoir, the average rose to five per 1,000 acres (Darby 1977: 57–9, 302; Heath 1982: 33; Millward 1985: 42–3).

The implications of population growth were considerable, not least in terms of where everyone was to live and work. Settlements recorded in the Domesday survey are enumerated in Table 1.1. The Lindsey (Lincolnshire) survey of 1115–18 includes 12 place-names in addition to the 492 recorded for the area in Domesday, while the Leicestershire survey of 1129–30 adds an additional 26 names to the county total of 296 (Slade 1956). Such discrepancies suggest either that the compilers were careless, or that the resources of

Table 1   Recorded settlements in Domesday

Derbyshire	46	Nottinghamshire	297
Leicestershire	296	Rutland	39
Lincolnshire	754		

(Sources: Darby 1977: 336; Millward 1985: 38)

minor settlements were included for Domesdsay purposes with those of an estate centre. The latter explanation best fits the Leicestershire case, where Lockington, Hemington and Long Whatton, appear as separate settlements in 1129–30 whereas in Domesdsay Book their resources were listed under Shepshed. In Derbyshire forty-three settlements lay waste at Domesday and another twenty-five were partly waste.

Settlement in the other counties of the region was also uneven, but possibly the most spectacular advances after 1086 were made in Lincolnshire. At Domesday there were relatively few settlements in the fenlands of Axholme in the north-west and in the south-east of the county, although these areas had been favoured for new settlement before 1066. Many pre-Conquest settlements were on land below 100 ft above sea-level. Axholme, where villages stood on islands of boulder clay surrounded by peat fen, the coastal saltmarsh, and the siltlands of the fens were especially favoured. The few new settlements above 300 ft were mainly in the upper valley of the Witham and the central wolds. In the two centuries after Domesday people came off the wolds and pushed out towards the fen edge. To cope with rising population some families restricted the number of children they bred, primarily through late marriage. More commonly, however, the response was to create new holdings, and this meant draining and reclaiming land. Highland parts of Lincolnshire were already showing signs of new settlement in the twelfth century, particularly to the north of Lincoln. Active land reclamation started in Axholme on the lower reaches of the Trent by 1189 and was still proceeding in 1337, while saltmarsh was being reclaimed in the north of the county early in the thirteenth century. From the mid-twelfth century there is evidence of new settlement in Kesteven, particularly in the fens and on the heaths of the Lincoln edge around Sleaford. Many of these fresh settlements were small enclosures of woodland, heath and marsh in what was already a densely inhabited county. In fenland Lincolnshire settlement led to the creation of new hamlets and monastic granges. The creation of sea-dykes and fen-dykes (causeways on baulks to keep the water at bay) was the work of whole communities, work that was not completed until the mid-thirteenth century, but its mark on the landscape remains today in areas such as Deeping St James and Market Deeping. This activity had the effect of creating in the Holland district of Lincolnshire the wealthiest area of England by the early fourteenth century.

Lincolnshire had relatively little woodland except in Kesteven but elsewhere in the region it was extensive. Much new settlement took place in woodland areas, hence the frequent references in contemporary documents to the practice of *assarting*, whereby woodland was cleared by grubbing up trees and bushes in order to make way for the plough. Pride of place in the East Midlands, perhaps for no other reason than that legends grew up about its associations with Robin Hood, is Sherwood, one of the region's royal forests. In Norman England Sherwood Forest covered about one-fifth of the county, predominantly the very poor, sandy soil stretching north from the county town which was thinly settled; even the gravel terraces of the Trent river valley had heavier settlement. The area developed under its own forest law and jurisdiction designed to safeguard the royal game. There were two forest courts, and the laws were enforced by a warden, verderers and rangers. Hunting parks were created within the forest, surounded by banks and timber paling designed to keep wild deer inside them. Clipstone Park, for example, was created between Mansfield and Edwinstowe. Several medieval kings from Henry I onwards used the royal hunting lodge in it, and John favoured a lodge nearer the Trent at Darlton (Kingshaugh) (Colvin 1963, II: 918–21, 970).

New settlement in the forest was generally late. Mansfield Woodhouse and Norwell Woodhouse were among a number of settlements which emerged only late in the twelfth or early in the thirteenth centuries as woodland was cleared on the keuper marl. Around the village of Tuxford, which was a staging point on the road to York, new settlement was taking place between 1292 and 1297. Although in 1329 and 1338 land was falling out of cultivation on two manors of the Sherwood area for lack of tenants, intakes from the waste continued until the eve of the Black Death. In the western part of the county new settlement was recorded as late as 1327. New settlement also took place in the Trent lowland including the areas of peaty soils (carrs) in north Nottinghamshire. Place-name evidence contains only forty-three clearing names, while of thirty-six examples of the place-name element *thorpe* – twenty-two of which were not recorded before 1086 – eleven were of parishes and two of villages, with the remaining twenty-three of much smaller elements.

Leicestershire was more densely settled at Domesday than its northern neighbour, but the county was unevenly populated. The absence of woodland suggests that settlement was already dense at the time of Domesday in the Vale of Belvoir and in the Welland and Wreake valleys. In these latter areas population density can be calculated at about 12 per square mile. Little new land seems to have been settled after 1086 here or in the Vale of Belvoir and the Soar valley. The contrast between these prosperous areas and western Leicestershire was marked. Here population density was around 2 per square mile, and the Charnwood Forest area was virtually empty, except for a scattering of named places along the margins of the forest. Not surprisingly colonization in the county during the twelfth and thirteenth centuries was predominantly in the forest area and the less settled and less fertile hilly region of west Leicestershire, especially in the coal measures north of Charnwood Forest along the Derbyshire border. At Swannington, on the western fringe of Charnwood, the local jury testified in 1293 that freemen were permitted to take in and cultivate land from the waste. Place-name evidence points to a landscape of medieval colonization in and around Charnwood, and the major restriction on settlement was the private hunting parks in this area (Stafford 1985: 21; Dury 1963: 81–3; Hinde 1985: 65, 205; Darby 1977: 26–7, 41, 43; Hallam 1981: 34–5, 94–5).

Leicestershire had at least thirty-four parks during the medieval period.

That at Barrow-on-Soar, set out early in the twelfth century, was probably the earliest; twenty-nine of the thirty-four date from 1200–1355. Bradgate Park, which existed as early as 1241, remains today as a remnant of one of these great medieval deer parks. Most parks were located with the greater estates in the west of the county, but their presence did not prevent movement into these areas, for between 1086 and 1377 the western part of the county's share of Leicestershire's population rose from one-fifth to one-third (VCH Leics III 1955: 135; Pye 1972: 236–9; Cantor 1970–1; Hallam 1981: 95; Millward 1985: 53–4).

Although new settlement in Derbyshire was extensive it took place notably late by comparison with other parts of the East Midlands, and it was limited by the nature of the terrain. The county's southern lowlands were the most densely populated. Nineteen settlements were recorded in pre-1066 sources, while thirty-five villages with new-settlement names first appeared in the records in 1086. In eastern Derbyshire at least sixteen villages are recorded in pre-Conquest sources, while a further twenty-nine villages with new-settlement names were first documented in Domesday Book. Post-1086 settlement seems to have been less marked in eastern Derbyshire than in the Pennines where heavy and late new settlement took place during the twelfth and thirteenth centuries. At least twenty-six new settlements were established after Domesday in the Pennine area, three of them after 1280. The county's woodlands were gradually being pushed back by colonization. Timber was cut for fuel and for building, and there is some evidence of the illegal building of houses within the forests and the clearing of land for farming. Reclamation of land for arable cultivation or improved pasture went on throughout the period in the county, particularly in the upland regions and east of the Derwent. Generally the land broken up for this purpose lay between 400 and 800 ft above sea-level. New lands were still being brought in from the waste right down to 1348 (Hallam 1981: 143–5). Apart from the Peak Forest the county had a second royal forest, Duffield Frith (or Forest). It belonged to the Duchy of Lancaster and was not designated as royal until 1399, but it was a hunting area at a much earlier date. Within it were several parks, each surrounded by palings, of which the most important was Ravensdale Park where there was a royal hunting lodge occasionally visited by Lancastrian kings (Colvin 1963, II: 989; Heath 1982: 41).

The expansion of a few settlements can be traced with some accuracy, particularly in the Peak. Wormhill in the extensive parish of Hope, was recorded as a settlement in Domesday Book. During the medieval period it played an important role in the affairs of the Forest of the Peak, and the villagers seem to have been pushing northwards into the Forest, to the brink of the Great Rocks Dale. In the process Wormhill was acting as the focal point for a frontier of expanding settlement. Thus Tunstead, a hamlet only a mile from Wormhill, came into existence early in the twelfth century, and Wormhill itself was evolving into a settlement in its own right by the mid-thirteenth century. This progress was confirmed when in 1273 a chapel was established in the village (Millward and Robinson 1975: 161–71).

The Land and the People

One of William the Conqueror's most significant moves after 1066 was to declare himself owner of all the land in England and then to redistribute it among his nobles. As a result, the king secured for himself a place at the head of medieval society and a dominant position in terms of the distribution of property. Immediately below him in the hierarchy stood the great territorial lords, both lay and ecclesiastical, who normally had extensive estates centred on a head manor. Next in order of descent came the lesser barons, the knights and the freemen, and beneath them the semi-free sokemen. Freemen and sokemen together held about 20 per cent of the land at Domesday, and the majority were living in the eastern part of England, particularly in Lincolnshire and parts of Leicestershire; indeed, the Domesday evidence for Lindsey suggests an area heavily peopled with small freeholders and cultivators. A further step down came the villeins, holding about 41 per cent of the land, and bordars and cottars. The latter group was numerous (approximately 32 per cent of the population) but held only about 5 per cent of the land. Villeins normally held standard tenement units while the bordars and cottars had only a few acres, probably obtained by colonizing and reclaiming marginal land. At the bottom the heap were the unfree (the serfs), found in greatest numbers in southern England and in a broad belt stretching north through the East Midlands. These status distinctions are no more than a guide, since Domesday terms were not consistent throughout the country, but they give an indication of the social ranks (Miller and Hatcher 1978: 22–3).

The estate or fief was the major unit of large-scale exploitation which supported the principal members of the ruling class in Norman England. It consisted of a number of manors that provided the framework within which

---

Plate 1.2   Oakham Castle, Rutland. The surviving late-twelfth-century hall succeeded an earlier timber hall, of which there is a record as early as 1086. The original hall was defended by a keep with a motte and ditch.

Oakham Castle hall is the earliest hall of any English castle to survive in such a complete form. It is particularly significant because it belonged originally not to a castle in the sense of a military stronghold, but to a manor house with no more than earthen defences.

The horseshoes are interesting. As the result of a unique right first mentioned in 1521, but of which no origin is known, the lord of the manor required every peer of the realm to forfeit a horseshoe on his first visit to the castle, or to compound for the same in money.

The hall was used for assizes at various times between 1229 and 1970, and most recently as a magistrates' court.

the tenants operated. Something like three-quarters of the total profits from land, as estimated by the Domesday commissioners, were shared between 100 priories, abbeys and bishoprics, and about 170 lay barons. Derbyshire's chief landowner in 1086 was Henry de Ferrers, with 114 manors in the county, and another 96 in 13 other counties; his principal seat was at Duffield. Hugh de Grantmesnil was Leicestershire's greatest landowner; his property included Barrow-on-Soar and land in thirteen other villages across the county. Already by Domesday the barons had begun to enfeoff 'knights' in portions of their property, a process which was eventually to create a numerous body of lesser and middling landlords. In Derbyshire these included Ralph Fitzherbert with nineteen manors. Some of the great estates survived intact in the eleventh century, thirteen in Nottinghamshire alone. Places such as Mansfield, as well as Bakewell and Ashford in Derbyshire, and Bolingbroke, Grantham and Kirton-in-Lindsey in Lincolnshire, were centres of such estates. Although found primarily in the upland areas of Derbyshire and west Nottinghamshire, great estates also survived where continuous royal control had preserved them, as in Rutland (Phythian-Adams 1986).

In the years down to the mid-fourteenth century this structure underwent considerable change. Villeins seem to have lost any remaining pretensions to freedom, although to picture them as sinking into servility may be an exaggeration since it is not clear to what extent they were free in the mid-eleventh century. Moreover, there were still means by which they could acquire freedom, including leaving the manor – either illicitly, or with the blessing of the lord – or gaining enfranchisement through the process known as *manumission*, usually for a cash payment. Freemen were numerous in the eastern quarter of the East Midlands. At least half of the land of Wigston Magna in Leicestershire (outside of the demesne) was held freely in 1086, while in seventy-three vills in the Guthlaxton and Gartree hundreds of Leicestershire in 1279, 39 per cent of tenants were free. Furthermore, by buying land and consolidating their possessions the Balle family in thirteenth-century Wigston Magna showed just how far a 'free' family was ready and able to go in organizing and improving its holdings (Hoskins 1957: 29, 49–52, 59). The number, if not the relative proportion, of freemen, probably increased through time because of their role in colonizing land. This seems to have been the case, for example, in Charnwood Forest and in the Lincolnshire fens.

Lincolnshire had a considerable number of sokemen around 1300; indeed, this was one of the wealthiest and freest areas of medieval England, hence the growth of population. The position of sokemen has been much disputed, particularly with regard to where they stood in the social hierarchy. It seems likely that originally they formed a distinct social group, and that individuals could hold free or unfree land. After 1086, however, their actual circumstances do not seem to have differed a great deal from those of villeins, and by the end of the thirteenth century much sokeland had been acquired by other social classes. In the later Middle Ages social status and forms of tenure could be separated, and tenure meant only the form of monetary payment and attendance at the appropriate court.

The Lay Landlords

By the time Domesday Book was compiled larger estates had been concentrated in the hands of a relatively small number of Norman tenants-in-chief holding their land directly from the king. Most English magnates had been deprived of their lands and replaced by Norman lords or other adventurers who had participated in William's Conquest. Of the Anglo-Danish aristocracy in Nottinghamshire in 1066 only one thegn, Toki, appears to have held really large estates in the county at the Conquest, and his lands (which also included property in Lincolnshire, Derbyshire, Leicestershire, Northamptonshire and Yorkshire) passed to Geoffrey Alselin whose chief seat was at Laxton. The roll of Norman magnates in Nottinghamshire also included Roger de Busli, William Peverel and Walter de Aincourt. The same picture can be painted elsewhere. Much of Sheriff Merleswein's land in Lincolnshire passed to Ralph Paynel, who also received some of Earl Morcar's property. Only one native holder of a baronial-size estate survived in Lincolnshire, and this was Coleswein; indeed, he was one of only two men in such a position south of the Tees. He held property over a wide expanse of the county although most of it was concentrated just to the north of Lincoln and in Kesteven (Wood 1948: 38; Hill 1948: 42–50).

A rough guide to the division of land in Lincolnshire is provided by the income from property in the county. In total it yielded about £3,500 of which some 14 per cent was from the king's own estates, 16 per cent was from a group of nine bishops' and abbots' estates, and 70 per cent was from the lands of secular lords, including about 4 per cent from the property of thegns who had survived the Norman settlement. Between the greatest and the least there yawned a considerable gulf. Seven of the most substantial landholders in Lincolnshire received more than half of the total assessed revenue, while at least sixty-five of the county's tenants-in-chief held property yielding under £30 annually. Taken in the round, Lincolnshire is probably typical of the region, with its local and non-resident barons and ecclesiastics, sub-tenants and knights, and the occasional survivor from the Anglo-Danish aristocracy (Platts 1985: 13–15).

The Norman lords sought to establish their authority by building castles, and fortification was particularly important during the wars between Stephen and Matilda, and again in the turmoil of King John's reign (1199–1216). The greatest of the castles were established by the Conqueror to consolidate his hold on the country, including the castles at Derby, Lincoln, Stamford, Nottingham, and Leicester. However, most if not all later castles were the work of private lords, particularly during the twelfth century. Leicestershire and Rutland have some twenty castle sites dating from the Norman period, while during the Middle Ages between twenty and thirty castles were built in Lincolnshire. Alexander, Bishop of Lincoln (1123–48), a great builder, was responsible for the castles at Sleaford, and just across the border in Nottinghamshire at Newark (as well as Banbury in Oxfordshire). Both Lincoln and Sleaford castles played an important part in the twelfth-century civil wars, and Stephen was captured at the battle of Lincoln in 1141. More significantly in the long run, medieval castles were the main residences of great lords, and the focal points of their extensive lordships (Millward 1985: 55).

The two most important administrative centres in Lincolnshire were at Lincoln and Bolingbroke. The earls of Chester, who claimed also to be the earls of Lincoln, asserted the right to be hereditary constables of Lincoln Castle, and at the same time they built themselves a fortress at Bolingbroke. The castle was still the centre of a great estate in 1608. Other barons also had their main residences in the county, including Gilbert de Ghent's at Folkingham, and these estates eventually acquired castles of their own. Baldwin fitz Gilbert built a castle at Bourne, Ivo Tailbois followed suit at Spalding, the Bardolfs built Carlton, and the Gresleys erected Swineshead. As the Middle Ages progressed the number of great honours declined, but a new group of landholders aspiring to be castle-builders emerged during the thirteenth and fourteenth centuries. A Robert de Tateshale in 1231 built a castle at Tattershall close to the Witham, and Anthony Bek, Bishop of Durham, in 1281 built Somerton Castle, south of Lincoln. Other older structures, no longer of military significance, fell into decay, including Stamford, Welbourne and Bourne (Rogers 1970).

A similar picture emerges from Derbyshire. Henry de Ferrers built Duffield Castle during the Conqueror's time and his family (later earls of Derby) kept it up, but it was despoiled in 1266, and little survives but the foundations of the large keep. Castles at Bolsover and Horsley were both built privately but came into Crown possession and remained so until the sixteenth century. The Castle of the Peak, built by William Peveril, fell into the king's hands in 1155 and was used as the administrative centre of the royal forest. Other castles were built at Codnor, Melbourne, Bretby, Castle Gresley and Mackworth. Less impressive, though important in their time, were the early motte-and-bailey castles found here and elsewhere in the region which were never rebuilt in stone and survive only as earthworks. Examples include Pilsbury in the Dove valley, and Hope, Hathersage and Holmesfield in the north of the county (Colvin 1963, II: 572–3, 681, 776–7; Renn 1968).

Leicestershire and Nottinghamshire have many earthworks recalling the early stages of Norman castle building, but none has been excavated (Phythian-Adams 1986: 28). The kings tried to control castle building and in 1176 Henry II ordered the Mowbrays, whose main estates were in Yorkshire, to demolish their castle at Owston in Axholme. The motte was partly levelled. The impressive earthworks at Laxton cover what may have been the finest motte and bailey in Nottinghamshire, although it was probably in ruins by 1300. Impressive earthworks still dominate the village of Castle Bytham in

Plate 1.3 The Castle of the Peak, Derbyshire. Built of stone on an almost inaccessible rock by William Peverel, bailiff of the royal manors of north-west Derbyshire to William the Conqueror, the Castle of the Peak is still to be seen today. Of the original eleventh-century work the north curtain wall towards Castleton is the most complete survival (although it has been repaired). The castle is protected by the natural lie of the land towards the east and west, and a large part of the south.

The castle came into the king's hands in 1155 and became the administrative centre for the royal forest. Henry II erected the keep in 1176, and this stands on the highest point of the site in a commanding position. Access was by a wooden outside staircase.

By the fourteenth century it was allowed to decay, and it was in ruins as early as the seventeenth century.

Lincolnshire. Lincoln Castle is still to be seen, as well as the stronghold of Tattershall Castle in the Witham valley, but there are few remains at Folkingham, Bolingbroke or Bourne, Sleaford or Stamford. Traces of the Norman castle at Belvoir have disappeared in successive rebuildings. Tattershall, one of the few Fenland sites chosen by a medieval lord, although begun by Robert of Tattershall in the mid-thirteenth century, was greatly enhanced by Ralph Cromwell in the fifteenth. It is a magnificent piece of brickwork, and the finest surviving tower to be built in England since the Norman keeps. Little survives in Derbyshire. Peveril is the best preserved, but only a fragment of Horsley remains, and one fourteenth-century wall of Melbourne Castle. At Bolsover the forecourt of the seventeenth-century keep stands on the foundations of an earlier one built 1173–9 (Barley 1972: 79; Pevsner and Williamson 1978: 27, 92, 249, 280).

Changes in lordship were inevitable in the course of time: the tendency was for the larger landholders to accumulate property from the lesser knightly families. The process of change can be most clearly demonstrated by comparing the Domesday findings with those of the Hundred Rolls for 1274–5. In Lincolnshire by the latter date thirteen estates warranted the title of barony. 'Baron' was a title often used for anyone who was a substantial landholder, but strictly speaking the title applied to tenants-in-chief whose relationship to the king was based on military service and the right to give counsel on important matters. Six of the thirteen Lincolnshire baronies could be traced back to the original Norman families, including the Gant, Deyncourt and Darcy families. The Gants were the wealthiest landholding family in Lincolnshire during this period, with possessions in villages throughout the county. The survival of so many Domesday families provided the county with an established aristocracy consisting of men with a commitment to the area. The same picture was not true elsewhere. In Nottinghamshire few of the Domesday lords survived for many generations; indeed, most of the tenants-in-chief listed in Domesday appear to have had little influence or longevity in the county. In these circumstances fragmentation of property tended to occur. Among the baronial fees which did not descend in direct line from their Norman founders in Lincolnshire property was already being divided by 1274–5, and the process was speeded up in the years down to 1311, largely as a result of line failure and military campaigns. The barons' rebellion against Henry III from 1258 also had a significant effect on the fortunes of several Lincolnshire families (Platts 1985: 20–30; Wood 1948: 39).

Fragmentation occurred when the lord granted parcels of land to the church or to favoured individuals. Finding land for younger sons, or division when the property came to daughters, could have the same effect. Thus in 1278 the estate of Walter de Merton at Kibworth Harcourt in Leicesteshire was divided between six relations and Merton College. The demesne was only reformed by an astute college purchasing policy over the following decade. Normally the land was scattered about the village fields and meadows. Where colonization came late in the Middle Ages consolidated properties were not unusual, and sometimes the lord used his authority to create a consolidated estate from a pre-existing conglomeration of property. Fragmentation seems to have been marked among all classes, and partible inheritance was practised by the freemen on the Holland fens, as well as elsewhere in the region. Freemen proliferated in the fens, but elsewhere bondmen constituted a large class. Although in their case the lord's supervision slowed down the pace of fragmentation, it occurred nonetheless. Certainly down to the Black Death the demand for land in the East Midlands could not be met merely by assarting, and while the practical convenience of consolidation made it a natural desire of many landowners, population pressure led to subdivision and, as a result, smaller sizes of property (Thirsk 1973a: 264–71).

The dissatisfaction with the king which led to the baronial rebellion was partly inspired by economic conditions. Over the period 1180–1220 prices, particularly of corn and livestock, doubled or even trebled (Harvey 1973). The lords' response was to curtail the practice of demesne leasing, which had been a feature of the early twelfth century. From the 1180s they again began to farm the land directly, urged on by the recognition that in inflationary times this was more profitable than fixed-rent leasing to tenants. For the knights, however, the situation was more serious. In effect, the class of knight was dividing into rich and poor. Many had been surviving on fees which were really too small to support them and their families, and the combination of inflation with the cost of equipping themselves to take part in the king's wars or to pay scutage (the sum demanded in commutation of military service in person) put them in an intolerable position. The result was a decline in the number of knights during the thirteenth century. In 1277 193 Lincolnshire knights assembled at Worcester to help check the Welsh insurrection, i.e. about one knight to every four settlements in the county. By 1324 the number was nearer to one to every five or six settlements. The expense of knighthood, and the amount of land a family needed to hold was becoming too great for many (Platts 1985: 30–6).

The Ecclesiastical Landlords

By no means all the land was held by lay patrons; the Crown, for example, held extensive properties in Derbyshire and Nottinghamshire, although hardly any in Lincolnshire, while the Church was one of the major landowners of medieval England. In the course of the post-Conquest centuries the Church came to own a considerable slice of the nation's landed wealth, and the bishops acquired the position of feudal magnates. The see of Lincoln stretched from the Humber to the Thames and included most of Lincolnshire, Leicestershire and

Rutland. The bishop's position in the land ranked with all but the greatest earls. His estates included property at Sleaford, Stow and Louth in Lincolnshire, while other land in the county belonged to the Archbishop of York – whose see included Nottinghamshire – and the Bishop of Durham. Derbyshire lay within the see of Lichfield. Moreover, the power of the Church lay not merely in its ecclesiastical landholdings, but also in its spiritual jurisdiction. The post-Conquest centuries saw a spectacular increase in the strength of episcopal government. In Lincoln, for example, an elaborate administrative machine was created which by 1250 had assumed the form it would keep throughout the Middle Ages. At the centre of this web was the bishop, a landed magnate, an adviser to the monarch, and an administrator on behalf of the Crown (Owen 1971: 20–1). The cathedral clergy also wielded administrative power. At Lincoln the dean and chapter claimed both civil and criminal jurisdiction over tenants living on their land, and similar rights belonged to the canons of Southwell Minster, where the king's justices held pleas at the south door of the church, and heard criminal cases in one of the canons' houses (Stenton 1965: 230–1).

Equally important in the course of the Middle Ages were the monastic foundations, which also became major landowners. At the time of Domesday Book the abbeys of Crowland, Peterborough, Ramsey and Westminster also had significant holdings in the East Midlands, but the transfer of substantial landholdings to the religious foundations still lay in the future (Mellows 1948). At the Conquest Derbyshire did not have any monastic houses, but Burton Abbey, founded in 1004 by the Benedictine order, held property in the south of the county bestowed upon it by its founder, Wulfric Spott, the owner of extensive estates in Derbyshire, Leicestershire, Nottinghamshire and south Yorkshire. Only ten Derbyshire manors were in church hands by 1086; the small quantity of church land in Nottinghamshire was predominantly in the hands of bishops. Over the following centuries, however, the growth of monastic estates disrupted local landholding, challenged hereditary rights, hastened the process of settlement, and contributed to the growth of the local land market. Some of the new foundations were to be found on land previously unsettled, as, for example, in north-west Leicestershire and the lower Witham valley. Moreover, Cistercian policy was to achieve solitude, and, coincidentally, to exert full tenurial and economic control by resettling villages. Thus the establishment of Rufford Abbey in the mid-twelfth century led to the disappearance of three villages, the establishment of a new settlement at Wellow and with it alterations to the parish boundary and the line of the road (Hinde 1985: 65, 205; Stafford 1985: 29–39; Barley 1957). No doubt some lay landlords were replanning villages in a similar fashion, but evidence of such activity is harder to come by.

From about 1130 the enthusiasm produced by reforming popes, and the beginnings of the crusades, brought a spate of monastic foundations. By 1200 there were over a hundred religious houses in Lincolnshire, compared with twelve in Derbyshire, twenty-four in Leicestershire, twenty-five in Notting-hamshire, and two in Rutland. During the two hundred years after 1066 several orders settled in Derbyshire. The Augustinian canons established houses at Calke and Church Greasley, as well as a small oratory in Derby and a large abbey at Darley. In 1172 they deserted Calke and moved to Repton Priory, while in the thirteenth century they established a small priory at Breadsall. The Premonstratensian order set up Dale Abbey in about 1160 and Beauchief between 1172 and 1186. Smaller houses in the county included the nunnery of St Mary-de-Pratis in Derby (1160), a house founded by the Cluniac monks in Derby but attached to Lenton Priory near Nottingham, and the leper hospitals in Derby, Alkmonton and Chesterfield (Hallam 1985: 55–69; Edwards 1966a: 210; Dury 1963: 87, 249; Wood 1948: 52–3; Platts 1985: 30–36).

In proportion to its size Lincolnshire had more monasteries than any county apart from Yorkshire. They were scattered throughout the county, ranging from large foundations such as Crowland and Bardney to smaller ones like Newbo in Sedgbrook, even the site of which cannot now be identified accurately. Crowland Abbey was the only monastic house in the county in 1066. During the twelfth century houses were set up at a great rate, and all the monastic orders are represented except for the Cluniacs. Among at least fifty priories, abbeys and preceptories established between 1130 and 1165 were ten belonging to the order started by Gilbert of Sempringham (the Gilbertines). County-wide five houses were royal foundations, thirteen were established by great magnates, four by bishops, and twenty-eight by members of the lesser nobility. Much of the initiative clearly came from the laity rather than from the monks. A great lord might set out to improve the church on his main estate, and ask a favoured monastery to send canons to man the new church. Examples in Lincolnshire include Baldwin fitz Gilbert's rebuilding of the parish church at Bourne, Henry fitz Eudo's efforts at Kirkstead, Ivo Tailbois' at Spalding, and Alan de Craun's at Frieston. Lesser gentry were moved by the same motives of establishing a memorial for themselves and engaging a religious community to pray for their souls. Hence the many smaller houses with perhaps half a dozen monks or nuns. Moreover, Lincolnshire land was valuable, and the distribu-tion of houses within the county reflects the monastic concern with financial viability. The Cistercian houses, for example, coupled their ideal of isolation with a keen eye for good farming land when siting a monastery. Almost always the value of the original estates was decisive in determining the location of the priory, a fact of some importance, although it does not detract from the genuine religious enthusiasm behind this vigorous movement (Rogers 1970: Owen 1971).

Nottinghamshire also had a cluster of foundations during this period. The first was the Benedictine priory at Blyth, set up by Roger de Busli in 1088. The great Cluniac priory at Lenton dates from the period 1109–14, and with lands scattered through seven counties it was almost certainly the county's richest. The Augustinian priories at Thurgarton and Worksop were built by great landowners of the county, Ralph, Baron Deyncourt at Thurgarton (1119–39), and William de Lovetot at Worksop (1123–40). As the twelfth century progressed houses multiplied: the Cistercian abbey at Rufford was founded in 1146 by Gilbert de Gand, Earl of Lincoln; the Benedictine nunnery at Wallingwells was erected by Ralph de Chevrolcourt in about 1140; and between *c.* 1154 and 1160 Thomas of Cuckney founded the Premonstratensian abbey of Welbeck, partly as a penance for his misdeeds during the civil war in the 1140s. The Gilbertine priory of Newstead was founded by Henry II about 1170, while Mattersey, another Gilbertine house, was founded in *c.* 1185 for six canons. Altogether twelve Nottinghamshire conventional houses were founded within a hundred years, and only one later addition was made, the Carthusian priory of Beauvale, set up in 1343 by Nicholas de Cantelupe, the Lord of Greasley (Wood 1948: 52–3, 102). Leicestershire was less well served, having no monastic houses of great importance. The Benedictines had a cell at Hinckley, and the Cistercians one at Garendon. Augustinian canons were responsible for Launde (1125), Ulverscroft (1134), Leicester Abbey (1143) and Owston before (1161). Other institutions included Burton Lazars Hospital near Melton Mowbray (Pevsner and Williamson 1984: 19–20).

Houses continued after 1200 to attract further gifts of land; Barlings Abbey, in the Witham valley east of Lincoln, for example, received 160 marks from William of Ingelby in 1267 towards the building and maintenance of a chantry chapel at Langworth; and in Nottinghamshire Thurgarton also continued to attract substantial gifts well into the mid-thirteenth century. Bequests to monastic houses were common in the wills of the pious, a trend encouraged by the fact that although most houses were initially endowed with one large manor, they later acquired property in a mass of small parcels of land, often scattered over a considerable area. As a result, by 1200 there were few villages in which no land was controlled by the Church. Thurgarton had three large, compact blocks of property around the priory itself, in the Nottinghamshire wapentake of Bingham, and across the Lincolnshire border in north Kesteven. It was the only Nottinghamshire house with extensive holdings in Lincolnshire. Overall income figures are difficult to evaluate, but Thurgarton's £250 in 1291 made it one of the wealthier houses in the East Midlands. Few houses in the region had incomes exceeding £300, and about 50 per cent had below £200 annually (Foulds 1980; 1984). If gifts ceased there was nothing except financial restraint to prevent purchases. Between 1253 and 1274 around 90 per cent of the land obtained by Prior John, the Almoner of Spalding, was by purchase, whereas over the previous two centuries property had primarily been acquired by endowment (Owen 1971: 47–57; Jones 1977: 41–3).

In Derbyshire by the time of the dissolution in the sixteenth century, land holdings of the county's religious houses, together with those of the thirty-one houses outside the county holding land within it, were considerable, particularly in the south and east, though rather less significant in the north-west of the county. This was despite the fact that the county had comparatively few religious houses within its borders. The larger houses had farms or granges in the county, mainly run by monks as extensive sheep runs, since wool was the most important saleable product of the monasteries. Religious houses played a pioneer role in farming the land, and they also took a hand in early industrial development; Dale, Burton and Beauvale Abbeys, for example, sold the rights to mine coal on their lands (Heath 1982: 35–40). The picture was not dissimilar in Lincolnshire, where the religious houses played a prominent role in the woollen cloth trade, and in fen drainage and settlement. Reclamation in the twelfth and thirteenth centuries resulted in the addition of arable, meadow and pasture to the siltland villages, and the establishment of granges and hamlets including those of the Benedictine houses of Crowland and Spalding (Hallam 1965; Darby 1983: 13–16).

Of these great foundations little has survived. Lenton Priory, despite being the most powerful monastic house in Nottinghamshire, has left few remains above ground, although excavation has revealed the plan of the twelfth-century church. Elsewhere in the county there are remains at Welbeck, Rufford and Newstead, incorporated in the country houses built on their sites (Pevsner and Williamson 1979: 19). Fragments of the priory at Repton in Derbyshire survive in the present school buildings, and remains have also been found at Calke Abbey. In Leicestershire, part of the churches survive from Launde and Ulverscroft, but houses at Bradley, Breedon, Charley and Kirby Bellars have almost entirely disappeared. A few remains of Mattersey Priory reflect the unwillingness of gentlemen to built houses near to the river Idle (Pevsner and Williamson 1979: 119, 305; 1984: 19–20). Ulverscroft, in the heart of Charnwood Forest, is the most complete Leicestershire survival, with extensive ruins of the priory church, the prior's lodging (now a private house), walls, ditches and fishponds. The ground plan of Croxton Abbey was recovered by archaeologists in the 1920s, and during the 1960s and 1970s the foundations of the chapter house at Garendon Abbey were unearthed by the Loughborough Archaeological Society (Millward 1985: 56).

The People

Over much of England the land was worked not by the lords, who cultivated directly between one-third and two-fifths of the arable land surveyed by the Domesday commissioners, but by a dependent tenantry. The divisions of status within the community were evidently complex at the time of Domesday, but there can be little doubt that English villages were not communities of equals.

Table 2   Rural population at Domesday

County	Villeins	Bordars	Slaves	Sokemen	Freemen
Derbyshire	1,858	738	20	128	—
Leicestershire	2,630	1,371	402	1,903	6
Lincolnshire	7,029	3,379	—	10,882	—
Nottinghamshire	2,634	1,180	24	1,704	—
Rutland	730	114	—	8	—
	14,881	6,782	446	14,625	6
England	109,230	81,849	28,235	23,324	13,553
East Midlands %	13.6	8.3	1.6	62.7	—

(Source: Darby 1977: 338)

Villages in the East Midlands were composed of lords, bond tenants, who owed their lord labour services in return for their holdings, and free tenants, who owed rents and certain non-servile services but were generally free to dispose of their land as they pleased. Lords exercised their greatest authority over demesne land, which usually consisted of one block, or possibly a group of furlongs or fields of reasonable size. They also had powers over the lands of their bond tenants, variously referred to as villeins, bordars and slaves (Table 2). Villeins were the most numerous across the country, accounting for 41 per cent or more in the East Midlands except in Lincolnshire where the proportion was 33 per cent. Their exact status has been a matter of debate, for both their obligations and their holdings varied considerably.

The standard tenement of freemen and villeins was the virgate, which comprised approximately 20–30 acres of arable and meadow, and the half-virgate, bovate, or oxgang, with common rights. Half-virgaters, and even virgaters, cultivated the land themselves with assistance from their family. Those with more land probably employed labour, albeit seasonally. Many of those employed in this way were likely to have been smallholding *villani*, bordars or cottars, although there were probably full-time labourers in the countryside as well. Bordars accounted for between 13 per cent (Rutland) and 26 per cent (Derbyshire) of the population of east midlands counties. Slaves (or *servi*) accounted for just over 10 per cent of the recorded population, and they seem to have worked almost entirely on the lord's demesne. Relatively few were recorded for the east midlands counties, Leicestershire apart, although it seems likely that this may have been due to under-registration (Thirsk 1973a: 264ff; Darby 1977: 73–4; Miller and Hatcher 1978: 24).

Most people in medieval England lived in village communities, and the majority of midlands villages were nucleated, with the houses grouped together around a church, a village green or a highway. A manor house (where appropriate), and other buildings including mills were also found within the settlement. Laxton, in north Nottinghamshire, retains much of its medieval character, with most of the houses still clustered around the church. Only the independent farms laid out in the 1720s and in the nineteenth century no longer conform, and many of the village farmers still live in the nucleated settlement. Of course there were a great many variations on this theme, but even where the open fields have disappeared village structures still survive. The houses at Barton-in-Fabis near Nottingham, for example, still cluster around the fourteenth-century church. Other villages in the county, including Linby, Calverton and Woodborough, spread out along a main street. The characteristic 'back lane', where the principal street was flanked on either side by footpaths or lanes providing access to the open fields, can still be seen at Laxton and Edwinstowe, while elsewhere the name itself still survives (in conjunction with Main Street), as at Ollerton. Usually this form produced a rectangular shape still found in Nottinghamshire and in Lincolnshire except in the fens where (with the exception of Axholme) the open-field system did not operate (Barley 1972: 95–6).

Village greens were not common in the East Midlands. Few Lincolnshire villages have one, except Market Staunton where it is the deserted site of an ancient market. In Nottinghamshire village greens still survive at Wellow, Car Colston and Clifton, while the small green at Ruddington may be the survival from a larger expanse of open land. Extensive market place areas can still be seen in the Peak District, at Monyash, Tideswell and Ashover for example.

At the centre of the community was the church. The Domesday Survey records forty-eight in Derbyshire, at least seventy-two in Nottinghamshire, fifty in Leicestershire and fourteen or fifteen in Rutland, but these are almost certainly underestimates (Heath 1982: 35; Weir 1986: 5; Phythian-Adams 1986: 38). What is not in doubt is that every parish was provided with a stone church during the medieval centuries, a remarkable witness not only to the enduring power of religious beliefs but also to the assumption of local magnates that they must provide a church for themselves and their tenants, appoint a priest, and provide a landed income for him. Thus in 1112 Bishop Robert Bloet consecrated the church at Thurlby by Bourne, which was endowed by Benceline, the mother of Ralf de la Mare, with half a bovate of arable land, an acre of meadow, and a toft, to which one of her knights added a further 2 acres of arable and one of meadow. By 1130 the endowment had been increased to a bovate of demesne, 3 acres of arable, and 2 acres of meadow (Owen 1971: 13). Ownership was represented by the right to appoint a priest, and patronage a form of property which could be bought and sold, or given away.

As a result of this burst of building, the Lincolnshire countryside has a remarkable heritage of parish churches, particularly in the area between Lincoln and Grantham, and the south-east towards Sleaford, Boston and Spalding. That part of the county was endowed with particularly good building materials and so produced perhaps the most impressive crop of medieval parish churches in the country. The Lincolnshire spire is the best of its kind in England (Rogers 1970: 40). Heckington, just east of Sleaford, has one of the

grandest churches in the county. It is built of Ancaster stone, the oolitic limestone from which Lincoln Cathedral and many of the county's medieval churches were constructed. Most of this stone came from the quarry at Ancaster, midway between Grantham and Sleaford. In addition, greystone was used for the marshland churches, and greenstone in the area around Louth. Ironstone is found near the Rutland border and in the north around Scunthorpe (Pevsner and Harris 1964: 27–8, 566).

About a hundred of Nottinghamshire's churches contain some Norman work, showing how much building or rebuilding went on before 1200. The county is too far west for oolite limestone. It does, however, have deposits of magnesian limestone, which was used for some of Nottinghamshire's most outstanding Norman churches, including the priory churches of Blyth and Worksop. The priory church at Blyth, a 'sad, badly treated fragment' of its former glory gives a feel for early Norman grimness (Pevsner and Williamson 1979: 77; Wood 1948: 49–51). Derbyshire has a number of Norman churches, the best of which are Melbourne, built on a near-cathedral scale, but the county's richest example of Norman architecture is the tiny Steetley Chapel (Pevsner and Williamson 1978: 275–9, 328). Leicestershire has several twelfth-century churches, and Rutland has excellent survivals at Tixover, with its massive grey Norman tower, and Tickencote, which has a particularly ornate chancel arch for a small church (Millward 1985: 56).

The influence of the church was not merely in its buildings but also in its priests and its services. All impropriators had difficulty finding qualified and conscientious priests. To raise the standards, diocesan bishops were encouraged to institute vicarages which would be the freehold of the serving priest, and Hugh of Wells, Bishop of Lincoln 1209–35, instituted more than 300 throughout his diocese (Stenton 1965: 217–21). Even so, the wide variety in the level of endowment enabled some clergy to live like gentry (Barley 1986: 141–2) while leaving many others to supplement their income in one way or another. In such a large body of men there were inevitably some criminals or men who now seem to have betrayed their cloth. The rolls of the justices of the peace in Lincolnshire between 1360 and 1375 are full of accusations of theft and violence, including the case of the two Spalding chaplains who stole gold and silver from a house at Whaplode. Others were accused of sexual misdemeanours, including Richard Johnson, vicar of Laxton, who was indicted in 1471 for having an affair with the wife of William Blyton of Wellow (Storey

---

Plate 1.4 Steetley Chapel, Derbyshire. Described by Pevsner as 'by far the richest example of Norman architecture in Derbyshire' (Pevsner and Williamson 1978: 328), this tiny chapel measures only 52 ft by 15 ft, but contains a wealth of mid-twelfth-century decoration. It consists of a nave, a slightly narrower and lower chancel, and an even narrower lower apse. The nave is oblong and the chancel square.

The nave and the chancel were roofless throughout the nineteenth century, but they were restored in 1880. However, the result is that some of what we see today is Victorian restoration rather than Normal original.

1984). Accusations were not necessarily well-founded, but it is clear that the Church had problems in recruiting, training and educating a competent body of men, and in filling the vacancies. In 1376, for example, Lincolnshire had just eighteen university graduates among its parochial clergy, while the parish chaplains who had the closest and most constant touch with the laity can hardly have inspired a great deal of respect (Owen 1971: 132–42).

These were only the inevitable problems of a Christian society. By the end of the twelfth century the religious needs of the settled population were reasonably well served by the system of parish churches and dependent chapels, while whatever the spiritual benefits that this brought, people were also aware of the presence and power of the Church through the duty of paying tithes. Although there was inevitably some resentment, this did not stand in the way of belief, and the Church accompanied the individual from baptism – preferably the same day as birth – to burial. It can be taken for granted that at least one daily mass was heard by many parishioners in most churches and many chapels. The full daily office was said in the collegiate church at Tattershall:

> The first bell for matins at Tattershall rang at 6 a.m., the second half an hour later, the last at 7 a.m. After matins solemn mass with organ and choral music was sung in the chapel of the Virgin and at the high altar a mass was also said. The first bell for vespers rang at 3 p.m., the second at 3.30 p.m., when the choristers said vespers and the compline of the Blessed Virgin; at 4 p.m. vespers for the day were to begin.
>
> (Owen 1971: 102)

In most parishes such an elaborate ritual took place only on Sundays, but the annual calendar provided a demanding schedule for parishioners to follow. Penance (confession) was obligatory at the beginning of Lent, and often before great festivals such as Christmas, Easter and Pentecost, while at some point in each person's life the various sacraments had to be shared. Moreover, the ecclesiastical authorities did what they could to ensure that Sunday was kept as a day of rest from secular labour, and that due observances were made in church. Episcopal visitations inevitably uncovered Sunday markets, and efforts were made to suppress these, while a whole string of festivals had to be observed in the course of the year. These in turn were often marked by special services and processions (Owen 1971).

Most villages had a mill. Watermills were used in the ninth century, and there is still plenty of evidence on the ground for their use in Leicestershire (Ashton 1977). During the twelfth century they were gradually supplemented by windmills, which was particularly significant for an area such as Lincolnshire, which lacks fast-flowing rivers, and by 1300 windmills were to be found throughout the county. They also spread to other parts of the region, including Nottinghamshire. (Conservationists anxious to restore Laxton to something of its former self in the 1970s even suggested building a half-size windmill based on the design of the old wooden post-mill.) Villages usually had a communal oven for baking bread, and a smithy to produce horse-gear, keys and locks, and basic agricultural implements. Within the village, houses and cottages were situated within an enclosed area of ground known as a toft (a back-yard) or a croft (a back garden and paddock). Chickens, geese and ducks could be run on this land, while vegetables grown to supplement the diet included beans, leeks and onions.

What little is known about family structure suggests that households were normally based on a nuclear family unit consisting of parents and children and one or more distant relatives, including a grandparent or the marital partner of one of the children. Parents often handed their tenements on to their childen in return for food and lodging; hence the occasional evidence of more extended family units. Household sizes varied, possibly increasing according to wealth. On the estate of Spalding Priory in 1267–68 the average household contained nearly five people, but on the larger holdings of 5–30 acres this could rise to over five, and over 30 acres to nearly seven. An average of five per household may be about right (Hallan 1981: 64).

No small houses have survived in the region from the Middle Ages, because they must have had a relatively short life, periodically being rebuilt, modified and extended. In the medieval period wood was the most widely used material, but few timber-framed houses survive. Newark has half a dozen (including the White Hart Inn), and there are scattered examples elsewhere including Nottingham and Southwell, while Stamford has more timber-framed buildings, mostly now plastered over, as well as being at the heart of the stone area.

The poor quality of local timber meant that eastern Nottinghamshire shared with Lincolnshire the construction form known as mud and stud, where a slight timber frame was protected by 6 inches or so of mud applied to laths. Almost any soil was suitable if mixed with chopped straw, and for preference also ballast (gravel or other small stones) and sand. These dwellings were easy to erect, requiring only the skills of the village carpenter, and the commonly possessed knowledge of how to dig and puddle the clay. Few have survived, except occasionally in Lincolnshire in the Witham valley, on the wolds and in the marshland. Mud was the single most popular building material for labourers' cottages in Leicestershire and Rutland down to the seventeenth and even into the eighteenth centuries. Surviving examples of these houses, often called cob cottages, in Rutland, Leicestershire and Nottinghamshire, are all found along the edge of the belt of good building stone. Since, on the limestone belt, numerous small quarries supplied rough stones for rubble cottages, this suggests that cob construction was only found when little good building stone was available. The crucial consideration was to keep the mud dry, hence walls were built on plinths of stone – in Leicestershire of boulders from the boulder clay, and in Rutland from rubble limestone – and were limewashed (Clifton-Taylor

1972: 287; Barley 1972: 100; Pevsner and Williamson 1984: 54–60, 449–50; Pevsner and Williamson 1979: 46–50; Seaborne 1964: 217–18).

The availability of stone in eastern Leicestershire and Kesteven was not necessarily beneficial to the poorest members of society because of transport costs. These were prohibitive until towards the end of the eighteenth century, although the prosperity of the wool trade helps to explain why stone became one of the normal materials for medium-sized as well as for large houses in the course of the fifteenth century. All the local quarries within a 25-mile radius of Stamford, originally opened for building churches and castles, were known in the Middle Ages, particularly those at Barnack, Ancaster and Clipsham. Oolite limestone, especially from Ancaster, had the highest reputation, and although Clipsham stone was widely used at Stamford its popularity was muted in the Middle Ages by technical problems. It was easily the hardest, and the saws available could not cut it accurately. In Derbyshire, carboniferous limestone and millstone grit from the Peak District were used for lonely farmhouses although their major use was to come much later as the material from which the county's distinctive dry stone walling was constructed. Brick was hardly used in the region before 1500, although there are a few examples, including the gatehouse of the Augustinian priory of Thornton in north Lincolnshire built in 1382 and Kirkby Muxloe Castle (1480–81) (Clifton-Taylor 1972: 79, 85–6, 96–7, 213).

Stone did not solve everybody's problems. Cruck houses were still built in an area stretching from the Derbyshire stone belt to Charnwood Forest, and some surviving stone-built houses have a cruck base to them. Many were thatched before tiles became available. Even so, roofing became increasingly sophisticated through time, and although the most common material was thatch a slater was employed at Rippingale in Lincolnshire as early as 1317 for work on the roof of William Inge's grange (Platts 1985: 77; Barley 1961: 24–5).

Most people lived in small homes. Cottagers are unlikely to have had more than one or two rooms, a hall and chamber open to the rafters in their homes; villeins probably had a two or occasionally three-roomed house; and freemen lived in something similar, although with farm buildings adjacent. Nor were they likely to have contained a great deal of equipment inside. Walls were bare, and the most noticeable feature would have been the open hearth for cooking and heating. In the absence of inventories before the sixteenth century little is known of utensils. Presumably most houses had a table, benches and beds, and while some may have had bronze or pewter cooking pots and pans the majority probably made do with earthenware.

It has been argued that merely in order to subsist families needed approximately 10 acres of arable plus pasture and common rights, but success was not guaranteed (Miller and Hatcher 1978: 147–52). The remarkable continuity of surnames in Kibworth Harcourt, Leicestershire, between 1280 and 1340 suggests a stable community with land passing from father to son, but it is difficult to be sure how representative this was (Howell 1976). Although opportunities were available during the eleventh and twelfth centuries to colonize new land in order to offset the impact of population growth – hence the efforts of freemen from Charnwood Forest in the west to the Lincolnshire fenlands in the east – by the thirteenth century such possibilities were increasingly rare, and as a result the size of the average holding declined.

Even firm lordship could not prevent property division, with the result that many holdings came to be of less than 10 acres. Among the Bishop of Lincoln's tenants on his manors near Stow around 1280 some 14 per cent were cultivating fewer than 5 acres, while at Elloe in the fenland at the same date there was about 1½ acres of arable, pasture and meadow per head of population. To some extent fragmentation may have resulted from the practice of partible inheritance, the division of an individual holding among a man's children. In the fenlands partible inheritance was the usual custom and here holdings were tiny because the land was so fertile. Nottinghamshire was predominantly a county of smallholders, many of them sokemen. By 1250–1300 the tendency towards smallholdings as a result of partible inheritance was clear. Partible inheritance probably existed in parts of Derbyshire as early as 1126. The sokemen were unfree and divided their holdings between their heirs. On the other hand, the case should not be overstressed; at Wigston Magna, for example, primogeniture, the descent of the property intact to the eldest son, always prevailed (Hallam 1981: 68–9, 103–4, 121; Hoskins 1957: 75).

The competition for land which produced these tiny holdings also raised the tempo of demand for employment among the many people who needed additional work in order to supplement their income. When labour was plentiful wages were depressed, and this induced some families to seek employment in other concerns, including making iron, salt and pottery, tanning and spinning and weaving. What this did for income is hard to say. In such conditions diet was naturally restricted. Bread, or in the case of north Derbyshire oatcakes, was the staple, supplemented by vegetables and pulses, and some dairy produce from livestock maintained in the croft, but few families ate meat. Fish was a regular item in Lincolnshire diets. Grimsby cod was nationally renowned in the thirteenth century, and herring was available in coastal towns and villages. Cheese was also an important part of the diet, with most villages in the region making their own from cows' milk. Overall, life was far from easy, and most families needed to perform a careful balancing act between achieving self-sufficiency and acquiring additional articles by trading in the local market (Hallam 1981: 66; Platts 1985: 77–83).

Law and Order

Overshadowing most peoples' lives was the lord. In medieval England self-government at the king's command placed a great deal of responsibility in the hands of powerful private individuals. In the countryside most people came into contact with three levels of local government: the king's officials; the Church, which was primarily concerned with religious offences; and the manorial court. Alternative jurisdictions existed in a few areas, such as the laws and customs relating to the Peak District lead industry (Kirkham 1968: 32–52). The manor court was the level at which most people encountered justice, but quite what the term justice implied is a matter of debate. Corruption was widespread; juries were packed; animals were unlawfully seized; and torture was not unknown. Medieval society was harsh and justice unequal. It was the world of that enduring local hero Robin Hood. No one is quite sure whether there really was a historical Robin, and even if such a man can be located in time there seems little doubt that the tales of Sherwood Forest and the Sheriff of Nottingham were later accretions to mythical tales rather than being original to the story. Even the social rebel, robbing the rich to pay the poor, appears to have been a later invention tacked on to the character of an honourable criminal who procured justice by guile and violence. In the words of his recent biographer:

> What is now pure adventure to the young or laudable social protest to the radical was at first a glorification of violence to young and old alike. Robin, whether real or legendary, was a product of a society where the threshold which separated lawful behaviour from self-help by force of arms was indistinct and easily crossed. It was a society where the exercise of local office and the enforcement of the law were often an instrument of political faction, a society where the defeated party might easily pay the penalty with their heads, a society in which men took to robbery and pillage under the pressure of famine and other adverse circumstances, a society in which crime was tolerated, in which local juries protected the criminals and in which gangs of knightly bandits might gain royal pardon for extortion, kidnapping and murder.
>
> (Holt 1982: 10)

While Robin Hood and his merry men may have made such activity honourable and meritorious, medieval England remained a harsh and uncompromising society in which to live.

The king's direct representative in the shires was the sheriff (literally shire reeve), a position which became significant during the eleventh century when the Anglo-Saxon shires were grouped together under provincial earls.

Although the earldoms disappeared after 1066 the office of sheriff grew in importance. The sheriff collected the king's revenue, maintained law and order, and held the county court – a regular meeting of the freemen of the shire to administer justice. In Lincolnshire it met every four or six weeks in Lincoln Castle, which was the sheriff's headquarters (Rogers 1966: 64–78). For legal and administrative reasons Derbyshire and Nottinghamshire shared a county court, and for many years a sheriff. The borough of Derby appears in the Nottinghamshire section of Domesday Book, immediately following the borough of Nottingham, and this anomalous situation was not resolved until Derbyshire was granted separate status in 1256 (Crook 1983: 98–106). As the sole representative of royal justice the sheriff's position was particularly formidable, and it is little wonder that the post was normally held by men of wealth. Before 1260 these were often men sent into the county from elsewhere, although thereafter local men were likely to hold the position (Platts 1985: 230–3).

The unsatisfactory nature of the king's justice produced the reforms of Henry II in the later twelfth century. He established regular provincial visitations by royal justices, which were to become the basis of the later assizes. Some of the initial circuits were enormous, stretching from Yorkshire to Kent, but by the end of the thirteenth century Leicestershire and Rutland were on a more compact itinerary whereby the judges visited Boston, Louth, Lincoln, Stamford and Grantham. Henry II also brought in changes in local policing functions, and perhaps most important of all, to improve efficiency and to reduce peculation, the office of coroner was introduced in 1194. If the primary function of the coroner lay with investigating sudden deaths, it was also necessary for him to play a role in the maintenance of law and order, and to act as a check on the sheriff at the county court. Initially each county had four coroners, although there were at least fourteen in Lincolnshire by 1300 (Platts 1985: 234). Leicestershire was divided into three separate jurisdictions: the Honour of Leicester, the borough and the shire, each with its own prisons, hence the need for more than one coroner (Lloyd 1980/1: 18–32). As a result of the appearance of coroners the almost untrammelled powers of the sheriff were considerably restricted in the course of the Middle Ages.

For most individuals the county and church courts were less relevant to daily life than the all-embracing manor court. The status of English villagers varied according to their degree of freedom, but the relationship between them was governed by the manor court. While even free tenants owed services and obligations to a lord, the extent of individual freedom determined how onerous the exactions would be, particularly in regard to labour services. Whether an individual was free or unfree could depend on the status of his parents or his land. Customary holdings, for example, imposed particular obligations irrespective of personal status. Of the three main classes of villager which predominated by the end of the thirteenth century, freemen usually worked 30 acres or more, and were sometimes related to minor gentry families, and cottagers had little more than their cottage and the surrounding land. More important as far as the lord was concerned, were the villeins since they were responsible for the majority of services and dues. But whatever their status individuals found themselves responsible for a wide variety of customary exactions ranging from money payments to demesne labour service.

The precise extent of an individual's dues varied between different places and across time, but they were determined at the manorial court. For most people the major contact with the law would have been in the form of the court leet. The manor court was usually held fortnightly by the lord or his representative in order to investigate trespasses, failure to perform labour service and other issues of local significance, particularly those affecting seigneurial prerogatives. These included land transfers, the unlawful pasturing of animals and brewing or baking rights. Manor courts also adjudicated in petty criminal proceedings. In effect, they were concerned with the customs and by-laws of the village. As such they were probably busiest in times of dearth. The Ingoldmells court leet in Lincolnshire heard 129 pleas of debt in 1315–16, and also found Gregory Roland guilty of stealing a bushel of corn from Robert Pepper's house at Langtoft (Platts 1985: 242).

Twice yearly the court leet, or sometimes the Hundred Court, took views of frankpledge, a twelfth-century development of the tithing system. This was the way in which ten, twelve or even more men were organized into groups to guarantee each others' good conduct. All free and unfree tenants were expected to be part of a tithing, the only exceptions being gentry, clergy and women. The occasion was also used for the tenants to swear fealty to the lord and to have their status verified and recorded for future reference. Manorial officers were also chosen at these courts, including reeves and dyke-reeves, haywards, stewards, ale-tasters, and the twelve eminent villagers who sat as the jury of presentment. The right to set up gallows on the manor was discussed at such sessions; in Lincolnshire during the 1270s and 1280s lords claimed the privilege in over one hundred towns and villages. How often gallows were used was another matter since most hanging in the Middle Ages was carried out by order of the royal justices. Occasional place-name survivals such as Gallows Inn in Ilkeston, or Gallows Knoll at Hopton, also in Derbyshire, serve as reminders of the frequency of execution venues in the Middle Ages (Cameron 1959: 379, 474).

Through the manor courts the lords were also able to impose obligatory customs and payments. *Merchet* was paid when the son or daughter of an unfree tenant wanted to marry, and *leyrwite* when a single girl became pregnant. A payment was required from those seeking permission to brew ale or to bake bread on the manor; in Stamford brewers' payments were known as *aletoll* and *brewsteresyeld*. Lords could also demand other tallages and aids, including customary eggs, geese and chickens at Christmas and Easter. At Sleaford in 1258 Thomas, son of Arnold farmed two bovates for which he paid a money rent of 6*d*., two fowls, twenty eggs, and 200 sheaves of rushes. Walter of Milnthorpe in the same parish also farmed two bovates, but he paid 4s. 3d. money rent, and provided two hens, twenty eggs and one quarter of oats. In order to hold and farm a lord's land tenants also had to pay *rents of assize*, normally rendered in cash, but even in the fourteenth century they sometimes paid in agricultural or industrial produce. Thus reclaimed land outside the village of Fleet in Lincolnshire was held by tenants against payments of salt, pepper and chickens. *Pannage* or *herbage* was paid for pasturing rights (Hosford 1968: 30; Platts 1985: 56–7).

On top of all these demands tenants were obliged to perform services on the lord's demesne. All the villeins at Sleaford in 1258 had detailed labour dues in addition to their money and kind payments. However, labour service varied considerably in practice. In some cases it could mean one – or in a busy period – two days' labour weekly, while on other demesnes a specific number of days was set aside for particular tasks. On the Leicester Abbey manor of Stoughton yardlanders owed two days' work a week for most of the year, but four days a week between 20 July and 29 September (124 days a year) in addition to ploughing, mowing, reaping and carting services. This seems to have been particularly onerous since on all other Leicestershire manors for which evidence survives demands were rather less heavy (VCH Leics II 1954: 173).

In a few places the lord's work was commuted into a cash payment, while some of the more wealthy tenants were able to hire agricultural labourers to do the work for them. Although Lincolnshire had many freemen, great care is needed to decide what the term really meant. Customary rents and services seem to have been more onerous in the county than in many parts of northern and western England, and even in the second half of the thirteenth century villeins' demesne works made up some 40 per cent of tenants' overall annual payments. Tenants obligations in terms of labour services varied according to the location and size of the manor. At Billingborough in Lincolnshire, for example, a villein spent annually two days ploughing, two harrowing, two sowing corn and flax, one day digging peat and another one sheep shearing, nineteen days reaping and a final three carrying hay and corn. At Hacconby, by contrast, the five villeins undertook only six days' work each during the year; while in the upland parish of Holywell in 1326 the villeins worked two days a week on the demesne for eleven months of the year, and eighteen days in August. It seems likely that in upland Lincolnshire lords were more successful in asserting their authority than was the case on the fen edges (Platts 1985: 64–5).

Through time changes took place in the extent and basis of freedom. In the prosperous years controls were relaxed, but when conditions were more difficult lords paid greater attention to customary dues and services. When demesnes were leased during the twelfth century some lords offered enfranchisement and commutation of labour services for a cash sum, but when they began to farm directly again after about 1180 the position changed as customary services became more valuable to lords than cash payments. Consequently efforts were made to tighten up or even increase their demands. Earlier tenurial arrangements were reinvoked, and administered more efficiently by farm managers. In many cases tenants were forced to acknowledge their liability to customary payments for which they had not previously qualified. On occasion this produced conflict. In 1279–80 the villeins of Mickleover in Derbyshire rebelled against the Abbot of Burton. The abbot seized their goods and chattles and a lawsuit ensued. Sokemen also suffered a decline in status in the century and a half preceding the Black Death. By the early fourteenth century lords were also taking greater care in collecting manorial dues. On the Abbot of Crowland's courts in Langtoft and Baston court business was recorded in increasing detail after 1300, suggesting greater attention to social and fiscal relationships on the manor. Possibly as a result, manorial profits rose considerably between the first and second decades of the fourteenth century (Hallam 1981: 163; Platts 1985: 52–71).

Farming

Nine out of every ten Englishmen lived in the countryside at Domesday, ekeing out a living from the soil. Prior to 1086 mixed farming was commonly found through much of England, although local conditions were reflected in recognizable specialisms. Lincolnshire was already noted for its cattle and pig rearing, and Leicestershire was important for sheep farming. From the Domesday Survey it is possible to gain a picture of the region's agriculture, which suggests that within the overall pattern of mixed farming, pockets of particularly rich arable land were found in parts of Leicestershire, Nottinghamshire and Lincolnshire. With the exception of the fens and marsh of Lincolnshire, the forests of Leicestershire and Nottinghamshire, and the upland moors of Derbyshire, much of the region was under arable. Meadow was recorded for the great majority of villages in Domesday, and substantial acreages were frequently found in parts of the East Midlands, particularly along the Trent and its tributaries in southern Derbyshire, eastern Nottinghamshire and northern Leicestershire. In these areas villages with 100 acres of meadow were not uncommon while quantities in excess of 400 acres were found in Lincolnshire, particularly on the coastal claylands of Lindsey and across much of Kesteven. By contrast, pasture is seldom recorded (Hallam 1981: 25; Darby 1977: 132, 148).

On the whole, while cereal production was the dominant rural interest, a heavy expenditure in human labour was required to make the land yield limited returns. Grain, particularly barley, was the most important food crop, as is clear from the number of mills recorded in Domesday – over 200 and possibly over 400 in Lincolnshire according to separate estimates, 123 on 89 sites or settlements in Leicestershire and 80 in Nottinghamshire. Sometimes groups of watermills were clustered together for industrial purposes, including ten at Derby for fulling, and in Lincolnshire fourteen at Tealby, thirteen at Louth and eight at Old Sleaford. However, Derbyshire had only fifty-two mills, just 15 per cent of the total number of places recorded, by comparison with 27 per cent in Nottinghamshire. Such evidence points to the importance of pastoral farming, and of small-scale settlement. The evidence of plough teams recorded in Domesday tends to confirm this picture. The heavy plough drawn by a team of eight oxen was the key to arable farming by 1086. It determined the method of ploughing in long strips of ridge and furrow, and the extensive balks and headlands, and it was a major determinant of the fertility of the soil, and therefore of agricultural yield. Fertilization depended almost entirely on the availability of dung, and on the number of ploughings each year (Darby 1977: 361; Platts 1985: 73; Stafford 1985: 24–8; Ashton 1977: 2).

Open-field farming was found throughout the East Midlands during the medieval period, although what this meant in practical terms varied considerably and has been much debated (Unwin 1983; Millward and Robinson 1975: 185; Baker 1963). Communal farming practices developed at different times and in different forms across the region. Lincolnshire was a well-settled county, and as a result its open fields probably developed early; indeed, it is possible that communal forms of agriculture existed in the county well before 1086 (Hallam 1965; 1981: 58–61). If communal farming of unhedged arable strips almost certainly predated the eleventh century, the fully fledged system of farming from a central village with two, three or even four large open fields (the classic or midland open-field system) was probably not organized until later in the Middle Ages. Between 1143 and the late twelfth century four upland Lincolnshire villages had a three-course crop rotation. There is an early thirteenth-century example from Rutland, and evidence for change from a two- to a three-field rotation at Galby in Leicestershire. Nottinghamshire and Leicestershire had plenty of examples of three-field systems by 1300. At Laxton the Mill Field was laid out by 1189, and the South (or Bottom) Field, the latest of the village's fields, by 1232; while Wigston Magna in Leicestershire had three fields by 1269–80 (Cameron 1980; Hoskins 1957: 63; 1950: 39). Four-fifths of Leicestershire's villages had three fields by the end of the Middle Ages, and a similar number in Rutland. Overall, it is probably safe to conclude that in the East Midlands the three-field system came into operation during the twelfth century and became common in the thirteenth.

The classic open-field system had a number of variants and some parts of the region had one- and two-field systems throughout the period. Two-field systems, sometimes known as infield-outfield (or the *breck* system), originated where the area of land available for tillage was large in proportion to the area which the village wanted to keep under the plough. The infield was a core of land maintained in permanent occupation along the lines of an ordinary open

Plate 1.5 Laxton, Nottinghamshire, the South Field. Laxton is the last village in England where the farmers still work their land in strips under the control of a manorial court. The South Field is one of the three surviving open fields, but it was once more extensive than it is today. Various enclosures since the seventeenth century have reduced the total acreage from over 500 acres to just 141 acres. The strips have also changed in size. When the village was reorganized between 1903 and 1908, many of the existing strips were amalgamated to form larger parcels which were better suited to the farming methods of the twentieth century. Whereas strips had seldom been more than one-half to one-third of an acre in the past, today most of them are about three acres in extent. However, the strip pattern can still be clearly seen on the ground, revealing the mosaic effect of different shaped and sized strips, and the curving edges of each strip, which originally came about through the effect of ploughing with a mouldboard plough. Although there have been changes, the village farming system is still based on the principles operating in the seventeenth century.

field, while the rest of the township apart from woodland constituted the outfield. In effect the outfield was a common, parts of which were intermittently used for cropping depending upon demand for resources. Usually such systems occurred on poor soil, as in the forest area of Nottinghamshire, and in the Derbyshire Peak District. Forty-five highland Lincolnshire villages had two-course communal crop rotations before 1200, and at the end of the Middle Ages two-field systems were still found on poorer soils in parts of Nottinghamshire and Lincolnshire. In addition, the two-course system continued to be observed on fertile land in populous marshland townships of Lincolnshire until the eighteenth and nineteenth centuries (Thirsk 1973a: 257).

Three-field systems were rare in upland Derbyshire, where cultivation usually involved two and sometimes just one field. In the latter instances spring-sown oats were harvested late in the year. Most of the one-field villages were found on the carboniferous limestone; they probably included Monyash and Sheldon, and it is at least possible that one-field cultivation was feasible because it was associated with the secondary occupation of lead mining (Millward and Robinson 1975: 182–3). Three-field villages in Derbyshire were found in areas with suitable soils and altitude, particularly on a level with or south of Derby, in the north-east of the county around Chesterfield, and in the lower Wye valley. About 80 per cent of the county's villages with three or more fields lay below 500 ft above sea-level, and 60 per cent of all the open fields were on clays (Hallam 1981: 115–17, 158–9).

The open-field system was a risk-sharing operation. Each of the great fields was divided into a number of separate units, the most basic of which was the 'land' or 'selion'. 'Lands', although of varying widths and lengths, were usually of less than half an acre in area, and either alone, or with a number of others, they formed a strip – which was a tenurial term rather than a unit of cultivation. A group of 'lands' uniformly cultivated formed a furlong, and each of the two or three open fields consisted of a collection of furlongs. Either the furlongs, or the fields, or both, were operated on a regularly rotating basis. One field would be given over to a winter-sown crop such as wheat or rye, the second would have a spring-sown crop such as barley or peas, and the third would be in fallow. As a result of ploughing with a mouldboard plough arable land in the open fields often took on the appearance, still widely apparent on the ground today, of ridge and furrow. Ploughs had a 'fixed' mouldboard which always turned the soil to the right. By ploughing round the clods that had been thrown up in the centre of the strip by the first cut, the soil of the whole strip tended to be heaped into a high ridge anything up to 3 ft high. Since the ridges improved soil drainage, by speeding up the run-off of surface water through the furrows which acted as gutters, the system was deliberately encouraged, particularly on heavy clay soils. It also ensured that good and bad land was fairly distributed, and that slopes and hillsides could be cultivated where population pressure was greatest. Stock was pastured on the arable and adjoining meadow in fallow seasons and in the period between harvest time and the next sowing. Strip cultivators had the right to graze a limited number of animals and to gather commodities such as timber and peat on the common pasturage or areas of waste. Although this system has now almost entirely disappeared from the English countryside it can still be seen in an attenuated form in the Nottinghamshire village of Laxton.

The communal nature of the open-fields system was emphasized by the role of the manorial court. The most difficult decisions faced by the court concerned crop rotations, and just how these worked is by no means clear. In some cases it seems likely that parts of fields were cultivated *en bloc*, reflecting the pressure of local needs (Thirsk 1964). However, the system was by no means static. Crop rotation and field reorganization was not uncommon. At Great Corringham in Lincolnshire the tenants' holdings were divided between the two halves of the village in 1200. What in effect was a two-field system was changed before 1600 to a four-field system but then reverted to a three-field system. More intensive rotations were adopted from time to time in conjunction with increased pressure of population. Traditional rotations were modified by the addition of peas, beans and vetches in increasing quantities from the mid-fourteenth century onwards (Thirsk 1973a: 258–62). Up to six different grains could be sown on a manorial demesne, and cropping on tenanted land was just as varied. Even the advantages to be gained from enclosure were discussed as early as the fourteenth century in Lincolnshire, while conversion of pasture and meadow to arable was common through the thirteenth and early fourteenth centuries.

Agricultural diversity and specialization is clear throughout the medieval period. Prior to 1350 Lincolnshire had two principal farming regions. The highland part of the county specialized in wheat, barley and sheep, while in the fenlands oats, and after 1300, maslin, sheep, cattle and dairy products were the main specialisms. Hemp and flax were also grown in the fenlands. Oats were probably the predominant grain in the county, although wheat was the most important crop in northern Lindsey and Kesteven. Sheep predominated among the county's stock, especially on the Lincoln Edge, the Lincoln Cliff and the wolds. The fenland was an important pastoral, and above all a cattle-rearing, region (Hallam 1981: 40–2). The areas of most meadow relative to arable were in the Lindsey marshlands, where lords must have specialized in livestock husbandry. Damp conditions probably determined the decision to divide land in almost equal proportions between arable cultivators and graziers. However, on the chalk wolds immediately to the west the imbalance was corrected by the emphasis on arable produce. A proportion of arable to meadow in the clays and fens of 3:1 is plausible, whereas in Rutland the proportion was more like 8:1, and in Leicestershire and Nottinghamshire 10:1. Such figures suggest that the proportion of meadow in Lincolnshire was considerable, and they also point to the variation in local farming practice (Platts 1985: 108–9).

Variation in agricultural practice was also found elsewhere in the region.

The usual course of winter crop, spring crop and fallow was followed in Leicestershire, but thirteenth-century evidence suggests no attempt was made to equalize the spring and winter crops. Oats were preponderant in the economy, while the importance of spring crops increased through time to represent something close to three-quarters of the total. New crops began to appear during the fourteenth century, including beans and peas (VCH Leics II 1954: 159–60). The Nottinghamshire evidence also suggests that oats were more important than other grains, while the number of dovecotes points to a sizeable grain output. Between 1255 and 1329 ten manors had fisheries, of which two were in the Trent and one in the Soar. Oxen, horses, and a large flock of sheep can be traced on one west Leicestershire manor. In the southern lowlands of Derbyshire, which included the Trent and Derwent valleys and the Pennine foothills, swine and sheep were common; indeed, sheep were numerous throughout the county. Goats were popular in some of the county's higher areas, but little is known about cropping beyond the obvious limitations on grain production imposed by upland conditions (Hallam 1981: 103–4, 154–5).

Finally, relatively little is known about farming practices. Some Nottinghamshire villages appear to have been short of manure. In Sherwood in 1327 tenants of one of the king's manors were permitted to collect the fallen leaves from the trees in Clipstone Park for manuring. Marling (the use of clayey soil to fertilize the land) was practised from an early date. Nottinghamshire had marl pits in 1279, and at least one person regularly marled his land at Cossall in 1294. Twelve marlpits dating between 1238 and 1457 are documented for Derbyshire, of which ten were in the rapidly expanding eastern and central parts of the county (Hallam 1981: 117–18, 161; Millward and Robinson 1975: 186).

To modern eyes the sparsely populated region with its dependence on the soil does not give much impression of wealth and comfort. Making a living from the land required unremitting toil in a struggle against landlords and weather combined. Yet many of those who came to England with the Conqueror in 1066 saw a land flowing with proverbial milk and honey. What the Normans recognized, and what cannot be determined simply from the bird's-eye view of 1086, was the phase of expansion which had begun in England probably in the tenth century, and which was to continue until the end of the thirteenth century. In this expansion the East Midlands played a leading part, even if it was not central to the lives of the great majority of people. That the perception was correct will become clear in Chapter 2.

Chapter 2

Prosperity and Decline, 1086–1348

During the two centuries after Domesday Book was compiled the East Midlands passed through a period of prosperity which helped to give it an economic unity. The signs of prosperity were numerous. Growing population and new settlement suggested a buoyancy which was also reflected in other aspects of regional life. Urban growth was an obvious pointer since towns were important as trading centres, quite apart from harbouring industrial development. Lincoln, the largest town in the region at Domesday, enjoyed unparalleled success partly as a result of its position at the head of the flourishing wool trade, which was itself a reflection of prosperity. Much of the wool, and indeed much of the commercial wealth of the region, was channelled through the great cathedral city and its feeder port, the newly emerging Boston. Crown charter grants of the thirteenth century point to a rapid expansion of local trading, and nowhere was the growth of such centres more pronounced than in Lincolnshire. The resultant increase in markets suggested a dynamism in local trading at the regional level. In addition to trade, industry was also on the move. Derbyshire lead, second only to wool among the region's industries, was also sold for export, and much of it passed through Hull and also Boston where it was exchanged for grain and other foodstuffs sent westwards. The focal point of the region, in every sense, lay in its eastern quarter. It was here that perhaps 70 per cent of the population lived, that the woollen industry enjoyed its great prosperity, and that the largest slice of local wealth was to be found.

The eastern part of the region was wealthy relative both to the other parts and also on a national level. Of thirty-eight counties (or, in the case of Yorkshire and Lincolnshire, divisions) for which comparable figures exist for the 1334 Lay Subsidy, Holland was clearly the wealthiest. Its standing reflected the remarkable prosperity of the coastal fenland settlements during the early Middle Ages, and all three divisions of Lincolnshire were above the national average. Apart from Rutland, placed sixth, the other east midlands counties fell below average, and Derbyshire on these figures was one of the poorest counties in England (Glasscock 1975; Schofield 1965: 504). Testimony to this wealth is found in church architecture. It is not just the monumental St

Botolph's in Boston which reflects the period; some of Lincolnshire's smallest villages can boast a church which serves as a reminder of the wealth flowing through the region, the same being true also of Leicestershire and Nottinghamshire. Even in Rutland large and attractive churches were going up during the century 1150–1250 in villages such as Clipsham, Little Casterton and Preston when the county's total population probably did not exceed 10,000 (Hoskins 1957: 58–9).

Unfortunately prosperity did not last, partly because it was built on shaky foundations. Communications in the region remained poor, despite the central role played by the Trent, and the inability of agriculture to increase output ensured that unchecked population pressure was always likely to precipitate a crisis when numbers outran resources. In addition, trading patterns altered as a result of the Hundred Years War. As a result, the prosperity of the eleventh and twelfth centuries was on the wane by the end of the thirteenth; indeed even for those who grew rich on the pickings of trade the years after 1300 contained nothing to compare with earlier times. The inhabitants of Grimsby complained of mud and sand in the haven in the 1280s, while the Boston wool trade peaked in about 1290. Throughout the region economic and social conditions were deteriorating by the early years of the fourteenth century, and disaster followed in the form of the Black Death and subsequent plague revisitations. Recovery was slow and faltering, and in 1500 the region was arguably less prosperous and less populated than on the eve of the Black Death.

Towns

In AD 1000 towns were of relatively little significance in the East Midlands. Although it is possible that the Vikings had given a stimulus to urban growth, particularly at Lincoln which seems to have enjoyed something of a reputation as an industrial centre between 960 and 1010, relatively few people lived in towns at the time of the Domesday Survey. Only nine boroughs were recorded in the Domesday Survey: Leicester, Derby, Nottingham and Newark, and five Lincolnshire settlements, namely Lincoln, Grantham, Torksey, Louth and Stamford. Lincoln, with a population of perhaps 5,000–6,000, was unrivalled for size throughout the East Midlands. To the south Stamford, with a population of about 3,000, was a regional capital of some importance, while Torksey had about 500 inhabitants, Grantham around 1,200, and Louth 600. Elsewhere in the region only Leicester with 322 houses and a population of between 1,000 and 2,000 stood on a par with the major Lincolnshire towns. Both Nottingham and Derby had fewer than 1,000 inhabitants (Darby 1977: 305).

Borough or market status did not necessarily imply a great deal of economic activity, and some places which did not have a formal status were locally important. Spalding lay between the sea and the marshy Lincolnshire fens, and its limited economy is clear from the references to fishing and salt making, the absence of watermills, and – for all practical purposes – woodland. Wirksworth, in Derbyshire, was relatively populous and prosperous, largely due to its lead mining interests, while Castle Bytham in Lincolnshire drew its wealth from ironworking. Other local places for which the Domesday entry suggests significant prosperity included Castle Donington in Leicestershire, and settlements which today are little more than villages, including Laxton and Edwinstowe in Nottinghamshire and Melbourne in Derbyshire (Stafford 1985: 46–53; Darby 1977: 318; Hinde 1985: 164).

The Conquest may have brought problems to the towns. As a regional capital Lincoln stood on a par with York and Norwich, although like York it seems to have suffered in the years after 1066. About one-fifth of its houses had been wasted by 1086, but it had at least five churches and was expanding beyond its limits. Thirty-six houses and two churches had been built beyond the city limits. The number of burgesses fell from 173 to 120 in Nottingham, and from 243 to 140 in Derby. However, there was also a more positive side to the Conquest. As an army of occupation the Normans proceeded to build castles in the major centres including Nottingham, Leicester and Lincoln. These were all part of William's method of imposing military control over his new kingdom. In Nottingham work began on a new Norman borough covering an area of about 120 acres and including the castle and a large market place within its perimeter. It lay to the west of, and was considerably larger than, the existing Saxon borough which covered a site of only about 32 acres. Leicester was also flourishing in 1086 with only four empty or dilapidated houses. Lincoln's position was strengthened by the decision to move the see of Dorchester from Oxfordshire to the town in 1072–73. The town became the capital of the largest English diocese, stretching from the Humber to the Thames, and in the wake of this move work began on building the cathedral. Finally, Oakham appears, according to its Domesday figures, to have been a large and thriving centre, although this seems to have been because five outlying settlements were included within its orbit for the survey purposes (Hill 1948: 44–5, 54, Chs IV, V; VCH, Derbys II 1907: 163; Barley and Straw 1971: 3–4; VCH Leics IV 1958: 2, 31; Hinde 1985: 221).

Medieval towns contained an assorted collection of merchants, craftsmen and shopkeepers – all of them operating on a small scale – and landless labourers in search of employment. But since urban life was highly competitive, towns tended to be overcrowded and many inhabitants lived in conditions of great poverty. A few towns developed a clear-cut economic base. Both Lincoln and Stamford, for example, built their prosperity on an urban cloth industry. Nor was it merely the larger towns which benefited from developments of this nature. Louth, in Lincolnshire, increased its prosperity by super-

Plate 2.1 Lincoln Cathedral. This view, taken from the castle, shows some of the infinite variety of architectural styles in modern Lincoln, with Elizabethan and Georgian houses lying in the shadow of the cathedral.

The cathedral was built following the movement of the see of Dorchester from Oxfordshire to Lincoln in 1072–73. It was completed in 1092, but after being damaged by fire in 1141, and an earthquake in 1185, it had to be rebuilt. Work continued through the thirteenth century, and the original structure has undergone many changes since that time. However, Lincoln is widely regarded as one of England's most distinguished cathedrals.

During the rebuilding, considerable changes took place. Although the limits of the original west front can still be seen in this picture, the front was widened into a screen and consequently deprived of the logic of its Norman predeccessor. Pevsner describes the outcome of this meshing of styles as 'curious rather than beautiful' (Pevsner and Harris 1964: 101).

The cathedral dominates not just Lincoln, but the countryside for miles around, and it must have been even more impressive when the great central tower (only just visible in this picture) and the two western towers had spires, between 1420 and 1549. The spire on the central tower was blown down in 1549, but those on the western towers remained in place until 1807.

imposing a cloth industry on to its established role as a regional marketing centre handling wool from the wolds and livestock from the marshlands. Craft gilds and fraternities, many of which were first recognized in the twelfth century, developed in the towns. Lincoln had at least eleven by the end of the fourteenth century, representing among others archers, barbers, cordwainers, fullers and masons. The gilds had only limited political power in the towns, but their social and economic influence was pervasive.

Town life also depended on the activities of merchants, goldsmiths and other groups. Significant Jewish communities were established in Lincoln and Stamford during the twelfth century, while the Church made a considerable contribution to urban development. A number of monasteries were situated near to towns, including Lenton Priory close to Nottingham, while rural monasteries owned houses in towns as a basis for marketing. Perhaps most significant were the friars, the travelling priests, who first appeared in the thirteenth century. For their work among the laity they naturally made their headquarters in towns, hence the fact that the four main orders each had houses in Boston, Lincoln and Stamford, while Grimsby had two friaries and Grantham one. Friars made a particular contribution in the provision of schools (Rogers 1970: 40; Platts 1985: 196–211; Hill 1948).

The county towns of Lincoln, Leicester, Nottingham and Derby enjoyed considerable prosperity down to the thirteenth century. Far and away the most important was Lincoln, dominated during the medieval centuries by its royal castle, its cathedral canons and its merchant gild. The new cathedral was completed by 1092. Thereafter, as churches were built and religious houses founded, the town came during the course of the Middle Ages to be heavily influenced by its foundations. Not surprisingly there were set-backs. Both in 1267 and 1275 the ruling elite was charged with oppression and misconduct, and when these accusations were revived in 1290 they provoked the intervention of the monarch (Hill 1948). Nor did the cathedral escape unscathed. It was badly damaged by fire shortly before 1146, and in 1185 it was split from top to bottom in an earthquake. Under the influence of St Hugh rebuilding began in 1192 and continued throughout the thirteenth century to produce one of England's most distinguished cathedrals, in the early English Gothic style. The great central tower was finally completed in 1311 and the small Norman west towers were crowned with additions around 1420. All three towers had spires, the central tower from 1311 and the western towers from 1420. The former was blown down in 1549 and the others were removed in 1807. Building on this scale was possible as a result of local prosperity. For his rebuilding programme St Hugh organized regular offerings, granted indulgences, and founded a gild for raising a cathedral building fund. The fabric fund was set up sometime before 1200 to receive legacies and offerings as well as endowments of land from wealthy individuals. The capacity to raise the sort of sums involved in maintaining the cathedral reflected not only its significance within the diocese, but also the prosperity of Lincoln and its surrounding area during

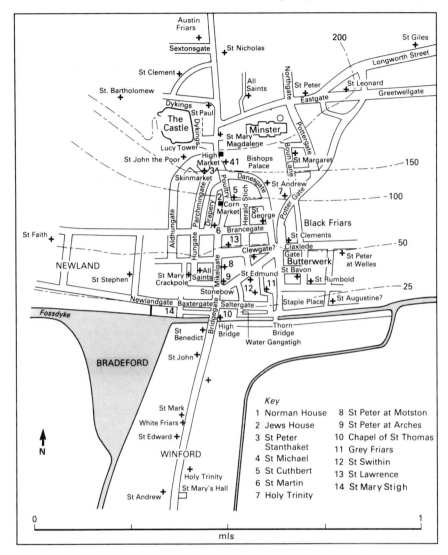

Figure 2.1 Medieval Lincoln, *c.* 1300 (after Hill 1948:244)

the twelfth and thirteenth centuries. Although much of the town was destroyed in a fire in 1123 Lincoln maintained its position as one of England's leading towns during this period (Hill 1948: 109–12, Ch. VII; Owen 1971: 41–3).

Most of Leicester's population of about 2,000 lived within the 100 or so acres enclosed by a wall raised on the foundations of the Roman defences, and even within these confines enough space was found for gardens and orchards. There were also seven parish churches, some of which may have resulted from

57

endowments by rich merchants in the years before 1143. As in Lincoln the cloth trade was vital to Leicester's economy, and the town's merchandise was sold as far afield as Boston and Stamford fairs. In 1202 Leicester stood fourth among medieval towns involved in the trade, behind Lincoln, York and Beverley. But cloth was not Leicester's only interest. At the beginning of the fourteenth century the town had nine tanneries and five footwear manufacturers. The attraction to tanners may have been the oak bark, since Leicester Forest reached almost to the walls of the town.

Medieval Leicester was dominated by its merchant gild, its abbey outside the walls, and its castle within the walls. The gild was confirmed to the town's inhabitants in the twelfth century, with the right to control trade. Membership was open to all traders and craftsmen (except females). The major trades group in the town consisted of people connected with the food supply, and they were followed by leather workers (including shoemakers), mercers, builders and metal workers. The role of Leicester Abbey, founded among the meadows of the Soar beyond the north wall of the town in 1143, was also important. Leicester merchants provided the chief outlet for the abbey's wool. In 1297–98, for example, Hugh le Mercer, one of the town's most important wool traders, was buying extensively from the abbey. The role played by the castle was equally significant, since the authority of its owners (the earls of Leicester and later the earls and dukes of Lancaster) eclipsed even that of the king, but this did not prevent burgesses from exercising increasing power in the course of the Middle Ages. Borough institutions were moulded from the relations between the earls and their stewards, and the burgesses (Phythian-Adams 1986: 43–8; VCH Leics IV 1958: 15–49; Millward 1985: 45–51; Pye 1972: 264–79).

Nottingham lay in the shadow of the Norman fortress built by William Peverel on the virtually impregnable Castle Rock. The English and French boroughs existed side by side, though maintaining a sense of independence as late as the seventeenth century. The French, or Norman, borough incorporated within its 80 acres the great triangular market place, one of the largest in England, and the two twelfth-century churches of St Nicholas and St Peter. Rebuilding of the castle in stone began during Henry II's reign, and the 'double borough' was further fortified with a bank, a ditch, and, from about 1267, a wall. In the course of the twelfth century the town acquired rights of self-government. By 1284 the burgesses had the right to elect annually a mayor and two bailiffs; and by the same charter the town was granted a second fair, this one of fifteen days, to complement the existing eight-day fair. Local prosperity was aided by the foundation of Lenton Priory *c.*1109–14, the wealthiest monastic house in the county. Around 1300 Nottingham's most widely acclaimed product was its leatherware, and its other major industry was cloth production. Iron and pottery making is known from the town's place names; bell-founding and alabaster working also took place (Cameron 1971: 71–2; Barley and Straw 1971: 3–5; Walker 1963; Owen 1945).

Derby was also important as a commercial centre, a fact recognized in the Crown grants to the borough after 1200. A charter of 1204 recognized the town's borough status and granted the right to hold a great market from Thursday night to Friday night. In addition it laid down that for 10 leagues around the town (excepting Nottingham) no one should work dyed cloth except in the borough; it also stated that the river Derwent should be kept free to voyagers. The burgesses, as in Nottingham, were allowed to form a merchant gild, which came to play an important role in town government. By 1330, however, the gild had been accused of acting oppressively, since merchants from outside the town were prevented from selling goods, except at wholesale prices, and only to the gild, particularly when wool, wool-fells, wine and lead were involved. The gild then resold the goods to the town at a profit (VCH Derbys II 1907: 163; Coates 1965: 110).

Urban development was by no means limited to the county towns, indeed one of the most striking features of this period is not merely the growth of existing settlements but also the increasing numbers of boroughs and market towns, which directly reflected commercial activity within the region. To found a borough was to invest in the settlement tenurial characteristics distinct from the rural surroundings, particularly the right to rent property without services, a right known as burgage tenure. It also implied a greater commitment to trade and handicrafts than to agriculture. The precise definition of a borough has been much disputed by historians. It is clear that not all the tenth-century boroughs retained this status into Domesday Book, while new boroughs emerged at various points during the medieval centuries. This was the case in the East Midlands and Table 3 gives an indication of which towns held borough status during the period. The list is not intended to be definitive. In Derbyshire, for example, Derby and Chesterfield would appear to have been

Table 3   Medieval boroughs in the East Midlands

Derbyshire	*Leicestershire*	*Lincolnshire*	*Nottinghamshire*	*Rutland*
Ashbourne	Hinckley	Barton-on-Humber	East Retford	Oakham
Bakewell	Leicester	Boston	Newark	
Castleton	Mountsorrel	Caistor	Nottingham	
Chesterfield		Gainsborough		
Derby		Grantham		
Wirksworth		Grimsby		
		Lincoln		
		Louth		
		New Sleaford		
		Stamford		
		Torksey		
		Wainfleet		
		Willingthorpe		

(Sources: Beresford and Finberg 1973: 85–149; Beresford 1981)

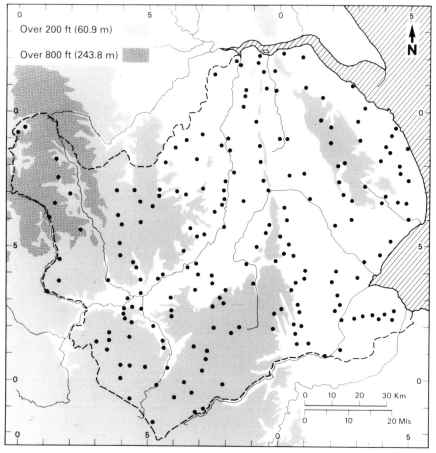

Figure 2.2 Medieval markets in the East Midlands

boroughs, although the latter did not have a mayor and corporation until 1598, while Bakewell was a mixed borough of burgesses and freeholders, and Ashbourne's attempt to attain borough status met with only partial success. Nottinghamshire was poorly served for boroughs, while in Leicestershire Lutterworth (1279), Ashby de la Zouch (1330) and possibly Castle Donington (1311) may also have had borough status (Coates 1965: 102; Unwin 1981: 234; VCH Leics II 1954: 177).

A number of new towns also date from this period, and such foundations in the Middle Ages usually reflected commercial considerations. None appear to have been founded in Nottinghamshire – with the possible exception of East Retford – and Rutland, but elsewhere they included Castleton (*c.* 1196) and Bolsover in Derbyshire; Belvoir (1076–1100), Mountsorrel (1148) and Market Harborough (1167–77) in Leicestershire; and Boston, Brigg (1183),

Sleaford (1123–47), and New Eagle (1345) in Lincolnshire. Castleton, now best known as a haunt for Peak District walkers, was built around a large market square and a church. The regularity of its pattern of lanes suggests a measure of formal planning from the beginning (Millward and Robinson 1975: 233). Castleton was not very successful, possibly because Peveril Castle lost its importance during the fourteenth century, but the same could not be said of Market Harborough, which was almost certainly deliberately created in about 1167–77 from the demesne of Henry II's royal manor at Great Bowden. As with most medieval new towns it was essentially a commercial venture. To this end it was deliberately located on the Leicester–Northampton road, near to a ford crossing the river Welland, and the whole plan, with its wide, funnel-shaped main street leaving plenty of room for the market and the annual fair, emphasized the importance of commercial activity. Not all new towns were a success, most notably in the East Midlands the ill-fated New Eagle. Appearing as it did just before the Black Death it is perhaps not surprising to find that the settlement made no noticeable progress (Mullins and Glasson 1985: 4; Hoskins 1949: 56–68; Beresford 1967: 416, 461–5, 475, 478).

A final indication of the buoyancy of commercial enterprise was the creation of markets and fairs. Domesday Book is an incomplete record of markets. None at all was recorded in Derbyshire, Nottinghamshire and Rutland. In Leicestershire, Melton Mowbray was the only place outside of the county town where there was a hint of trade and commerce. Lincolnshire was rather better recorded, with markets at Barton-upon-Humber, Spalding, Louth, and three or four minor centres. Even this list must, however, be incomplete. Over the next two centuries the number of markets proliferated. The climax of their creations in England, as the result both of royal grant and the spontaneous action of interested parties, was in the thirteenth century. Monarchs began to accept a fee in return for granting market rights to manorial lords. For their part the lords received regular tolls from traders. As a result, during the thirteenth and early fourteenth centuries the number of identifiable markets increased, a development which coincided with the rise of horses – in place of oxen – hauling, to speed the movement of goods to the market. The East Midlands was in the forefront of this change (Langdon 1984: 37–66).

It was at the point when seigneurial economic strength was at its maximum in the thirteenth century that many of the markets of the region were founded. This must have coincided with an increase of tenant production for the market, partly to raise money to pay rents, fines and taxes. Whatever the direct profit made by a landlord from a market, and this seems never to have been large, the indirect significance of setting up such trading centres was obviously considerable. On the other hand, in Nottinghamshire seigneurial control may have been weakening by the late thirteenth century, and it is possible that quite apart from the implications for their income landlords turned to market creation as a means of restoring their economic control (Unwin 1981: 231–7).

Table 4   Markets founded in the East Midlands, *c.* 1200–1349

County	1200–49	1250–99	1300–49	Before 1349	Total
Derbyshire	5	14	4	6	29
Leicestershire					37
Lincolnshire					120
Nottinghamshire	3	12	7	6	28
Rutland	0	1	2	2	5

(Sources: Britnell 1981: 210; Coates 1965: 108–9; Unwin 1981: 235–6; Platts 1985: 135–7; VCH Leics II 1954: 175)

Known market creations during the Middle Ages are given in Table 4. In Derbyshire both Derby and Chesterfield appear to have been market towns well before 1200. They were probably the only substantial centres of their type, although other parts of the county traded through market towns near the border such as Nottingham and Burton on Trent. In addition, Ashbourne, Bakewell and Repton held markets by ancient custom, and, as ecclesiastical centres, their marketing functions may pre-date the Conquest. By the mid-fourteenth century twenty-one Derbyshire settlements had been granted both markets and fairs, a further four places had markets only, and Bakewell, a fair only. Two-thirds of the markets and fairs recorded before 1350 were established or recognized between 1200 and 1275. Since many of the markets and fairs were granted to individuals prepared to 'buy' commercial privileges from the Crown, social and political factors helped to determine distribution. Larger landowners who had influence with the Crown, tended to be able to acquire charters. Thus the Earl of Derby obtained market rights at Hartington, and the earls of Lancaster acquired rights at Melbourne and Wirksworth (Coates 1965).

In Nottinghamshire the major period of market creations was in the late thirteenth century, suggesting a rough parallel with neighbouring Derbyshire, but market rights were not granted to the county's wealthiest inhabitants in the manner of Derbyshire (Unwin 1981: 234–7, 248). Possibly the most significant development was in the county town itself, where the spacious, funnel-shaped market place, built at a meeting of several communications networks, encouraged Henry I to require the men of Nottinghamshire and Derbyshire to go first to Nottingham to sell their wares (Platt 1976: 27). In Leicestershire only Melton Mowbray and Belvoir are known to have had market privileges before 1200, but another twenty-three settlements had gained similar rights by 1300. Altogether medieval Leicestershire had a total of thirty-seven official market towns, most of them situated on the main routes emanating from Leicester. The east and west-central portions of the county were the least well served (VCH Leics II 1954: 175–7). In Rutland, Overton and Oakham were the only markets in the reign of Henry III, but further grants were made for

Uppingham in 1281, Empingham by 1318, and for Belton, Barrowden and Burley during Edward III's reign (VCH Rutland I 1908: 216).

Finally, in Lincolnshire more than fifty markets were chartered between 1270 and 1347, coinciding with colonization and reclamation as increasing numbers of villagers set out to produce surpluses for the market. Markets were to be found in eighty-five townships and villages, of which five had two weekly markets. Twenty-five other places had a market which was probably chartered but for which no grant has survived, and five of these had two markets. Altogether the county was served by at least 120 markets, a relative density of 1 to every 24 square miles compared with 1 to every 36 in Derbyshire. Topography and social structure clearly influenced market location. Many were found in the siltland townships of the fens or along river valleys, and in the marshlands and wolds of east Lindsey. Urban centres such as Grimsby, Lincoln and Grantham tended to have a retarding effect. At the height of the period of market creation most people in Lincolnshire probably needed to travel no more than three or four miles to a chartered market, and there were doubtless more unchartered trading centres even nearer to hand. Fairs were almost as numerous as markets in the county, many of them being licensed by the same charter. Most lasted three days, but some for as long as eight or even fourteen. Boston and Stamford fairs were the most renowned in the county during the thirteenth century, although they were not alone as focal points for large-scale marketing. The longer fairs were sustained by visiting buyers and sellers from other regions of the country, particularly in Boston where the range of goods included wool, hides, fells, lead, canvas, grain, livestock and fish for export, and furs, silks, wines, hawks and spices for import. Some of the larger fairs were promoted by influential families or religious houses, although most of the major ones were situated on the coast or near to navigable waterways (Platts 1985: 135–44).

How far did the markets help to promote intra-regional trade? In Nottinghamshire, traders seem to have preferred markets within the county boundary, but by contrast the high incidence of Derbyshire markets found close to the county borders suggests the opposite pattern (Unwin 1981: 240; Coates 1965: 104–7). On the other hand the large number of markets is indicative of the communications problems of medieval England. Something of the importance of a particular centre can be judged from the proximity of other markets. In Lincolnshire centres such as Lincoln, Boston, Grimsby and Grantham did not face market competition from nearby rivals. As a result, the county came over time to consist of a series of sub-regions each dominated by a large town, but the transition from this situation to a 'county' identification with Lincoln at the centre depended on improved communications. This position was certainly developing in the thirteenth century, and an indication of progress can be measured from the Lincoln Parliament of 1301. When Edward I called this particular assembly in the county town the task of provisioning the 200 members involved the whole county. Goods were brought from all parts of Lincolnshire, and it is significant that they came primarily by road despite the fact that the Parliament was held during the winter months (Pelham 1951: 16–32).

Not all of these boroughs and markets were of similar importance. The most significant centres in early fourteenth-century Leicestershire included Melton Mowbray and Market Harborough, Ashby de la Zouch and Lough-borough (Hoskins 1957: 60), while important centres elsewhere included Newark and Mansfield in Nottinghamshire, Chesterfield in Derbyshire, and a string of Lincolnshire towns. Almost invariably commercial activity seems to have been the spur to urban development, and towns such as Stamford, Grantham and Newark were important because they lay on major com-munications arteries in addition to having significant trading interests. Stam-ford prospered during the Middle Ages as a centre of trade and manufacturing. Apart from benefiting from its strategic position on the Great North Road, it was also fortunate in lying between the wool producing fenlands to the east and Leicestershire and Northamptonshire to the west. The town was ideally situated both as a marketing area for raw wool and for the production of cloth. Weavers, dyers and fullers all appear in the town's twelfth- and thirteenth-century records, although the absence of a craft gild organization suggests that their importance should not be overplayed. Ironically, although the town's ancient customs and liberties were confirmed in 1202 it did not receive borough status until 1462, by which time its greatest years were long past (Rogers 1965: 34–57).

A number of towns played a significant local marketing role, among them Chesterfield and Mansfield. Chesterfield, the major town of north-east Derbyshire, was first mentioned in 955. It was a market town during the twelfth century even though its earliest charter was 1204. The original market lay on a cramped site adjoining the church, and by 1199 the 'new market' had been laid out on the west side of the town, where it is still to be found. This did not immediately supersede the earlier market which was still functioning on a Tuesday in the thirteenth century. Chesterfield is an early example of how town planning helped to complete the transition from rural manor to small town, while its prosperity depended upon the cloth industry, well established

---

Plate 2.2 Boston, Lincolnshire. A nineteenth-century print showing the harbour and a few fishing vessels. In the foreground there is little evidence to suggest that Boston enjoyed the status of one of England's premier ports in the thirteenth century, when it was also one of the wealthiest towns in England. The basis of this prosperity was the wool trade, and much of the export came from the east midlands counties.

For evidence of this long-past prosperity the eye is drawn to the background of the picture where the imposing presence of St Botolph's church, lying just to the north of the market place, is to be seen. It is one of the largest of English parish churches, and the Stump, 'the most prodigious of English church steeples', is 272 ft high (Pevsner and Harris 1964: 463). The church was begun in 1309, and its massive presence is a reflection of Boston's medieval wealth. However, the town's glory days were relatively short-lived, and since the later medieval period it has been a port of only minor significance, though it remains an important market centre for the fens.

by the early thirteenth century. The town also had interests in woollen cloth manufacture, tanning and a range of specialist craftsmen working leather, among them shoemakers, glovers, saddlers, girdlers, pursemakers and bottle-makers. Ashbourne was also laid out as a planned town in the thirteenth century, while Bakewell, Castleton, Bolsover and Wirksworth were all recognizable as towns (Blanchard 1967: 383; Bestall 1974: 25–44, 66, 69–70; Riden 1977: 5–15).

Mansfield appears to have been a market centre during the twelfth century, which is hardly surprising since the settlement was a natural centre for the exchange of goods between the limestone area to the west, and the relatively lower sandstone region to the east. As the centre of an important royal manor and the meeting place for the soke court it also drew considerable numbers of people when the court met. In 1227 the men of Mansfield were granted a market charter, and although this was surrendered when the Crown granted the manor and soke to Henry de Hastings in 1238 the market continued to function. From a population of 250–300 in Mansfield and its immediate surrounds at Domesday numbers rose steadily, possibly doubling between 1100 and 1300 (Crook 1984: 26–7; 1985).

The towns of medieval England, large or small, were trading points, and the number of creations in this period reflected the abundance of trade and the fragmentary communications network. The cost of moving goods overland meant that most of the markets established in the thirteenth and fourteenth centuries served a small and primarily local market area. In addition, most of Derbyshire's market towns were situated on or close to major streams, although this probably reflected density of settlement rather than being a direct consequence of any widespread use of river and valley routeways. This did not ensure the success of all the markets which were established. Competition was considerable in south-east Derbyshire, and it was here that those markets described in the fourteenth century as little used or moribund were primarily found. As communications improved, competition among market towns increased, to the extent that by the mid-seventeenth century about two-thirds of market towns no longer held a regular market (Coates 1965: 107). The same was true in Nottinghamshire. Several townships which received market charters in the thirteenth and early fourteenth centuries increased in relative importance in the settlement hierarchy between 1086 and 1334, including East Retford and Colston Bassett, but in other places the market made no perceptible difference, and some even declined. The smaller the settlement the more likely it was to grow when awarded a market. By 1600 only nine markets were left in the county, most of them located in settlements which had developed into towns. The other twenty-one medieval markets had all decayed since the fourteenth century, although the most notable period for decline appears to have been the later fifteenth and early sixteenth centuries. As in Derbyshire the implication is that people were physically able – and presumably financially able as well – to travel the greater distances. The road network played a crucial role in this process – it was the markets situated on main through roads which tended to survive – and by 1600 an urban hierarchy was developing based on the six major market centres which came to dominate the remaining rural settlements of the county (Unwin 1981).

This weeding-out process took time, and an indication of the state of towns in the region immediately prior to the Black Death can be gained from the lay subsidy returns of the 1330s. On a national level Boston ranked fifth and Lincoln seventh among the greater towns, with Newark trailing at 24, Nottingham at 26, Stamford at 29 and Derby 36. The most significant figures, however, are those which relate to the Lincolnshire settlements along the coast and around the Wash. Within the county only Lincoln and Boston were larger than some of these settlements, several of which probably had populations of 500–1,000, including Saltfleetby, Wrangle, Leake, Benington, Freiston and Spalding. Their assessments were considerable. While, for example, assessed wealth in Newark amounted to £390, much higher figures were recorded in Pinchbeck (£675), Spalding (£630) and Holbeach (£495). Altogether twenty-seven places in Lincolnshire, but just the county towns (not including Oakham) and Newark elsewhere, had assessed wealth of £225 or more. The Lincolnshire figure included almost every fenland township in the Holland division. Many of these were not recognizably towns although a number of the larger settlements figure in lists of ports and were clearly involved in a flourishing coastal trade. Mablethorpe and Ingoldmells also benefited from this activity. Local prosperity was partly connected with land reclamation and with the rich arable land which could sustain a sizeable population, as well as salt making, fishing and fowling, and these figures help to account for Holland's rating as the wealthiest part of England. The subsequent retreat from the margins of cultivation around the mid-fourteenth century meant that these places made no further progress, but there is no doubt that in the 1330s the balance of urban wealth lay firmly in the eastern part of the region (Platts 1985: 189–96; Darby 1976: 179–83).

Communications and Trade

The problem of communications within the region was considerable. The Danes made good use of the river routes, wintering in Nottingham and Repton during the 860s after penetrating the area along the Trent. All five of the Danelaw boroughs were situated on navigable rivers. Indeed, by Domesday the waterway system was well established. The main axis was the Foss Dyke, a 7-mile long artificial channel possibly constructed by the Romans for drainage if not for navigation, and almost certainly still in use shortly before 1066. It linked the river Witham – connecting Lincoln to the Wash – to the river Trent, which was navigable from the Humber as far as Burton. Such was the importance of this link that anyone impeding the passage of boats on the Nottinghamshire Trent was liable to a fine:

> the water of the Trent, and the Foss (*fossa*) and roads towards York are so regulated (*custodiuntur*) that if anyone impedes the passage of boats or if anyone ploughs or makes a ditch within two perches of the king's road, he has to pay a fine of £8.

The burgesses of Torksey were entrusted with the responsibility for conducting the king's messengers through Lincolnshire to York. In addition, the Welland was navigable as far as Stamford.

The major towns were all significant trading points, and usually they stood at the interchange of vital communications points. Lincoln's position on the Witham and the Foss Dyke ensured good communications throughout the region. As such it both fed on the buoyancy of the regional economy and was itself an important factor in the well-being of the county. Gainsborough linked the city with north Nottinghamshire and south Yorkshire; Newark with Nottinghamshire and Derbyshire; and Sleaford, which created a link with Kesteven and Holland, acted as a staging post for the transport of goods to the town. By water, goods moved rapidly along the Witham and via the Foss Dyke to the Trent; indeed, possibly the most significant symbol of Lincoln's economic position was the reopening of the Foss Dyke to traffic in 1121 – it may have been blocked shortly after 1066 as a result of the town's post-Conquest troubles – and the prosperity of Torksey (Barley 1936: 10; Hill 1948: 173).

Much the same was true of Nottingham, situated not merely on the Trent but also on one of the two overland routes through the region, the London–York road, where it crossed the Trent. The town's position on the Trent was of vital importance. Charles Deering wrote in the mid-eighteenth century that:

> It appears plainly by Domesday-Book, that the River Trent was
> Navigable before the Conquest, whence there is no doubt, but that a
> good Share of Trade, was carried on, between Nottingham and other
> Places by Water. Time immemorial, the which, after the Conquest has
> been increasing proportionably to the Increase of Trade in general.
> (Deering 1751: 91)

A charter of *c.* 1155 gave the town's burgesses the right of toll over all people passing along the river as far as East Retford, and the river was used for the transport of lead from the Peak District, coal from the Cossall and Selston area of Nottinghamshire, and a variety of other goods including alabaster, wool, timber and corn. This situation gave a particularly favourable position to Nottingham merchants. They were exempt from tolls on the river as far as the Humber, and they came to possess what amounted to a virtual stranglehold over the trade of Nottinghamshire, parts of Derbyshire, Leicestershire and north Warwickshire (Cameron 1971: 72–3).

On land two of the old Roman roads, the Fosse Way and Ermine Street, cut across and through the region. The combination of water and overland transport was vital, and tended to influence settlement patterns. Just as Nottingham stood on the London–York road where it crossed the Trent, so Stamford was situated where the Roman road crossed the Welland (Darby 1977: 301–2; Owen 1945: 14; Stafford 1985: 9–15). Even so travel was tedious. Travelling light on horseback in 1319 it still took five days to move between Cambridge and York, while to accompany goods on the journey was even more complex. On route for the same destination carrying cloth and furs another group from Cambridge spent two days travelling to Spalding, a journey accomplished in two boats, a third day travelling overland to Boston, two further days in a single boat to Lincoln, one more day reaching Torksey, and two more to make York. Tedious or not, considerable distances were covered. The obedientiaries of Durham Cathedral Priory regularly travelled to Boston fair to make their bulk purchases, carrying them back by boat to Lincoln, overland by cart to Torksey after the Foss Dyke had silted up, along the Trent and Ouse to Boroughbridge and from thence by road (Barley 1936; Platt 1976: 81).

Throughout the period the river network was vital for the movement of bulky goods. The central artery through the region was the Trent and frequent attempts were made to ensure free passage. In 1322, for example, a royal official was appointed with the task of arresting all those who tried to prevent traders with victuals and goods from passing up the river to Nottingham. Produce was brought overland in the fourteenth century from Derby and elsewhere to avoid the shallows and rapids in the river between Sawley and Wilford. It was then carried to a wharf east of Trent Bridge, before being dispatched downstream. In return corn was traded along the river between Gainsborough and Nottingham. Wool for Boston went one of two ways: either by river to Newark, and then by carts or packs overland through Claypole and Sleaford; or along the Trent to Torksey, and then along the Foss Dyke and the Witham. Although the Foss Dyke is known to have been used in 1319, by 1335 this route had closed, and all water-borne trade had to go by the Humber. This may be why an agreement of 1414 for the transport of alabaster from the Chellaston quarries in Derbyshire stipulated that the goods should be carried to Hull (Wood 1950: 5–6). Quantities of stone must also have been moved by water, particularly for the building of fenland churches (Barley 1936). Since the countryside north of Nottingham was particularly unsettled in the early fourteenth century the Trent was the only reasonably safe communications route between the Midlands and the north of England. Despite its importance the river was occasionally blocked, and this, with the silting of the Foss Dyke, was indicative of an about-turn in the prosperity of the region's overseas trade by the early fourteenth century.

Overseas trade was a further indication of local prosperity, and the mushroom growth of Boston during the twelfth century is indicative of the significance of international markets. Founded in the period 1086–1113, Boston was the great success story of Norman commercial enterprise. It is not mentioned in Domesday Book, but within a century it had become one of England's premier ports and trading centres. The town was built on a narrow strip of land sandwiched between the river Witham on its western side and the Barditch, a ditch and internal bank, to the east. The central focus of the settlement was the bridge across the Witham – which may date from as early as 1142 – and the adjoining market place, with St Botolph's church just to the north. The settlement was defended by a ditch, probably before 1200, but urban expansion was such that expansion beyond the ditch had occurred by the thirteenth century. By the early fourteenth century something in the region of 5,000 people must have lived in the town. Boston's tax valuation in 1334 was exceeded only by London, Bristol, York and Newcastle (Harden 1978).

The basis of Boston's prosperity was the export of wool, primarily from Lincolnshire, which produced wool regarded as second to none in both quality and quantity, and also from religious houses and private estates throughout Leicestershire, Nottinghamshire and Derbyshire. Well over half the wool exported from England in 1275 passed through Boston, and a record 10,280 sacks were exported from the port in 1290–91. On the other hand, trade was dominated by overseas interests. Of 307 merchants and sailors (apart from Italian firms) paying customs duty on wool exports through Boston in 1287–88, among the larger merchants responsible for thirty sacks or more only three were readily identifiable as Englishmen. They included Gilbert de Chesterton of Grantham with eighty-seven sacks, and the same man exported at least 100 sacks in 1290. In 1297 the English were still a minor force, with just fifteen Englishmen, mostly from Lincoln and Grantham, exporting 144 sacks between them. The proportion seems to have gone up in the early years of the fourteenth century, with a number of substantial merchants from Lincoln, Spalding, and Grantham, in addition to those of Boston, exporting through the port (Lloyd 1977). To supplement the wool trade Boston also carried on a flourishing export business in Derbyshire lead and fenland salt.

Boston developed links with northern Europe as well as the Mediterranean. Most of its wool export went to Flanders, Italy and Germany, and local merchants imported commodities for consumption in the region; thus wine was sent via the Witham to Lincoln, for the bishop, and also to Grantham, Newark, Nottingham, Castle Donington, Spalding, Stamford and Leicester. The extent of the port's trading interests was considerable. By 1323 the merchants were trading with London, Jutland, Friesland, Cologne, Scotland and Ireland. But it did not last; from about 1290 the wool trade began to move away from Boston. It was still the second port for wool exports in the 1330s, but it had lost ground and as trading interests and routes changed during the fourteenth century – particularly with regard to the Italian trade – the port's fortunes slipped into reverse gear (Dover 1972; Carus-Wilson 1962–3: 183–201; Lloyd 1977: 123, 140).

Elsewhere in Lincolnshire both Grimsby and Gainsborough enjoyed overseas trading links during the Middle Ages, though neither of them on the same scale as Boston. It was ironic that Grimsby, further north on the Lincolnshire coastline, did not enjoy the same prosperity as Boston during the medieval period, since it had greater administrative independence (Rigby 1984b: 51–66). Grimsby was a marketing and manufacturing centre which served a small hinterland in the Lindsey marshes, extending at most 9 miles around the port. Local craftsmen concentrated on supplying food, clothing and buildings, while the merchants were primarily interested in coastal rather than overseas trading interests. Grimsby's overseas links were mainly with Scandinavia and the Low Countries. Exports included grain, cloth and wool, while among the incoming goods were timber, corn and wine. Grimsby's coastal trade involved the carriage of foodstuffs north to Newcastle in return for coal, and south to London. However, while the leading burgesses dealt in grain, coal and herrings, they were in a different league from the international traders of Boston and Lincoln (Rigby 1984a: 45–6; Gillett 1970). At Gainsborough the town's bailiffs received a three-year grant of quayage in 1298 to build a quay against the inundations of the Trent. In 1322 the town was named as one of the ports to supply the king with corn, and in 1401, along with Nottingham and Newark, it was requested to build a barge for the king's service. Gainsborough also benefited from the decay of Torksey in the fifteenth century. Its trading interests almost certainly included Derbyshire lead and Sherwood timber (Beckwith 1967a: 3; Platts 1985: 145–51, 187).

Industry

The industrial prosperity in the East Midlands during the early Middle Ages was built on relatively slim foundations laid in the eleventh century. The major industrial interest recorded in 1086 was the mining of lead in the Derbyshire Peak District. Domesday Book noted what seems to have been lead smelting sites at Matlock Bridge, Bakewell, Ashford and Crich, and three at Wirksworth. Silver production may have taken place in the royal manors of Matlock Bridge, Ashbourne, Parwich, Darley and Wirksworth, although Derbyshire galena had a low proportion of silver compared with Yorkshire and the Mendips. On the other side of the region specialized iron works were found at Stow and Castle and Little Bytham in Lincolnshire, and salt making went on in many east coast marsh villages. Fisheries were found in various parts of the region. Although the towns were probably centres of commerce rather than of industry, a few urban industrial activities are known. Pottery was manufactured in several places including Stamford – which is known to have had a thriving industry from the tenth to the thirteenth centuries – Lincoln and Torksey in Lincolnshire, Leicester, Nottingham and Derby (Darby 1977: 299; Kilmurry 1980; Stafford 1985: 53–60; Fuller 1970).

In general terms manufacturing in this period has to be seen as rural craftwork rather than anything remotely resembling modern industry, particularly in Lincolnshire which has always been primarily an agricultural county, even though a number of places became centres of local industry with a variety of craftsmen. In 1332 a high proportion of villages had a resident smith, although little is known about where these men obtained their iron ore. Some was extracted in Lindsey, but it is likely that more was brought from Derbyshire. A few other specialist metalworkers were found in the villages, including the occasional plumber and locksmith, while carpenters were ubiquitous in the countryside (Platts 1985: 120–3). Despite this proviso the eastern part of the region contained the most important industry of this period.

Woollen cloth was possibly the most important manufacturing concern in the medieval East Midlands. In Lincolnshire large flocks were grazed on the wolds from at least the eleventh century, and the marshlands also provided excellent grazing land. As a result, wool became a major product in the county. It was the principal commercial occupation of the monastic houses, several of which leased warehouses in Boston and other places to facilitate their overseas trade. Although fleeces were originally cleaned and spun within the household, the development of the Flemish cloth industry raised demand and transformed many English graziers into international suppliers. However, local interest did not stop with producing raw wool. Simultaneously cloth production moved into the full-time cloth producer's town-based shop. By the thirteenth century production was taking place on a capitalistic merchant-orientated scale, with the various processes of spinning, weaving, fulling and dyeing separately controlled. Lincoln and Stamford became widely known as English cloth-producing centres, with Lincoln specializing in finely finished high-quality cloth, and Stamford in a particularly fine type of cloth bought for kings and great men such as Archbishop Becket, which must have resembled the chain-mail of a hauberk (Owen 1971: 66–68; Platts 1985: 126–8).

The wool trade also flourished elsewhere in the East Midlands. In Nottinghamshire religious houses were trading with Flemish and Florentine wool merchants from the thirteenth century, and here, as elsewhere, the fourteenth century proved to be the golden age for the trade. Flemish merchants resided in the county and local men were domiciled abroad in order to promote the trade. Nottingham itself benefited from King John's grant in 1199 of a merchants' gild with the exclusive privilege of manufacturing dyed cloth or cloth designed to receive a dye within 10 miles of the town. It was a move which helped to turn the town into a regional centre for cloth manufacture. Newark merchants, in common with those of the rest of the Midlands, were compelled to export their wool from Boston, where the staple was fixed in 1369. The town's wool trade was controlled by the mayor and twenty-four aldermen. But the trade did not last. By the fifteenth century it had begun to wane, and the demand for wool revived only with the growth of framework knitting in the eighteenth century. Wool for the European market was also produced in Derbyshire, with much of it being exported through Hull and Boston (VCH Notts II 1910: 340–3; Blanchard 1967: 419–22).

Lead mining ranked second to wool production in this period. The Derbyshire lead mining industry was stimulated by the demand for the soft lead produced in the Peak District for roofing in England and the Low Countries. As the major English source of lead, the Derbyshire industry flourished down to the mid-fourteenth century, though with periodic booms and slumps. The fragmentary statistical material which has survived shows that in the Crown's lordship of the High Peak, expansion of production in the late twelfth century was followed by decline down to the 1240s, and then by a brief recovery before yet a further regression down to the end of the century. However, elsewhere in the Peak the situation was rather different, with production rising in the manors of Bakewell, Ashford and Youlgreave to about 1340. Further evidence of expansion on the eve of the Black Death is suggested by a labour shortage, which resulted in miners being impressed from the Dartmoor area to work in the Peak (Blanchard 1971: 124–5; 1967: 283–6; Carr 1965: 210).

In the course of this period wool and lead came to represent the major parts of a much more extensive range of pursuits including coal mining, the production of millstones in Derbyshire, pottery and leather goods, and a whole range of local craft occupations. Although coal mining was not mentioned in Domesday there is evidence to suggest that extraction had certainly commenced by the thirteenth century. Coal was being mined in the Nottingham area by 1257, while the earliest mining lease among the papers of the Middletons, who owned estates west of the town, dates from 1316. Across the border in Derbyshire Beauchief Abbey was granted lands and rents at Swanwick in about 1300 by the lord of the manor of Alfreton, with licence and liberty to dig for coal. The grant was confirmed in 1316, and for the next two centuries the mine was worked on lease to laymen. Coal was also mined on the Leicestershire and south Derbyshire coalfield during the thirteenth century (Smith, R. S. 1964; Johnson 1953; Owen 1984: 20–22; Pye 1972: 342).

Pottery was another significant local industry, mentioned in Domesday at Lincoln, Stamford and Torksey. Stamford, as an important economic, political and military centre, was a prosperous town in the tenth century. Its pottery was already sold widely before the Conquest, but after that markets opened up throughout the Midlands and eastern England. Stamfordware has been found all over Lincolnshire and further afield up to a radius of 120 miles from the town. However, the vigour and prosperity of the early twelfth century proved to be shortlived, and the growth of the industry in Nottinghamshire

and elsewhere brought production in Stamford to an end by the mid-thirteenth century (Kilmurry 1980). No potters were listed at Lincoln, Stamford or Torksey in 1332, and although this does not mean the industry had completely died out the major trading interests of the earlier period had probably fallen foul of small-scale competition from other centres such as Bourne and Toynton (in the Lincolnshire wolds).

Leicester seems to have had a flourishing leather industry. Leather working is known as early as 1199, and various interrelated leather crafts were established by 1300. Tanning flourished in Newark from about 1280. Evidence of salt making in the Lincolnshire fens during the two centuries after Domesday is derived from charters and a number of rentals, surveys and account rolls. Although few salt makers were recorded in the 1332 tax listings, many craftsmen may have fallen below the tax threshold; in any case these activities were part-time occupations co-existing with arable cultivation and of only marginal financial benefit to the families involved. Fishing was well established, both along the Lincolnshire coastline and also on the rivers Witham, Ancholme and Slea. There were around thirty fisheries near Bourne in 1086. On the coast Grimsby and Boston were the primary fishing centres, though fishing was secondary to trade in Boston and was not yet especially important in Grimsby. It was only in the fifteenth century that Grimsby fishermen began to venture out of the Humber and as far afield as Iceland (Allin 1981: 2; VCH Notts II 1910: 337; Hallam 1959–60; White 1984: 29–37; Platts 1985: 125–6).

Elsewhere natural resources encouraged the concentration of artisans in small-scale local industry. Building stone was quarried around Stamford, but elsewhere – as in Lincoln – the transport costs ensured that only the wealthiest members of the community had stone-built houses. The prior and monks of Lenton in Nottinghamshire received permission from the king in 1429 to quarry stone in Sherwood Forest, and thereafter stone was carried to Nottingham from various parts of the county. In some parts of Lincolnshire by the fourteenth century brick was coming into use for both church and house building. Although relatively expensive to make, bricks were cheaper to obtain than stone brought long distances. Also significant from the thirteenth century until the Reformation was alabaster working, which provided a large output of ornamental work for churches in the region and further afield. The carvers (sometimes known as kervers) of Nottingham, Derby and Burton on Trent obtained a reputation for the high quality of their work over many generations.

Plate 2.3 Heckington Church, Lincolnshire. The magnificent spire of St Andrews Church, Heckington, marks the beginning of a row of fen-edge villages stretching south to the Northamptonshire border at Market Deeping. Helpringham, Great Hale and Swaton all have fine churches, but all give pride of place to Heckington, which is one of the most outstanding churches in a county where fine churches abound.

St Andrews was built as a piece, of Ancaster stone, during the flowering of the Decorated style in the early fourteenth century. It is 164 ft long, and the spire is about 180 ft high.

The raw material was quarried at Tutbury, near Burton, Chellaston, south-east of Derby, and Red Hill, south-west of Nottingham (Edwards 1966a: 231–3; VCH Notts II 1910: 330; Platts 1985: 128–35).

By the middle decades of the fourteenth century the prosperity of the early Middle Ages had passed. Population growth, always uneven but generally upwards, had slowed to a virtual halt. New settlement and land colonization, such a feature of the immediate 1086 period, had virtually come to an end, except perhaps in Derbyshire. The limits of settlement had effectively been reached, and the village economy was increasingly under threat from the division of land which had taken place in order to accommodate rising numbers. The signs of prosperity – growing numbers and sizes of towns, flourishing local and overseas trade, and developing industry – were all to be seen, but the scale of economic activity needs to be kept in perspective. The expansion of known market facilities during this period suggests an active exchange of goods. Coupled as it was with land colonization and, in Lincolnshire, reclamation, it suggests a growing desire – or perhaps necessity – to produce for the market. As a result there is evidence to suggest that more goods were being moved, and probably over greater distances, within the region. While the number of new markets argues for an inadequate communications network, the provisioning of the 1301 Lincoln Parliament provides salutary evidence that it was possible for goods to be moved over quite long distances, by road, even in winter. This is not, of course, to deny that waterways were the most significant means of moving goods, with the Trent occupying a role as central commercial artery for the region which it was to continue to play at least until the coming of the railway. Boston's overseas trade also increased the movement of goods within the region. By the thirteenth century the East Midlands was flourishing, as a result of intra-regional trade and communications, but prosperity proved to be short-term. The blocking of the Foss Dyke by 1335 and the decline of Lincoln together symbolized the end of the golden age and ushered in the austerity of the later Middle Ages.

Chapter 3

The Black Death and its Aftermath, 1348–1500

In June 1348 bubonic plague hit the Dorset town of Melcombe Regis. The Black Death, as it came to be called in the nineteenth century, had finally crossed the Channel after sweeping across Europe from central Asia. In the months that followed it raged through England and Scotland, subsiding only in 1351. Perhaps a third of the population of England died in the catastrophe. On its own this was bad enough, although economic historians now believe that recovery began remarkably quickly in the aftermath of the plague; but the cumulative impact of further plague outbreaks in 1361–2, 1369 and 1375 proved to be more than the country could stand. By the third quarter of the fourteenth century the population of England had fallen to between one-third and one-half of the level reached before 1348; there was little further growth before 1500. The adjustment that was required to a new situation took various forms: falling prices, rising real wages, changes in the management of demesne lands and the extent of labour services, the abandonment of cultivation on land which had been only marginally economic, and, in the longer term, village desertion. The purpose of this chapter is to describe how the East Midlands fared in the aftermath of the disaster, but it needs to be born in mind that while for individuals, for families and for whole villages successive visitations of the plague brought devastation in their wake, for the community as a whole the situation was not all bad. Living standards appear to have risen; manorialism gradually collapsed; and villeinage faded away. For those who survived, the fifteenth century was not such a bad time to be alive, and even the lords, who might have been expected to suffer in the changed circumstances, often showed remarkable resilience.

The origins of the mid-fourteenth century crisis pre-dated the Black Death. Wetter conditions were already affecting the region by the late thirteenth century, and the years 1315–22 witnessed widespread distress, particularly during the great European famine of 1315–17 when late rains prevented the ripening and harvesting of corn. The gains of land in Lincolnshire during the twelfth and thirteenth centuries proved to be short-lived; from the 1280s many areas were being affected by rising water tables. Rainfall was heavier and coastal innundations more regular after 1300, reducing arable areas and deterring some landlords from pastoral farming. The onset of wetter weather affected arable, meadow and pasture lands in Lincolnshire, not merely in the low-lying fenlands but also in much of Lindsey. Few parts of the county except the chalk and limestone uplands seem to have escaped the effects of waterlogging. Taxation figures reflect the extent of the crisis even before 1348, while the decline of coastal salt production in the marshes was further evidence of the community responding to changing conditions. The balance was only partially redressed by a shift of emphasis from pastoral to arable farming in the marshlands and some clay areas. This usually meant a reduction in the amount of meadow, which, because it was often found near rivers and marsh, was the first land to become waterlogged (Hallam 1965: 123; Platts 1985: 117–19).

Industry and trade were also in difficulty. Lincoln's heyday proved to be short-lived, and the gradual silting of the Foss Dyke highlighted the change of fortunes. By the late thirteenth century trade was already beginning to avoid using the canal, and in 1335 the men of the county of Lincoln petitioned the king and council, pointing out that the Foss Dyke was so obstructed that it could no longer be negotiated by boats and ships. Various efforts were made to restore the waterway during the fourteenth and fifteenth centuries, and its importance is clear from a claim as late as 1518 that revival of the now decayed city would be made possible if the Foss Dyke could be made deeper, wider and longer (Barley 1936). Elsewhere the cloth industry in both Leicester and Nottingham was in decline before the mid-fourteenth century. In Leicester the industry appears to have been migrating from the town by the early fourteenth century, and only one fuller – described as a poor man – appeared in the records in 1322. Conditions in the region were obviously changing even before the Black Death, but the crisis of the mid-fourteenth century produced an entirely new environment.

Population and Settlement

In the absence of good data measuring the impact of the Black Death on population trends is fraught with difficulties. The most recent figures suggest that the population of England was somewhere between 4.5 and 6 million on the eve of the Black Death, but probably only 2.75 to 3 million by 1377 (Hatcher 1977: 68–9). Figures for the East Midlands (see appendix) suggest an overall population of around 332,000 in 1377, or, using the same multiplier, nearly 700,000 in 1348. This figure may have been below the maximum previously achieved, since evidence from Lincolnshire suggests that there had already been a retreat from the margins of cultivation by the 1340s. It also seems possible that the post-1315 famine may have reduced the population level either directly or as a longer-term result of malnutrition (Platts 1985: 154).

How far the region was typical of national trends is a matter for debate. In Lincolnshire the population may have fallen from roughly 385,000 in 1348 to around 212,000 by 1350, and a rough estimate that the region lost half of its population would probably not be far from the truth. One indication of the devastation is that vacancies among clergy in the year March 1349–50 totalled 44.8 per cent of the 553 benefices in the archdeaconry of Lincoln, and 36.5 per cent of the archdeaconry of Leicester. Densely populated areas seem to have been the most severely affected. Consequently in Derbyshire, with its scattered settlements, the impact of the plague may have been less catastrophic than elsewhere, with population declining by perhaps no more than one-third (Blanchard 1967: 472–3). A few small villages failed to survive, including North Cadeby on the Lincolnshire wolds, Middle Carlton in the west of the county, and Ambion in Leicestershire, while the catastrophe seems to have sealed the longer-term fate of a number of others, among them West Wykeham, to the west of Louth (Darby 1976: 190; Platts 1985: 162–7).

Possibly more significant than the single outbreak of 1348–51 was the recurrence of plague over the following decades. After a further outbreak at Palterton in Derbyshire in 1362 there were no tenants left, and the land remained uncultivated for twenty-five years. Selective visitations of plague during the thirty years after 1349 were particularly damaging in Nottinghamshire. The heavy clayland arable of the northern wolds was labour intensive and all villages required a certain number of able-bodied males merely to carry out the agricultural routine. In smaller villages the margin between sufficiency and insufficiency was therefore low, and by the early decades of the fifteenth century there is evidence to suggest that some villages were in considerable difficulties, among them Thorpe-in-the-Glebe (Heath 1982: 44; Cameron and O'Brien 1981: 64). Further outbreaks of bubonic plague in 1361–62 and in 1369 neither upset the overall distribution of population in Lincolnshire, nor prevented gradual recovery, but there is widespread evidence of land being under-used, losing value, or simply falling out of cultivation. Other indications of decay include derelict windmills and watermills, dilapidated houses, untenanted messuages and tenements, and derelict dovecotes (Platts 1985: 169–78). Reductions in tax assessments also point to post-plague problems. In Leicestershire the assessments of 1334 were cut in 1445 by 38 per cent in Melton Mowbray, 40 per cent in Wigston Magna and 60 per cent at Humberstone (VCH Leics III 1955: 137; Hoskins 1957: 83–8).

It was the later outbreaks of plague which served to hamper the process of recovery. The low point of national population may have been reached in the mid-fifteenth century when a figure of 2 to 2.5 million is not unreasonable, even in the 1520s a figure of 2.25 to 2.75 million may not be far from the truth (Hatcher 1977: 69). Economic historians have argued that falling population

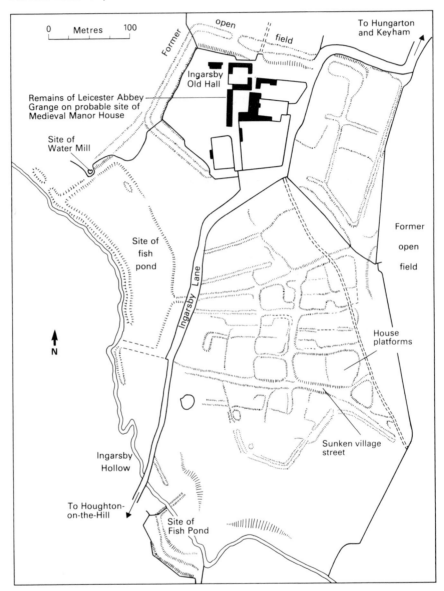

Figure 3.1   Ingarsby: a deserted village site (based on Millward 1985: 61)

produced both a shortage of labour and of tenants, which in turn depressed estate revenues. With the labour shortage came also a rise in wages, and falling prices. But the timing of these changes has to be kept in perspective. Agricultural prices and in many cases estate revenues do not seem to have been seriously affected until the 1370s, thereby confirming the view that it was not merely the Black Death which brought a fundamental realignment of the economy but the successive epidemics of plague down to the 1370s.

A clearer indication of the impact of plague is derived from changes in the pattern of settlement. The region suffered more than its fair share of desertions and shrinkages (Table 5). In relative terms, Leicestershire, Nottinghamshire, Lincolnshire and Rutland were among the most heavily depopulated of English counties (Beresford and Hurst 1972: 39), but it is clear that the impetus towards desertion came in the second half of the fifteenth century, long after the Black Death, and that it was not only recent settlements which were affected. More than 70 per cent of the places suffering depopulation in Derby-shire and Nottinghamshire had been founded before the Conquest. Whereas just 12 per cent of known desertions in Leicestershire date from *c.* 1350–1450, 60 per cent date from the period 1450–1700. Among them was Ingarsby, one of the best documented of Leicestershire's deserted villages, whose earthworks are still clearly visible today. Much of the manor was granted to Leicester Abbey in 1352, and in the years which followed the monks managed to acquire complete possession. Finally, in 1469 the village became a grange of Leicester Abbey, and although the abbey may have hastened the process, it seems just as likely, on the basis of surviving tax figures, that the village had long been in decline (Millward 1985: 60–2).

Table 5   Deserted medieval villages in the East Midlands

Derbyshire	33
Leicestershire	69
Lincolnshire	220
Nottinghamshire	67
Rutland	13
	402

(Source: Beresford and Hurst 1972: 34)

Most of Leicestershire's deserted villages lie in the east of the county. The prosperity of this particular area may have been more severely affected than other parts of the region. Similarly in Lincolnshire at least twenty-seven villages disappeared in the second half of the fifteenth century. Among Not-tinghamshire's deserted villages from this period is Keighton, which is men-tioned in documents relating to the affairs of Lenton Priory. Traces of the village are still to be seen on the University of Nottingham's campus, but they are by no means as dramatic as the earthworks which mark Thorpe-in-the-Glebe. Other villages, while not disappearing, certainly declined in size. In Leicestershire, Galby had thirty-three families in 1381 but only fourteen in 1563, and Wigston Magna suffered a sharp population decline after 1377. The timing of desertion or of shrinkage seems to have reflected less the immediate impact of the Black Death than reorganization of the agricultural community which took place thereafter (see below) (Edwards 1966a: 211; Dury 1963: 91; Dodgshon and Butlin 1978: 140; Hoskins 1946; 1950: 35; 1957: 15–35; Beresford and St Joseph 1958: 108; Cameron and O'Brien 1981).

Landlords and Tenants

In the aftermath of the Black Death the regional economy had to return to some sort of normality, and the evidence suggests that this took time. Even in the mid-fifteenth century the agrarian economy of south Lincolnshire was still depressed, and Spalding, a town of nearly 3,000 people in the mid-thirteenth century could boast less than 800 inhabitants in 1485 (Hallam 1967: 86–95). But while few landlords benefited from the changing circumstances after the plague their tenants generally found life less restricted.

The financial problems of the lords after 1348 were considerable. Many lesser lords had trouble making ends meet. In Lincolnshire, some found their income from rents shrinking following the famine years 1315–22 (Platts 1985: 161). In the 1340s, 126 Lincolnshire knights were listed as holding knight's fees, although 109 of them held property which was valued at less than £40 per annum, the level at which the qualification was fixed in 1300. The character of the greater lordships was also changing as old-established families died out and were replaced by men with national rather than local interests. Some were men who received the king's favour as a result of military or domestic service, and several were members of his household who chose to administer their estates from afar. Among the latter group were Philip le Despenser, who gained control of the Goxhill estates in Lincolnshire around 1300. The result of this trend was that the county's most substantial landholders turned out to be men with much less local contact than had been the case in the past.

On the other hand it would be wrong to picture a devastated, poverty-stricken picture of landlords in the aftermath of 1348 or even of 1370. As much as anything, it was competence or otherwise in management and administration of estates which determined their fortunes. But this may be to overstate the case, especially as one of the features of the period seems to have been the lack of scope for financial improvement. Leasing demesnes, abandoning direct cultivation, shifting to sheep farming, and reducing labour services made the conditions of tenancy easier. The old order simply could not be maintained (Dodgshon and Butlin 1978: 136). Of the few local families that prospered during the period, probably the best example is the Willoughbys of Eresby, Lincolnshire. The family had baronial connections in the thirteenth century and had acquired baronial status by the fifteenth. Even so, such families could not hope to compete for influence with those who were active in the Hundred Years War. However, of the wealth brought back to England by the nobles returning from France relatively little found its way into Lincolnshire, which was already becoming predominantly a region of small local gentry families (Platts 1985: 38–43).

For much of the fifteenth century lords were involved in feuds, rivalries, and ultimately in the Wars of the Roses. This did not prevent them from building although it did impinge on what they put up. Historically the most important work was that of Ralph, Lord Cromwell (1393–1456). In the 1430s he started building Tattershall, a majestic tower house in Lincolnshire, and almost simultaneously he was responsible for Wingfield Manor in Derbyshire, the most important baronial residence to survive in England from the mid-fifteenth century. Both houses are uniquely important nationally. He was followed by William, Lord Hastings, who built the castles at Ashby de la Zouch and Kirby Muxloe. In 1461 Hastings acquired the manor house at Ashby, and the same year he was granted Belvoir Castle from which lead was taken for his building work at Ashby. Thirteen years later he acquired a licence to crenellate his houses at Ashby, Bagworth and Kirby, and to make parks at each. As a result, he built the great tower at Ashby, and from 1480 he started building at Kirby Muxloe. Ashby was the larger of the two, but both represented domestic buildings of moderate defensive strength which he turned into fortified houses, reflecting the uncertainty of the times. Freestone was brought 11 miles from Alton quarry, and rough stone for the foundations from a number of places in the vicinity of the house, while lime was carried 9 miles from Barrow-on-Soar, and roofing lead came down the Derwent from Wirksworth. The walls were of brick made, as at Tattershall, by Flemings. Work at Kirby Muxloe was brought to an untimely end when Hastings was beheaded in 1483 (Peers 1975). The uncertain conditions for house building were also reflected at Gainsborough Old Hall, a timber-framed, unfortified structure built in the 1460s, but plundered if not partially destroyed in 1470 by opponents of the owner Sir Thomas Burgh. It was repaired in brick (Emery 1985). In Leicestershire, Thomas Grey's unfortified Bradgate Park also dates from the late fifteenth century (Beresford and St Joseph 1958: 57–8).

The lawlessness of the Middle Ages which induced men to fortify their houses culminated in the baronial struggles known as the Wars of the Roses. The number of barons in England may have declined since the Conquest, but the power struggles remained. In Lincolnshire by the early fifteenth century the two most powerful magnate families, Lord Cromwell of Tattershall and Lord Beaumont of Folkingham were irreconcilably opposed. They sought to rally the local gentry behind their particular cause, and in turn to line up behind greater magnates such as the Dukes of York and Suffolk in order to maintain their influence. The feud produced the sacking of Stamford and Grantham in 1461 – an event which arguably marks the beginning of the civil wars – and the

disastrous revolt against Edward IV in 1470. These two incidents, meagre contributions to the wars though they may seem at this distance in time, were more action than Nottinghamshire had to endure, although rival armies several times passed through the county. It was in Leicestershire, however, that the conflict ended. In August 1485 Richard III was residing at his Bestwood hunting lodge outside Nottingham when news arrived that Henry Tudor had landed at Milford Haven. Richard marched south through Leicester to the final struggle at Bosworth Field on August 22. The Tudor dynasty had arrived, and the baronial struggles were almost over although a number of subsequent, if less historically significant, conflicts included the Battle of Stoke in Nottinghamshire two years later (Storey 1970; Wood 1948: 112–26).

The religious lords suffered in this period, although in their case largely from a change of fashion in regard to the Church. The loss of popular support for monastic foundations is clear from the lack of gifts. The laity became more interested in their parish churches and money was spent on making them more attractive. New aisles were added, large windows replaced narrow wall slits, clerestory windows were added (as at Laxton and the Muskhams in Nottinghamshire), carved sepulchres, rood screens and chantry chapels appeared. The great and the good preserved their memories beneath effigies and tombs which are still to be seen in many parish churches, among them in Nottinghamshire Sir Adam de Everingham's alabaster tomb at Laxton, and that of Sir Robert and Sir Gervase Clifton at Clifton. Among a number of fine fifteenth-century towers are those at St Bartholomew's, Kneesall and St Peter's, Shelford (Wood 1948: 107–8; Pevsner and Williamson 1979: 158, 308). The parish church's gain was the monastic house's loss. At Crowland, in the Lincolnshire fens, by the fifteenth century the monks in their role as landlords were treated as an anachronism no longer worthy of respect. Considerable hostility was directed at the Abbey's wealth, and both Crowland and other fenland houses incurred great displeasure when they strengthened their position through further land purchases (Raban 1981).

The major impact on lords and tenants alike was the altered circumstances in regard to services and dues. For landlords tenants were hard to find for vacant holdings and hard to keep, so that a movement away from demesne farming was speeded up. From the late thirteenth century lords were again abandoning demesne farming, and the impact of the Black Death was to speed the process up so that by the mid-fifteenth century few lords worked their

---

Plate 3.1 Kirby Muxloe Castle, Leicestershire. The castle was begun in *c.* 1480, and constituted part of the extensive building works of William, Lord Hastings. Work stopped abruptly when Hastings was beheaded in 1483.

The castle is built in brick, and both the controller of works and the master mason visited Tattershall, probably to study the brick keep or the gate tower of the 1430s. Stone was used only for the doorways and windows. Kirby Muxloe is really a fortified manor house laid out round a single courtyard. No compromise was required with pre-existing work, though the castle is on the site of a moated fourteenth-century house.

demesnes directly. In Derbyshire cultivation was abandoned and estates leased during the years which followed Thomas of Lancaster's rebellion in 1322, and at Melbourne direct cultivation was given up as a result of the Black Death. Most of the county's lords with demesne had abandoned direct cultivation by 1377. On twelve manors held by lay lords in Leicestershire between the mid-fourteenth century and 1427 the demesnes were leased out; the trend was particularly clear after 1348. By the fifteenth century most of the large demesnes had been leased (Blanchard 1967: 27–45; VCH Leics II 1954: 182–5).

As lords abandoned their demesnes, tenants avoided dues. There seems to be little doubt that the tenantry benefited in various ways from the changing conditions of the late fourteenth century. They could move in search of better wages and conditions even if moving might be a breach of feudal obligations. An important feature of this movement was migration to London and other urban centres, and movement from the Midlands to the capital appears to have been on the increase. Those who remained were able to obtain better conditions because with tenants hard to find lords had to give up labour services. In 1381 only three of Galby's thirty-three families still had villein status, the rest having gained emancipation in one way or another. By 1500 service had effectively disappeared from the region (Hoskins 1950: 35).

One consequence of this change was the declining influence of the manorial court and the need for justice to be exercised on a wider canvas. At the same time the Crown decided from about 1300 to tackle some of the problems of local government by appointing temporary commissions to inquire into specific matters in the localities. Normally, the commissioners were local knights and gentry who could be expected to know the area. Commissions could be established for any number of causes, including road and bridge repair and the collection of taxes, but in the longer term the most significant was the commission issued to keepers of the peace. Although initially their powers were limited and they needed the cooperation of the sheriff, the value of these men soon became apparent and in 1361 they were upgraded to the position of justices of the peace. Not only did this move bring royal justice to the shires, it also gave the individuals appointed influence beyond their manors, and their powers were extended to cover the more serious crimes brought before sessions, including murder and robbery.

Despite periodic attempts to abandon the office of justice of the peace, it became apparent that it filled a gap in the legal and administrative relationship between central government and the localities. The authority of the sheriff was waning and the Crown was increasingly reluctant to use the coroner. Consequently in 1461 the position of the justices was enshrined in law. In future they were to take responsibility for indictments. These had previously gone to the sheriff's tourn, the twice-yearly sessions he held in each hundred of the county to administer summary jurisdiction. The £20 property qualification introduced in 1439 ensured that all JPs would be men of local standing. On the other hand, numbers were small; legislation of 1388 provided for six justices in each county, and in 1390 this figure was raised to eight, but by the late fifteenth century it was usual to have up to twenty in the more populous counties. They met four times a year – hence the term quarter sessions – largely to deal with the violence which permeated medieval society (Moir 1969: 15–25).

Who served in the office of justice? The most substantive evidence for the East Midlands comes from Derbyshire where numbers on the commission rose from twelve in 1429 to twenty-six in 1504. Normally they included the chief steward for the Duchy of Lancaster, who was often an important national figure and a midlands landowner. Peers with local estates were appointed, including the Lords Audley and Lord Cromwell, while the two Derbyshire peerage families of Grey of Codnor and Blount usually had a representative. Down to 1457, and again from 1483, there were normally two or three gentry who were 'imported', men with land in the county but a base beyond its boundaries. Being on the commission was not the same as attending sessions, and it is clear that the bulk of the work was undertaken by Derbyshire gentry even though they constituted only between one-quarter and one-half of the named justices in the first half of the fifteenth century. This proportion rose later in the century, possibly since they did the actual work, but also as part of a general increase in numbers. Willingness to sit on the bench was reflected in the fact that it became the preserve of a small group of working magistrates. A quorum of two was normal, occasionally with three or perhaps four sitting at particular sessions. Ralph Pole of Radbourne, John Curzon of Kedleston and John Tunstead seem to have undertaken most of the work from the mid-1430s until 1460, while one family, the Vernons, constituted a regular presence on the bench in the first half of the century. As the bench increased in size towards the end of the century it came to be dominated by small lay landowners, and the burden of work was also shared around (Wright 1983: 93–109).

Finally, as a result of the decline of service after the Black Death the nature and size of landholdings also underwent change. In general the average size seems to have grown larger, with the number of very small holdings diminishing as a result. By accumulating land, particularly where customary dues were no longer payable, tenants were able to prosper, and many became employers of labour. By the early sixteenth century about 28 per cent of Leicestershire's taxpayers depended on wages (VCH Leics II 1954: 197). High wages due to labour scarcity may have deterred some people from taking on more land than the family could manage, particularly since arable farming seems generally to have been in difficulties during the course of the fifteenth century. With markets glutted and prices depressed, marginal lands were no longer cultivated, thereby adding to the process of depopulation.

Land also seems to have changed hands more frequently, although this may have been a temporary phenomenon as property passed into the hands of formerly landless men. At Kibworth Harcourt in Leicestershire, for example, the high turnover of surnames in the late fourteenth and early fifteenth centuries resulted from the temporary dislocation of the normal pattern of hereditary descent of land; the return of the old stability by the seventeenth century suggests that this was not a long-term decline in the attachment of individual families to certain parcels of land. Overall, those families surviving the plague enjoyed a higher standard of living than their predecessors (Howell 1976: 139; Dodgshon and Butlin 1978: 129–30; Platts 1985: 183–4).

The Transition to Pasture

The arable sector of the East Midlands economy was depressed throughout the fifteenth century. In Derbyshire tenants were able to improve their property in the years of low rent following the Black Death. From 1416, however, the evidence increases for falling rents and unused land. Initially, except for one or two areas in the Trent valley, this seems to have reflected a decline in rent per acre rather than a contraction of land under the plough. Although reduced in numbers, the remaining population had increased the size of their holdings and reorganized the fields (sometimes through agreed enclosure, particularly in the Peak), to maintain the area of tillage. Animal husbandry was found to be increasingly profitable, partly because falling rents pushed up real incomes and enabled tenants to carry more stock. Even so, by the 1430s land was being abandoned.

The slackening of demand for arable produce was not matched by any loss of demand for wool; indeed European cloth makers still prized Lincoln-shire wool. The greater profitability of sheep in the county precipitated a major shift towards pasture in the later fifteenth and early sixteenth centuries. In turn this furthered the process of depopulation and desertion, while bringing prosperity to only a few of the county's farmers. The position was much the same in Leicestershire. Sheep farming was moderately important in the county from the twelfth to the fourteenth centuries, especially in the north-east on the lands of the religious houses, and in the Charnwood and Leighfield forest areas. The movement to enclose for pasture reached a peak in the county between 1490 and 1510, and produced the depopulation of entire villages in some cases (VCH Leics II 1954: 189–93; Platts 1985: 178–82).

Nor was the trend towards pasture farming limited to the sheep runs of Lincolnshire and Leicestershire, as is clear from Derbyshire. Tenants began during the course of the fifteenth century to find animal husbandry profitable; falling rents had the effect of raising their incomes, thus enabling them to improve their holdings to keep more animals. As a result, the pasture areas of the county suffered much less than their arable counterparts. In general terms between 1377 and 1540 both sheep and cattle farming were profitable in Derbyshire, and down to the 1430s the whole county prospered; the evidence of falling rents and unused land, with the exception of one or two places in the Trent valley, seems to have represented a reduction in rent per acre rather than a contraction of land under the plough. By increasing the average size of holdings, and reorganizing fields, a smaller population was able to maintain the area under tillage. Rents remained steady after about 1450, particularly in the major stock breeding area of the county, the north-west. There is some evidence of depression in animal husbandry and tillage in the north-west over the years 1450–1475, and in the south all forms of pastoral activity slumped between 1440–60 and had hardly recovered by 1540. In the north, by contrast, from the 1460s and 1470s the local economy benefited from a considerable expansion of pastoral farming. Prosperity also brought an increase in arable farming to the area, with the paradoxical result that the poorer arable of the Middle and High peak was in demand while in the traditional home of arable in the Trent and Derwent valleys rents were stagnant and land went out of cultivation. Consequently by the 1530s the north of the county was dominant in sheep breeding, and had an important dairy industry. What in effect had taken place was a reorientation of the county's economy, from the dominance of tillage in its own right to its subordination in the interests of pastoralism. The result was a change in the fabric of the economy with stagnation and decline on the previously important alluvial soils of the Trent and lower Derwent valleys, but growing production on the limestone soils of the north-west (Blanchard 1967: 111–12, 235–6).

Urban Decay and Trade Depression

The evidence for widespread decline, particularly among the larger towns of late medieval England, has accumulated in recent years, and the east midlands towns were no exception (Dobson 1977). However, coinciding with decline came greater independence in local government jurisdiction for a number of the larger towns of the region. Urban decay was not merely a result of the devastation caused by the Black Death, although the impact of the plague on population was serious enough. Lincoln's population fell from possibly 7,000 in 1300 to only 4,000 by the early sixteenth century, and Stamford's dwindled from about 2,000 to 1,200 between 1300 and 1500 (Platts 1985: 218ff). Urban populations continued to fall even after the visitations had finished. In Derby, for example, the population was about 1,300 in 1377 but only 1,130 as late as 1524 (Blanchard 1967: 316–19). More significant for decline was the collapse of the cloth industry, which brought depression to some of the region's major towns even before 1348, and which helps to account for the relative decline of some of the region's largest towns at the national level. Boston, ranked fourth and Lincoln sixth, among provincial towns (excluding London) in 1334, had slipped to twenty-second and fifteenth place by 1525, while Stamford had gone from twenty-eighth to thirtieth (Darby 1976: 243).

The clearest example of decline in the East Midlands was Lincoln. The town's charter of 1409 turned it into a county borough distinct from the surrounding county of Lincolnshire. It gained the right to elect its own sheriffs who would hold their county courts along with the old city courts (Hill 1948). However, this independence came as the town slipped from the position of a major regional centre, which it had enjoyed in the twelfth century, into the status of an important county town (Dodgshon and Butlin 1978; 142). Much of the reason for this was the decline of the wool trade; the removal of the staple to Boston in 1369 was merely the last straw for the town's beleaguered cloth industry. The continuing demand for Lincolnshire wool after 1350, which was partly responsible for the conversion of arable to pasture, did not bring prosperity to the county town. Cloth making moved away to avoid gild restrictions, and local Lincolnshire weavers worked in their own homes for a local market (Platts 1985: 182).

Leicester's experience was similar to Lincoln's. Various privileges had been assumed in the town by the early fourteenth century, and thereafter the borough gradually developed in a coherent form. By 1360 control of the fair had been wrested from the Duke of Lancaster and taken over by the mayor and a small committee of burgesses. Legislative functions in the town were being exercised by a special group of burgesses, and one indication of the significance of local government affairs in the town was that in the course of the fifteenth century mayors were increasingly men of substance within the community. From the late thirteenth century the mayor's prominence in local affairs became more noticeable, and during the fourteenth century the post seems to have been held predominantly by merchants, including mercers and wool merchants, and a few innkeepers and vintners. The position of town clerk also evolved during the fifteenth century. Eventually by legislation of 1489 the ancient bodies which had regulated the life of Leicester made way for a single institution which was soon to become the corporation of seventy-two burgesses and a mayor. The group consisted of twenty-four members of the bench, who were the controlling factor, and forty-eight new comburgesses. While all this was going on, however, the cloth industry was migrating away from the town, particularly during the course of the fifteenth century (VCH Leics IV 1958: 18–29, 38, 48).

Nottingham also achieved independence while suffering the impact of a declining wool trade. Powers to act as justices were granted to the mayor and recorder in the town's charter of 1399 and to 'four other upright and lawful men of the town to be selected by the Mayor'. County justices were not to interfere in town business. To preserve a foothold in the boroughs the Crown appointed recorders; Nottingham's first known recorder took up his office in 1399. Finally, in 1448 Nottingham received formal incorporation as a county

Plate 3.2 St Mary's Church, Nottingham. An impressive, cathedral-like building, second only to Newark as the largest parish church in Nottinghamshire. St Mary's was probably a Saxon minster which was rebuilt in Norman times, and what we see today is almost entirely fifteenth-century. It is built on a cruciform plan. The nave has six bays and aisles.

The earliest parts of the present building are the south porch and a recess in the south wall of the south transept, which are early-fifteenth-century. The windows are wholly perpendicular.

The church has experienced some rebuilding and additions through time, of which one of the most notable is the Chapter House, built by Bodley in 1890. This was in the anticipation – in the event unrealized – that St Mary's would become the cathedral church of the diocese of Southwell, created in 1884. In the event this honour fell to Southwell Minster.

---

under the name of the mayor and burgesses of Nottingham, and it was separated from the shire unit of which it had previously been a part. Under the 1448 charter the town council was restricted to the mayor and seven aldermen, one of whom was to be mayor, for life, and they were to be JPs. The charter was confirmed in 1462 (Owen 1946). However, all this was achieved while Nottingham's cloth industry declined. In 1378 the fair was reduced from fifteen to five days, and by 1433–34 Nottingham was listed as 'an impoverished town'. The town's trading connections with Hull and Boston became increasingly precarious; indeed, the link with Boston via the Foss Dyke was severed. However, as with other towns in the region, Nottingham still had wealthy merchants able to act as MPs, to build substantial town houses for themselves, to take responsibility – in this case – for rebuilding St Mary's in the fifteenth century, and to found chantries and almshouses (Barley and Straw 1971: 5, 7).

Evidence of urban difficulties is not limited to the county towns. Over much of the region the picture was of stability if not of actual decay, with little indication of prosperity. In Lincolnshire the decline of the county town had severe repercussions for other places, particularly Torksey, which relied on Lincoln to generate its trade along the Foss Dyke, and the decline of overseas trade largely as a result of falling demand for cloth had severe repercussions for the ports. The indications of faltering economic activity are not difficult to find. During the fourteenth century the Trent navigation, and Nottingham's links with Boston and Hull – the main artery for the exchange of goods during the twelfth and thirteenth centuries – became increasingly precarious, partly because the rising water table produced flooding and made changes of river course more difficult to control. The cutting of communications through the Foss Dyke was symbolic of a new set of circumstances. Changing trade routes during the Hundred Years' War affected Boston, because the focus of trade moved towards London and the southern ports. Midlands cloth was diverted through London, while Derbyshire wool, which had in the past normally passed through the east coast ports, went south through London and Southampton. A large proportion of Derbyshire's imported manufactured goods now came from the south, and dyestuffs for Leicester were carried overland from Southampton (Blanchard 1967: 439; Platt 1976: 78).

Under the circumstances it is hardly surprising that the decline in trade through Boston which commenced towards the end of the thirteenth century could not be halted. For the town the result was catastrophic. What had been the most prosperous community in Lincolnshire before 1350 could not sustain this position, particularly from about 1430, and it has sometimes been cited as one of the clearest examples of late medieval urban decline. At its peak Boston's trade had rivalled that of London, but then a period of what amounted to disastrous decline set in. While Hanseatic cloth exports reached new peaks after the Treaty of Utrecht in 1474, Boston was not part of this expansion, and by the early sixteenth century exports of 100 cloths a year were exceptional, a far cry from the 2,500–3,000 annually in the 1390s. Silting in the haven, the decay of the Foss Dyke, and the decline of Lincoln, all contributed to the failure, and by 1563 the population probably did not exceed 3,000, about half the level of 1377. The town did not go down without a fight. In the early fifteenth century efforts were made to revive local fortunes by challenging the monopoly of the Germans in Europe's far northern waters. Boston vessels began to fish in Icelandic waters, and to trade to Iceland, but it proved impossible to break the hold of the Hansa trading ports. However, the situation was not all gloom and despondency; Boston remained a major regional market centre and the only sizeable town in one of the richest areas of early sixteenth-century England. In St Botolph's, the 'stump', it had not only one of the largest of English parish churches, but a spectacular reminder of the wealth which had once accrued from the wool trade (Carus-Wilson 1962–3: 199–200; Rigby 1985).

Grimsby experienced hard times even before 1300, with complaints by its merchants about interference in both its local and international trade. Unlike Lincoln and Boston it seems to have enjoyed something of a recovery in the second half of the fourteenth century. The church tower was rebuilt and a new gaol and a common hall erected. But this proved to be short-lived, and by the mid-fifteenth century the town was again in great difficulty. Its population, which may have reached 2,000 in the mid-thirteenth century, declined to probably no more than 1,400 in 1377, and to perhaps only 850 by 1524. The remaining townsmen were poorer than their predecessors, a result, partly, of the decline of the haven, which like many east coast ports was affected by silting (Rigby 1984a: 47–54). Overall, a combination of the disruption of trade caused by the French wars, a decline in the quality of locally produced wool, the collapse of cloth making in some of the region's larger towns, and silting in the ports (at both Boston and Grimsby), served to undercut the major trading links which had been established in the early Middle Ages.

Decline was not the order of the day everywhere. Stamford, Grantham, Sleaford, Gainsborough and Louth all saw important building by and for the wealthy in the later Middle Ages, an indication of continued prosperity among some members of the urban community. These remained centres of commerce, although Sleaford and Gainsborough slid into the relative position of being little more than rural market towns. Stamford and Grantham benefited from their position on the Great North Road, and from their continuing interest in the wool and cloth trades. Overall, however, for Lincolnshire towns the fifteenth century was a bad time as their populaces retreated to the countryside in the relatively favourable farming conditions after 1348. The towns did not recover until the nineteenth century (Platts 1985: 218–29).

Elsewhere estate rentals in the Derbyshire market towns of Bakewell, Ashbourne and Wirksworth slumped between 1300 and 1450, and had only recovered slightly by 1540. The picture is of falling population and abandoned buildings. The same picture may not, however, have been true of Derby and Chesterfield, where cloth production tempered any tendency towards decline. Chesterfield remained active in the dyeing trade, and by the mid-fifteenth century it was a significant centre of textile production. Partly as a result a two-way overland traffic seems to have developed in which Derbyshire lead was carried to Southampton in return for dyestuffs (Blanchard 1967: 335–41, 399; Bestall 1974: 87, 89).

The absence of further market creations after the mid-fourteenth century is further evidence that towns were not making the same progress as before the Black Death. Many of the existing centres went through a period of economic difficulty; indeed, nationally, possibly one-third of all markets disappeared between the thirteenth and the sixteenth centuries, although many of these can have been little more than village markets. In Derbyshire, markets have continued in an unbroken sequence in around one-third of the places originally selected during the Middle Ages. But many other sites were failures. In 1330 the right to hold a market and fair at Sandiacre had not been exercised since the grant was made in 1252, a reminder that while charters granted a right to hold a market they did not imply that one was ever held. Ilkeston market had a chequered existence, being periodically discontinued and revived down to the nineteenth century. Sixty per cent of Lincolnshire's village markets disappeared, although almost all of the small urban markets survived. Among those failing to make the grade in Leicestershire was Stapleford Park, where only the old market cross remains as testimony to the village let alone to the market (Thirsk 1967: 467–73). Inevitably market failure had a great deal to do with depopulation caused by the Black Death, but it must also have represented the 'illusory optimism' of some of the lords who bought market charters in the thirteenth century, and thereby overinflated the network. This excess had largely been shaken out by the early sixteenth century (Coates 1965: 101; Hilton 1985: 10).

If, as has sometimes been suggested, the creation of a market was a landlord ploy to assert economic control in the community, it might be expected that the change in relationships after the Black Death would contribute to the decline in numbers. Evidence drawn from Nottinghamshire suggests that such a link is too simple since several small markets were still functioning between 1400 and 1450. It seems possible that increasing taxation by the late thirteenth century induced the tenantry to enter the money economy, and an obvious way of doing this was by marketing their produce. By sponsoring and taking a profit from markets, lords encouraged a change in the legal and economic position of their tenants. However, by the fifteenth century reduced population levels tended to favour the tenants' demands for higher wages and free status, with the result that many of the initial requirements for small rural markets disappeared. The need to sell grain for tax purposes diminished, and what began to take place was the centralization of the market economy. When this occurred it did so in the smaller market towns rather than in the village markets (although some of these survived because of their physical location), which was to have longer-term implications for the growth of urban populations (Unwin 1981: 251).

Industry

Although the evidence is often sketchy, industry appears to have suffered as badly as other sectors of the economy in the aftermath of the Black Death. This was particularly the case with the cloth trade, the most prosperous branch of early medieval manufacturing. It was far from disappearing, but particularly in the towns it was not faring as well as in the past. This was partly because cloth making was increasingly located in the countryside, particularly where pastoral farming was dominant. In the Derbyshire townships of Rowsley, Nether Haddon, Alport and Stanton, the communities enjoyed a significant cloth industry over the years 1355–1380. By the 1370s the industry was providing work for about one-quarter of the populations of Baslow and Nether Haddon, while at Rowsley between 1379 and 1381 Bartholomew the Tailor set up an enterprise offering work to almost one-third of the villagers. Unfortunately these developments proved to be short-lived; numbers dwindled from about 1380 and the fulling mills fell into decay (Blanchard 1984: 232).

Derbyshire lead miners also experienced difficulties in the wake of the Black Death. The rural economy of the Peak District suffered although it would be too much to say that the industry was brought to a standstill (Carr 1965: 214). Because it was labour-intensive, it was particularly affected by the Black Death, and at Ashford production had ceased by 1353. Recovery set in within a few years, but not enough to carry production back to its earlier levels; indeed, at the end of the fourteenth century output may have been only about half the level of a century before, and even in the post-plague boom of the 1380s it was only a fraction of the levels achieved in the heyday of two hundred years earlier. Production declined further during the first half of the fifteenth century, then recovered, and went on to grow quite substantially from the 1460s (Blanchard 1971: 127–9).

Lead production during this period was also affected by other factors, noticeably a shift in the centres of production towards the mines north of the Wye. During the 1430s, and 1440s, when around 200–300 tons of ore was mined annually, 450–600 local people found summer work in the shallow workings. However, mining was one of several occupations for many of these people and it is not always possible to distinguish them in tax lists since dual-occupationalists preferred to be known as farmers. Elsewhere in the Peak employment was to be found in textile production (Blanchard 1972; 1984: 232–3).

Many other industries in the region were on such a small scale that it is difficult to be sure how badly they were affected after 1348. Hints of hard times can be gained from the decline of salt making on the Lincolnshire fenlands (Hallam 1959–60: 87). Insufficient coal may have been raised in these years for the plague to have registered a significant check to the industry. The evidence is thin and rather scattered. In Derbyshire the West Hallam pits were leased to a mining consortium in 1379 and 1398 (Postles 1979: 221–2). Coal seems to have been in continuous use around Nottingham by the late fourteenth century, and in 1457 William Arnalde granted to the Prior and Convent of Beauvale the right to mine in Selston. Two years later the Prior of Lenton acquired from the Carthusians of Beauvale part of their underground coal at Newfield (VCH Notts II 1910: 325). From about 1460 coal mining became significant for the Willoughbys of Wollaton, and although nothing is known about output, coal was regularly being sold from the estate by the end of the century (Smith, R. S. 1964). On the Leicestershire and south Derbyshire coalfield the evidence of mining is firmer by the fifteenth century, and production was probably spurred on by the shortage of woodland in Leicestershire, although it is impossible to say anything firm about levels of output and sales (Owen 1984: 22–7).

Other forms of extractive industry can be conveniently grouped under the heading of quarrying. In Derbyshire, this included plaster and lime burning, alabaster manufacture, the production of building stones including slates, freestone, cob-stone and crest-stone, as well as millstone and grindstone production. Individual parts of the county had their particular specialization, with limestone working dominant in the 'White Peak' (carboniferous limestone area), and gritstones in the 'Dark Peak' further to the north (Blanchard 1984: 235).

Some processes were probably less affected than others by the impact of plague. The Nottingham school of alabaster carvers flourished in the second half of the fourteenth century, and by the following century the town was the centre of a nationwide industry. Other centres of carving developed in Lincoln, Derby, Tutbury and Chellaston, while as the reputation of the local carvers grew so also did their overseas trade. Evidence of their work is found as far afield as northern Spain and Iceland. However, the sixteenth-century Reformation dealt a severe blow to the carvers. The Nottingham school probably did not survive beyond the mid-sixteenth century, but memorial tombs were still being made after that date in Burton and Chellaston (Edwards 1966a: 233–4).

The prosperity of the East Midlands was already fading before the Black Death swept through the region in the mid-fourteenth century, but by 1500 the region was a pale shadow of its former wealthy self, perhaps no part more so than Lincolnshire. While conditions for tenants on the land generally improved after the mid-fourteenth century, for most other people there was little cause for rejoicing. The later Middle Ages were years of economic and related difficulties, even if the quality of church architecture and the continuing demand for wool suggests the need for caution when discussing the reality of the slump. Population declined in the fourteenth century and failed to recover in the fifteenth. Landlords became increasingly sceptical of making money from the traditional mixed pattern and as they turned their land down to grass in the late fourteenth and fifteenth centuries many villages either shrank or were deserted. In turn the change of land use reflected a recognition that tenants were hard to find, and that they could not be expected to accept the conditions they had previously tolerated. By 1500 villeinage had quietly died.

Lack of demand as the population failed to recover from the impact of plague affected local industries, while changing trade patterns brought Boston's meteoric rise to a grinding halt. Towns such as Lincoln, Leicester and Nottingham, which had relied heavily on their cloth industries, found themselves in the contradictory position of losing their major concerns while

Plate 3.3 Derbyshire Alabaster. The second panel of a fifteenth-century triptych from the Derbyshire school of alabaster carvers. The Nottingham school flourished in the second half of the fourteenth century, and other centres developed at Tutbury and Chellaston as well as Derby.

This example comes from Elham Church, Kent, but, such was the reputation of the local industry, that requests for alabasters came from all over Europe, and evidence of the carvers' work has been found as far afield as Spain. The panel is believed to represent Henry II and Thomas Beckett.

gaining greater governing powers. The extent of urban decay needs to be kept in perspective, since not all the region's towns suffered in the changed circumstances of the later fourteenth century. Smaller towns, particularly those beyond the reach of gild controls, flourished, often because they were able to sustain a cloth industry where their larger neighbours were failing. On the other hand, many of the market towns which had been so precipitously founded in the early Middle Ages failed to survive the downturn in the economy.

Modern scholarship does not regard the Battle of Bosworth in 1485 as quite the clean cut through history which was once imagined. However, this symbolic final act of the Middle Ages occurred as the prolonged depression in the East Midlands following the Black Death came towards an end, and as the devastating impact on Lincolnshire became fully apparent. Whereas the county had been the dominant area of the region since the Scandinavian settlements of the tenth century, and had usually ranked among the ten wealthiest counties in England during the early Middle Ages, its position slipped during the fifteenth century, and the trend proved irreversible. From lay tax assessments it is clear that while the whole region took a pounding Lincolnshire decisively lost its position as one of England's wealthiest areas. On the basis of the 1334 Lay Subsidy returns, assessed wealth per square mile was calculated at £20.4 for Rutland, £16.6 for Lincolnshire and between £6.6 and £13.7 for the other three counties, with Derbyshire the poorest of all (Darby 1976: 141). By the early sixteenth century this situation had begun to change. Although in 1515 Holland was still above the national average it had fallen to nineteenth out of thiry-eight in a comparative table of wealth. Lindsey and Kesteven were now below average and occupying twenty-eighth and twenty-ninth places respectively. For Lincolnshire there was to be no recovery; between the early seventeenth and early nineteenth centuries it was never able to climb above twenty-seventh out of thirty-nine and by the latter date it was firmly rooted below the other east midlands counties (Buckatzsch 1950). This was not so in 1515 when Lincolnshire's demise had still to be balanced by change elsewhere; the region's other counties were all below average, and growth since the mid-fourteenth-century had been slow (Schofield 1965: 504). The rise of the western counties lay beyond 1500.

Part two

The East Midlands in the Early Modern Period, 1500–1750

Chapter 4

The Land and the People

By the early years of the sixteenth century the prolonged aftermath of the Black Death in England was coming towards an end, and from the 1520s sustained population growth was accompanied by significant economic development. The number of taxpayers in the Lay Subsidy returns increased between 1524–25 and 1543–45 in Derbyshire (by more than 18 per cent (Sheail 1972)). Leicestershire and Lincolnshire, the three east midlands counties for which details survive, although it is possible that the later record is simply more accurate thus distorting the size of the increase. The trend was sustained into the seventeenth century, but from the 1630s a long period of relative stagnation set in before a renewed upsurge of population and economic growth marked the period from about 1740. In the two and a half centuries between 1500 and 1750 late medieval decline was finally arrested and a process of change instituted which brought England to the threshold of industrialization. Such change was vital. The characteristic feature of the medieval community was the small, more or less independent community. The self-sufficient relationship between communities was limited by communications, and the events of the fourteenth century had revealed how easily population could outrun resources, and with what devastating effects. An industrial society could not be built on such foundations. The years 1500–1750 were a period of transition as the insularity which characterized medieval England gradually broke down.

The process of change was complex. Considerable efforts were made to increase output from the land by reorganizing and improving agricultural practice. This permitted local specialization and greater sophistication in the techniques of selling agricultural goods. In turn, marketing required improved transport facilities. Ease of movement not only helped to encourage local trade, it also made possible the expansion of industry. Perhaps most crucial of all were changes which took place in the towns, not so much in terms of population growth as in function. County towns played an increasing role as regional centres. They became the focus of the fiscal, judicial and political concerns of the whole shire, and many gentry families began to maintain fine town houses, built in the classical tradition. Examples can still be seen in Derby (the Devonshire house in the Cornmarket) and Nottingham (the Willoughbys' house on Middle Pavement). The gentry brought their wealth to town, and in the course of the period 1500–1750 county capitals assumed a dominant role in the provision of high-order goods and services, and brought a coherence to the regional economy. Moreover, towns lower in the hierarchy also grew in stature. The business of the community became more organized, and the proliferation of market towns which characterized the thirteenth and early fourteenth centuries was replaced by a smaller number of more important centres. Market towns had often been established at the junction of farming countries, and they were usually the focal points of communications, but many of them also began to take on more consistent industrial roles. Some towns, and the areas around them, even came to specialize in the production of particular craft goods for regional and national markets (Everitt 1979: 106; Langton 1984: 148–50).

Although these changes were taking place nationwide they were nowhere more apparent than in the East Midlands. At the beginning of the period Henry VIII was able to describe Lincolnshire, following a visit in 1532, as 'one of the most brute and beastly of the whole realm' (Bindoff 1982, I: 131), but this would have been less than honest by 1750. The economic ties which had been so important before 1300 were re-established during this period and further developed. The Trent was again an artery of fundamental importance to local trade, indeed, this was arguably its heyday as a critical supply line for the movement westwards of grain from Lincolnshire and Leicestershire, and east-wards of cheese, lead – if the Derbyshire lead industry was to continue to flourish – and coal, since the growth of mining around Nottingham took place only because of the supply lines. Moreover, coal mining and framework knitting, the new leading industries of the region, were firmly established in the western quarter, around the county towns of Nottingham, Derby and Leicester, rather than the ailing Lincoln. It was this area which after 1750 was to become the central focus of economic activity, reflecting a remorseless shift in the balance of population and wealth. By 1750 Lincolnshire was still the most populous of the counties, but it now contained only 35 per cent of the region's people.

The significance of local ties must not, however, be overestimated. Not all goods were sold within the region. No area of England could avoid the pull of the London market, even if in general the period was one in which the focus on substantial market towns helped to generate regional intra-dependence. Nor was it merely the London market which deflected attention away from the region. Events initiated elsewhere had a profound effect on local development. The dissolution of the monasteries altered the pattern of land holding, the civil wars disrupted trade and commerce, and finally it was at Derby that the last serious attempt to restore the disgraced Stuart dynasty finally came to grief in 1745. The growth and development of the East Midlands between 1500 and 1750 has to be seen in the context of these national movements.

Population

The general trend of population in this period was of an increase down to the 1630s, after which only slight rises occurred before the 1740s (see appendix). Leicestershire provides the clearest example from the East Midlands; 8,750 families were recorded in the 1563 ecclesiastical census, which suggests a total population of 35,000–44,000. By 1603 the number of households had risen to about 13,825, an increase of 58 per cent in forty years. Parish register evidence confirms this startling late-sixteenth-century increase, which took place despite recurrent outbreaks of plague. Wigston Magna, for example, suffered in 1592 and 1598, and again in 1602 and 1609, while epidemics ravaged Loughborough in 1551, 1558, 1609–10 and 1631 (Griffin 1967–8). This increase during the sixteenth century apparently came to an end early in the seventeenth century, and between 1630 and 1660 many villages were scarcely replacing themselves – a pattern which can be confirmed from the Hearth Tax returns for 1670, and the population return of 1676 made for the Bishop of Lincoln. The Hearth Tax returns for Leicestershire show 14,486 households (excluding the county town), suggesting a population two-thirds greater than in 1563, but only 5 per cent in advance of 1603. The ecclesiastical census total for the same area in 1676 reveals 39,000 Anglican communicants, Roman Catholics and protestant non-conformists, from which a figure of 44,000 for total population can be calculated. The different calculations do not all agree, but they confirm that the rapid population increase of the later sixteenth century had come to an end in the course of the seventeenth century. Further estimates prepared for the Bishop of Lincoln suggest continuing stagnation into the eighteenth century, with high levels of mortality. Only from about 1740 is it possible to trace a further sustained population rise (VCH Leics III 1955: 138–45). At Wigston Magna numbers doubled in the hundred years to 1620, but there followed fifty years of stability before they began to increase again – largely through in-migration in search of work – towards the end of the century (Hoskins 1957: 211).

Elsewhere the upward movement is clear enough but the trend is less obvious. In 1563 Derbyshire had a total of 10,615 households, which on a multiplier of 4.5 or 5.0 suggests an overall total of between 47,000 and 53,000 (Riden 1978: 64). Figures derived from the Hearth Tax returns of the late seventeenth century suggest that numbers had risen to a minimum of around 70,000 in the 1660s. They began to rise more steeply through the eighteenth century (Edwards 1982b: xliii). It also seems likely that the balance of population in the county was tilted towards the industrial, or semi-industrial districts. In 1635, for example, 65 per cent of the county's able-bodied males were to be found in the Wirksworth, High Peak and Scarsdale hundreds (Dury 1963: 98). The overall increase almost certainly masks occasional mortality crises. The best known of these was the outbreak of plague at Eyam when 260 people from 76 families died in the twelve months from September 1665, but this was only one of a number of such instances. Between October 1586 and November 1587, for example, Chesterfield was ravaged by plague, and two further outbreaks occurred before the end of 1609 (Daniel 1985; Riden 1984: 101–10).

Lincolnshire's population may have been in the region of 110,000 in 1563, rising to 116,000 in 1603 (Hodgett 1975: 65–6). Between 1563 and 1723 population in the archdeaconry of Lincoln – i.e. all the county except a small part of the north-west – rose by 14 per cent, but this was not a straight-forward increase. The birth-rate was high in 1600–1640, but it slowed down after the Civil War. Moreover, the rate of increase varied across the county. Over much of Lincolnshire, population was stable throughout the seventeenth century, falling sharply by a quarter in the southern wolds. By contrast, numbers rose in the Holland fens and the Isle of Axholme, which suggests, since the fenlands were not particularly healthy areas, that any increase was a result of migration from areas suffering stagnant or even falling population. Incomers to the fens were almost certainly looking for land, partly as a result of changes in agriculture which led to the enclosure of the heavy claylands – often for pasture – and partly as land became available after reclamation (Holmes 1980: 18–23). There is some evidence to suggest that falling child mortality may have helped to raise population by the early eighteenth century. The death rate of infants (0–1 year) in two fenland parishes declined from 262 in Leake and 246 in Wrangle per 1,000 in the period 1654–1703, to 233 and 226 respectively between 1704 and 1753 (West 1974).

For Nottinghamshire the evidence is thin. Population seems to have risen steadily down to the third quarter of the seventeenth century, before a mortality crisis from which full recovery was not achieved until the 1780s. J. D. Chambers' view was that from 17,818 households in the late seventeenth century (90,000–95,000 people – which may indicate a slightly high multiplier) the county population rose steadily, and by 1725 it was between 30 and 40 per cent higher than in 1670, most of the growth having taken place between 1690 and 1720. However, this picture does not accord with more recent estimates which suggest stagnation for much of the first half of the eighteenth century both locally and nationally, and Chambers himself found evidence of population reversals in the 1720s as a result of heavy epidemics, particularly between 1727 and 1729 (Chambers 1966: xi, 82).

Overall, after a long period of recovery from the fourteenth into the sixteenth century, population began to rise steadily, but variably across the region. If the experience of Leicestershire – which has been the most closely studied – is in any way typical, it would seem that the pattern of growth accorded with national population trends for the period. In addition, this period saw the first considerable movement of population. As framework knitting developed during the seventeenth century it attracted migrants towards the centres of the industry around Nottingham and Leicester. The increase in numbers at Wigston Magna towards the end of the seventeenth century was partly a result of the attraction of employment, and by 1698–1701 17 per cent of the population had found employment as framework knitters (Hoskins 1957: 211–12). In Nottinghamshire between 1674 and 1743 a sample group of industrializing villages increased their population by 47.8 per cent while in a group which remained predominantly agricultural the increase was only 12.7 per cent (Chambers 1957: 20). On the other hand village industrialization does not seem to reflect, as was once believed, the onset of land hunger. Recent studies of both Nottinghamshire and Leicestershire suggest that there was no firm link between a land shortage brought about by engrossment and enclosure and industrialization (VCH Leics II 1954: 229; Rogers 1981; Mills 1982).

The Church, the Dissolution of the Monasteries, and Local Society

Few local people in 1500 can have anticipated the major social changes which were to occur during the following century, largely as a result of religious upheaval. Lollardy had briefly established a hold in the region in the fourteenth century, particularly around Leicester which was only a few miles from John Wycliffe's home parish of Lutterworth. Four inhabitants of Nottinghamshire were examined before the Archbishop of York in 1396 and compelled to renounce Lollardy; and two arrests were made at Newark in 1418–19 on suspicion of Lollardy (Wood 1948: 109–10). This background was significant, but it was the poverty of the individual parish churches which must have been the most obvious feature of religious life at the beginning of the sixteenth century.

Lincolnshire in 1526 had some 632 parishes, served by 1,312 clergy. Clerical numbers were almost certainly in decline, and from Visitations it is clear that non-residence was widespread due to the poverty of many individual livings and the need to support the higher echelons of the church establishment. Some clergy were failing to celebrate mass and to maintain church fabric, although in general the education of ordinands appears to have been better in the early sixteenth century than it had been a hundred years earlier, and both pastoral and liturgical duties were performed with some regularity (Bowker 1968). The picture was similar in the archdeaconry of Leicester. Again plenty of evidence survives of poorly educated and non-resident clergy, but this did not mean they were neglecting their cures. The root problem seems to have been that livings simply did not produce sufficient income, since 60 per cent yielded less than £10 a year (Fuggles 1970–1). Indeed, six livings in the county yielded less than £5 in 1534, of which two were in the county town (Hoskins 1940–1). It was a situation which may well have been exacerbated by the movement towards pastoral farming, which was less tithe rewarding than arable. Poverty was also a problem for the monastic houses. By 1500 Lincoln had fifty-one monastic houses, containing around 500 men and women who had taken vows, although numbers seem to have fallen as a result of the financial squeeze. Behaviour also left something to be desired, with occasional evidence of gambling, excessive drinking and failure to maintain the vow of chastity. Apathy, and neglect of religious duties also came high on the list of accusations levelled against the members of the houses (Hodgett 1975: 9–19).

It was from this platform that reform of the Church took place in the early years of the 1530s following Henry VIII's decision to break with Rome. Locally the reformation was probably of less significance for the community than the dissolution of the monasteries at the end of the 1530s. The attack on the religious houses had a far-reaching impact. In 1535 a vast survey of the Church's wealth was completed in the form of the *Valor Ecclesiasticus*, and a year later commissioners were sent to visit all monastic foundations. Their wealth varied considerably. Lenton Priory had the greatest gross income in Nottinghamshire (£418) while Broadholm Nunnery enjoyed less than £19. Across the border, incomes in Leicestershire varied between the £724 of Leicester Abbey and the £21 at Bradley (Jack 1965–6: 28). By the first Act of Dissolution, passed in 1536, all the smaller houses (those with a clear yearly value of less than £200) were threatened with dissolution. Some forty of Lincolnshire's houses fell into this category, although only twenty were suppressed in the summer and autumn of 1536, while of Nottinghamshire's thirteen houses six were surrendered under the terms of the first Act. Newstead, Beauvale and Wallingwells secured a stay of execution, but only by paying a large fine (Cameron 1975: 50–2). Several Derbyshire houses were also exempt in 1535, including the Premonstratian Abbey of Dale which paid £166 13s. 6d. for exemption, only to be surrendered two years later (Johnson 1980: 49).

While this was in progress, however, the Pilgrimage of Grace broke out. Trouble flared in Lincolnshire on Sunday, 1 October 1536 when a group of armed men under the leadership of a shoemaker known as Captain Cobbler took possession of Louth church. The disturbances quickly spread to Horncastle and then to the rest of the county. A mob marched first on Sleaford and then on Lincoln, but the revolt ended as quickly as it began. By 13 October it had collapsed leaving one of the leaders, Robert Aske, to flee back into Yorkshire where he became a leader of the Pilgrimage of Grace. Although it began as a popular revolt, the Lincolnshire rebellion was taken over by the gentry, whose motives were less clearly religious than local in origin. Consequently it did not prove easy for the Crown to counter since few loyal men could be found within Lincolnshire. The gentry might have suppressed the rebellion, but they were disillusioned by their exclusion from power (James 1970), while the clergy were opposed to the religious legislation and its economic consequences (Bowker 1972). It is not surprising that Henry VIII took full vengeance by executing the known ringleaders – and, in the case of Lord Hussey, some who had simply failed to do anything. By contrast, in Nottinghamshire George Talbot, Earl of Shrewsbury, on hearing the news of the Lincolnshire disturbances, began to collect levies in the county and from the surrounding shires. He was joined by the earls of Rutland and Huntingdon, with the intention of sealing off the north by making the Trent a line of defence, precautions which in the event proved unnecessary, although Shrewsbury received twenty-five monastic manors in the county as a result (Wood 1948: 130–1; Bindoff 1982, I: 165). In the aftermath of the revolt the government was able to confiscate the property of abbots who treasonably took part. It was also provided with an excuse for completing the process of dissolution, and with the demise of Crowland on 4 December 1539 the last of the Lincolnshire houses disappeared (Hodgett 1975: 22–41).

The attack on the Church destroyed many of its buildings and its treasures. The commissioners were ordered to raze monastic houses to the ground, although the instruction was amended to removing the stairs and gable-ends while leaving the walls standing – in order to save cost. The Reformation did not stop there. In Edward VI's reign chantries were swept away, chapels were destroyed, many hospitals were dissolved, and it proved difficult to keep local schools going. Even the parish churches came under attack, quite apart from the cathedral at Lincoln where large parts of the episcopal lands were surrendered in 1547 and the holy shrines were sacked (Rogers 1970: 50). For the most part little of the religious houses in the East Midlands has survived, although in a number of cases private houses were raised on their foundations. In Nottinghamshire, Newstead, Rufford and Welbeck, contain traces of their religious background in the foundations (Pevsner and Williamson 1979: 302, 365). Elsewhere Grace Dieu, an Augustinian priory of 1240 on the northern fringe of Charnwood Forest was turned into a residence by John Beaumont in 1539. By the end of the seventeenth century most of the buildings had been demolished to form one of the most picturesque monastic ruins in Leicestershire (Millward 1985: 67). In Lincolnshire houses on the sites of Thornton and Sempringham were planned but never finished, while Calke Abbey in Derbyshire and Langley Priory in Leicestershire are examples of country houses built on monastic sites after the original buildings had been cleared away.

The Landed Estates

The impact of the dissolution of the monasteries varied partly according to the landed possessions of the houses. These were considerable in Lincolnshire and in Leicestershire – about 70,000 out of 500,000 acres in the latter case (Jack 1965–6: 12) – but much less in Nottinghamshire. Much of the land was alienated by the Crown over time and passed either to the more prominent members of county society or to rising families climbing into landed society. Consequently ex-monastic land played a prominent part in the rise of some gentry and the increased prosperity of a number of yeoman families. In Lincolnshire, beneficiaries included Charles Brandon, Duke of Suffolk, Edward Fiennes, Lord Clinton and Saye, and Thomas Manners, later the first Earl of Rutland. The result was to consolidate the power of these families at the head of county society. By contrast, Sir John Willoughby of Wollaton, one of Nottinghamshire's more substantial landowners, had ready cash but acquired little land, perhaps because his association with the houses at Beauvale and Lenton ensured that any application for land would not be viewed favourably. The Talbots, earls of Shrewsbury, were probably the family to benefit most in Nottinghamshire and Derbyshire from the dissolution, and they depended on royal bounty rather than purchase (Cameron 1975: 53–5).

The acquisitions of lesser men also had some impact on the social structure. Seven local gentry, and six royal officials, received grants in Lincolnshire between January 1538 and July 1540, but it was usually men with some standing in the county who purchased ex-monastic property. The Carrs of Sleaford were an exception. While not unknown before the dissolution, they purchased sufficient monastic acres to suggest that the family fortunes were based on them. As a result, Lincolnshire acquired a number of aristocratic families who dominated some parts of the county, while the increased acreage of many gentry gave them a greater hold over the district than would have been possible fifty years earlier. Even so some areas, particularly the fens, still had few prominent landed families, and the difference between the better off and the poorer gentry remained considerable. At one extreme were gentlemen with estates worth over £300 a year, including Sir Francis Ayscough of Stallingborough; Sir Edward Dymoke of Scrivelsby, and Sir Robert Tyrwhit of Kettleby. By contrast, Anthony Cony, Thomas Flete and Thomas Pulverton, all of them gentlemen of Holland, had rents of only about £10 a year. Nottinghamshire also acquired a number of new families as a direct result of the dissolution, notably the Cartwrights, Coopers and Bolles (Hodgett 1975: 49–58, 63–6; Cameron 1975: 57–8).

If the dissolution of the monasteries did not produce the wholesale emergence of a new class of gentry, there were some notable incomers during this period, and with them some great houses consciously designed as demonstrations of the power and wealth of the families who built them. Possibly the most famous of the incomers were the Cavendishes of Suffolk who arrived in Derbyshire to take up the monastic lands awarded to William Cavendish, one of the commissioners appointed by Thomas Cromwell to visit and take the surrender of various religious houses. He married Elizabeth Hardwick, the twenty-seven-year-old daughter of an obscure Derbyshire squire, sold his Suffolk estates and bought the Chatsworth estate of his wife's brother-in-law. Work began on the first Chatsworth House, but before completion Sir William died leaving his widow with six children and the supervision of 375 workmen. In 1568 she married – as her fourth husband – the sixth Earl of Shrewsbury who had responsibility for Sheffield Castle, Sheffield Manor, Wingfield Manor, Tutbury Castle, Worksop Manor, Buxton Hall and Rufford Abbey. During the course of the marriage Hardwick, Bolsover, Welbeck Abbey and Oldcotes Hall were added. By the time Shrewsbury died in 1590 Bess had a considerable income, much of which she used in building during the last eighteen years of her life. The old manor house was converted into Hardwick Old Hall between 1587 and 1591, and after her husband's death Bess employed Robert Smythson to build Hardwick New Hall. The two buildings together cost around £5,500 (Durant and Riden 1980; 1984: lvi), and she also spent time and money transforming her other houses (Durant 1977; Heath 1982: 52–5). The estates descended through Sir Charles Cavendish, the youngest son of her second marriage.

Across the border in Nottinghamshire the most important house built in the Elizabethan period was Wollaton Hall, constructed in the 1580s for Sir Francis Willoughby, again to a design by Robert Smythson, who worked extensively in the region. The Hall, built at a cost of £8,000, was constructed of Ancaster stone, although great quantities of bricks were made on the site and some walls probably have a brick core with stone facing. It admirably succeeded in its major purpose, which was to impress. To complement the house the grounds were landscaped with attractive walks and rides, and trees were planted. Also in Nottinghamshire Wollaton was matched by the sixth Earl of Shrewsbury's magnificent Worksop Manor, again probably to a design by Smythson. As at Wollaton formal gardens and plantations were laid out, but the house was destroyed by fire in 1761. Although plans were drawn up for a replacement which would have been on the scale of Blenheim, this was only partially completed, and when the property came into the hands of the Duke of Newcastle in 1839 he pulled it down. After the dissolution Welbeck passed to Sir Charles Cavendish (son of Bess of Hardwick) and from him to his son, the first Duke of Newcastle. Smythson drew up major rebuilding plans, but only a small part of them was executed (Pevsner and Williamson 1979: 365–6, 390–2). In Leicestershire Belvoir was rebuilt in the 1520s by the first Earl Manners, but the county has no Elizabethan house of major importance. Torksey Castle was built in the 1560s by Sir Robert Jermyn, but Lincolnshire's most remarkable Tudor house was Grimsthorpe Castle. This thirteenth cen-

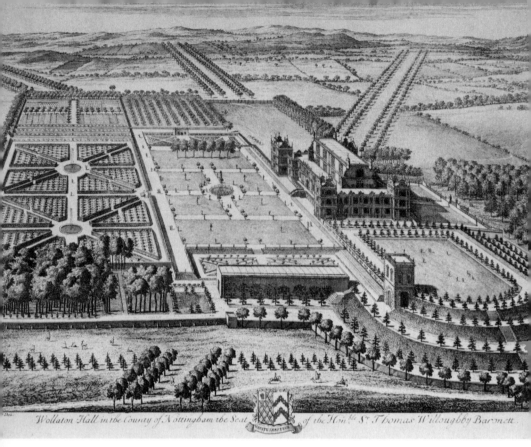

Plate 4.1 Wollaton Hall, Nottingham, an engraving by John Kip (*c.*1650–1722) from the painting by Leonard Knyff (1650–1720). This is a typical Knyff–Kip production. Knyff drew a great number of bird's-eye views or plans of mansions and parks of the aristocracy, which Kip engraved. No real attempt was made to portray perspective, but considerable attention went into displaying the formal garden layouts, many of them of Elizabethan date. This was the case at Wollaton, where the formal garden was replaced during the eighteenth century by a landscaped park. Only a relatively small area of garden remains today.

The hall was built by Robert Smythson for Sir Francis Willoughby in the 1580s, largely of Ancaster stone, and is regarded as the most important Elizabethan house in Nottinghamshire and one of the most important in England. It was built as a showpiece in a prominent position, and despite the growth of Nottingham around it, even today it is remarkably 'visible' locally. It is distinguished from earlier Elizabethan houses by its all-round symmetry, and the raised central hall, although by contrast with the exterior, the interior is disappointing.

Wollaton Hall was bought from the Willoughbys in 1925 by Nottingham Corporation, and since 1926 it has been used as a natural history museum. The grounds were reduced in size when the corporation sold off part of the land for housing development, but Wollaton Park, with its industrial and agricultural museums, remains a favoured haunt of Nottingham people on Sundays and bank holidays.

---

tury castle was greatly enlarged in the sixteenth century by the Duke of Suffolk, although his alterations are now obscured by later work. Nor is it only the larger houses which have survived as a memorial to their builders. Many sixteenth and seventeenth-century small halls and manor houses are still to be seen in the Derbyshire countryside today, among them Holm Hall near Bakewell and Aston Hall near Hope (Edwards 1982a: 1).

Events during the civil wars were not kind to local property. The sixteenth-century castle at Belvoir was destroyed, and was rebuilt by the eighth Earl Manners between 1654 and 1668 at a cost of £11,730. Damage and destruction occurred at various Nottinghamshire houses, including Shelford and Wiverton, and the homes of the Suttons at Averham and the Cartwrights at Ossington. Newstead was looted by the Nottingham garrison in January 1644, and Welbeck had been stripped of furniture, pictures, plate and linen (Wood 1948: 201–2). In these circumstances it is not surprising to find building activity resuming. Nottingham Castle, severely damaged in the civil wars, was demolished by the Duke of Newcastle, and a new baroque mansion was erected in its place during the 1670s at a cost of £14,000. The first house at Thoresby was built between 1685 and 1687, while Belton House in Lincolnshire has been described by Pevsner as 'perhaps the most satisfying among the later seventeenth-century houses in England'. Sir John Brownlow, the owner, laid the first stone in March 1685. Grimsthorpe Castle received a new front in 1685, and a further plan to remodel this part of the house was drawn up by Vanbrugh only thirty years later. Building took place during the 1720s (Pevsner and Harris 1964: 452; Colvin 1970). Post-Restoration buildings in Derbyshire include Sudbury Hall, while considerable work took place at Chatsworth between 1687 and 1707, and the grand style of the house was emulated at Calke Abbey in 1703. Burley-on-the-Hill in Rutland was built by the second Earl of Nottingham 1696–1700 to replace an earlier house destroyed in the civil wars, at a cost of £30,657 (Plumb 1955). Important houses in Leicestershire from this period include Stapleford Park (*c.* 1670–80) and Stanford Hall (1697–*c.* 1703). Finally, a number of surviving smaller country houses from the post-Restoration period have also survived in the region, including Gunby Hall in Lincolnshire (1700).

The Homes of the Lower Orders

For those beneath the gentry in the rural social structure a recognizably modern society was emerging in this period. Serfdom in its classic medieval form had effectively disappeared from the countryside, although what appears to have been the last large-scale reference to serfdom in England survives in a report of 1570 by a jury enquiring into the existence of serfdom in the Duchy of Lancaster manor of Long Bennington in Lincolnshire (Hosford 1960). Hoskins has noted the increasing role of the money economy, which played only a marginal part in the life of Wigston Magna villagers during the Tudor era, but became much more significant in the course of the seventeenth century. Even so, the relative self-sufficiency of the community was enough to protect it against outside pressures:

> It was this economy, which lived almost entirely off its own resources,
> that enabled the peasantry of all classes from the yeoman down to the
> cottager and labourer not only to stand up to the catastrophic rise in
> prices of the later sixteenth century, but even, for many of them
> (labourers included) to improve their position; and it was this same
> economy which enabled the village to withstand for so long the
> disintegrating effect of Parliamentary enclosure and not to collapse at
> the first blow.
>
> (Hoskins 1957: 193–4)

Though self-sufficient, Wigston was still prey to outside forces. During the
seventeenth century it had 'an incessantly active land market', while the Hearth
Tax assessments suggested 'a greater tendency to differentiation between
social classes' than in the Tudor century. This development of a recognizable
social pyramid produced an economic gulf with the appearance of a native
gentry 'sprung from the minority of successful peasantry'. Property was also
passing into the hands of outsiders, not all of whom chose to reside in the
village, while towards the end of the period the development of framework
knitting tended to undermine the cohesive unity of the community (Hoskins
1957: 193–8, 212).

Hoskins has also written of a great rebuilding between 1570 and 1640
affecting Leicestershire and much of the East Midlands. In Leicestershire this
was predominantly in timber-framing, except in the stone area of the east of the
county. Panel filling was usually wattle-work, but there is also evidence from
the county of brick nogging, although drastic remodelling and alteration has
left few examples from this period in an unaltered form. Stone was still the
accepted building material – even for cottages – when it could be quarried
locally, and stone slates were used particularly in Rutland, Leicestershire,
Kesteven and north Derbyshire. In the latter area during the later seventeenth
and eighteenth centuries thatch was replaced by slate as roofing material for
stone cottages, and stone itself replaced the older cruck of timber-framed
structures. Cob cottages with solid walls (as distinct from mud and stud), were
still built in parts of Leicestershire and Rutland, and in Nottinghamshire. A
very few examples survive from this period, mainly along the edge of the best
good building stone (Seaborne 1964). It is now easier to find lengths of garden
wall in that material. Few of Lincolnshire's surviving mud and stud cottages in
the Witham valley, on the wolds and in the marshland, are older than the
seventeenth and eighteenth centuries (Barley 1961: 100).

Gradually, however, the urge to build in brick gathered momentum, and
this brought what may best be seen as an extension of Hoskins' great rebuilding. At Laxton in Nottinghamshire the rebuilding in brick dates predominantly
from the period *c.* 1730–1780, while in Lincolnshire it can scarcely have begun
before the late eighteenth century. The distinctive red brick of many east
midlands villages suggests the houses belong almost entirely to the century

Plate 4.2 Housing for the lower orders, Melbourne, Derbyshire. These cottages are on Potter Street, at the junction with the Castle Square, where they face across the site of the market towards Melbourne Castle. Although extremely difficult to date, they are almost certainly of eighteenth-century origin. They are of a box-frame, half-timber construction (which has been cut into to insert the windows), built on an ashlar (stone) base, and infilled with brick. The upper storey, like many of the buildings in Melbourne, is a later addition, hence the dormer windows. The original roofline is still visible on the left-hand side of the picture. On the right of the picture is a later, two storey building with (on the top storey) windows which are characteristic of a framework knitting workshop.

1770–1870. Brick spread haphazardly – Nottingham, for example, had little brick building before the reign of James I – but by the eighteenth century it dominated much of the country. Its spread in the East Midlands can occasionally be documented. Thus at Crowle (Lincolnshire) in 1649 the manor court jury presented William Occorbie for making bricks on the common and selling them out of the manor. The use of brick in Nottingham escalated from about 1660 until it became the brick city which it is today. By the eighteenth century virtually every new house in the town was of brick, and the same was true for the Trent valley. By the end of the century even the humblest cottages were brick built (Pevsner and Williamson 1979: 46–50; Clifton-Taylor 1972: 35–7, 104, 218–19; Barley 1986: 183). A timber-framed house could be given a new lease of life by having the panels filled with brick, or by cladding a frame completely in brick. Piecemeal improvements of this sort can be of almost any date (Pye 1972: 581–2).

Whatever the relative merits of building materials there is also some evidence to suggest change in house construction over the Tudor period, and with it increasing wealth. One-room houses were still quite common in mid-Tudor Lincolnshire, but they were fewer in number. Whereas two-thirds of inventories for the county in the 1530s fail to mention distinct rooms, only one-third of those for 1572 omit reference to specific parts of the house. By the first decade of the seventeenth century the structural division between house

113

and parlour was common in Lincolnshire, Nottinghamshire and Leicester-shire. Such a change reflected the growing wealth of Lincolnshire farmers, even if it took time to turn money values into household comforts (Barley 1961: 46, 78–96). At Coningsby, on the edge of the fen, there were houses of four, five, six and even eight rooms in the early seventeenth century, which marked it off as a village of some wealth (Beckwith 1982: 9–12). Elsewhere the number of four-roomed houses seems to have grown substantially by 1635.

By the first half of the seventeenth century Lincolnshire houses, if they were the normal two-room buildings, had a hall and a parlour, while larger houses usually had one or more chambers, used for storage purposes rather than as sleeping quarters. Only houses with four rooms or more tended to have a kitchen. Most houses were thatched, although the pantile spread westwards from Lincolnshire during the seventeenth and eighteenth centuries. Floors were usually of earth even in the better homes. Few examples survive, although the evidence of inventories suggests that social divisions in housing affairs were becoming apparent. In the Trent valley villages north of Newark there was a clear distinction between labourers and craftsmen, most of whom had no more than two rooms, and richer farmers with two parlours, three or more service-rooms and chambers for corn or cheese (Barley 1961: 151–3).

After 1660 among smaller houses in the region it seems clear that while the poorer labourers were probably still living in houses of one or two rooms, the five- to seven-room house was increasingly common. They seem to have become the standard home for craftsmen and husbandmen, and in a village such as Norwell in mid-Nottinghamshire, where there were no yeomen, they must have been more or less the standard type in the post-Restoration period. Inventory evidence for the years 1689–1708 from Clayworth in the same county reveals that James Searsey, George Norton and William Gabitas had, at most, three or four rooms, while the wealthier majority had between five and seven. George Norton's was probably the simplest house, consisting merely of a hall, parlour and kitchen (Perkins 1979: 7–8). Inventories show how common it was to make additions to houses. In the Trent valley the usual extension involved a new parlour, with a chamber over it. However, it seems that parlours were still rooms for sleeping, and the use of upstairs chambers for storage (for keeping seed corn or for ripening cheeses) continued because before the later eighteenth century few houses had a cellar. Brick continued to spread, without overwhelming, the vernacular tradition in the area (Barley 1961: 203–10).

Finally there were always those for whom any kind of properly constructed house was a luxury. Migrant workers in Charnwood Forest in 1604 were said to have found themselves temporary abodes including a 'sory "cote" pytched unto a nooke of a rock of stone'. This was reported to be the home of a poor basket maker who, 'for his own succour made the same of Stickes and turffes, but paid no rent or fine' (Coones and Patten 1986: 228). In the Derbyshire Peak, Daniel Defoe found a lead miner and his family living in a cave where not only had the husband been born but his father and grandfather before him:

> There was a large hollow cave, which the poor people by two curtains hanged cross, had parted into three rooms. On one side was the chimney, and the man, or perhaps his father, being miners, had found means to work a shaft or funnel through the rock to carry the smoke out at the top. . . . The habitation was poor, 'tis true, but things within did not look so like misery as I expected. Every thing was clean and neat, though mean and ordinary. There were shelves with earthen ware, and some pewter and brass. There was, which I observed in particular, a whole flitch or side of bacon hanging up in the chimney, and by it a good piece of another. There was a sow and pigs running about at the door, and a little lean cow feeding upon a green place just before the door, and the little enclosed piece of grounds I mentioned was growing with good barley.
>
> (Defoe 1971: 463–4)

Similarly forms of rock house were also to be found in Nottingham, largely because of the town's sandstone base. Houses were cut into the natural scarps and the flanks of roads sunk into the rock, and according to one seventeenth-century commentator anyone desperate for a house had simply to go to Nottingham with the right tools 'and work himself a hole or burrow for his family' (Barley 1986: 278).

Local Government and Society

The changing structure of local society as witnessed by the rise of some new families and the decline of others was also reflected in the sphere of local administration. The *ad hoc* nature of local government which had allowed considerable room for local flexibility and had left central government with relatively few powers in medieval England was increasingly formalized during the sixteenth and seventeenth centuries, largely as a result of the Tudor reforms. As a result, down to 1835, local government was roughly divided between the responsibilities of the county, the borough, and the parish. It was not a hard and fast distinction. Parts of Nottinghamshire fell within the responsibility of the Peculiars of Southwell and Scrooby, while Sherwood Forest came under forest law. This was revived for an area south of the Trent by Charles I in the 1630s, as a means of improving his income, and it continued to be enforced beyond 1660, although by then it was primarily in order to defend traditional privileges rather than to represent the rights of the monarch (Seddon 1978). At the same time it was important to preserve the forest, if only to ensure the availability of timber for shipbuilding. Perhaps the most abiding impression is the absence of conformity in local government. At one extreme a sizeable town such as Gainsborough was governed into the nineteenth century by a manorial court – a medieval institution designed for running the country-side – while at the other extreme a decayed port like Grimsby retained all the paraphernalia of a separate borough despite having a population of only 500–600 in the early eighteenth century when Gainsborough was nearer 3,000 (Beckwith 1968: 9).

Medieval administration was centred on the county, headed by the sheriff, and the manor court. A good deal of latitude was permitted to the nobility and gentry, allowing them to exercise power in the countryside through courts leet and baron. Such a situation was inimical to the Tudor monarchs' desire for a strong central administration, so a series of reforms was introduced to bring the greater magnates under the discipline of the law and to enable central government to obtain what amounted to a monopoly of violence within the state. The major carrot dangled before the greater landowners was the position of lord lieutenant, a post established on an *ad hoc* basis during Henry VIII's reign primarily to deal with specific military issues in particular counties. Even before the sixteenth century the right to call out and command the local levies had been removed from the sheriff by special commissioners for array appointed periodically by the Crown, and the lord lieutenancy was a further development. The duties of the post could include mustering men for the king's service in time of war, or for suppressing rebellion. Thus in 1536 Henry VIII made the Duke of Suffolk and Earl of Shrewsbury his lieutenants to command the forces raised against the Pilgrimage of Grace (Wood 1948: 145). A statutory basis for the post was provided in 1550, although appointees remained temporary until 1585 and Nottinghamshire, for example, had a permanent lord lieutenant only from 1626. Derbyshire shared a lieutenancy with Staffordshire 1585–90, and Leicestershire and Rutland were associated for lieutenancy purposes for much of the period before 1642 (Sainty 1970). The principle of one lord lieutenant for each county was established during the seventeenth century. Although occasionally a knight held the position, normal-ly it was filled by a local peer on the assumption that it should be occupied by men with considerable status in the county. However, this was not a rigid stipulation; the decision to appoint the lord treasurer, Lord Burghley, in Lincolnshire in 1587, for example, brought in a man who can rarely have been resident locally. Burghley was able to perform the office because the principle of appointing deputy lieutenants – usually from among senior gentry in the county – was established in the course of Elizabeth's reign.

Although the lord lieutenancy was primarily established for military purposes, by the end of Elizabeth's reign new functions were being added. The lord lieutenant began to wield considerable influence in patronage, including the selection of justices of the peace, and he also became a vital channel of communication between the county and central government. Finally, the lord lieutenant's growing power inevitably circumscribed those still remaining in the hands of the sheriff, although it was only during the course of the seventeenth century that the gentry began positively to try to avoid the post and even then the position remained important during election years (Holmes 1980: 80).

It was the role of the justices which expanded most significantly during this period. As the old communal courts gradually disappeared the justices became the men who enforced the criminal code, but they also acquired a whole range of new duties as a result of Tudor social legislation. Perhaps not surprisingly the principle was established that they should be drawn from among the established members of society. Established families with large estates and country houses came to form the backbone of local government. They assembled quarterly as justices of the peace to undertake a whole range of legal and administrative functions. In their administrative role they were responsible for overseeing the regulating of wage rates and conditions of apprenticeship, controlling alehouses, and looking after roads and bridges. Above all they became responsible for assessing and levying rates – particularly the poor rate – when parishioners, churchwardens or constables defaulted. As a court of law the justices were empowered to try offenders, although it was customary for capital offences to be reserved for the king's justices in the assizes. Justices could also act alone, or in pairs, in the countryside, to examine alleged offences, issue warrants or summonses where one person alone was charged, and convict for profane oaths, tippling and failure to attend church.

Quarter sessions were a county institution, except that Lincolnshire was divided into three for this purpose, with Lindsey, Kesteven and Holland each exercising separate jurisdiction. Within these divisions magistrates meeting at a particular town did not of necessity deal with business for the whole division. In Holland, the sessions held at Boston were for business relating to the northern sub-division, while those at Spalding were devoted to the affairs of the south. Normally sessions moved from one centre to the other on consecutive days, although it was unusual for justices in one sub-division to appear on the bench of another (Olney 1979: 5–8). This also occurred in Nottinghamshire although some justices sat at two of the three centres as quarter sessions moved from Nottingham to Newark and to East Retford. Additional adjournments were held in Blyth and Mansfield, particularly during periods of unrest, and when individual communities were in turmoil justices adjourned to the village in question. Special sessions were held at Gunthorpe in 1621, 1625, 1629, 1631 and 1641 (Copnall 1915: 3; Welby 1974; Chambers 1966: 51).

The result was to give increasing importance to quarter sessions as the justices helped to strengthen executive power in the counties, which had been relatively weak before 1460. Although central control was still exercised in relation to the appointment of justices, considerable attention was paid to

117

loyalty so that families began to appear in the commission for generation after generation. The number of justices varied over time. In Nottinghamshire they increased during the reign of James I, but were then cut back by Charles I in the 1630s. On the whole, however, numbers tended to increase partly due to the workload, but partly through pressure from the localities since individual families were reluctant to find themselves omitted. Even so, access to the bench was closely guarded. In six commissions of the peace issued for Leicestershire between 1621 and 1636 thirty-two resident families were represented, fewer than one in ten of the county gentry (Fleming 1981/2: 26). In 1623 the Earl of Huntingdon, lord lieutenant, noted that only eighteen justices were actually resident in the county, but although as a consequence some areas were under-represented, he only recommended three new inclusions (Huntington Library, HA5471).

This situation changed with the aftermath of the Civil War. Although justices retained many of their pre-war powers, particularly after 1650 the social status of those serving on the bench fell. In Lincolnshire they were mainly minor gentry, with a few military officials and rising lawyers. These, the 'mean men', as they were called, became the backbone of local administration, replacing members of the old county elite. They could not survive the Restoration. Only about one-fifth of those serving on the 1658 commission were reappointed after 1660 (Holmes 1980: 206–7, 219). Further trouble was in store when, towards the end of the century Charles II and James II purged the commissions. In Holland, no sessions were held in the latter part of 1680 because a number of active and useful magistrates had been removed from office. Unfortunately, as this implies, the prestige of being in the commission came to outweigh the duty of serving, and many families were satisfied merely to find their names mentioned. In Kesteven between 1680 and 1685 nineteen of the thirty-six families resident in the county and named in the commission failed to act, and only five attended more than half the sessions. Nor was this unusual since a similar lack of attention to duty can be seen among the magistrates of the Horncastle sessions between 1665 and 1673, and among the Lindsey coast commissioners of sewers in the decade before the Civil War (Holmes 1980: 81–3).

If the major responsibility of the justices was in keeping the peace, possibly the most significant additional development in their work lay in the area of controlling the poor. In 1563 the justices were entrusted with the duty of seeing that the new poor rate was collected. This supplemented their powers to deal with the apprenticeship of children (1549–50), and was in turn developed in the role given to them in 1575–7 to maintain houses of correction. The piecemeal legislation of the sixteenth century was codified in 1597 and 1601. Exactly how these powers were carried out in practice is difficult to determine in the absence of quarter sessions records before the seventeenth century. A few examples survive, however, which suggest that responsibilities were taken seriously. At Leverton, near Boston, from 1563 poor law relief was collected from the thirty-six villagers deemed capable of making a contribution. Although much of the money collected went to relieve the impotent poor of the village, sums were also given to collectors from hospitals and poor houses throughout the country, among them the new hospital at Louth (Hodgett 1975: 97–9).

The executive functions of local government were largely carried out by the high constables, who were appointed by quarter sessions usually from among the lesser gentry. In seventeenth-century Nottinghamshire Bassetlaw had a high constable for each of its three divisions while the five smaller hundreds had one each. Over time the quasi-magisterial powers which they possessed were gradually reduced, while the burden of administrative duties increased. In particular the power of the high constables to call meetings of petty constables for administrative purposes was curtailed in 1737. The duties of the high constables included presenting and repairing decayed bridges, enforcing the use of prescribed weights and measures, overseeing the transportation of vagrants and collecting county rates.

County justice was overseen by the clerk of the peace, who received only a nominal salary but could charge professional fees, while finances were in the hands of a treasurer. Nottinghamshire was divided into two parts for financial purposes, and the officers involved were responsible for overseeing payments for gaols, the transport and maintenance of vagrants, pensions to maimed soldiers, the provision of bread for gaoled prisoners, and other necessities. For these duties the treasurer for south Nottinghamshire received £18 a year, and his northern counterpart £9 (Chambers 1966: 55–9).

The second level of local government in the countryside was the parish. Although originally this was a unit of ecclesiastical jurisdiction attached to each church, the parish developed civil duties through time. Its governing body was the vestry, sometimes co-opted, and sometimes elected; and it was empowered to raise a rate for the upkeep of the church, the roads, and, most significantly from the sixteenth century, the poor. Some parishes were run by a small group of leading farmers, while elsewhere – Sutton Bonington in Nottinghamshire, for example – a considerable number of the inhabitants concurred in corporate action. In some parishes public meetings were called to advise the vestry on particular decisions, whereas in others no such consultation appears to have taken place. Parish officers were annually chosen from among the parishioners, and they were not paid. The justices appear to have taken little interest in appointments, and generally to have allowed parishes to be self-governing, although they did expect constables to attend quarter sessions. The vestry met frequently to pass the accounts of the poor law officers, the constable and surveyor of highways, and the Field Master. The latter post was found in a number of parishes, including Laxton in Nottinghamshire, and the duties included letting the common grasses of the parish. The best example of how parish government worked is provided by surviving 'town' books. Those for the Nottinghamshire village of Clayworth 1674–1710 and for Barrow-on-

Monday Jan 27 '77

At Breakfast Mary Cooper Eat her Broth
and laid the remaining part of her Breakfast
in the Window and offord to Eat it, I took it
away and Said I would lay it by for her
She then began to Swear & Scold, damn'd me
be a Gallows look, Get Bastard Rogue
the Gallows Groans for me and damn his
Soul it will Soon have him and kept
repeating over the above words and Oaths
above half an hour

29 She the Said Cooper thro Aggravation hear
that they had plenty of Bread & Bear to
Supper Supply'd after the old Peoples had Eat
their Supper for Long Milk for a Child above
Old Told her if She was Ill or any thing
was the Matter with the Child I would give it
Milk or any thing Else but as She & the Child
was well I did not See any Occasion to give
Milk for her the hasty Milk for the Child I
thought that at this time was Sufficient
She then began to treat me in an Insolent
Manner & Call'd me a poor Nasty Dog
Damn'd my Soul to Hell and wish
the Divil was picking my Bones
and Repeated the Same Oath as she Did
on Monday - - - - -

30 Scold very Much was 40 Minutes
Dressing a Child and did no work but
Sat by if fire till after Ten O Clock

31 Morning Damn'd me for a Clam Viny
Nasty Dog and that Sarah Southorn was
my Whore and if She Cooper Should See
the Divil picking my bones, with a great
Number of more Oaths And Saucy Language

Plate 4.3 Excerpt from the Town Book, Ashby-de-la-Zouch, Leicestershire. 'The Town Book' contains lists of settlement certificates received and given, examinations, removal orders, etc., compiled from about 1721 to 1760. It also contains one page, reproduced here, of 'Behaviours' in the workhouse, dating from 1777. Although this is not particularly typical of entries in the book, it gives the kind of intimate detail which is often lacking in more conventional documents. The writer's unpopularity with Mary Cooper comes through clearly enough from the fact that on four separate days she finds reason to loose off a string of invective against him (Leicestershire Record Office, DE 432/1).

Humber in the early eighteenth century, for example, provide a fascinating account of the parish officers and their duties as well as the finance of local government (Rogers 1979; Barley 1938).

Farming

Although the traditional structure of farming typical of medieval England continued through much of this period, enough change took place to suggest a significant deviation from the pattern of the past, and with it came a rise in output. Some changes were long-term and hard to measure. Rye, a major field crop in medieval Leicestershire, was less widely cultivated by the seventeenth century, while wheat and barley became important through most of the region. Other changes were more obvious, and included improved cropping patterns and rotations, reclamation and enclosure. It is impossible to measure the overall level of change by the mid-eighteenth century but there seems little doubt that collectively these developments helped to bring about a substantial improvement in output.

Although the common field system has sometimes been portrayed as inimical to improvement (Kerridge 1967: 107–8) enough evidence has come to light to suggest that such a stark view is untenable. In the sixteenth century various specialisms developed within the region. On the eastern uplands of Leicestershire and in Rutland farmers often had above average sheep flocks, in the Vale of Belvoir the speciality was growing corn for the market, and around Market Harborough they fattened beef (Thirsk 1967: 89–91). Within the common field system itself room existed for innovation and adjustment to the proportion of acreage devoted to arable and pasture. Farm sizes increased, strips or 'lands' were gathered together into larger holdings, and piecemeal enclosure produced closes for new fodder crops, dairying and fattening. Contemporary observers regarded the best farming as being found on enclosed land where convertible husbandry was practised. There is widespread evidence for the cultivation of turnips and artificial grasses, as well as more limited interest in hemp and flax, hops and woad. In 1591 and 1592 woad growing occupied 40 acres at Wollaton. The leaves were picked two or three times a

121

year, and this gave employment – albeit briefly – to more than 1,000 people not merely from Nottingham, but also from the adjoining villages of Chilwell, Beeston, Radford and Basford (Thirsk 1978: 5). In north Lincolnshire Drayner and Burrell Massingberd were using improved rotations and new crops including clover, coleseed and turnips on their estate in the later seventeenth century. However, the Massingberds were exceptional in an area which remained backward in agricultural practice until the 1820s and 1830s (Holderness 1972a).

Cattle and sheep were central to open-field farming, both for their manure, and also for their meat, milk, skins, tallow and wool. Areas of permanent pasture were maintained for breeding and fattening. Defoe remarked on the graziers of Leicestershire, and on the sheep and horses of Lincolnshire:

> The sheep bred in [Leicestershire] and Lincolnshire are, without
> comparison, the largest, and bear not only the greatest weight of flesh
> on their bones but also the greatest fleeces of wool on their backs of any
> sheep of England: nor is the fineness of the wool abated for the
> quantity; but as tis the longest staple so tis the finest wool in the whole
> island. . . . These are the funds of sheep which furnish the City of
> London with their large mutton in so incredible a quantity.
>
> (Defoe 1971: 408–9)

Horse breeding was also important in the region, with noted fairs at Ashbourne, Nottingham, Mansfield, Newark, Horncastle, Belton and Leicester. Meadowland alongside the Trent, Witham, Soar and Ancholme was used for dairying, and the rich pastures of the Vale of Belvoir became famous for the production of Stilton cheese (Thirsk 1985 I: 94–102).

Greater light is thrown on the pattern of agricultural change by looking at what by the sixteenth century were the distinctive farming regions of the East Midlands. The vale of central Lindsey, an area of mixed husbandry, was situated between the limestone cliff and the wolds, the Trent valley in west Lindsey and the vale of west Kesteven. It was an area of nucleated villages and common fields. As population increased the fields moved into the pastures until villages were hard put to find enough grass for their stock. To combat these shortages farmers used 'leys', the temporary laying down to grass of parts of the arable in the common fields and the sowing of legumes such as clover to add to soil fertility while yielding heavy crops of hay. Average farm sizes were about 20–30 acres of arable, meadow and enclosed pasture, and nearly always the commons were carefully regulated. The principal crops in Lincolnshire were barley, wheat and peas. On the claylands the trend was to stock the pastures more intensively and to enclose or to use leys in order to 'borrow' ploughland for additional grass.

The second farming area of the region was in the uplands, consisting of the Lincoln cliff and heath, the wolds south of the Trent, and the limestone and millstone grit moorlands of Derbyshire. In Derbyshire farmers were primarily concerned with cattle and sheep, and large breeding flocks were kept for ewes' milk cheese. Derbyshire was not the most productive county. In 1620, according to the justices, Derbyshire produced little grain except oats, and was not able to supply more than half its own needs, hence the dependence on grain imports along the Trent (Chambers 1957: 38). However, there is evidence to suggest efforts were already being made to increase cultivation in the area. Oats and peas occupied the most ground. The stock-rearing, cattle-feeding region lay in the central sector of the county, particularly the Dove and Derwent valleys, but many farms supported large flocks as well as bullocks. By-employment made it possible for men to make a living from the land. The Trent claylands were predominantly common field territory, where the nature of the soil did not encourage the early adoption of new fodder crops such as turnips and clover. Sheep-barley husbandry was found on the wolds and limestone heath of Lincolnshire. The sheep were pastured on the slopes of hills and folded by night on the cornfields. Barley was the chief cash crop closely followed by wheat. Sheep far outnumbered cattle, and were the mainstay of the local economy largely because of the poor quality of the soil. Change was not impossible. Turnips were introduced in the early eighteenth century, with the result that upland farmers who had previously rented pastures on the marshlands to the east in order to fatten their sheep could now keep them at home, and cattle became the chief occupants of the marshland pastures. The upland farmers replaced their stock of sheep sent to the marsh with droves of Scottish cattle. Sheep flocks came to average about 100 in the first half of the eighteenth century on the wolds, although as the price of wool began to fall the economy ran into difficulties (Thirsk 1985, I: 99–106).

A third area of the region is the less fertile but extensive wooded areas, including Sherwood Forest in Nottinghamshire, Charnwood in Leicestershire, and Leighfield in Rutland. Although the forest district was still extensive in Nottinghamshire, only 50 or 60 square miles survived in Charnwood, while Leighfield was disafforested about 1630. On the sandy infertile soils of the forest areas the farming pattern involved retaining a small amount of permanently enclosed land near the homesteads, while leaving the rest open, common to the villagers' sheep and cattle. Brecks, or temporary enclosures, were made to bring land under tillage for periods of five or six years. The arable was used mainly for growing oats or peas, followed by barley, and then rye, oats again, and lastly 'skegs', a form of oats. Within Sherwood Forest much of the land consisted of gorsy heath, cony warrens and sheepwalks, but the lack of demand for land was such that in the eighteenth century it became the centre of some large parks and stately homes. Over time some of the waste was slowly improved by temporary cultivations, cropping for five or six years, and then returning to grass. In a few areas convertible husbandry was possible, and by the mid-eighteenth century turnips and clover were grown. Large flocks of sheep were kept in order to improve soil fertility, and inventory evidence suggests that it was possible to make a tolerable living from forest land (Thirsk 1985, I: 95, 106–11).

The Lincolnshire marshlands represent a fourth farming area, running southwards from the Humber along the line of the coast until they meet the fenland of Lindsey near Wainfleet. Near to the sea is saltmarsh, much of it reclaimed land; further inland is middle marsh, with soils consisting mainly of boulder clay. Saltmarsh was the richer and more valuable land, but it was subject to the risk of flooding and erosion by the sea, while the middle marsh had a greater element of arable. Livestock was central to marshland farming. Mixed husbandry was also practised on the marshlands of Holderness and the coastal strip of Lindsey. The specialities of these areas were cattle and sheep fattening *and* wheat growing. Consisting as they did of bolder clay, silt and peat carrs, when properly drained the clay made good cornland, and both regions were grazing grounds for fat stock *and* a granary. Beans were the main fodder crop, and wheat the main cash crop. In general the marshlands were well populated with prosperous corn-and-cattle farmers, many of whom were rich squires and yeomen. It was not easy to find a poor man in the area (Thirsk 1967: 32–6).

The prosperity of the Lincolnshire wool trade was sufficient to encourage the use of reclaimed land for sheep rearing. During the sixteenth century a strip of silt deposits forming saltmarshes up to 10 miles wide, and stretching from the Humber to the Wash near Boston, was reclaimed piecemeal from the sea, and in the course of the seventeenth century some of those lands were occupied by inland landholders anxious to rent grazing land for fattening sheep. This practice began around 1600 as a result of a forage crisis which afflicted the traditional mixed farming further inland. The utilization of these first-rate grazing lands helped to overcome the problem (Perkins 1977a: 7; Holderness 1974). On the other hand these offcomers were the more substantial of the inland farmers, and their demand for marsh pasture drove up rents and forced out many of the smaller men who traditionally dominated the area (Thirsk 1985, I: 111–13). By the eighteenth century a shift was taking place in the business. The traditional situation in which the county's wool clip had been far more important than any sales of mutton, gave way to a changing pattern as the result of alterations in supply and demand. In addition to the growth of demand for cotton goods, the Lincolnshire sheep farmers were affected by mid-eighteenth century developments in demand for various types of wool. This included a move to develop long-woolled sheep, which undercut Lincoln-shire farmers. The result was a steady decline in the profitability of wool on permanent pasture, and a change from making profits by selling fleeces to concentrating on mutton.

Finally, the fen region in the north-west of Lincolnshire and a large area surrounding the Wash including Holland and parts of eastern Kesteven and eastern Lindsey, also practised a pastoral system of husbandry. Numerous drainage projects were put forward, but none produced a fundamental alteration in the local economy, which remained a district of pastoral husbandry. The richest asset was the abundant summer grazing. The arable was meagre; the average holding had no more than 10 acres under the plough, on which the chief crops were barley, wheat and pulses (Perkins 1977a: 12–18, 38–40).

The two major developments relating to farming practice in this period, reclamation and enclosure, were both designed to increase the productivity of the land. Reclamation took place in various parts of the region. In the forest regions landlords established plantations, which they cultivated for building timber, coppice wood, and other purposes. Derbyshire coppices produced wood for charcoal and for pit props. Derbyshire also witnessed considerable reclamation between 1500 and 1650 (Fussell 1951: 11; Thirsk 1985, I: 121–4). New pastures were gained from the sea in the Lincolnshire marshlands, and considerable effort went into constructing and maintaining sea walls. River embankments also needed maintenance, while fen drainage permitted an extension of the cultivated acreage.

Fen drainage was not a new idea in the seventeenth century. Since the thirteenth century the commissioners of sewers had been responsible for undertaking works designed to prevent inundation, and during the sixteenth century various commissions were responsible for attempts to control flooding and for encouraging small drainage schemes. But the sixteenth century was one of discussion and experiment by comparison with the seventeenth (Jones 1986; Darby 1983: 41–51). The change of emphasis from small-scale local projects to efforts at draining the whole area can be dated from James I's declaration in 1621 that he was unwilling to allow waterlogged lands to lie waste and unprofitable, and that he would undertake drainage work himself for a recompense of 120,000 acres. Action, however, had to wait until the accession of Charles I, when in 1626 the king concluded an agreement with the Dutch entrepreneur Sir Cornelius Vermuyden. In return for one-third of the drained land, Vermuyden was to raise the capital and provide the technical expertise needed to drain the fens of Hatfield Chase and the Isle of Axholme, around 60,000 acres in all. Part of the king's interest arose from being lord of the manors of Hatfield and Epworth, and the crown claimed half of the drained land, leaving the fenmen, who had previously enjoyed the whole area as common pasture, what was left after entrepreneur and monarch had taken their share. The Crown appears neither to have known about nor to have cared about the profitable farming of the fenmen, which would inevitably be affected by drainage.

The advantage of using Vermuyden was that he arrived with new techniques. His aim was to abandon the older methods of keeping the river channels clear in favour of cutting a new river channel to make the water flow faster and to keep the rivers from silting up. Between 1626 and 1636 Axholme was drained, with impressive results, as new land was cultivated, new settlers arrived, and in some cases wages rose considerably. The disadvantage was that Vermuyden arrived without local acceptance, and with every intention of

Plate 4.4 Fen drainage, Crowland, Lincolnshire. For centuries the village of Crowland was surrounded by water, until drainage schemes led to a transformation of the fen lands. This view shows Crowland High Wash, west of the village of Crowland, with the river Welland in the background, and in the foreground the New River.

A second point of interest worth noting is the pattern of envelope ploughing, so called because of the pattern created by the movement of the plough from a centre line in four directions.

succeeding by fair means or foul. The men of the Isle of Axholme were faced with losing two-thirds of their common land and the dislocation of their traditional farming. They argued that the expropriation was wholy illegal, and they mounted a strenuous campaign of opposition. For his part Vermuyden was under pressure to complete the project without paying too much attention to the demands of the fenlanders. The predictable result was an outbreak of popular anger, rioting and, when Vermuyden's men began work in Haxey Carr during the summer of 1628, assaults. In the process one of the fenlanders was killed, an event viewed with complacency by the Crown, whose resources were placed at Vermuyden's disposal in order to quell the riots. The ringleaders were proceeded against in Star Chamber, and lesser men were imprisoned. Thereafter work was able to progress without noticeable interruption partly because government assistance was forthcoming when further riots occurred during the 1630s. Vermuyden was even accused of inventing riots or inflating their seriousness to secure the continued assistance of central government.

Vermuyden's lack of scruple in his efforts to keep order on the Isle of Axholme was matched by his manipulation of the legal proceedings in the 1630s. The fenmen set their faces against any division of the land, but the commissioners after surveying the land apportioned Vermuyden's one-third, and suggested a division of the rest which would have left the commoners a mere 6,000 acres. Vermuyden had purchased the Crown's share, and he wanted a legally binding agreement to bring his plans to fruition. After a series of dubious legal moves he managed to secure a title, and the men of Axholme were silenced at least until 1642. Overall, the scheme represented a formidable example of the deployment of royal authority to crush the fenlanders who were forced to watch their traditional economy being dismembered.

Vermuyden's success was more difficult to repeat where private landlords had rights in the common fens, and therefore had to be considered in any large-scale drainage operation. A way was found, however, since the commissioners of sewers were given statutory authority to legitimize drainage operations and to compel the participation of recalcitrants among the local landowners. This authority was exercised in a number of operations, including the drainage of the Ancholme Level. In August 1635 the local commissioners of sewers condemned lands in the villages alongside the river Ancholme belonging to men who had failed to pay a deliberately high rate set three months earlier. The commissioners then sold the 5,827 acres to Sir John Monson, a local landowner who, by the spring of 1639, drained the fen. Finally, the Crown also backed drainage schemes in south Lincolnshire, particularly after Charles I's resolution in 1633 to have 'the whole level of fens in county Lincolnshire drained'. The South Forty Foot Drain, cut in the 1630s, provided a negotiable river from Bourne to Boston, and the fens north of Boston between the Witham and the Wash were also drained in the 1630s (Darby 1983: 88–91).

The progress of enclosure varied during the course of this period. In the sixteenth century it was regarded as an unmitigated evil, and the East Midlands was affected by the related problems of unemployment and depopulation. Returns from the enclosure commissions of 1517–19 reveal that more than 4,000 acres had been enclosed in both Nottinghamshire and Lincolnshire, and nearly 6,000 in Leicestershire. Enclosing activity gathered momentum during the century. At Foston in Leicestershire more than half the open fields were converted to pasture before Anthony Faunt, the lord of the manor, enclosed the village in 1575 (Millward 1985: 71). The enclosure commission of 1607 reported the enclosure of more than 12,000 acres in Leicestershire, and by 1640 one-quarter of the county had been enclosed. Over 13,000 acres in Lincolnshire had been enclosed and converted to pasture.

None of these figures will bear close scrutiny, and recent estimates suggest that the extent of sixteenth-century enclosure was minute by comparison with the seventeenth century. The important point is that here was the beginning of a change from arable to permanent pasture which later generations were to applaud and to take further. It could be justified both technically and economically. On the Lincolnshire wolds and limestone edge and in the eastern uplands of Leicestershire enclosures were used to extend the area of sheepwalk, and to increase the quantity of sheep feed in winter. In south and parts of east Leicestershire new closes on the heavy clay soils were used for cattle fattening, and the area was already beginning to supply beef to other parts of the Midlands and to London (Thirsk 1967: 240–55).

Enclosure in the seventeenth century was much less contentious than previously – partly because tenants had joined their landlords in favouring the process – and was almost certainly on a much wider scale than in the sixteenth century. There were good economic reasons for this. Across the country the period 1660–1750 was characterized by falling agricultural prices, especially for cereals. This trend culminated in two decades of depression between 1730 and 1750, notwithstanding the efforts of central government to offset the farmers' difficulties by encouraging grain exports. Evidence for depression can be found in all the east midlands counties (Mingay 1956; Chambers and Mingay 1967: 41). The reaction of landowners and farmers alike was to try to increase the productivity of the land, and to this extent the light-soiled areas, notably those of East Anglia, outcompeted their rivals elsewhere. With dairy product prices holding steady many owners saw the answer to their difficulties in terms of a change of land use. This was particularly true of the heavy claylands of the East Midlands, which were better suited to permanent pasture than the open-field mixed farming commonly practised.

The result was a burst of enclosing in the 1660–1750 period, although it was generally of a more piecemeal and small-scale nature than after 1750. Unfortunately, partial enclosure of this nature has left little by way of a written record, which makes it difficult to be precise about the extent of change. In Lincolnshire and Rutland about two-thirds of the land was enclosed by non-parliamentary means, while in Nottinghamshire almost one-quarter of the pasture district was enclosed by 1700 (Chambers 1966: 151). Early enclosure on the Lincolnshire claylands was particularly vigorous in central Lindsey, where the soil was suited to pasture and land was often flooded by the river Witham. Twenty-nine Lindsey villages were subject to some form of enclosure during the seventeenth century. Sixteenth- and seventeenth-century evidence from the county suggests that the marshlands were the earliest enclosed, while the light-soil areas of the wolds and heath remained relatively little affected. Stock rearing was the usual impetus behind enclosure (Johnson 1962; Johnson 1983). Possibly 45 per cent of Nottinghamshire was already enclosed by 1759, and the movement was most obvious in the pasture region of the Trent valley, particularly in the parishes where one or two landowners predominated. The farmers of Cotgrave agreed in 1717 to enclose one of the four common fields in order to remedy a grassland shortage, while even parishes enclosed by Act of Parliament often had an earlier enclosure history, as at Beeston near Nottingham where the Nether Field was enclosed in 1610, probably for pasture (Cossons 1958). Enclosure by agreement also took place frequently in the Peak District, especially where dairying and stock breeding were practised (Thirsk 1985, I: 136–7).

Similarly Leicestershire saw a steady transformation of the open fields into permanent pasture. Village after village of the Vale of Belvoir was enclosed during the second half of the seventeenth century almost certainly for the purpose of fattening cattle, dairying and horse breeding (Chambers 1966: 219). Over the period 1660–1760 seventy-three places in the county were enclosed, and by 1730 more than half the county was already enclosed; indeed, recent estimates suggest that the critical period for enclosure in the county was during the seventeenth century when perhaps one-third of the total acreage was affected. By 1730 the limits of enclosure by agreement had been reached, which explains why the county was in the forefront of the parliamentary enclosure movement when it began to gather momentum in the second half of the eighteenth century (VCH Leics II 1954; Thirsk 1985, I: 117–21). A further 35 per cent of the county was enclosed between 1760 and the end of the century (Wordie 1983: 496–8).

Two results followed from enclosure in the region before 1750. First, the transformation of land use, particularly in Leicestershire which changed from a predominantly arable to a predominantly pastoral county (VCH Leics II 1954: 220–3). Second, enclosure, while not necessarily bringing total depopulation, could bring shrinkage, and population shift. Before enclosure the midlands open-field system, including the Lincolnshire claylands, was classically village-orientated with communal cultivation regulated in a manor court. Such a system was immediately threatened by the land use change associated with enclosure. The enclosure returns for 1607 show that in Lincolnshire 199 farmhouses, and 140 barns, cottages and stables had decayed, while 312 farm houses had been turned into cottages, and a further 440 farm houses had been made into cottages and allowed to stand empty. At the same date Leicestershire had 172 houses of husbandry said to be decayed (Reed 1981: 67). Of course not every area was affected. In the fenlands, for example, townships often consisted of several manors, and since as a result communal regulation could not be wholly decided within the manorial court the sense of community was focused on the village rather than the manor (Thirsk 1967: 39).

Taken altogether the evidence of change in the east midlands countryside suggests that this was a period of significant development in the East Midlands countryside. Population grew perceptibly, even if the rate of change varied across the region and through time, and alterations in structure were important. Land passed into the hands of lay landlords, the old social restrictions of the manorial system were finally laid to rest, and partly as a result agriculture was able to break out of the debilitating strait-jacket which had been such a feature of medieval England. As the manorial system broke down, responsibility for local government passed to the county and to the parish, to a more formalized system largely conceived in Tudor England and built upon down to the nineteenth century. Some evidence, particularly from inventories and housing, suggests relative wealth in the farming community, while the enthusiasm for reclamation – with the exception of fen drainage for which there were extenuating circumstances – and for enclosure suggests that the farming community was reacting to demand for its products. Possibly after 1660 it was also responding to depressed prices.

Chapter 5

Towns, Trade and Industry

Towns as we know them are a distinctive product of nineteenth- and twentieth-century society. Until the mid-eighteenth century it was not always possible to distinguish them from the larger villages of the surrounding countryside. Clark and Slack have suggested that the readily recognizable characteristics of pre-industrial English towns were a concentration of population, a specialist economic function, a complex social structure, a sophisticated political order and a distinctive influence beyond their immediate boundaries (Clark and Slack 1976: 4–5). Towns depended on their hinterlands, both for a regular supply of food and also for the raw materials required in industrial production. As a result they acted as a market, and a focal point for the local transport network, and these functions helped to stimulate the commercialization and development of the agrarian economy; indeed, economic activity was drawn into towns, and this helped to widen local marketing areas. Towns also became the centres for service specialisms such as banking and insurance, law, medicine, education, entertainment and local government. Finally, through their open, competitive and acquisitive societies, which differed from the countryside around them, they helped to develop a new consumer ethos (Corfield 1982: 96–8; Abrams and Wrigley 1978: 295–309). Perhaps the most distinctive characteristic of this period was the emergence of a number of substantial market towns in place of the proliferation which marked medieval England; indeed, urban growth was primarily based on marketing facilities.

This relationship was largely a result of the small size of the urban community and the depression which overtook many towns towards the end of the Middle Ages, reaching a low point in the mid-sixteenth century. John Leland, for example, referred in the early sixteenth century to the 'much decayed' towns of Lincolnshire, and settlements in the east of the region, including Lincoln and Stamford, Grimsby and Boston, were among the most affected (Rogers 1970: 50; Hodgett 1975: 135). Leicester was also one of the clearest examples of sixteenth-century urban decay (Abrams and Wrigley 1978: 159–85). However, by contrast with other parts of the country, including the West Midlands, urban revival did not involve the growth of new towns.

Indeed, from the sixteenth century to the present the county towns of Derby, Leicester, Lincoln and Nottingham – four of the five Danish boroughs – have been among the region's largest, while Grimsby (the fourth town in population terms in the 1950s) was a medieval borough of some significance. Consequently economic development produced an increase in the importance of the older towns rather than the growth of new cities, partly because the major towns had developed close to good water communications and, more fortuitously, partly because of their proximity to the coalfield.

In the sixteenth century none of these towns was particularly sizeable. Nottingham's population rose from about 3,000 in the early sixteenth century, to perhaps 3,500 by 1600, and to 5,000–6,000 in the 1670s; by 1739 it was well over 10,000 (Chambers 1966: 82–3). Leicester may have been slightly larger in the mid-sixteenth century than Nottingham, but it increased more slowly, reaching 6,000 in 1700 (Thirsk 1985 I: 89), and about 8,000 by 1750. Lincoln, the major town of the region during the Middle Ages, had little more than 2,000 inhabitants in the mid-sixteenth century and probably not much more than double that total two centuries later (Hill 1966; 146–7). Derby, a town of 1,300 people in 1524 and perhaps 2,000 in the 1560s (Blanchard 1967), had increased to just over 6,000 in the mid-eighteenth century. Even in 1700 the combined populations of these county capitals, the largest towns in the region, probably represented no more than 4 per cent of the total population of the East Midlands. No other town had more than 4,000 inhabitants in 1750, and only Boston, Gainsborough, Hinckley and possibly Newark topped 3,000. Two centuries earlier even market towns of more than 1,000 were unusual: in Derbyshire, for example, only Chesterfield and Wirksworth exceeded this figure in the sixteenth century (Riden 1978: 69).

During this period a significant change took place in the relationship between town and countryside. A number of towns were appointed county boroughs in their own right with the liberty to exercise full powers of local government. Some, although not all (Chesterfield and Louth, for example) of these municipal corporations returned two Members of Parliament. The form and nature of the corporations was by no means standard, and even the titles of members of corporations varied. In Lincolnshire by the eighteenth century the chief magistrate of the borough was normally referred to as the mayor, but Grantham was governed by an alderman and twelve justices of the peace, and Stamford was under the control of an alderman, twelve comburgesses, and twenty-four capital burgesses, which, according to Defoe, 'abating their worships' titles, is, to me, much the same thing as a mayor, aldermen and common council' (Defoe 1971: 420). Members of corporations acted as justices of the peace during sessions. A town clerk, recorder, coroner, and other officials were employed by each corporation. The independent corporations identified by the Royal Commission of 1835 are given in Table 6.

Lincoln's corporate powers included regulations and duties laid down for the mayor, the justices, coroners, members of the common council (the

Table 6   Municipal corporations in the East Midlands by 1835

Derbyshire	Leicestershire	Lincolnshire	Nottinghamshire
Chesterfield	Leicester	Boston	East Retford
Derby		Grimsby	Newark
		Grantham	Nottingham
		Lincoln	
		Louth	
		Stamford	

twenty-four) and the common clerks. The city had considerable judicial pow-ers; indeed, privileges were claimed which were similar to those of the city of London. At the same time, however, Lincoln was poverty-stricken, and the city fathers had considerable difficulty collecting sufficient rates to run the town. Since the town's poverty sprung from the decline of its traditional cloth trade, much of the city government's time was spent obtaining exemptions from royal taxation; some efforts were also made to promote trade by favouring 'natives' rather than 'foreigners' within the town. Thus in 1524 it was laid down that only freemen of the city could sell bread and that not even apprentices and journeymen could bake until they had their freedom (Hodgett 1975: Ch. 8).

Town parishes had the same responsibilities as those of the countryside. This was not always helpful, particularly in the six tiny parishes of Stamford and the fifteen in Lincoln. Conversely, in some places the duties of parish officers had become sufficiently onerous to permit a degree of professionalism. St Peter's vestry in Nottingham appointed George Pindar as overseer in 1718 on a salary of £4 a year, which was raised in 1727 to £5, and one shilling for every certificate of settlement. Parish constables had their expenses met by their own parishes (Chambers 1966: 59–65). Such diversities of experience were also reflected in the wide variety of roles performed by manor courts. While in some parts of the region they were disappearing in the face of enclosure, at Gainsborough the great court baron, court leet and view of frankpledge of the Hickman family retained considerable importance in town government into the nineteenth century. Twice a year the owners of certain tofts in the town formed the jury; their duties included upkeep of the highways (Wright 1982: 7–9).

Nottingham, the largest town in the region by 1750, generally attracted praise from visitors. In the 1530s John Leland wrote that:

> Nottingham is both a large town and well builded for timber and plaster, and standeth stately on a clyminge hill . . . The market place and street both for the building on the side of it, for the very great wideness of the street, and the clean paving of it, is the most fairest without exception of all England.
>
> (Leland 1907: 94)

In the late seventeenth century Celia Fiennes described Nottingham as 'the neatest town I have seen . . . all the streets are of a good size all about the town' (Fiennes 1947: 72). By the time of her visit brick and stone were rapidly replacing the older wooden-framed buildings, and fine houses in the town reflected the prosperity of some of its leading families. It was a description with which Daniel Defoe readily agreed; in his view Nottingham was 'one of the most pleasant and beautiful towns in England' (Defoe 1971: 451). Early in the sixteenth century it was known as a town of gardens. In 1504 Nottingham consisted of a central core of tenements with a few associated gardens or other properties clustered around the Market Square, an outer ring of tenements and gardens, and on the periphery a number of closes, barns and gardens (Mastoris 1985: 38). This pleasant situation persisted into the eighteenth century. In 1720 there were about 2,000 dwellings and 10,000 inhabitants, and the town was noted for its spaciousness. A number of elegant houses in the town date from the early eighteenth century; the Exchange Building, erected in the Market Square in 1724 to a plan designed by the mayor, cost £2,400 (Bryson 1974: 74, 77). Even by the time Badder and Peat mapped the town in 1744 little suburban development had taken place beyond the Norman town.

Leicester did not enjoy the same reputation. Leland noted in the 1530s that 'the whole town at this time is builded of timber' (Leland 1907: 14), and by the mid-seventeenth century it was considerably decayed. John Evelyn described it in 1654 as 'the old and ragged city of Leicester, large and pleasantly seated but despicably built, the chimney flues like so many smiths' forges'; while another commentator described it in the 1670s as 'an old, stinking town' (Bray 1906: 204; Ellis 1976: 87). Leicester's problem was that as the medieval wool trade passed away, no adequate substitute appeared to take its place. The result was that a town of perhaps 3,000 people in the 1520s had, in the words of its historian, 'no marked industrial character'. Indeed, it was little more than a market town, and more than half of those admitted freemen during the sixteenth century were involved in the provision of clothes, food and drink. Although 'a leaning towards the leather and allied trades was becoming evident by the first quarter of the sixteenth century', the town still depended for its prosperity on the surrounding countryside (Hoskins 1963; 1955). The way out of this malaise came only towards the end of the seventeenth century with framework knitting. By 1714 the town was reputed to have 500–600 frames, supposedly giving employment to 7,600 people, although this must have included the knitters in surrounding villages and even then the proportion is unlikely. Even so, framework knitting was the industry which converted Leicester from a county town and market into a major manufacturing centre. The marketing functions remained significant, however, and a new exchange was built in 1748 (Simmons 1974, I: 97–101, 110–12).

At the end of the seventeenth century Derby, like Nottingham and Leicester, was in the process of changing from a county and market town into an industrial centre. In 1693 it had 694 houses, 76 malthouses, and 120 alehouses

– it was noted for its ale – and during that decade a new water supply was created by George Sorocold using a floating waterwheel on the river Derwent (Rippon 1980: 95). The turnpiking of local roads, the improvement of the river Derwent in the 1720s, and the building of Lombe's silk mill, all contributed towards the development of industry in the town. Celia Fiennes noted some of the changes towards the end of the seventeenth century: 'the River Derwent runs by the town and turns many mills, and the water engine which turns the water into the pipes that serves the town'. She found the market place 'very spacious, well pitched, a good Market Cross', while in about 1700 the town was described as 'neat, large, well-built, and populous' (Fiennes 1947: 169–70; Cox 1700a: 428). For Defoe Derby was

> a fine, beautiful and pleasant town . . . it has more families of gentlemen in it than is usual in towns so remote, and therefore here is a great deal of good and some gay company. Perhaps the rather, because the Peak being so near, and taking up the larger part of the county, and being so inhospitable, so ragged and so wild a place, the gentry choose to reside at Derby, rather than upon their estates, as they do in other places.
>
> (Defoe 1971: 457)

Sixteenth-century Lincoln was a shadow of its former self. The common council minutes, beginning in 1511, point unmistakably to decline: private individuals were forbidden to pull down houses or to export building material, despite the fact that the houses were empty and no money was available to renovate them; and a petition for relief in 1528 declared that Lincoln was eight or nine parts fallen into ruin. William Lambarde, writing in 1584, declared Lincoln to be in a pitiful state (Hill 1956: 19–39). John Evelyn in the 1650s found it 'an old confused town, very long, uneven, steep and ragged'; while Daniel Defoe described it as 'an ancient, ragged, decayed, and still decaying city'. Only the upper part of Lincoln escaped the general gloom; here Defoe found 'some very good buildings, and a great deal of very good company' (Bray 1906: 207; Defoe 1971: 410–11). Lincoln's manufacturing was bound up with the local countryside, from whence came the resources for milling and malting, brewing and tanning, the staple trades of the town. Only as the eighteenth century progressed did it begin to enjoy a modest prosperity as demand increased for wool, corn and meat products in London and the West Riding (Hill 1966: 100, 138–9).

Outside the county towns the old coaching towns are among the best documented. Stamford still had the buildings and the institutions of its illustrious past, but its economy had faltered to the point where much of the population was on the verge of destitution. In 1548 the number of parishes was cut from eleven to six, and thirty years later the town council was concerned by unemployment and poverty. Even in 1524 the town had fewer households than

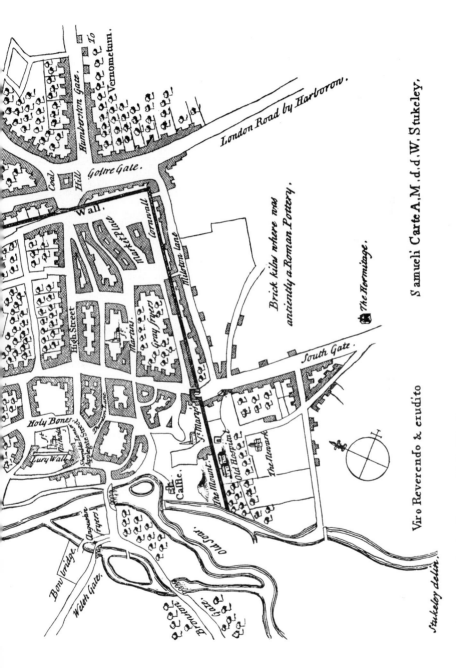

Figure 5.1 Leicester in 1722 (after Simmons 1974: 108–9)

Plate 5.1 Stamford, Lincolnshire, the Bull Running. The annual bull running on 13 November was a popular event in Stamford until the nineteenth century, when it fell victim to the movement to suppress cruel sports.

Although attempts were made to end the running during the 1780s, it was only after the passing of the 1835 Cruelty to Animals Act made available legal grounds for prosecuting participants that anything was done. In 1837 the Society for the Prevention of Cruelty to Animals laid charges against eight men involved in the 1836 running. In November 1837, encouraged by the Home Office, the magistrates posted notices of severe punishments which would be imposed if the running was repeated, and 240 special constables were enrolled. Even this could not bring such a popular event to an end, but in 1840 670 inhabitants signed a petition commiting themselves to assist personally in suppressing the running as long as no outside help was sought. This proved more than enough to bring the custom to a halt.

Spalding and not many more than some of the larger fenland villages. From then until the mid-seventeenth century population growth remained slow, and it was only after about 1660 that some revival seems to have occurred. The number of households increased from 242 in 1524 to 282 by 1665, but then more rapidly to 470 in 1705 and to 856 by 1788. Part of the problem, as in Leicester and Lincoln, was the absence of an adequate replacement for cloth. Even when prosperity returned towards the end of the seventeenth century no single trade was dominant, although leather working, weaving, and wood and stone crafts were the most important. Depression brought decay and the silting of the Welland, and it was the decision to clear this and to encourage trade which seems to have been behind Stamford's recovery in the course of the seventeenth century. This permitted the town to malt and transport the barley crop of the surrounding countryside (Rogers 1965: 58–76). As a result, travellers found much to enthuse about. Celia Fiennes found Stamford to be 'as fine a built town all of stone as may be seen' (Fiennes 1947: 67). To Defoe it was 'a very fair, well-built, considerable and wealthy town' (Defoe 1971: 420), but this was before a fire destroyed large areas in 1727 (Wright 1982: 14, 16). Stamford and Spalding are full of particularly good examples of early Georgian architecture, the one in stone and the other in brick. Stamford today is a Georgian town, developed on the basis of Great North Road commercialism, and still featuring many of the grey stone buildings of the period, including the Assembly Rooms (1725), and other houses from the 1730s onwards (Rogers 1965: 77–90).

Grantham was centred around a market place where the road to the south-west joined the Great North Road. In about 1700 it was said to be 'rich and populous' (Cox 1700b: 1418), while to Defoe it was 'a neat, pleasant, well-built and populous town', with a good market, good trade, and considerable wealth. Despite his criticism of the Great North Road, he found both Grantham and Stamford 'famous . . . for abundance of very good inns, some of them fit to entertain persons of the greatest quality' (Defoe 1971: 419, 429, 441). Defoe also liked Newark, a town of perhaps 2,700 people in 1600, which benefited from its local marketing functions as well as the movement of people along the Great North Road, and goods along the Trent. Although timber-framed in the sixteenth century, it was rebuilt in brick from about 1660, and by the early eighteenth century according to Defoe it was 'a very handsome well-built town' (Barley 1949; Defoe 1971: 410). By the 1740s the population may have exceeded 3,000, and Handley House stands today as a monument to its eighteenth-century wealth (Wood 1937b: 24).

The decline of overseas trade hit the seaports hard; both Boston and Grimsby came, by the eighteenth century, to be more important in coastal than in overseas trade (Hodgett 1975: 83–90). Boston had relied for its prosperity on the trade in raw wool, and this suffered when the practice spread of turning the wool into cloth prior to export. In 1592 Queen Elizabeth discharged the port from certain tax payments because of its 'poor estate'. Even so, a few cloths and skins continued to pass through the port, and a small amount of wine was imported. Despite silting, vessels continued to reach the town, helping to facilitate inland trade. Boston acted as a supply centre for south Lincolnshire and as a port outlet for much of its produce. Goods from Northumberland and Durham were landed in the town, and fen produce was shipped off, much of it for London. Around 1700 it was said to be, 'and long hath been, a famous and flourishing town' (Cox 1700b: 467) while Defoe found it 'a handsome, well-built sea port town . . . large, populous . . . full of good merchants and has a good share of foreign trade, as well as Lynn' (Defoe 1971: 414). In fact, this was rather optimistic. In 1683 only eleven vessels sailed from Boston to London, and by 1700 it was losing out to Hull as a port for the transhipment of midlands goods; indeed, it had been replaced by King's Lynn as the principal port on the Wash. By 1709 it was ranked nineteenth among English ports for registered shipping, but despite the growing significance of

Gainsborough it remained the main port in Lincolnshire, and even in 1750 its population was still around 3,000 (Wright 1982: 20–21).

Grimsby's population was around 850 in 1524, but it was a town in decline. By the 1570s its seaborne trade was insignificant (Gillett 1970: 98–104), and a century later it may even have been smaller than the neighbouring village of Clee. By then Grimsby was only one-sixteenth the size of Boston. Only two or three merchants were left in the town, and despite dredging no ships cleared for foreign parts in 1704 and only two entered. The coastal trade was doing a little better, but hardly prospering. In George I's reign the vicar estimated that only 98 families lived in the town, and the parish registers suggest a population of between 500 and 600. For Defoe it was 'a good town . . . but an indifferent road for shipping' (Gillett 1970: 169; Jackson 1971: 44; Defoe 1971: 413).

Of other towns less detail is known. The East Midlands had one resort in the seventeenth century, Buxton, renowned since the sixteenth century for its waters but much criticized for its accommodation. Richard Blome commented in 1673 that the town would have more visitors 'were there better conveniences of lodging and entertainment', and both Charles Cotton in 1681, and Celia Fiennes a few years later expressed similar sentiments. The accommodation according to Fiennes was so bad that 'few people stay above two or three nights its so inconvenient' (Burton 1977; Fiennes 1947: 103). A few years later Daniel Defoe also criticized the lack of lodgings (Defoe 1971: 469), and this chorus of unfavourable contemporary opinion evoked Lord Macaulay's scathing remarks in the 1840s to the effect that:

> the gentry of Derbyshire and of the neighbouring counties repaired to Buxton, where they were lodged in low rooms under bare rafters, and regaled with oatcake and with a viand which the hosts called mutton, but which the guests suspected to be dog.
>
> (Macaulay 1913, I: 335–6)

Even in 1750 a passing traveller found himself 'in a very wild and drery situation' when he spent the night in Buxton, but a growing interest in the countryside, and of tourism in general meant that the town was popular despite its deficiencies of accommodation, and he found 'much company there and a dancing partee' (Garlic 1982).

The proliferation of market towns which characterized the medieval period had not merely come to an end by 1500, but it had gone into reverse; indeed, far fewer markets were to be found in the sixteenth century than had been the case three hundred years earlier. Derbyshire could boast twenty-eight markets in the medieval period but only nine or ten by the late seventeenth century, recovering to twelve in 1792 (Coates 1965: 107). Leicestershire's thirty markets of the early fourteenth century had become just thirteen in 1673, and twelve in 1693 (Everitt 1973: 216). Over the period 1500–1750 the other east midlands counties could also boast far fewer markets than previously: Lincolnshire had thirty-seven in the sixteenth century, falling to thirty-one by the end of the eighteenth; Nottinghamshire had nine and Rutland two throughout the period (Thirsk 1985, II: 410). Market density was greatest in Leicestershire, and thinnest in Derbyshire and Nottinghamshire. Many of those that had survived were in a parlous state. At Waltham-on-the-Wolds in Leicestershire the market was described in 1670 as being 'very inconsiderable and in a manner disused'. Decline, however, was an uneven process, and in the sixteenth century some markets were expanding and a few new ones were being founded. The market at Ketsby in Lincolnshire, for example, came into being in 1524 (Thirsk 1967: 466–75).

The other local towns of any significance were the markets which had survived the weeding out process since the Middle Ages. The local significance of these places still varied quite considerably. Defoe mentioned the smaller Lincolnshire towns of Brigg, Castor, Louth, Horncastle, Bolingbroke, Spilsby and Wainfleet, but commented that 'as these are all inland towns they afford little remarkable'. Spalding he admitted was 'pretty well built and well inhabited', but he was 'very glad when I got out of it, and out of the rest of the fen country' (Defoe 1971: 413, 415). Loughborough and Melton Mowbray were market towns 'of no great note', Mansfield was a market town 'without any remarkables'; Chesterfield was 'a handsome populous town, well-built and well inhabited', though with 'little or no manufacture', while Wirksworth was a large and well-frequented market town (Defoe 1971: 409, 457, 460, 479). What Defoe does not seem to have spotted, despite his passionate interest in trade and manufacture, was the early development of industry in some of these centres. Mansfield, for example, had thirty or forty frames in the town by 1727, while Hinckley, the centre of hosiery manufacture in Leicestershire, was a town of 2,250 by 1717, and even before the *Tour* began Wirksworth had been described as 'the chief town in the Peak, and the greatest market for lead in England, because near this town . . . are the furnaces where they melt down their lead-ore with great fires' (Cox 1700a: 433).

Defoe, of course, was not always an accurate reporter. His disparaging comments about Chesterfield, for example, were clearly undeserved. Tanning, shoemaking and the other leather trades were the most important sixteenth century manufactures in the town, with the wealthiest single group of townsmen being the tanners. The wool industry was also significant in the town during the sixteenth and seventeenth centuries, and hosiery knitting emerged as the most important branch of textile production in the eighteenth. Iron making was important, while many people pursued a dual occupation, some, for example, combining butchering with farming. This is not surprising since Chesterfield was first and foremost a market town, with much of its economic activity centring around the weekly market and its annual fairs (Riden 1984: 123–81; Bestall and Fowkes 1984: 41–53).

Falling numbers were not an indication of declining trade, but a reflection of the changing function of market towns. In fact, this represented the first stage in what eventually was to be the social and economic dominance of towns in English society, as the purely local function was superseded by a provincial role. It was reflected in the size and function of market towns. The characteristic Tudor market town had a population of perhaps 600–1,000 and occasionally 2,000 inhabitants, and the more important were beginning to specialize as the movement of goods increased; in the East Midlands, for example, a number were concentrating on livestock. Large sheep markets were held in Loughborough and Market Harborough, and the latter was also one of the principal horse markets of the area. Derby, by contrast, was a corn market, furnishing corn brought along the Trent to the miners and quarrymen of the county. Specialization was possible because traders were prepared to travel longer distances. Doncaster wool market was attended in Charles I's reign by merchants from places throughout the East Midlands. It is clear, in fact, that even in the sixteenth century, cattle, sheep and horses were driven considerable distances to markets throughout the Midlands (Thirsk 1967: 478–539). Over

---

Plate 5.2 Newark, Nottinghamshire, an etching of the Market Place by Edward Eyre, *c.* 1778. Although the dating is uncertain, the etching dates from only a few years before the Hon. John Byng described Newark market place as containing 'much good building, and beauty', and even today visitors cannot but be struck by this elegant Georgian market place.

On the left of the picture is the town hall, built *c.* 1774–76 of Mansfield stone by Carr of York. Also to be seen on the print and still there today is the sixteenth-century half-timbered Queen's Head. Newark in the late eighteenth century was a flourishing market town which enjoyed considerable prosperity as a result of its road and river traffic. On the south side of the market square the Saracen's Head and the Clinton Arms stand as reminders of the pre-railway-age, genteel, passenger traffic that frequented the town.

the period 1640–1750 wool and corn was sent from Lincolnshire into Yorkshire; malt was sent from Mansfield and Worksop into Derbyshire; stock from
Leicestershire and Nottinghamshire went to the Birmingham area and into
south Yorkshire, corn went from north Derbyshire to Manchester, and considerable numbers of cattle were driven south from Lincolnshire to the London
market (Thirsk 1985, I: 89–92; Hey 1980: 176). In the later years of the
seventeenth century Celia Fiennes noted that Chesterfield had 'a great market
like some little fair, a great deal of corn and all sorts of ware and fowls', while at
Uppingham in Rutland – hardly a major centre today – she found another
thriving market, with dealing in corn, leather, yarn and cattle (Fiennes 1947:
96, 161).

What was town life like at this time? It was certainly dangerous given the
number of places which are known to have suffered fire disasters. At least
nineteen towns in the region suffered severe fire damage in the seventeenth and
early eighteenth centuries, among them Loughborough with three disasters,
Barton-upon-Humber, Grantham, Stamford, Hinckley, Tuxford, Worksop
and Spalding with two each. At least 100 houses were destroyed at Hinckley in
1728, and damage estimated at more than £20,000 occurred in the fire at
Spalding in 1715 (Jones *et al.* 1984). The first fire in Tuxford was on 8
September 1702 when:

> betwixt the hours of five and six at night a dreadful fire broke out by
> casualty in Tuxford in this county which in less than three hours burnt
> down and consumed the dwelling houses, barns, stables, cow houses
> and out-houses of the inhabitants of Tuxford together with their corn
> and hay and most of their several household goods and household
> stuff . . .

Damage, which was mainly to the property of the town's poorer inhabitants,
was estimated at nearly £4,000 (Beckwith 1967b: 59–60).

While some towns suffered recurrent conflagrations, others were luckier,
and Lutterworth, in Leicestershire, provides an example of everyday life in a
market centre with 300 families in the seventeenth century. Lutterworth was
essentially a farming community which transformed itself into a business
centre only on fair and market days. For the rest of the time it operated more or
less like a village. Until the mid-sixteenth century much of its trading function
had been concerned with the wool trade, but thereafter its major concerns
became livestock and corn. Lutterworth became an exchange centre for
livestock, since it stood on the droving route from the north-west to the
south-east, and by the seventeenth century two or three professional stock
dealers had settled in the town. Although there were no corn dealers as such,
many people were involved in the middle trades of milling and baking.
From the mid-seventeenth century the number and variety of businesses in
the town was also on the increase. Permanent private shops with their own

Table 7 Specialities of market towns in the East Midlands, 1500–1640

Corn	Boston, Bourne, Brigg, Burton on Trent, Chesterfield, Derby, Gainsborough, Grantham, Hinckley, Horncastle, Loughborough, Lutterworth, East Retford, Sleaford, Stamford
Malt	Burton on Trent, Derby, Grantham, Mansfield, Stamford
Cattle	Brigg, Gainsborough, Newark, Uppingham
Horses	Hinckley, Leicester, Louth, Market Harborough
Sheep	Grantham, Horncastle, Loughborough, Market Harborough, Sleaford
Swine	Hinckley, Horncastle, Louth, Mansfield, Melton Mowbray
Poultry	Boston
Linen and hemp	Donnington (Lincs)

(Source: Thirsk 1967: 589–92)

premises (as opposed to market stalls) were beginning to appear (Goodacre 1978).

Fairs retained a vital significance through the period, and the first reliable list of 1756 shows that they were held in seventeen places in Derbyshire, fourteen in Leicestershire, forty-five in Lincolnshire, fifteen in Nottingham-shire, and two in Rutland, a total for the region of ninety-three (Thirsk 1985, II: 429–33). Nottingham's major fair was the annual Martinmas fair at Lenton, about a mile from the town. According to Charles Deering, writing in 1751:

> Our Nottingham Shopkeepers till within these 60 years last past, did not venture to go long journies, but depended upon the great annual Martinmas Fair at Lenton, where they used to buy their mercers, drapers, grocers, and all sorts of goods they wanted, brought thither by the Londoners, and others.
> (Deering 1751: 92)

Individuals travelled considerable distances to make their purchases. In the 1630s John and Thomas Hatcher of Careby in Lincolnshire visited Newark, Grantham and Nottingham fairs to buy oxen, bulls, bullocks and steers; Stow Green, Spilsby and Waltham – all in Lincolnshire – for steers; Corby and Rothwell in Northamptonshire for steers and cows; Melton Mowbray and Fotheringay for geldings. Kitchen requirements regularly induced John Careby to travel from his home on the Kesteven heath to the fen fair of Stourbridge and Peterborough (Thirsk 1957: 137, 176). Whether such travelling was typical is less clear since in the later seventeenth century sellers and buyers seem usually to have travelled within a 20–25 mile radius (Thirsk 1985, II: 441). According to Deering, by the eighteenth century the willingness of Nottinghamshire merchants to travel to distant markets 'has given them an opportunity of buying their commodities at the best hand, and contributed much to the increase of the number of wholesale dealers in Nottingham, whilst Lenton Fair is dwindled to a very inconsiderable Market' (Deering 1751: 92).

Overall, during this period a more mature marketing system was emerging under the pressure of transport changes and greater competition, but markets and fairs were not the only places at which goods were bought and sold. Lincolnshire inventories for the period 1535–1700 reveal a considerable number of 'shopkeepers', predominantly butchers (48 per cent), but also considerable numbers of mercers (25 per cent), drapers (11 per cent) and chandlers (6 per cent). Seventeenth-century Chesterfield had grocers and chandlers, mercers, drapers, ironmongers, and even a confectioner. How many of these were shopkeepers in the twentieth-century meaning of the term is not known, since seventeenth-century shopkeepers kept a mixed stock in trade. Butchers, for example, were invariably farmers as well. Many must have been farmer-grazier-dealers selling their meat in the local market town, and only two in five of Lincolnshire butchers' inventories mention a shop (Barley and Barley 1962). The Lincolnshire evidence suggests a general trend towards a greater element of private trading in the East Midlands, particularly for corn, sheep and wool. This movement gathered momentum through the period, as inn yards, parlours, shop doorways and farm gates became effective trading places. Regionalism and provincialism remained paramount in 1750 (Thirsk 1967: 545; 1985, II: 501; Hey 1980: 190).

Transport and Trade

One reason that fewer, more specialized market towns were able to do the business previously scattered around a large number of smaller ones lay with improvements in the transport network. In the mid-sixteenth century parishes were made responsible for road maintenance. Each year from 1555 a surveyor was elected by the parishioners, and it was his duty to call upon others to spend several days repairing the roads. Such an *ad hoc* system reflected the relative lack of importance attached to the highway, although plenty of evidence survives of worn surfaces being replenished by lines of flagstones known as causeys, some of which can still be seen on the ground today (Hey 1980: 64–71). Efforts were made to present parishes at quarter sessions when road surfaces became intolerable. In 1658 the inhabitants of Duffield, Derbyshire, were presented for failing to repair Cowhouse Lane, which 'ought by them to be repaired being used for all carts and carriages'. Similarly the overseers of the highways at Gainsborough were ordered by Lincolnshire quarter sessions in 1663 to set aside a number of 'common days' to fill the middle part of a street with gravel. Once this work was done the house owners were to ensure that the street was properly paved (Derbyshire RO, Quarter Sessions 1658). Nottinghamshire quarter sessions also contain numerous examples of presentments (Copnall 1915: 69–77). Apart from Chesterfield and its neighbouring townships of Newbold, Tapton and Hasland, no other north Derbyshire parishes consistently levied highway rates over any number of years during the period 1700–60. The resultant poor conditions were reflected in proceedings at quarter sessions. Somercotes was indicted in 1738 and 1746 on account of the fact that the Nottingham–Alfreton road was 'ruinous' (Hopkinson 1979: 17).

Bridges were a further problem. Fine examples of stone-built bridges survive from as far back as the fourteenth century, including Bakewell bridge in Derbyshire, but upkeep posed a considerable problem. From 1531 the justices had the right to levy a county rate for bridge upkeep, and over time they accepted responsibility for a considerable number of strategic river crossing points. Derbyshire JPs accepted responsibility for thirteen bridges on the river Derwent from Cromford northwards, and they spent considerable sums on widening and repairing them. In 1687, for example, £120 was spent on Grindleford bridge. Generally, justices proved reluctant to take over bridge maintenance, preferring to leave the task to individual parishes, although George Sitwell showed considerable interest in repairs to the bridge over the Rother at Renishaw when his iron interests were involved (Riden 1985: xxix–xxx). As a result, indictments regarding bridge repairs are as numerous in quarter sessions as for roads. During the seventeenth century in Nottinghamshire thirty-eight bridges were sources of parish presentments, including a warrant in 1634 against the inhabitants of West Stockwith and Misterton 'who refused contributions of divers sums on them imposed for repair of Stockwith Bridge and other bridges there ruinous' (Hey 1980: 75–7; Copnall 1915: 80–8). On the other hand local responsibility was not entirely neglected. Between 1729 and 1739 thirty-nine Derbyshire villages built or rebuilt their bridges, and bridge building was widespread in the region during the second half of the eighteenth century (Nixon 1969: 138; VCH Leics III 1955: 82).

Presentments did not necessarily bring overnight improvement and passengers and goods alike had to brave what can only be described as variable conditions. In the later seventeenth century the ever intrepid Celia Fiennes described the miles between Castleton and Buxton as 'very long', while between Uppingham and Leicester she encountered 'very deep roads . . . I was near 11 hours going but 25 mile – as they reckon it – between Wansford and Leicester town' (Fiennes 1947: 109, 162). Parts of the Lincolnshire fenlands were subject to flooding for much of the year, and in the summer of 1709 Bishop Wake's coach overturned between Horncastle and Boston. When he eventually managed to free himself from the vehicle he took to his horse (Wright 1982: 22). Daniel Defoe wrote at length on the poor road surfaces which were hampering trade between the midland counties and London. He was particularly critical of the two north–south roads passing through the East Midlands, the Great North Road, and the road from Northampton, through Market Harborough and Leicester to Nottingham. Travellers found themselves bogged down in the stiff Leicestershire clays, before moving on to a 'hard and pleasant' road for 30 miles through Sherwood Forest on the sandstone (Defoe 1971: 429–30, 441).

Defoe was preaching to the converted by the 1720s. In the seventeenth century the events of the Civil War, and the introduction of a postal service, revealed the need for an efficient mapping system, and reliable road surfaces. Increasing internal trade highlighted the problem. The solution adopted came in the form of turnpike trusts, non-profit-making ventures by which money was raised to improve a road, and then repaid from tolls levied on passengers and goods. Down to 1750 the turnpike system developed piecemeal across the country. Roads from London were among the earliest to be turnpiked, including the two east midlands roads so heavily criticized by Defoe. In 1725–6 an Act was passed to facilitate turnpiking the Great North Road from Grantham to West Drayton, just north of Tuxford. At this point the road passed on to the Bunter sandstone, which provided a firmer foundation. The other north–south route was improved by a series of Acts. In 1725–6 the road from Market Harborough to Loughborough was turnpiked, and in 1737 and 1738 legislation was obtained to improve the roads from Loughborough to Nottingham and to Derby (Cossons 1934: 9–11). The latter of these routes opened up the road to Manchester. Legislation in 1725 facilitated the turnpiking of the Manchester–Buxton road, which permitted broad-wheeled traffic into the Peak for the first time (Hey 1980: 23). Its significance was further enhanced when the Loughborough–Derby road was continued to Ashbourne to join a link from the Buxton–Manchester road (Pye 1972: 314; Edwards 1966a: 317; Chambers 1957: 11–13). Both roads proved beneficial for the carriage of coal, and this was also why the Turner family sponsored a scheme to rebuild the road from their pits near Swanwick to Matlock. The need to move heavy goods, particularly lead through the High Peak to Bawtry, was also reflected in the Act to turnpike the Bakewell–Chesterfield–Worksop road in 1739 (Hopkinson 1979: 18–19). By 1750 the Great North Road had been turnpiked south from Grantham, through Stamford to Wansford Bridge where it joined an earlier improvement (Wright 1982: 23).

The condition of these early turnpikes was variable. In 1739 the Great North Road to the north of Grantham was described as 'a narrow paved causeway for horses, with an unmade road on each side of it' (Wright 1982: 23). On the Market Harborough–Leicester road in the 1720s carts and men were hired to remove gravel from pits near the road, and spread it to form a track about 14 ft wide. Twelve labourers were allotted 2 miles of road each, and instructed to drain the road surface, and to prepare gravel and other material for the parish teams to lay when the time for statute labour came around (VCH Leics III 1955: 79, 81). In Derbyshire, the early projectors were said to have 'too closely imitated the defective system on which roads had been previously set out' (Farey 1811 III: 225). On the other hand, the growth of overland traffic in the seventeenth and eighteenth centuries suggests that conditions were improving. Long-distance carriers became well established during this period. Derby had services to the capital by the 1630s, and a Chesterfield man, John Armitage, described himself as 'London carrier' in his will of 1661. By 1715 road carrying services from London were reaching all parts of the region (Table 8), and in 1751 Nottingham was served by 22.5 overland carrier services each week, of which three were London connections and approximately one-third came from more than 30 miles away (Hey 1980: 211–13; Turnbull 1977: 24–29). According to Charles Deering

> That the Trade to and from this Town by Land-Carriage is considerably advanced for this last Century is manifest in this, that in the Year 1641, there were but two, and now there are nine Carriers in this Town, besides those who pass through it.
>
> (Deering 1751: 91)

Table 8 Principal destinations of road carrying services from London to the East Midlands, 1715

Derbyshire	Ashbourne, Derby, Tideswell
Leicestershire	Ashby de la Zouch, Hinckley, Loughborough, Lutterworth, Leicester, Market Harborough, Melton Mowbray
Lincolnshire	Gainsborough, Grantham, Lincoln, Louth
Nottinghamshire	Newark, Nottingham
Rutland	Erpingham, Oakham

(Source: Chartres 1977: 90–93)

Turnpikes were designed with both passengers and goods in mind. Nottingham, Worksop and Mansfield developed as turnpike junctions due to their importance in the local exchange of coal. In 1764 the coal owners were said to have 6,000 tons of coal waiting to be sent along the Belper–Nottingham road, but held up as a result of the state of the road. The majority of funding for routes west from Grantham and Lincolnshire came from Lincolnshire land-owners anxious to improve the exchange of coal and corn. However, it was the movement of livestock which chiefly benefited from road developments. By the later seventeenth century east midlands livestock farmers were already selling to Manchester, Sheffield and Birmingham (Henstock 1969: 33, 41–2), while an overland drove route passed through Mansfield, Newark, Stamford and Uppingham south towards London. Animals were sent from Leicestershire and Lincolnshire, and the trade was particularly important for the latter county with the collapse of wool prices (VCH Leics II 1954: 220; Perkins 1977a: 12–13). According to Daniel Defoe:

148

The vast consumption of wool in Norfolk and Suffolk is supplied chiefly out of Lincolnshire, a county famous for the large breed of sheep bred up for the supply of the London markets, as the western manufacturers are supplied from Leicestershire. Leicester, and Northampton and Warwickshire having an innumerable number of large sheep, which, as is said of Lincolnshire, are bred for the London markets, the wool consequently is of an exceeding long staple ... the rest of the Leicestershire wool-merchants, who do not bring their wool southward, carry it forward to the north, to Wakefield, Leeds and Halifax; here they mix it with, and use it among the northern wool.

(Defoe 1727, II, pt II: 55–9)

By 1740 families such as the Massingberds of Ormsby regularly sold their animals at Smithfield, and geese were driven from Lincolnshire to the capital (Beastall 1978: 7, 16–17).

Although it took time to improve the road system this was not necessarily vital for trade since so many goods moved by water. The river Trent was the central artery, even though its trading function was hampered by the presence of sixty-seven shallows and twelve fords between Wilden Ferry (Shardlow) and Gainsborough (Hopkinson 1959: 24). Vessels were still able to reach Nottingham and even Burton on Trent with difficulty, but Nottingham corporation consistently refused to countenance improvements west of the town, despite petitions in favour from Chester, Middlewich, Nantwich, Stafford, Lichfield, Tamworth, Uttoxeter, Birmingham, Coventry, Newark, Gainsborough and Derby, as well as the merchants, ironmongers and cheesemongers of London and Westminster. When improvement proposals were put forward Nottingham threatened to stop *all* traffic going beyond Trent Bridge, as, for example, in 1698. The initiative for this move came from William, Lord Paget, and in 1699 he obtained legislation to make the Trent navigable between Wilden Ferry and Burton. In addition, he received a monopoly of the wharves and warehouses between Trent Bridge and Burton, which was particularly useful to a man who was the leading landowner of the Burton district, and interested in the local collieries. Paget found the task of completing the navigation rather more difficult and expensive than he had expected, and by 1711 it was still not finished. Although when an attempt was made in 1714 to pass further legislation which would have helped Paget to improve the river, Nottingham corporation voted £50 to be spent opposing the scheme, by 1720 the upper Trent navigation was largely fulfilling the aims of its promoters (Wood 1950: 20–1; Owen 1968).

Efforts to improve linking waterways also ran into difficulties. By letters patent of 1634 Thomas Skipwith was empowered to make the river Soar navigable between Leicester and the Trent to facilitate the movement of coal (Thirsk and Cooper 1972: 349–51). Although he carried out work for several miles from the Trent, possibly as far as his house at Cotes, he was forced to

149

leave off in the end for lack of finance, and the improvement decayed. Improvements of the river Derwent between Derby and the Trent were persistently obstructed by Nottingham corporation, a policy which inevitably produced friction with Derby corporation. Numerous attempts were made between 1638 and 1719 to improve the river Derwent between Derby and the Trent. According to one contemporary commentator 'whoever stood for Parliament-man and gave hopes for effecting of this [the Derwent navigation] has commonly been chosen'. Lead merchants and ironmongers from London petitioned in favour of various bills which were introduced into Parliament, on the grounds that such 'ponderous commodities' as lead, iron and millstones were costly to transport overland. Newark favoured improvements, to permit the sale of grain in Derbyshire. Opposition came predominantly from vested interests in and around Nottingham. In 1696 the town corporation petitioned against any scheme to improve the Derwent on the grounds that it would reduce the trade of Nottingham, Leicester and Loughborough, ruin the Trent as a navigation, lower the rents of lands, and impoverish the land carriers. Three years later the corporation was reported to have put chains on Trent Bridge to prevent traffic moving to the west, and in 1717 £100 was voted towards opposing any further Derwent scheme. Opposition also came from freeholders, copyholders and farmers in villages near to the Trent, most of whom argued that the price of corn would be slashed, and tenants would not be able to pay their rents. Legislation was finally obtained in 1719, and the first vessels reached Derby in 1721 (Willan 1936: 36, 38, 40–5; Chambers 1957: 11; Heath 1982: 115).

Improvements took place on some of the Lincolnshire waterways. The commissioners of sewers managed to maintain the river Witham as a navigable waterway between Lincoln and Boston during the sixteenth century, although the crucial Foss Dyke was in a perilous condition. This neglect resulted from the decline of trade in Lincoln and Boston, but the corporation of Lincoln had no intention of accepting the closure of the Foss Dyke without a struggle, and in the 1520s scouring work was undertaken to clean up the waterway. However, this seems to have been only a temporary improvement, and by the middle of the century the Foss Dyke was apparently little used (Hodgett 1975: 81). Further efforts to put it into reasonable condition came in the seventeenth century. Legislation in 1671 enabled Lincoln corporation to improve the waterway at Torksey. When this proved less than wholly successful the corporation leased the waterway in 1740 to Richard Ellison on a 999-year term at £75 per annum. In return for the toll profits Ellison was required to maintain a depth of 3 ft 6 in. throughout the length of the navigation. Restoration of the Foss Dyke was mainly completed by 1744, at a cost of over £3,000, and the price of a chaldron of coal in Lincoln immediately fell from 21s. to 13s. By 1780 the Ellison family had made a fortune from its agreement with the corporation (Wright 1982: 21–2, 35). Less successful was Francis Mathew's plan in 1655 to link Great Yarmouth with York along the existing waterways, partly to facilitate the movement of Derbyshire and Nottinghamshire coal to Boston (Willan 1936: 9, 26). Finally, one other scheme which produced results was the Stamford canal of 1570, a 9½-mile navigation beside the river Welland from Stamford to Deeping St James. There it rejoined the river through Spalding along a navigation to the Wash, which was completed between 1664 and 1675. Coal, groceries and agricultural produce were among the goods carried.

The importance of the Trent becomes apparent when its trading function is considered. Until the Burton breweries began to use the river for the sale of beer to the Baltic, in the 1740s, trade was almost entirely regional or coastal rather than overseas. The river was vital for the development of mining in the region. Wollaton's proximity to the Trent was of considerable significance from the time coal mining started, and the Strelley family were inspired to begin working their pits in the 1540s by the prospect of selling coal in Leicestershire and Lincolnshire, in addition to Nottinghamshire. The Wollaton pits sent coal into Derbyshire, in addition to enjoying a flourishing trade along the Trent to Gainsborough, and Sir Francis Willoughby is reputed to have paid the men who brought stone from Ancaster to build Wollaton Hall with baskets of coal (Girouard 1983: 84). In the later sixteenth century the Willoughbys had warehouses and a staff of servants at Gainsborough, from whence their coal was distributed to neighbouring villages. By 1615 the Willoughbys were selling cheap coal as well as glass – made at Wollaton – in Southwell, Newark, Grantham, Lincoln, Boston, Torksey, East Retford and Gainsborough (Smith, R. S. 1964). Without good water communications the coal industry struggled. This was especially the case on the south Derbyshire–Leicestershire coalfield where production was confined within narrow limits by the difficulties of selling coal at a distance. Throughout the seventeenth century expansion of production was limited by the excessive distances between pits and consumers and the lack of population growth and industrial expansion within its confines. Measham colliery, for example, sold most of its coal in 1724 by road to customers within a 10-mile radius. The most distant customers were at Burton on Trent (13 miles), Hinckley (15 miles) and Shenton (18 miles) (Griffin 1969: 196; Owen 1984: 82).

From the beginning, Nottinghamshire coal was exchanged for grain (VCH Notts II 1910: 283–4); in 1655 16,000 tons of coal a year were passing along the Trent to Newark in return for corn and malt. A similar pattern was true of Derbyshire largely because the expansion of numbers working in the lead industry produced a local food crisis by the 1620s. According to one contemporary 'the hardcorn gotten therein will not serve above one half of the people', and as a result the county relied on Danzig rye brought along the Trent from Hull (Fisher 1961: 73; Chambers 1957: 38). By the 1690s coal was also sold in Northamptonshire in return for barley (Thirsk 1985, I: 134). The grain trade was an important subsidiary of the Derbyshire lead industry. Lead was predominantly moved overland to Bawtry and Worksop, and then along the

Plate 5.3 Nottingham. This prospect, by Thomas Sandby R.A. (1723–98), was first printed in Charles Deering's *History of Nottingham*, published in 1751. It shows the town from what is today the West Bridgford side of the river, and it contains a number of interesting features. In the background is Nottingham, with the castle on the left, stretching across to St Mary's on the right of the picture. In the centre are the meadow lands which were overbuilt in the nineteenth century, and the foreground shows the river Trent with the old, seven-arched, Trent Bridge. The barges hauling goods along the river are a reminder of the vital significance of the river for trading purposes.

Idle, with grain passing in the opposite direction. The route seems to have been established in medieval times although the sixth Earl of Shrewsbury (d. 1590) was the man who had done most to establish Bawtry as an outport for lead, iron and millstones from the Peak. George Sitwell of Renishaw used this route in the mid-seventeenth century for the sale of iron, despite the inadequacies of the Idle for navigational purposes (Riden 1985: xxi–xxii).

The river was also used for carrying raw materials and other goods that were required in the industrializing towns of the Midlands. In the sixteenth century London merchants had factors or agents at Gainsborough, and in 1604 Sir William Hickman – lord of the manor of Gainsborough – agreed with various citizens of London to establish shops and warehouses for them. Such was the volume of business in the town by 1636 that the annual three-day fair was lengthened to nine days, and a second fair of similar duration was permitted. A boatmaster contracted to the Wollaton pits claimed in 1606 that

he had taken coal to London and returned with goods for sale at Lenton Fair, near Nottingham. Groceries and luxury goods were among the largest items coming up river by the end of the seventeenth century, and the iron trade was particularly important. In 1719, for example, Leonard Fosbrooke of Wilden Ferry carried over 100 tons of Swedish iron up the Trent to Burton and from thence to Birmingham by land carriage. In 1751 Charles Deering stated that Nottingham was supplied by river with grocers' goods, oils, wines, hops, bar iron, block tin, pitch, tar, hemp, flax, deals, Norway oak, and other timber (Deering 1751: 91). However, the story was not always one of success. Sir Percival Willoughby, encouraged by London factors, attempted in 1695 to break the monopoly of the Newcastle colliers on the London coal trade, but failed.

Surviving Hull port books give an indication of the volume of trade passing through Gainsborough by the early eighteenth century. As early as 1693 some lead was going from Derby via the Trent to Hull and in 1704–5 lead was the largest single item. The cargo of the *Content* of Stockwith, bound for Yarmouth, indicates something of the range of goods carried: lead, mill-stones, ironmongers' wares, bellows, scythe stones, saws, iron bushes, English iron, English earthenware, canvas, linen, and woollen yarn. Agricultural produce was also carried, including 90 tons of cheese in the first six months of 1705. During the 1720s, according to Defoe, 4,000 tons of cheese went down river every year. Malt and grain also passed through Gainsborough, and after 1699 so did Burton ale. Deering wrote of the regular downriver Nottingham trade as consisting of coal, lead, timber, corn, wool, potters' wares and cheese from Staffordshire, Cheshire and Warwickshire (Owen 1968: 255–6; Wood 1950: 11; Beckwith 1967a). Cheese production in south and east Derbyshire also depended on the Trent since much of it was sent by river to London. Arable produce also crossed the region, with Lincolnshire corn being sold in north Derbyshire mining communities (Henstock 1969: 33), although the poor state of the river Witham between Lincoln and Boston ensured that little was sold to London before the second half of the eighteenth century (Lewis and Wright 1973: 9–10). Burton ale was sent downriver because it kept well (Owen 1978: 32–4, Ch. 4). Some hosiery goods were also sent by water to Gainsborough, in return for groceries, wine, oil, plaster, and flintstones for the Staffordshire potteries (Henstock 1969: 41). When Daniel Defoe passed through Nottingham and Hull in the early eighteenth century he summed up the importance of the Trent. At Nottingham he wrote of how:

> the Trent is navigable here for vessels or barges of great burthen, by which all their heavy and bulky goods are brought from the Humber, and even from Hull; such as iron, block-tin, salt, hops, grocery, dyers' wares, wine, oil, tar, hemp, flax etc. and the same vessels carry down lead, coal, wood, corn; as also cheese in great quantities, from Warwickshire and Staffordshire.

When passing through Hull he commented that its trade included

> all the lead trade of Derbyshire and Nottinghamshire from Bawtry wharf . . . the cheese brought down the Trent from Stafford, Warwick and Cheshire, and the corn from all the counties adjacent, are brought down and shipped off here.
>
> (Defoe 1971: 450, 454, 528)

Industry

During this period industry had more in common with small-scale manufacturing than with modern industrial practice. Village and town craftsmen were to be found throughout the region. Leather workers and shoemakers, carpenters and blacksmiths abounded in Lincolnshire. Inventories for more than 300 carpenters have survived for the period 1550–1700, of which nine out of every ten relate to villagers. Hemp and flax were widely grown in the fens, providing employment for women in the curing process as well as affording an occupation for spinners and weavers (Thirsk 1967: 40). They were also cultivated in

Nottinghamshire where, in 1617, 200 people were presented at quarter sessions for soaking flax and hemp in the Trent, a practice that had been outlawed in Henry VIII's reign (Copnall 1915: 61). Weavers were to be found in most Lincolnshire villages, as were masons and builders, while potters and basket makers resided in a handful of places, and even the occasional soap boiler (Barley and Barley 1959). The number of tradesmen's families varied between 8 and 20 per cent, and averaged 15 per cent of all the families in rural Lindsey. Of the 1,320 inventories that survive for the area over the period 1660–1800 twenty-two were for carpenters and joiners, twenty for weavers, fifteen for smiths, and thirteen each for butchers and innkeepers. In the small Derbyshire market town of Melbourne in 1695 fifty-four men were employed in twenty-nine different trades or crafts. Elsewhere in the county at the end of the seventeenth century a few farmer-weavers were still to be found pursuing a – declining – dual occupation (Thirsk 1985, I: 133, 143). Many people enjoyed the benefits of a by-employment. In winter farmers could transport coal, charcoal, malt, bricks, tiles, slates, timber and building stone, as a means of supplementing the living they derived from the land. Small-scale lime burning was widespread, while in the forest areas considerable work was available thinning, cutting, stacking and transporting timber.

Perhaps the most important of these traditional, rurally based local industries was leather working. Among new additions to the freedom of the city of Leicester in the sixteenth and seventeenth centuries leather workers made up about 19 per cent of the total, and they virtually monopolized the mayoralty. The link here, as in the Lincolnshire fens and the area around Newark, where leather working also flourished, was with cattle rearing. Indeed, the conversion of arable land to pasture in the vicinity of Leicester seems to have been a vital stimulus to the industry, with the result that local butchers seem during the sixteenth century to have been more interested in supplying the tanners with hides than the townspeople with meat (Clarkson 1958).

In the longer term, however, conditions were changing. The sixteenth-century concern with projects produced notable results in the East Midlands, including the knitting schools founded in Lincoln and Leicester by 1591 (Thirsk 1978: 19, 39, 66). Even rural Lincolnshire could not avoid the passage of time, though it retained a past heritage longer than the industrial parts of the region. By the 1840s village weavers were virtually gone, and tailors were becoming general outfitters and drapers; otherwise, the employment profile of rural Lindsey was little different in the 1840s from what it had been in the early eighteenth century (Holderness 1972b). Part of the reason was that Lincolnshire failed to develop any real manufacturing interests. Whereas in sixteenth-century Leicester it was still possible for leading tradesmen to be graziers or farmers, this was unlikely to be the case by the eighteenth century. By the time Celia Fiennes and Daniel Defoe passed this way there were already signs that industrial production was on the increase, and it was not the old wool industry on which they commented but framework knitting (Fiennes 1947: 73; Defoe 1971: 408, 454).

The wool industry which had been so important to the medieval East Midlands had lost much of its impetus, although wool was still a major product. Down to the sixteenth century the production of long-staple wool was negligible in England, but enclosures for sheep farming provided better grassland and the predominantly short and fine medieval wool of the region was slowly replaced by a longer and coarser staple. Short wools were still produced in Leicestershire and Lincolnshire in the early eighteenth century although in lesser quantities than in earlier times. However, by the end of the seventeenth century most of the wool in these counties was long wool, a transformation which had taken place since the mid-sixteenth century. The finest Lincolnshire wool was from the wolds and the poorest from the salt-marshes. During the seventeenth century the fleece of the Lincolnshire breed deteriorated, and it was not until the eighteenth century that attempts were made to rectify this situation. Derbyshire wool was mainly of the coarse, short-staple variety, although some finer wool was probably produced by the small forest sheep, as was the case in Nottinghamshire (Bowden 1962: 26, 31–2, 37).

For making better-quality kerseys and broadcloths West Riding manu-facturers used wool from the Midlands, either by itself or mixed with coarser wool from the north. East Anglia and the west of England took most of the finest and longest wool produced in Lincolnshire and elsewhere in the Mid-lands. As a result, West Riding manufacturers made journeys to the wool-grow-ing areas of Lincolnshire and Leicestershire to acquire their raw materials, and by the second quarter of the seventeenth century wool was regularly brought to the Doncaster market from Nottinghamshire, Derbyshire, Lincoln-shire and Leicestershire. Lincolnshire wool was important for the West Riding worsted industry which developed after 1660 (Bowden 1962: 69–71).

These developments could not hide a significant shift in the region's textile interests which was primarily associated with the framework knitting industry. Hand knitting was established in the East Midlands during the sixteenth century, at Nottingham by 1519, and at Leicester by 1597. It coin-cided with the growing fashion for knitted stockings rather than cloth hose, and it made use of local wools while also proving to be a useful supplementary form of employment (Thirsk 1973b). In the 1580s the Rev. William Lee of Calverton in Nottinghamshire invented the stocking frame, and although initially viewed with some scepticism this came into widespread use from the 1630s for the knitting of worsted stockings. William Iliffe introduced the frame at Hinckley before 1640, while Nottingham had two master stockingers as early as 1641 (Wells 1972: 48). By 1664 some 650 frames were to be found in the East Midlands, and during the second half of the seventeenth century the industry spread among the villages of the fertile claylands south of Leicester and of the Trent and Soar valleys as well as the poorer soils of Sherwood and

Charnwood forests (Chapman 1972: 7, 33, 35). While London remained the centre of the trade and the major location of silk knitting, the East Midlands became increasingly important for the knitting of worsted yarn, partly because it used the long wool from the midlands sheep. Once the trend was set in motion it could not be halted. By the end of the seventeenth century Nottingham had added silk to its worsted knitting, and in the eighteenth century it turned to cotton. Silk knitting also came to the Derby area by the early eighteenth century, in connection with Lombe's silk spinning operations (Thirsk 1973b).

Framework knitting began, and indeed continued, as a domestic industry until mechanization occurred from the 1840s. In the early eighteenth century the typical knitter was an artisan with little more property than his frame, his furniture, and the odd sheep, cow, or pig – a situation little different from that of a medieval village weaver. Thus Daniel Venn of Wigston Magna left three cows and a pig as well as four frames at his death in 1680 (Thirsk 1985, I: 127–8). Such men were still to be found in the countryside in the mid-nineteenth century, but by then the industry had become considerably more specialized. In Nottinghamshire it developed originally in the forest areas, and the villages continued to play a significant role even after the industry became town-based. At least thirty-one south Nottinghamshire villages had a framework-knitting-based economy (Rogers 1981).

Even in the first half of the eighteenth century the trend was towards locating the industry in the larger towns. By 1751 more than 1,200 of the 3,000 frames in Nottinghamshire were to be found in the county town, and at about the same time Leicester was said to have 1,000 frames. The result was migration into the towns since knitters worked directly for hosiers who provided their raw materials and bought their finished goods. As early as 1710–15 Nottingham had at least sixty-nine master framework knitters, Leicester fifty-eight, Hinckley fifty-six, and Wigston twenty-eight. Numerous villages also had up to half a dozen master framework knitters. Apprenticeship indentures for the years 1710–15 refer to masters living in fifteen different south Derbyshire locations near to the Nottinghamshire border, some of whom still had a considerable agricultural interest. But the movement into the larger settlements was irreversible. By 1739 Nottingham had fifty master stockingers. The hosiers found in the town the necessary mechanical skills they required for servicing, repairing and improving the stocking frame. Nottingham was known for its ironwork in the late seventeenth century, and by 1739 the town had fourteen framesmiths, twelve needle makers and eight frame setters-up (Thirsk 1985, I: 127, 133–4; Wells 1972: 48–9, 61–3).

The movement of the industry from London to the East Midlands requires some explanation. William Lee's invention failed to catch on in the Nottingham area, and knitting on the frame was established in London partly because the early manufacture was mainly for silk hose and luxury goods. The production of silk hose initially forged the link with the East Midlands.

Nottingham needed silk to pursue its interest in silk hose, and a link with London proved to be useful as a means of facilitating the sale of midlands produce. These conditions alone are not sufficient to explain the wholesale movement of the industry to the region in the first half of the eighteenth century, as a result of which by 1727 there were reputed to be 500 frames in Leicester, 400 in Nottingham, and 3,750 in the surrounding villages. At least another 800 moved from London between 1730 and 1750. Three reasons can be offered for this shift in location. First, the London base of the industry suffered from conflict between the hosiers and the Framework Knitters' Company. Since the Company's control of the knitters was limited for all practical purposes to the area around London, and entrepreneurs wished to move beyond its jurisdiction, the East Midlands was attractive because it had built up a nucleus of the industry during the seventeenth century. London continued to play a vital marketing role for the East Midlands, selling its hosiery to southern and central Europe, and by 1750, to America. To sustain the London connection hosiers often apprenticed a son to London to retain the contacts which enabled the region to feed the capital with cheaper and more standardized products.

Second, framework knitting was well suited to lowland Britain because in the seventeenth century it did not need coal and water power. Other lowland areas already had economic activities which preoccupied their capital and labour. Nottinghamshire, Derbyshire and Leicestershire did not have a strongly established woollen cloth industry, and the area's abundant low-cost labour was clearly an attraction. In addition the ready availability of capital is clear from the growth of the industry. Wealthy individuals saw it as an opportunity for small-scale (and small-risk) investment, by building knitters' cottages or by owning frames – which cost only £5–£10 and were not subject to obsolescence. Other sources of capital were maltsters – partly because inns often acted as distribution and collection points – and for the larger hosiers, Smith's Bank in Nottingham, which performed a valuable service lending money and providing a bill-discounting service (Chapman 1972).

By the early eighteenth century the silk industry had also migrated to the East Midlands. It had expanded in Spitalfields as the result of an influx of Huguenot refugees from France in the 1680s, and the attraction of the Derby area arose from the town's specialization in silk production and the availability of the river Derwent for providing water power. The first attempt to spin or 'throw' silk by power-driven machinery was made at Derby in 1702. This failed, but a larger factory was built by Thomas Lombe between 1718 and 1722. Driven by a Dutch waterwheel constructed by the water engineer George Sorocold, this was partially based on the plans of a successful similar venture in Italy. It provided yarn of a superior quality to any other manufactured in Britain, and as a result it helped to break the London monopoly of silk supply, and to hasten the migration of framework knitting to the East Midlands. The Derby mill produced silk almost continuously down to 1890, and the site of it

Plate 5.4 Derby, the Silk Mill. In the centre of this print is the silk mill built for Thomas Lombe in 1717–18, which superseded the smaller Dutch Silk Mill built for Thomas Cochett in 1702 (on the right). The print is undated, but the weir was built for the arm of the Derby canal which comes in on the left, so the picture is post-1796.

The mill wheel and the mill-wright work for the Cochett mill, and the mill work for the Lombe mill, were both by George Sorocold, one of the most important water works engineers of the eighteenth century. His best-known work involved the installation of public water supplies, on which he was active in various towns during the 1690s and 1700s.

The original mill has now gone, and on the site today only some stone foundation arches and the (altered) tower survive. The present mill was rebuilt after a fire in 1910, and today houses the Derby Industrial Museum.

Sorocold's earliest engineering work for which firm evidence survives was in connection with the bells and chimes of All Saints Church, Derby, and in the background of this print can be seen the fine perpendicular tower of the church (which has been Derby Cathedral since 1927) dating from the 1520s.

---

can still be seen today (Chambers 1957: 14–15; Wells 1972: 49–50; Cooper 1982: 37–46).

The region's extractive industries grew and flourished during this period. Derbyshire millstones enjoyed a national reputation; in the 1720s they were among the major exports mentioned by the petitioners in favour of an improved navigation of the river Don, and later the trade was helped by the turnpiking of roads in the north-east of the county (Hey 1980: 140–1). Celia Fiennes commented on the Ecton copper mines near Ashbourne:

> they dig them like a well but secure the side with wood and turf bound with the wood like laths or frames across and long wayes, to secure it.
>
> (Fiennes 1947: 109)

However, it was coal, iron and lead which were arguably the region's most important extractive industries during this period, and all enjoyed prosperity among the inevitable periods of difficulty.

Coal mining in the sixteenth century was most notably connected with the Willoughby's enterprise at Wollaton, but the steady growth of demand brought into production large mining ventures elsewhere, including north-east Derbyshire. At Wollaton, mining developed towards the end of the fifteenth century with the move to deeper pits. Profits already exceeded £200 in 1500, and rose to more than £500 soon afterwards, but this proved to be a peak which could not be sustained. Periodically they even fell below £200, though in odd years such as 1584 and 1586 they exceeded £1,000, and they are reputed to have been sufficient to finance at least one-third of the cost of Wollaton Hall (Girouard 1983: 83). Even so, the scale of operations at Wollaton in this period was probably exceeded only by some of the north-eastern collieries. By the 1540s the Strelley family were beginning to raise significant amounts of coal at their pits in Strelley and Bilborough. At the end of the century, however, production was declining.

During the sixteenth century most coal was sold to domestic consumers. Local purchasers included Lenton Priory (before the dissolution), and the families at Wollaton Hall and Belvoir Castle. Efforts were also made to use the fuel commercially. Glassworks were established at Wollaton in 1615, the aim being to employ local coal in producing the glass, which could then be sold on the London market. Calculations suggested that it would cost £1 2s. 7d. to sell a ton of Wollaton glass in London. By 1616 two furnaces had been erected, and the following year weekly profit amounted to £1 10s. 4d. The enterprise did not last long, however, coming to an end in 1617 (Smith, R. S. 1962).

When coal production faltered towards the end of the sixteenth century the Willoughbys came to an agreement with Huntington Beaumont. The Beaumonts, a Warwickshire family who moved into Coleorton, were the most important mining family on the south Derbyshire–Leicestershire coalfield in the sixteenth century, and early in the 1570s they entered into a partnership with the Willoughbys. Although the precise business relationship is obscure the agreement led to the expansion of mining around Coleorton. The agreement was signed by Nicholas Beaumont, and it was his son Huntington who was largely responsible for overseeing mining developments. In 1601 Huntington Beaumont leased the Wollaton pits from Sir Francis Willoughby. Two years later he took over a 21-year lease of the Strelley pits which the Byrons of Newstead had obtained in 1597. He was soon producing a steady output of coal, but he ran into marketing difficulties. In 1604 he undertook to deliver 7,000 loads of coal at Nottingham bridge each year, for onward transmission to London. However, this particular sale was never as profitable as he had hoped. By 1618 his capital ran out, and so did the patience of his backers. Beaumont was imprisoned in Nottingham for debt, and the merchants who had put up financial support entered into possession of Strelley and worked the colliery for the last seven years of the lease (Smith, R. S. 1957, 1962; Owen 1984: 31–5). Despite Beaumont's failure mining continued. The collieries at Cossall and Trowell were worked in the 1650s and 1660s. They declined after 1672, and mining was not resumed at Trowell until 1720. Trowell Field was the centre of the Willoughbys' mining operations from 1730 until the 1760s, and profits averaged around £1,000 a year in the early 1730s before falling to £263 between 1738 and 1748 (Aley 1985: 292–5).

Coal was also mined on a significant scale in Derbyshire during the seventeenth century, in the north-east of the county where George Sitwell of Renishaw was particularly active in the 1650s, and by the 1690s at Denby, Smalley and Heanor. Shallow pits were worked over large areas of the county's coalfield, including almost every parish of Scarsdale Hundred. Many small pits were sunk to expose the shallow coal seams. Coal was required for brick making, lime burning, pot making, malting, and for domestic heating. Production was still largely by small partnerships, with the miners tilling the fields when demand fell and when the pits needed to drain. The more enterprising colliers leased larger pits from landowners, or managed them on their behalf (Hardy 1955–6). The Turners of Alfreton were among the most important families involved with the seventeenth-century Derbyshire coal industry (Hopkinson 1957).

The expansion of mining on the south Derbyshire–Leicestershire coalfield was considerable from the 1570s, not merely under the Beaumonts' influence at Coleorton, but also around Staunton Harold and Lount, as well as at Measham, Swadlincote, Gresley and Newhall. The result was 'a quite remarkable expansion of the coalmining industry in Leicestershire and South Derbyshire in terms of both output and spatial extent' (Owen 1984: 50–1). However, the impetus was not maintained, and from the 1620s the industry was beset by considerable expansion problems in the absence of improved forms of transport. Production does not seem to have increased significantly in the course of the seventeenth century, largely because of distribution problems, and it probably remained at about one-tenth of total midlands output around 1700 (Owen 1984: 62–4, 79).

On both coalfields coal was easy to work because much of it outcropped near to the surface. From the Middle Ages onwards the usual practice was to sink a new shaft rather than to drive long headings into the coal, and, to ensure continuity of production once a shaft came into production, work began on sinking what was expected to be its successor. In these circumstances haulage and ventilation were not usually major hazards, but drainage was a recurrent problem, and led to the introduction of Newcomen engines at Coleorton in 1727 and at Wollaton in the 1730s (Heath 1982: 79; Pye 1972: 347; Edwards 1966a: 237). By contrast the earliest engines in Derbyshire were introduced at Staveley in the 1760s, and Alfreton by 1775 (Hopkinson 1957: 318). The importance of this new technology was not lost on John Wilkes who became the most influential mineowner on the coalfield, with pits at Swannington,

Coleorton, Newbold, Worthington, Measham, and Oakthorpe. Altogether, output may have topped 40,000 tons annually. However, from the coalfield as a whole output probably did not increase significantly even by the mid-eighteenth century, although changes took place in the distribution of pits. Many of the less important areas lost their mining concerns, and outcrops of low-grade coal seem to have been exhausted by the early eighteenth century. Limited markets were still restricting the size of the industry (Owen 1984: 118).

Iron was made in Derbyshire during the sixteenth century. Sir John Zouch erected the first blast furnace in the East Midlands at Codnor, Derbyshire, in 1582. Eight years later it was taken over by Sir Francis Willoughby of Wollaton, who considered, but never built, a second furnace. The enterprise did not contribute much towards relieving the family's financial problems, since it lacked sufficient capital to become a major local concern (Smith 1967). By this time iron was also being made elsewhere. The earls of Shrewsbury were instrumental in promoting the industry around Chesterfield. A blast furnace is first mentioned at Stretton in 1593, and a furnace and forge had been built at Barlow by 1605–6. Blast furnaces were also erected in the Rother valley early in the seventeenth century. At Wingerworth, for example, a furnace and forge were erected in about 1600 by the Hunloke family (Riden 1984: 149). Further south, on the Ashby coalfield, there is evidence of blast furnaces at Staunton Harold and Harshorne, and a forge at Whitwick, operating during the seventeenth century (Cranstone 1985).

The result of these early schemes was that by 1650 five blast furnaces were at work near Chesterfield, and in 1657 nineteen iron works were operational in eleven different parts of the Scarsdale Hundred of Derbyshire. One manufacturer, George Sitwell, was making considerable quantities of iron, much of which was shipped along the Idle and Trent for London and abroad. Bar iron was sent to Nottingham, Derby, Sheffield and Boston (Riden 1985). In 1672 more than a hundred smithies were recorded in the north Derbyshire parishes lying in the vicinity of Sheffield. Local gentlemen who owned furnaces and forges included William Bullock of Norton, a gentleman-manufacturer on a considerable scale in the 1660s with axes and hoes valued at £190 (Thirsk 1985, I: 134). However, in general terms the industry promised more than it could pay, and production declined towards the end of the seventeenth century, almost certainly as a result of competition from Swedish imports. By 1740 only four furnaces were in blast in Derbyshire, producing around 800 tons annually, and a decade later four bar iron forges were producing 650 tons. One furnace and four forges were at work in Nottinghamshire. By this time the industry had passed into the hands of a group of masters with Quaker connections, but little progress was made after 1690: 'in the local iron industry the seventeenth century lasted until 1750' (Edwards 1966a: 235–7; Chambers 1957: 5–9).

Lead production remained as uncertain in these centuries as during the later medieval period. From the 1460s until at least the 1530s production increased (Blanchard 1971: 129) but, following a further period of depression, expansion on a much larger scale commenced after 1560 with the introduction of the reverbatory furnace. As a result, the industry was able to expand as demand grew during the sixteenth century (Riden 1984: 163–7). It also became more labour intensive. In 1433 lead mining employed only 1,100 men, but by 1580 this had increased to 9,000, by 1597 to 10,000, and in 1649 to at least 12,000, and one estimate suggests that 20,000 men, women and children were partly dependent on the trade as an occupation in 1642. By the early years of the seventeenth century more than half the national output of lead came from Derbyshire (Daniel 1977; Dias 1981: 53). By 1635 production of smelted lead was averaging 2,000 tons yearly, and the justices stated that at least half the able-bodied males were engaged in lead mining. As lead came to be used by the Staffordshire potters for glazing, and as white lead was made for use in paint manufacturing the industry developed quickly. By the later seventeenth century the majority of veins which bore ore at an outcrop had already been discovered, and thereafter searching for veins went on mainly to determine the best locations for shaft sinking (Carr 1965: 215–16; Willies 1979: 120). However, the industry remained wedded to its traditional image as a labour-intensive and small-scale concern, as is clear from the hundreds of mines which continued in existence. It was a situation encouraged by the local lead laws which gave the individual rights to develop lead workings, with the result that the typical miner remained an independent figure, a man such as Bryan Melland of Middleton-by-Youlgreave, whose inventory in 1635 listed corn on the ground, haystacks, kine, bullocks, a heifer, and various mining tools (Thirsk 1985, I: 140).

In the course of the eighteenth century greater capital resources were required as the surface mines were worked out and lead had to be brought from greater depths. Daniel Defoe found a miner 'at work 60 fathoms deep, but there were five men of his party, who were, two of them, eleven fathoms, and the other three, fifteen fathoms deeper' (Defoe 1971: 467). Deeper mining required improved drainage, initially by hydraulic pumps, and later by one of two different methods, both of them expensive. The first was to dig a drainage level, known as a sough, which was designed to lower the water level in the mines to allow lead to be extracted. More than 300 soughs have been listed, of which at least three date from before 1650, sixteen from before 1700, and another sixty-five from the first half of the eighteenth century. Only about one-third can be dated with any accuracy, but it seems likely that the great majority were sunk during the first half of the eighteenth century. Most were small and ran for hundreds rather than thousands of yards, but there were some notable exceptions. Cornelius Vermuyden began the construction of a sough of more than 1,000 yards under Cromford Moor between 1632 and 1651. This was twice replaced, the second time by the Cromford Long Sough, which was deeper, half as long again, and technically more difficult (Willies

1979: 137). According to one estimate £30,000 was spent on Cromford sough between 1673 and the mid-eighteenth century, while £35,000 was spent on a 2-mile sough at Stoke between 1724 and 1734, and £30,000 at Yatestoop on a 2¼-mile sough between 1743 and 1764 (Willies 1986: 263).

Although waterwheels were used in Lathkilldale, the major alternative to the sough was the steam engine. The first Newcomen engine introduced into lead mines was erected at Yatestoop mine, Winster, in 1717. A second engine followed in 1721, and possibly a third by 1728. Much of the impetus came from the (Quaker) London Lead Company, which sent agents in the 1720s to try several ores at Winster and Wensley. As a result of these trials the Company established a smelt mill, and a cupola reverbatory furnace at Ashover in 1735. New furnaces were built east of the Derwent near the coal seams (Raistrick 1977: 82–4, 119–20; Edwards 1966a: 268; Ford and Rieuwerts 1983: 22–3). Engines were not cheap to run. Unlike coal mines, which utilized the poorer quality coal, and had relatively little real fuel costs, the lead mines had to acquire their coal at the market price. In the longer run this proved prohibitive and after the 1720s no further engines were set up until the 1740s, and wherever possible soughs or waterwheels were used for drainage. Where engines were employed the result was deeper mines. Shafts might well be 5 or 6 ft in width, and 300–1,000 ft deep. An engine naturally increased capitalization: according to one estimate, the amount of gear employed at a mine seldom exceeded £100 value, but this could rise to £1,000 when an engine was erected (Willies 1979: 117–18).

In 1750 it was still possible to look across the East Midlands and to see a landscape fundamentally unaltered since 1500. The towns, and particularly the county towns, were larger, but they did not yet dominate the countryside around them. Some of the numerous small market towns had shrunk, but others had become much more firmly established as centres of regional trade. On land only one or two roads had been substantially improved from the trackways and paths of medieval England, while on water the Foss Dyke was open but the river Trent had yet to benefit from a major improvement scheme. Behind this superficial glance, however, significant changes were taking place. The towns might not yet have grown, but they were becoming recognizable centres not merely of trade, but of the many service sectors of the economy. Framework knitting had visibly grown to become a new and thriving industry in the region, while the extractive industries were all more securely based and profitable. Above all, goods were being moved backwards and forwards across the region whatever the state of the roads and waterways. By 1750 the preconditions existed for the more fundamental changes which were to transform the region in a way no one could have foreseen.

Chapter 6

The East Midlands and the Nation

The restructuring of the economy which took place during these two and a half centuries was accompanied by significant developments in local society brought about by the religious changes of the 1530s, the disruptions of the Civil War period, and later the troubles associated with the Glorious Revolution in 1688 and the Jacobite uprising of 1745. New families and houses appeared in the countryside, and the foundations of modern local government were laid in country and town alike. But just how far were the localities aware of these major national movements? The question is easier to pose than to answer. In medieval England localities had distinctive characteristics of their own. Barons' revolts and political insurgence may have taken place within the region, but consciousness of the nation, and of national events, seems to have been limited. This was no longer true by the eighteenth century, but the process of enlightenment is not easy to trace. Historians have argued that although the sense of national identity was increasing through the sixteenth and seventeenth centuries, with it came an even more powerful sentiment, at least for the period 1640–60: a sense of county identity. The gentry, it is alleged, were more concerned with their own locality than with the wider world beyond, and this insularity helps to explain many of the loyalties particularly of the Civil War period; indeed, this permits an explanation of the Civil War in terms of a revolt over the way in which individual communities had been treated by Charles I's increasingly interventionist government. It is a view which has many supporters since most counties had at the very least few neutralist gentry at the outset of the war, men who believed in closing ranks behind county boundaries in an effort to protect the administrative integrity of their shires against disorder. To an extent this was a result of the significance given to the county by Tudor legal reforms, which turned it into an important agency of local government. It was for this reason that county towns grew in importance during the period. The separatist tendencies among the Derbyshire gentry were reflected in a desire to preserve the framework of local society in a peaceful fashion, but this played into the hands of cliques who were committed and determined to drag the county into the Civil War conflicts (Fletcher 1973: 42). This same isolationism may have been responsible for the failure of the East Midlands Association, since local loyalties divided the counties rather than uniting them (Beats 1978: 174).

The reality of these county islands is now questioned, particularly by those who believe that there was a much greater appreciation of national issues than has perhaps been recognized. If the gentry were first and foremost interested in their own locality, they also had ties to the wider community and to the nation. Moreover, the evidence is that in areas such as the East Midlands, which were hardly remote from London, national issues were of fundamental importance. Clive Holmes has recently argued that it is incorrect to see Lincolnshire as an insular county community in the seventeenth century, and much of what follows is an attempt to place the East Midlands firmly into the context of national events, particularly as it became more involved with them, from the sixteenth century onwards.

Reformation and Dissension

The impact of national events at the local level obviously varied, but some indication of growing awareness of the relationship between locality and nation can be gained from looking at events prior to the civil wars. Perhaps the major discontinuity in English history with a significant bearing on the localities during the sixteenth century was the Reformation. Henry VIII's break with the Pope may have produced the Lincolnshire rebellion, but this particular outbreak of popular hostility should not obscure the remarkable equanimity with which the East Midlands greeted the constitutional upheaval of the 1530s. As for the spread of Protestantism, this seems to have taken place only slowly in Lincolnshire (Bowker 1981). Although the phrasing of wills may not always be a reliable guide to religious loyalty there is evidence to suggest that Lincoln was less conservative than York in its approach to change. Catholic preambles fell from 98 per cent of wills before 1546 to 38 per cent during Edward VI's reign, before returning to 80 per cent under Mary, and falling again to less than 5 per cent during Elizabeth's reign. On the other hand many testators were looking for a compromise. In Edward VI's reign 29 per cent of wills were Protestant in form, but one-third were neutral, and even in Elizabeth's reign 45 per cent expressed no preference (Lucas 1985: 62). Among the clergy, in both Lincolnshire and Derbyshire the response to change was slow, but most bent with the winds of change of dogma and doctrine and remained in their posts (Johnson 1980: 61).

The longer-term impact of changes in religion was limited. Few objections seem to have been voiced as rood screens were removed, the altar was simplified, and communion was offered in both kinds. Loyalty checks on leading local figures were periodically carried out to ascertain their sympathies, and of 396 clergy in the archdeaconry of Lincoln tested in 1576 only one was 'vehemently suspected' of not conforming. Changes took place among the clergy, most obviously in terms of marriage; of 400 clergy in the archdeaconries of Lincoln and Stow in 1576 well over half were married, and the proportion rose by the end of the century. The church buildings themselves do not seem to have benefited. This was an undistinguished period for church building. Few churches were built in Lincolnshire between the medieval period and the later eighteenth century. None of the fifteen Nottinghamshire churches dating from between the Restoration and the early nineteenth century is architecturally important, while only All Saints Derby (1723–5) is particularly noticeable in Derbyshire (Pevsner and Williamson 1979: 26–30; Pevsner and Williamson 1978: 37–42). Perhaps the major change was that as preaching became more regular, seating became desirable if not essential.

Puritanism became a significant factor in religious life only towards the end of the sixteenth century. Twenty-three Lincolnshire clergy were suspended from their cures for refusing to subscribe to the three articles of 1577. Nottinghamshire had a number of nonconformist clergy by 1590, and Scrooby, at the point where the boundaries of Lincolnshire, Nottinghamshire and Yorkshire converge, was a particularly noted centre of separatism. In 1606 a group of Puritans in the village seceded from the Church. One of their leaders was the postmaster, William Brewster, and another of the separatists was William Bradford of Austerfield near Bawtry. Brewster had previously been in trouble for practising the puritan habit of repeating sermons in the parish church. The separatists divided into two groups based on Gainsborough and Scrooby, and individually they migrated to the Netherlands in 1608. Brewster and Bradford were among migrants to America on the *Mayflower* in 1620. Anabaptists were to be found in Lincoln and Gainsborough by the 1630s (Hodgett 1975: 168–88; Marchant 1960: 139–66; Watts 1978: 41–50; Holmes 1980: 41).

Religion produced divisions within the community, but it is not now regarded as a critical factor in the causes of the Civil War. More important was the distrust and resentment of central government which grew in intensity during the first forty years of the seventeenth century, and particularly in the localities from the years of Charles I's personal rule. Whatever the merits of Charles I's government in the 1630s one of the chief effects was to produce suspicion and distrust about its motives. Eleven out of forty-five Nottinghamshire gentry refused to contribute to the forced loan of 1625, and the efforts to secure a free gift produced only £70. The east midlands counties were as reluctant as elsewhere to meet Charles I's taxation demands, particularly in regard to ship money.

Provincial opposition to Charles I was revealed at its most open over the collection of ship money during the 1630s. At first this was regarded as a legitimate imposition on the community. Virtually the whole requirement was paid in 1635 and 1636, and even in 1637–38, the year of John Hampden's celebrated case questioning the legitimacy of the king's discretionary power, 90 per cent was collected. The real evidence of a collapse in cooperation comes from 1639, when only 19 per cent was paid (Rutland paid nothing at all), a state of affairs which reflected local fears of the consequences of ship money for the economic and social stability of each county community. Charles's demand for money and men for his war with the Scots produced a breakdown of peace and quiet in the localities, and the elections of 1640 were fiercely contested as a result. The deterioration in ship money payments from Lincolnshire was marked, with 20 per cent outstanding in 1637, 24 per cent in 1638 and 82 per cent in 1639 (Gordon 1911: 157–60). Although this partly reflected an inadequate collection procedure, the fact that the decline was more noticeable than in the neighbouring counties of Leicestershire and Nottinghamshire suggests deeper resentment at Charles's personal rule, and in parts of the county this must have been connected with fen drainage.

Most of the drainage schemes in Lincolnshire initiated during Charles I's reign took place in the teeth of opposition, particularly from the fenlanders who, deprived of their rights, resorted to force. The suppression of riotous activity was justified on the grounds of the benefit likely to accrue to the nation by converting unproductive and waterlogged acres to valuable arable. In fact, the king's major interest was the profit he stood to make from the land made over to him in the transactions. By contrast the fenlanders may have found themselves with drained land, but it was now reduced in acreage by between one-half and two-thirds. It is hardly surprising to find that what had been in the sixteenth century, and indeed remained down to 1625, a politically quiescent county, was a hotbed of political ferment by the end of the 1630s. Charles I managed, by his policy towards the fenlanders, to induce considerable opposition towards himself and the policies he represented (Kennedy 1983). The county's twelve MPs elected to the Long Parliament in 1640 included three sheriffs who had resisted paying ship money, and a number of men who had been prominent in resisting the forced loan in 1627. Almost all leaned to Presbyterianism or Independency in religious affiliation (Keeler 1954: 54–5). Nor perhaps is it surprising to find that by the following year tempers were frayed. In April 1641 enclosures were broken down at Pinchbeck, and elsewhere ditches were dammed, banks breached, sluices torn down, and cattle driven into the arable enclosures. The riots became more intense at harvest time as the participants sought to take away the newly reaped crops (Holmes 1980: 121–30, 138, 154–7). In 1639 commoners and fenmen made an attempt to dispossess adventurers in the Lindsey Level by cutting the banks and flooding the land, with consequent loss of crops on the ground (Darby 1983: 89–91). Under cover of the Civil War most of the drainage work was undone, and the fenlanders achieved on a grand scale what others were doing along more modest lines – they were paralysing local government in an attempt to undermine the authority of a monarch who had persistently upset local governors.

The Civil Wars

As a consequence of its geographical position the East Midlands could hardly avoid involvement in the conflicts of the 1640s, but this does not imply that local people were anxious to participate in civil war. As Charles I journeyed north early in 1642 a number of petitions were presented to him, including one from Rutland when he was *en route* between Stamford and Grantham, and others from Nottinghamshire and Lincolnshire when he reached York at the end of March. Both the latter counties urged him to return to good relations with his Parliament, and a copy of the Nottinghamshire petition was used as the basis for one prepared by the gentry of Derbyshire. This lack of commitment has been seen as a triumph for provincialism, as individual counties and towns sought to protect their integrity by holding a neutral position. It was an attitude adopted by the leaders of Derbyshire opinion in March 1642, and throughout the summer their major aim was to keep the county free from the growing conflict. The Lincolnshire gentry were equally unwilling to commit themselves to either side in the summer of 1642. They raised a troop of horse:

> only for the preservation of peace within themselves, in that they
> resolve (having thus discharged their duties both to the King and the
> two Houses of Parliament) not to embark further by sending any forces
> out of the county, to aid either side, but as much as in them lies, to
> endeavour accommodation.
> (Morrill 1976: 37)

Neutrality in this case, resulting from the turmoil in the fens during 1641 and 1642 – and the government's apparent powerlessness to do anything about it – produced a perceived threat to the social hierarchy and to property; in other words, neutralism in Lincolnshire was primarily a result of general uneasiness about the ability of central government to deal with local insurrection (Holmes 1980: 149–57). Throughout the war period the fenlanders fought to reclaim their lost rights, paying little attention to either of the main parties in the struggle (Lindley 1982).

The king's presence in Leicestershire served to draw the county into war at an early stage, but again the evidence is of reluctance among the gentry to become involved. Many of the county's Elizabethan families had declined by

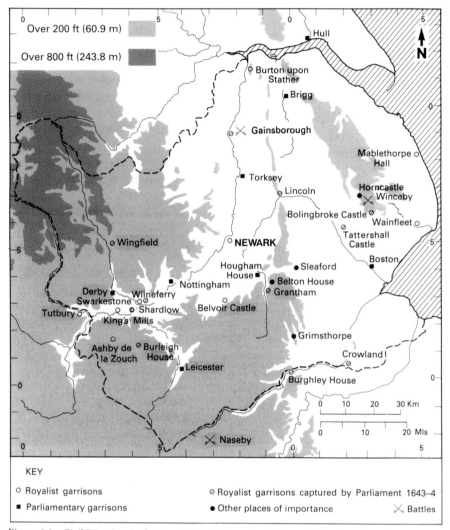

Figure 6.1 Civil War sites in the East Midlands (based on Palmer 1982: 48; and Holmes 1980: 162)

the end of the sixteenth century, and in a few cases were being ousted by new ones, including the Halfords and Hartopps. Of forty-three families holding some county office between 1621 and 1640 the civil war allegiance is known for only thirty-five, of whom twenty-three were royalist and twelve parliamentarian. However, few Leicestershire men proved ready to leave the county to follow the royal standard. On the whole, both the townsmen of Leicester and many of the gentry were prone to indecision at least until the two leading local families, the Hastings and Greys, declared for the king and parliament respectively. Even then the royalists were greatest in number but not in fervour, and the parliamentarian cause was upheld by a relatively small group of activists, mainly in the south and east of the county (Everitt 1969; Fleming 1981–2).

Leicestershire's dilemma was not untypical; across the country moderates sought to avoid war, but as they agonized extremists were seizing the initiative. Derbyshire's lord lieutenant, the Earl of Rutland, strove to preserve unity in the summer of 1642, but the county's neutralist stance was broken when Sir John Gell garrisoned Derby for the parliamentarians towards the end of the year. Thereafter Derby was parliamentarian for the duration of the conflict, while the county as a whole tended towards royalism, especially in the northern and western areas. Chesterfield changed hands no less than five times (Fletcher 1973; Brighton 1981).

Once hostilities commenced Nottinghamshire was at the centre of civil war action. Charles I was at Newark on 11 July 1642 and at Nottingham ten days later. The following month he returned to the town to raise his standard, despite efforts meantime to seize the county magazine for Parliament. Nottingham represented a strong point for the king, a bridge over the Trent which he could use to marshal his northern influence for a march on London. Unfortunately for the king only a handful of men from the East Midlands rallied to his standard. As a result the royal army moved towards Shrewsbury, and the first battle of the war – Edgehill – was fought outside the region. Sir John Digby, the Sheriff of Nottinghamshire, attempted to secure the county for the parliamentarian forces. He occupied Newark in December 1642, but was frustrated in his intention of taking the county town. It soon became clear that the county's peers and gentry were predominantly royalist, leaving a relatively slight list of gentlemen who supported the parliamentary cause (Wood 1948: 172–7).

Lincolnshire activists for both sides in the early months of the conflict were sufficiently aware of the neutralist sentiment to make no real attempt to insist on the wholesale involvement of the county in military preparations. In general terms the county lay within the sphere of parliamentary interest. Just over the border, however, was the great royalist fortress of Newark Castle, which played a major part in the struggles, while a string of royalist manor houses were fortified and garrisoned for the fight. The men of Newark not only resisted all attempts to take the town, including three major attacks between 1643 and 1646, they even rejected an order to surrender when instructed by the king himself. Newark's role was twofold. Its main task was to keep open the London road for the king's army by controlling the river Trent crossing (and, coincidentally, hindering the movement of parliamentary troops from East Anglia into the north); and second it flew the king's flag in the area, by encouraging the smaller royalist centres at Belvoir Castle in Leicestershire, Welbeck, Shelford and Wiverton in Nottinghamshire, and Belton House in Lincolnshire. Overall, participation in the war was determined by local issues and by the influence of the greater landowners. Even in the fens, where parliament's chief strength in the region lay, Crowland remained an effective outpost of royalism until April 1643.

In the initial stages of the war the royalists were on the offensive, and the major local interest was in the Earl of Newcastle's proposal to push southwards. For this purpose Newark was particularly important, and one of the major obstacles was the parliamentary stronghold of Nottingham. At the end of 1642 John Hutchinson and the parliamentary committee resolved to hold the town as a garrison, and early in 1643 measures were taken to fortify it with roadworks and earthwork ramparts. By June it was clear that the site was too large to defend, and the ardent parliamentarians withdrew to the castle, taking the town's fourteen cannon with them. Various attempts were made by the royalists to break this particular pocket of resistance. In September 1643 royalists raided the town and built a fort at Trent Bridge which it was intended to occupy for the king. However, the raiders were repulsed, and the fort was captured and occupied as part of the castle garrison. It remained a source of contention throughout the conflict. In April 1645, for example, an attack from Newark surprised the fort and it had to be further strengthened (Butler 1949).

The need to break the resistance in Newark was vital to the parliamentary forces. To organize themselves for the task they formed the East Midlands Association on 15 December 1642, one of the earliest examples of regional cooperation. The Association consisted of the forces of Derbyshire, Leicestershire, Nottinghamshire, Rutland, Northamptonshire, Buckinghamshire, Bedfordshire and Huntingdonshire. (An attempt to match this alliance on the royalist side came early in 1643, when, according to Sir Edward Nicholas, the counties of Leicestershire, Derbyshire, Nottinghamshire, Lincoln and Rutland petitioned Charles I – who agreed to the request – for a commission associating the counties) (HMC, Hastings MSS 1930, II: 89–90). From the beginning the parliamentary east midlands grouping was weakly conceived, lacking geographical and territorial feasibility. The armies of the Association never combined properly together and their performance on the battlefield was disastrous. The Association was eventually dismantled in October 1644 (Beats 1978). Before that time the first attempt to besiege Newark came in February 1643 under a joint army from Nottinghamshire, Derbyshire and Lincolnshire. Not merely did this fail, it resulted in a series of counter-attacks from Newark which strengthened the king's influence in Grantham and Sleaford. It was the threat of renewed royalist influence in the area which led Cromwell to march north from Crowland in April 1643, with his new model army, but following his withdrawal a new wave of raids occurred, this time towards Lincoln and Louth. The king's army, under the Earl of Newcastle, several times prepared to march south on London. After Gainsborough was taken, Lord Willoughby of Parham, Parliament's lord lieutenant in Lincolnshire, withdrew from Lincoln to Boston, and Cromwell from Stamford to Peterborough. But the royalists failed to push forward, partly for fear of leaving Hull in parliamentary hands, and as a result the parliamentary forces regrouped around King's Lynn from

Plate 6.1 Newark, Nottinghamshire, the Queen's Sconce. A large, bastion-trace fort, the Queen's Sconce is perhaps the most impressive extant work of the kind in this country. It lies at the Mill Gate end of the town, covering Markhall Bridge, where the Fosse Way crosses the river Devon, on a slightly elevated spur of gravel giving a wide view across flat meadows to the north and west. In total it covers a little over three acres.

The civil war fortifications at Newark reflect the town's position as a royalist stronghold. They are the most impressive in England, with several small redoubts, batteries, and sconces in the fields surrounding the town, the most impressive of which is the Queen's Sconce.

where the Earl of Manchester passed to Boston and advanced on Horncastle, capturing Bolingbroke Castle on the way. At Winceby on 11 October 1643 the royalists were defeated, Newcastle withdrew into Yorkshire, and Lincolnshire returned to parliamentary hands.

173

This did not prove to be the end of the story. Early in 1644 Newark was again besieged, this time by Sir John Meldrum with 2,000 horse and 5,000 foot, mainly drawn from Derbyshire, Leicestershire, Lincolnshire and Nottinghamshire. The town was relieved on 21 March by Prince Rupert, who scattered the parliamentarian horse before moving on to take Lincoln two days later. The fortifications of the county town, and those of Gainsborough, were dismantled, and the garrisons at Crowland and Sleaford were thrown out. Fears were expressed for Boston before it was relieved by troops from King's Lynn. Once more the parliamentarians marched on Lincolnshire, under the leadership of the Earl of Manchester and Oliver Cromwell. On 25 April they reached Stamford, and troops were sent to drive the royalists from Sleaford and Grimsthorpe. Lincoln was occupied in early May, after considerable resistance during which the cathedral was damaged. The army crossed the Trent at Gainsborough, leaving Newark on one side, and proceeded to defeat the royalist forces at Marston Moor. After this the thrust of the war passed into the west country, although the Newark stronghold continued to launch raids in the locality. Torksey House and Hougham House were attacked and small pockets of royalists at Stamford and Crowland were encouraged in their resistance.

Leicestershire, meantime, had been spared the worst excesses of the strife, and serious problems arose only towards the end of the conflict. In May 1645 the royalists besieged Leicester with 5,520 men, and on 30 May Prince Rupert began a bombardment. The walls were breached, and the royalists proceeded to sack the town. To counter this threat Fairfax lifted his siege at Oxford and marched north to relieve Leicester. After defeating the king in one of the decisive battles of the Civil War, at Naseby just over the border in Northamptonshire, he proceeded to Leicester, which surrendered on 18 June. The king's cause was now in terminal decline, but both Ashby and Belvoir castles continued the resistance. They were besieged in the autumn of 1645, and fell to the parliamentarians in the early months of 1646 (VCH Leics II 1954: 114–17). Meantime the parliamentarians were able to concentrate their attentions on Newark. In late November 1645 the Scottish army arrived before the town, and it was besieged for the next twenty-six weeks. Conditions became intolerable with an outbreak of plague in March 1646, and by early May the town was described as 'a miserable stinking infected town'. But when the king was arrested by the Scots at Southwell on 5 May resistance could no longer be sustained and surrender followed on 8 May 1646 (Royal Commission on Historical Monuments 1964).

The second civil war carried much less threat to the area but was none the less significant. Following the fall of Pontefract Castle at the beginning of June 1648 the king's adherents moved on through Doncaster and the Isle of Axholme, to take Lincoln on 30 June. Parliament sent Colonel Edward Rossiter to counter the royalists, who in turn moved on to Gainsborough and Newark. Rossiter finally caught them at Willoughby-on-the-Wolds in Nottinghamshire, and his overwhelming victory decisively crushed royalist hopes in the East Midlands (Wood 1937a: 146–55; Hensman 1923; Holmes 1980: 200–3).

Allegiances during the civil wars were by no means fixed, partly because local issues were often the main determinants of loyalty. The men of Axholme flooded the Isle to keep out the king's soldiers largely because they associated the hated drainage commissioners with the king, but they also resisted Parliament when they were ordered during Cromwell's rule to return the lands they had appropriated. For many people life seems generally to have gone on as normal. Only in the fens, and in the towns, did major changes take place as a result of the struggle. In all the fen areas the drainage schemes were abandoned and the commoners reoccupied the land. It was some years before these areas recovered from the setback (Rogers 1970). Among the towns, Grantham, Lincoln and Gainsborough all suffered. Gainsborough, twice besieged, was particularly badly affected. Outside the towns, however, the situation varied. While Wingfield Manor in Derbyshire suffered siege, counter-siege, bombardment, and considerable damage, Wollaton Hall, just a few miles from Nottingham, was insignificant in the fighting, although it was garrisoned by a company of parliamentary foot in September 1643 to prevent a similar move by the Newark royalists. In May 1644 it bought its protection from the royalist Earl of Newcastle, but it soon fell back into parliamentarian hands. Between 1643 and 1647 the Civil War cost the Wollaton estate £793, three-quarters of which went in payments to the parliamentarian, royalist and Scottish armies. Work on the estate seems, however, to have proceeded as normal (Kirkham 1971–73; Hodson 1962).

The Interregnum and Beyond

The impact of the Civil War was felt not merely in the military but in the personal manoeuvrings of the period, and for some families it was as much as they could do to survive at all. Royalists in financial trouble before the war had to endure not merely defeat on the battlefield but the sequestration of their estates. In a number of cases, particularly among leading supporters of the king, this proved ruinous, while others barely survived after years of considerable hardship. In Nottinghamshire Sir Gervase Clifton did not take up arms, but his leanings were clearly towards the king. As a result all his estates were sequestered, and in January 1647 the committee for compounding set his fine at £12,120. This was reduced to £7,625, and after half of the fine was paid and obligations were given to pay the remainder, the sequestration was ended (Seddon 1980: 37). Clifton was relatively lucky. Sir Gervase Scrope of Cockerington in Lincolnshire spent a good deal of time in a debtors' prison, and his son was found to be 'in worse condition'; while Sir Philip Tirwhitt found himself with 'scarce bedds left for himself and children . . . to lye on', in order to pay his composition fine of nearly £3,000 (Holmes 1980: 178, 220).

Charles II's restoration in 1660 was widely welcomed, particularly by the gentry who hoped and believed the challenge posed by the Interregnum governments to the social order would soon be at an end. There was no guarantee that this would be the case, but the speed with which the 'natural' rulers returned in force to the commission of the peace suggested a desire to put the past behind them. In Lincolnshire only about one-fifth of the justices who served in 1658 survived the Restoration. The rest were replaced by eminent royalists, the Fanes, Tirwhitts, Husseys, Monsons, Thorolds, Dallisons and Scropes, together with a number of men who although they fought against the king in the 1640s refused to participate in the radical developments beyond 1648 (Holmes 1980: 219). Perhaps in no area was the old order more successfully restored than the Church. A number of parish livings in Derbyshire were augmented during the Interregnum – although the gains were lost again in 1660 (Clark 1980) – but in general terms few people had much patience left with the experiments of the previous two decades. Some of course could not wait for change to come. On 17 August 1660 three men entered Kibworth Beauchamp parsonage and summarily evicted Parson Yaxley and his household. His wife, sent packing in her underclothes, rallied support from parliamentary veterans for an attack on the parsonage, which ended with Mrs Yaxley being shot and blinded by one of the evictors (Pruett 1978: 16–17). Yaxley had made many enemies – converting the font into a horse trough had not helped – and such precipitate action was not copied everywhere; indeed, it may well be that while Charles II did what he could to secure a compromise church settlement, he was outmanoeuvred by a combination of pressure from the provinces for a church on traditional lines, and from the Cavalier Parliament which forced on him a series of intolerant measures.

The re-establishment of conformity was brought about relatively quickly, not merely as a result of legislation but also through the enthusiasm of the local gentry. As early as September 1660 a campaign of persecution began, with one Nottinghamshire JP, Peniston Whalley openly expressing the view that JPs should bring the Puritans to book whatever the king might have declared. Possibly as a result, Nottinghamshire seems to have been one of the counties where puritan incumbents were most likely to find themselves prosecuted in quarter sessions. Thirty-eight puritan ministers were ejected from their livings in Nottinghamshire (Wood 1948: 202–3). Ejected nonconformists accounted for about one-fifth of Leicestershire's parish clergy, but many other parishes were also affected, either by the removal of conforming ministers where evicted loyalists were restored or by resignations from poor livings by incumbents anxious to corner better ones. As a result, between 1660 and 1662 about half of the county's parishes must have seen a change of minister (Pruett 1978: 23). Among Derbyshire's 135 clergy in 1660, forty-five were pre-Civil

War ordinands, but many of the Restoration clergy lacked full legal title to their livings. During the years 1660–62 Anglicanism was re-established in the county, along with the procedures and administrative practices of diocesan government. By 1662 a conservative settlement was acceptable, and the old church order seemed less of an evil than had once been believed (Clark 1983). Even so, turnover among the clergy was considerable.

Restoration of the old order also meant persecution of those who failed to conform. The local militia was given the task of watching the disaffected, to prevent their meetings and to put down any possible resistance to the restored monarchy. Fears of a nonconformist revolt led in 1663 and 1665 to considerable numbers of arrests in Nottinghamshire, and through the decade the militia was occasionally used against conventicles. However, such apparently draconian action was not necessarily as formidable as it might seem since the dissenters showed little evidence of disaffection, and the militia was too small and too slow to react to have been of any great use if an uprising had taken place (Seddon 1982). Even so Presbyterians unwilling to rejoin the Church were inevitably affected. Corporations were purged at Grantham, Lincoln, Boston and Stamford, while in Lincolnshire at large by 1680 the bulk of the Presbyterian families who had participated in the restoration were no longer represented on the commission (Holmes 1980: 220–4). But it was the Quakers who suffered most of all. The term itself was reputedly first used during the trial at Derby of George Fox in 1650 (Heath 1982: 148), and thereafter the region seems to have been something of a Friends' stronghold. There were between 500 and 1,000 Friends in late seventeenth-century Leicestershire, and they were strongest in the valley of the Soar and the Vale of Belvoir. At least 50 of them were imprisoned in 1661 and 1662, and others were periodically fined or imprisoned in the years down to 1689 (Evans 1952). In Lincolnshire the south Holland Quakers were subjected to intense pressure. Meetings were broken up by soldiers, and individuals were imprisoned: 78 Quakers were persecuted in 1665, 72 in 1670 and another 11 in 1671. The vigour of the attack on nonconformity was partly inspired by fears of a reaction against the Restoration, and when this was not forthcoming the intensity of persecution fell away. In many places nonconformists enjoyed toleration as a result of local neglect or the half-hearted execution of the laws. For most of the time the attitude was one of benign neglect. The gentry connived at dissenters because persecuting them no longer seemed essential to sustaining their social and political hegemony (Holmes 1980: 228–34). The level of tolerance reached a point where Castle Donington had a Quaker constable whose responsibilities included oversight of the town's Quakers.

As a result, nonconformity was far from extinguished. Nottinghamshire had thirty-seven conventicles in 1669 (fourteen Presbyterian, eleven Quaker, six Baptist and six Congregational) attended by around 2,000 worshippers. Most were small meetings held in private houses, except in the county town where the Presbyterians, Independents and Quakers had built a formidable

following. In 1669 Leicestershire had fifty-six conventicles, which made it moderately nonconformist rather than a dissenting stronghold. The thirty-one conventicles in the south of the county had an average attendance of fifty-eight, while the other twenty-five scattered about the rest of the county had an average attendance of thirty-two (Sanders 1934: 104; Evans 1949: 11). Bishop Compton's survey of 1676, which was designed to find the number of people and the number of dissenters across the country, reveals the extent of conformity despite considerable confusion in its compilation. These figures are for the total communicants of fourteen years and upwards (Table 9). From them it is clear that the region had only a small number of Catholics, fewer than 1 per cent in each of the counties except Derbyshire (1.2 per cent) (Wood 1948: 206; VCH Leics II 1954: 69). There seems to have been little cause for alarm.

Table 9 Conformists and non-conformists in the East Midlands, 1676

County	Conformists	Catholics	Dissenters	Total
Derbyshire	49,553	596	928	51,077
Leicestershire	39,191	148	1,166	40,505
Lincolnshire	84,907	580	2,595	88,082
Nottinghamshire	35,325	169	1,569	37,063
Rutland	9,718	61	110	9,889

(Sources: Whiteman 1986; Cox 1885; Guildford 1924)

Beyond 1660 life returned to some sort of normality, and beneficial developments in the region included a resumption of fen drainage. Earlier drainage works had been ruined by war-time riots, but it was now Parliament to whom would-be projectors needed to turn for legal authority, and in 1661 Sir John Monson secured legislation for his Ancholme drainage. The Deeping Fen adventurers also obtained legislation, in 1666 and 1670. The drainers now had to rely on the established courts to uphold their rights. The new procedures gave the drainers the proper legal rights which Charles I had never been able to offer them, and which the fenmen respected (Holmes 1980: 226–8; Fletcher and Stevenson 1985). On the other hand there seems little doubt that fen drainage remained in an unsatisfactory state until well into the eighteenth century (Darby 1983: 88–91).

The next test for the local community came in 1688, and little support was forthcoming in the East Midlands for James II when William of Orange arrived in the west country during the autumn of that year. James II's policies

Plate 6.2 Belper, Derbyshire, Field Row Chapel. A congregation met in Belper from the 1670s, and by the later eighteenth century it had become Unitarian in persuasion. In the 1780s the entrepreneur Jedediah Strutt joined the group, and it was he who erected the chapel in 1788. The chapel is of squared stone with hipped slate roofs. It was originally rectangular with the entrance at the south end, but the east and west wings were added in c. 1800, and box pews put into them. The chapel has a south gallery. Strutt's gift is commemorated in a monument of 1797.

had been widely resented. In Leicestershire the Whig Earl of Rutland had been removed from the lord lieutenancy in favour of the Earl of Huntingdon, an uncompromising Tory. When lords lieutenants were instructed to question their deputies and justices on the possibility of repealing the Test Act and penal legislation the dissaffection became apparent. Huntingdon posed the king's 'three questions' in February 1688, and although five of his hand-picked deputies agreed to them, only one justice followed suit. Several families, including the Abneys, Verneys, Noels and Packs, discreetly absented themselves, while four or five others simply refused to answer (VCH Leics II 1954: 120). A meeting at Sleaford in November 1687, when the questions were put to the Lincolnshire elite, revealed the extent of disaffection since most of the gentry refused to associate themselves with James's policy; and while the lord lieutenant, the Earl of Lindsey, obeyed orders from the king he did so with obvious reluctance (Holmes 1980: 250, 252). Catholics and dissenters alike were mistrustful of James. Only William Thorold, of the ten Catholics added to the Kesteven commission of the peace by James in 1685, actually attended sessions. When it came to the crunch in 1688 neither nonconformists nor Catholics turned out for the king, while the bulk of the Lincolnshire Tory gentry refused to resist, but also failed to raise a finger in support of James II.

When the revolution came, William Cavendish, Earl of Devonshire, was one of the northern leaders. This was a particularly significant role given the expectation that William of Orange would land somewhere north of the Trent and march south. Devonshire's territorial overlordship in Derbyshire gave him considerable influence and on 21 November 1688 he entered Derby with perhaps 500 men. The county had a higher than average number of Catholics (Table 9), and it is possible that his reception was less than overwhelming. In any case, he moved on the following day to Nottingham where support was stronger. Among the families joining him there were the Howes of Langar, who raised a regiment of horse, and probably also the Earl of Stamford and John Coke of Melbourne. On 24 November Devonshire was among those who addressed a meeting at the Malt Cross in Nottingham to explain the rising, and a few days later any lingering doubts on the part of the local gentry were dispelled when Princess Anne fled to Leicester, and then Nottingham (VCH Leics II 1954: 120). Devonshire was able to call out the Derbyshire militia and most of the county responded. When, on 8 or 9 December, Princess Anne set out for Oxford, she was accompanied by most of the principal local gentry. Devonshire received a dukedom for his role in the revolution. In Lincolnshire there were rumours of resistance towards the end of 1688, and the Bertie family prepared to defend Grimsthorpe from a body of 1,500 cavalry which was reputedly in Northampton putting everyone to the sword. But when the gentry met at Sleaford in mid-December they sent an address to William assuring him of their support (Wood 1940; Hosford 1976; Holmes 1980: 251–3).

Beyond 1688 it became apparent that the destructive forces of religious dissent had been greatly exaggerated. The seemingly staggering number of licences taken out for meeting-houses under Article 19 of the 1689 Toleration Act was not, as some contemporaries claimed, an indication that a new wave of sectaries was spreading across the land, but a response by already existing congregations wishing to move premises or to open new ones. In both Nottinghamshire and Derbyshire Presbyterians numbered little more than 4 and possibly 5 per cent of the population, and even these figures may have reflected the influence of William Bagshawe's preaching in Derbyshire, and the importance of Nottingham's High Pavement Presbyterian chapel where 1,400 'hearers' met weekly. Leicestershire had 2,750 Presbyterians, 1,170 Independents and 935 Baptists. Overall, Independents represented about 2 per cent of the east midlands, and Baptists slightly below 1 per cent. The latter were strong in Lincolnshire where General Baptists had been established since the 1620s. Dissent flourished on the Isle of Axholme and in the fens, reflecting the political and religious radicalism stirred up by fen drainage projects (Watts 1978: 278, 283; Rogers and Watts 1978).

From these returns two further conclusions can be drawn. First, dissenters tended to congregate in a few centres, usually towns. This was clear as early as the 1670s when the three Nottingham parishes contained 389 dissenters, or 11.7 per cent, compared with an average for the county of only 4.2 per cent. By contrast, the county's second largest town, Newark, recorded none at all. Other relatively high concentrations were in villages, including Calverton 52 (29%), Cotgrave 54 (20%), Flintham 40 (19%), North Collingham 60 (17%), Everton 29 (15%), Willoughby 24 (15%), and Kneesall 45 (14%) (Guilford 1924). In Leicestershire by the early eighteenth century 11.9 per cent of dissenters but only 6.8 per cent of the county population lived in the county town, while in Lincolnshire 19.4 per cent of dissenters lived in Lincoln, Boston, Gainsborough and Spalding, which contained just 7.9 per cent of the county's population. In Nottingham something like 2,000 out of a population of 8,000 were dissenters (Watts 1978: 286, 449). Second, dissent flourished among textile workers. Around 1720 in Nottingham a quarter of the fathers whose children were baptized at High Pavement chapel were stockingers. The chapel was in St Mary's parish where, by the time of Archbishop Herring's Visitation in 1743, roughly 10 per cent of the parishioners were dissenters. This compares with two-thirds of the parishioners of the town's other two parishes. These figures also seem to represent a high point for dissent. By 1743 Presbyterianism had collapsed in rural Nottinghamshire, and survival in the county town was largely due to the continuing role of High Pavement chapel. Elsewhere the pattern was similar. Derbyshire experienced a considerable decline in dissent, especially during the period 1689–1772, and particularly in the Trent valley area (Austin 1973).

A more serious threat to local peace was posed in 1745 when the rebel Jacobite army reached Derby before turning back from a final assault on London. The town was occupied for three days in December that year by the rebel forces of the Young Pretender. This was no accident; indeed, the significance of Derbyshire was not lost on the Pretender. The county undoubtedly had an undercurrent of Catholic recusancy, and Derby itself was a town with a strong Jacobite element. The coming of the Pretender was well advertised, giving the local gentry an opportunity to take precautionary action, but the different attitudes in the county towns suggest the extent of Jacobite sympathy varied. In Derby a meeting was called at *The George* on 3 October, at the expense of the lord lieutenant, the Duke of Devonshire. The Tories reputedly favoured calling out the local militia, but this was opposed by the Whigs who suspected the loyalty of its members. Instead the Whig view, which prevailed, was that a 600-man special force should be raised, which would be organized in two regiments under Lord Hartington and Sir Nathanial Curzon. Such a move suggested that although the county's upper and middle-class inhabitants were keen to resist Bonny Prince Charlie, they could not be sure of the sentiments of the lower classes. The Duke of Newcastle, lord lieutenant of Nottinghamshire, and a leading government minister, looked on Nottingham as a key town in the defence of the kingdom; indeed, the original rendezvous point for all regular forces assembling to defend the Hanoverian dynasty was Nottingham.

Nottingham was not in particularly good shape to defend itself, partly because Chapel Bar, the last surviving relic of medieval fortifications, had been pulled down in 1743. In mid-September 1745 Nottingham's inhabitants were ordered to collect their arms to be viewed by the magistrates. Since it was obvious that most of these were not fit for use, Newcastle was asked to order sufficient arms for 1,000 infantry and to dispatch them with all haste to the town. Early in October meetings were held to attract subscribers to volunteer regiments, and the Duke of Kingston, a deputy lieutenant, was given powers to raise the troops. Money came from every level of county society including Lord Middleton (£400) and William Levinz (£100) (Wood 1945: 75–6). Even so, the reluctance of Nottingham to pay for its own defence soon became apparent.

By the time the rebel forces reached Ashbourne on 3 December 1745 it

---

Plate 6.3   Ashbourne, Derbyshire. A print taken from the anonymous *History and Topography of Ashbourn* (Ashbourne, 1839). The print shows the main London–Manchester road running through the town, the Elizabethan grammar school on the left, the late-seventeenth-century mansion house of Dr John Taylor on the right, and Pickford's waggon passing the grammar school.

Ashbourne was rebuilt in brick during the eighteenth century, at a time when it enjoyed some prestige as a fashionable social centre. It was regarded as an adjunct to the Lichfield intellectual circle associated with Dr Erasmus Darwin and Dr Samuel Johnson. The mansion house was enlarged and refurbished in late-eighteenth-century style by Dr Taylor, whose visitors included his friend Dr Johnson.

Ashbourne's prosperity is well demonstrated in this print. Several of the houses on the left-hand side of the street were the homes of well-to-do maltsters. The town reflected a concentration of wealth which produced substantial town houses, and was similar in many ways to larger centres such as Newark, Chesterfield and Ashby-de-la-Zouch.

was clear that local resistance would not be sufficient to repel them. The Duke of Devonshire's volunteer regiment, the 'Derbyshire blues', panicked, and he led them to Nottingham to try to save face. Even here they were not secure, and when the Pretender reached Derby on 4 December, Devonshire moved on to Mansfield and later to East Retford. As a result, Derby was occupied by the Pretender and his army, some 6,000 troops were billeted in the town, and both money and recruits raised. The troops appear to have behaved in a civilized manner in the town, and the decision to retreat ensured that Nottingham escaped depredations altogether. Whether its hastily called volunteers would have given any better account of themselves than those of Derbyshire is uncertain, but preparations had at least been made in the town for the arrival of the Highlanders. Shops were shut, and people packed their goods and plate, especially when it was rumoured that on 5 December the rebels would march through Nottingham to Loughborough. Newcastle was even told the following day that the Highlanders had taken the town (Eardley-Simpson 1933; McLynn 1979; Wood 1945).

Nottingham's fears were not matched in Leicester, where the rebels might well have been welcomed. The corporation did little more than send out messengers to 'wait and send accounts of the motions of the rebels'. No troops were raised, and only the Protestant dissenters showed much inclination to resist. Many citizens prepared meat and drink for the rebels and prayed for their success, and it was rumoured that the corporation secretly put together a welcoming address (VCH Leics IV 1958: 126). All this reflected the long-standing Jacobite sympathies of the town, partly through its links with the Earl of Huntingdon, whose influence in this direction outweighed the Whiggish views of Stamford and Rutland. In addition, the high Toryism of the corporation helped to make religiously inspired Jacobitism a real force locally (McLynn 1983). In the event, however, the Young Pretender turned back at Derby, and posed no further threat to the region. The Duke of Kingston's regiment was involved in hounding the rebels back towards Scotland.

In the two and a half centuries after 1500 the isolation of the old medieval society was finally broken down, to be replaced by not only a more integrated region but also a more socially and economically advanced one. In 1500 the majority of people lived in isolated communities, paying service to a manorial court, and exchanging their goods in a local – but small – market. Industry was relatively unimportant, and only a few towns could boast a really significant role in the community. By 1750 such a picture would be inaccurate if not misleading. The money economy affected every aspect of daily life, law and order had passed into the hands of the county and the parish, towns and industry had developed, and trade had grown. Most individuals were probably better off in 1750 than their counterparts in 1500. Ashbourne, Melton Mowbray, Louth and Newark are among the local towns which all contain examples of fine eighteenth-century town houses. The evidence of house sizes and furnishings also suggests greater prosperity. Perhaps above all the insularity of the community had been broken down. Changes in farming practice had helped to increase productivity and to make specialization possible. In turn, this was possible because communications had improved. Tiny communities clustering around a small market town were a thing of the past. Many of the early medieval markets disappeared, as a smaller number of more active centres took their place. A hinterland of 50–100 miles made for greater sophistication in marketing, and it also emphasized the importance of the town. County towns grew in size and esteem as local government and service functions came to be located in them, while other towns developed for all sorts of reasons, including trade and passengers along the Great North Road, and manufacturing concerns. Trade itself was made possible by limited improvements to the road network, and by the exploitation of water transport resources. Without such developments the local coal and iron industries could never have made the progress they did. Structurally, the decline of the medieval cloth industry did not mean the end of demand for east midlands wool, but the textile manufacturing replacement for cloth came in the form of framework knitting and related concerns. By 1750 the importance of Nottingham, Leicester and Derby, the growth of framework knitting, coal, iron and lead mining, and the focus of the transport improvements were all pointing distinctively towards a shift of interests in the region away from the now decaying Lincolnshire towards the new industrial area stretching roughly from Mansfield and Chesterfield through Derby and Nottingham south to Hinckley and Leicester. It was in this area after 1750 that the greatest changes were to occur. Finally, the isolation of the East Midlands could no longer be maintained. Events during the civil wars, and reaction of the fenlanders to drainage schemes, revealed an awareness of the national scene which could not be reversed. Local government, far from becoming an autonomous autocracy beyond 1688, as is sometimes maintained, remained subject to central government discipline. The sensitivity of Westminster to the provinces was clear down to 1715 in the manipulation of positions on the commission of the peace, and although intervention was less marked thereafter, central oversight remained during the eighteenth century. By 1750 the region was both more functionally coherent in terms of its economic and trading concerns and also more aware of its place in national society. This was the base upon which the modern East Midlands was constructed during what was to be in many ways the heyday of the region.

Part three

The East Midlands in the Industrial Revolution 1750–1900

Chapter 7

The Growth of a Regional Economy

The changes in the structure of the East Midlands between 1500 and the middle of the eighteenth century were significant in themselves, but as nothing compared with the century and a half which followed. In the latter, the classic industrial period, a rapidly growing population came increasingly to be centred in the industrial heartland of the region between Mansfield and Hinckley. Textile production, coal and iron output and, during the nineteenth century, engineering, helped to place the region on a firm industrial footing, while in the countryside agricultural output increased substantially. Intra- and inter-regional trade flourished as road, water, and later rail communications made possible the movement of people and goods on a scale never previously envisaged. Indeed, change was so fast in this period that the river Trent, long the central communications artery, reached its peak of importance early in the nineteenth century only to go into almost permanent decline when the railway superseded waterborne transport. The canal age, 1760–c. 1830, produced regular trade patterns because most shipments travelled relatively short distances, and the pressure for canal building arose from the recognition that local trade would benefit. This was nowhere better demonstrated than in the movement of coal and iron eastwards from Nottinghamshire, Derbyshire and Leicestershire in return for agricultural produce. In this period the functional coherence of the region was at its most clear-cut, but it was to be merely an interlude before the railway altered the pattern once again.

Above all, these years were notable for urban growth on a scale which turned the larger towns into foci of attention bonding together the villages and townships around them. It was not merely the rise in the urban population which was significant, but the increasingly important role of towns within the community. Their marketing function remained, at least in the large centres of population, but towns now come to offer a host of services to the community which gave them a dominant position over their hinterlands. It was in towns that services tended to centre, that workhouses were often built, that hospitals were opened, and from which new provincial newspapers emanated. Migration patterns into the industrial areas served towards the same ends. Growth also brought social problems on a scale unmatched in the countryside. Municipal reform in the 1830s eased the task of tackling these difficulties in the corporate boroughs, at least by contrast with the rural areas and the smaller towns where the structure of local government remained unchanged until towards the close of the nineteenth century.

These developments helped to foster an awareness of the region. In the early modern period men had been predominantly concerned with a geographically limited area known as their 'country', but through time a growing coherence and unity of character among the different regions came to be generally recognized. By the early nineteenth century regions were identified with particular issues, and economic differences lay at the root of this pattern of fragmentation. A uniformity of character developed within them based on a provincial city, and as regional centres increased in significance, so also did culture. Interest in and use of dialect seems to have become more intense and self-conscious towards the end of the eighteenth and in the nineteenth centuries. Pulling against these regional forces were national trends. As has been shown, no locality was untouched by the Reformation and subsequent religious changes because of their impact on forms of worship; by the seventeenth century the civil wars revealed that if a man's first loyalty still lay with his 'country', national events could no longer be held to take place without reference to the localities. Central government oversight of local government was just one way in which the region was made more aware of its relationship to the nation.

This trend towards integration between region and nation could not be reversed. The spread of information through the medium of the provincial newspaper was making London news accessible to large numbers of people, and central authority began to be required for all levels of local administration. Whereas seventeenth-century enclosure had usually been by agreement, sometimes ratified in the courts, from the 1750s almost all enclosure took place as a result of parliamentary legislation. Similarly turnpike trusts, canal and later railway companies, all required statutory backing. In the course of the 1830s the reformed poor law gave greater control to a central board of commissioners, while the individual borough charters were superseded by uniform constitutions. Thereafter neither countryside nor town – although the former came nearer than the latter – could escape the meddling of central government in its efforts to preserve law and order and to produce healthier towns. The mass of social legislation passed by mid-Victorian Parliaments rendered the localities increasingly dependent on Westminster for their powers.

The conflicting forces of regional distinctiveness and national integration were tilted sharply in the latter direction during the 1840s by the railway. Samuel Smiles was not alone in recognizing that 'the locomotive . . . virtually reduced England to a sixth of its size'. Goods and men could now move freely. The restrictions imposed on the routes of canals by terrain were conquered by the railway. London was able to exert an influence over the regions which it had previously lost to the canal-based regional capitals in the late eighteenth century. The railways set in motion powerful forces in favour of national integration, even if the mid-nineteenth-century decades during which they were built were precisely the period when regional cultural cohesion reached its zenith. It may be no coincidence that with the coming of the railway national organizations, including trade unions, at least became possible, while mass political campaigns such as Chartism and the agitation against repeal of the corn laws were countrywide movements. If it was between the mid-eighteenth and the mid-nineteenth centuries that the region could be most clearly identified as having functional coherence – before the railway again altered the balance of relations between London and the provinces – after 1850 the transport restraints which made short-distance migration and short-range trade attractive fell away. Although the Midland Railway, based as it was on Derby, gave some coherence to the East Midlands in the mid-nineteenth century, by 1900 the restrictions which were so important in maintaining regional intra-dependence had largely disappeared. The effect of the various changes chronicled below was to produce a sense of regional identity only for it to fragment again before the present century (Langton 1984).

Population

Perhaps the most striking feature of the period 1750–1900 was the growth and movement of population within the region. In 1750 the total population of the East Midlands was probably just short of half a million. By the time of the first census in 1801 it had grown to 657,000; half a century later it had reached 1,227,000 – a rise of 87 per cent – and by 1901 a further increase of 67 per cent took the overall figure to two million (see appendix). Behind these crude figures lay a significant structural shift. While Derbyshire and Nottinghamshire increased their share of the total, Lincolnshire's proportion declined sharply. Although Leicestershire's proportion remained much the same, the county experienced significant internal movement, particularly after about 1850 as the eastern part of the county steadily declined and the balance of population came to be concentrated in the industrial towns of the western part of the county (Table 10).

The decennial censuses are of some help in providing a picture of the pattern of population growth in the region. For the first three decades or so of the century large parts of Derbyshire, Leicestershire and Nottinghamshire approached and even exceeded national growth rates. The slowest increases were in the agricultural lowland areas of the eastern parts of Nottinghamshire and Leicestershire, and in Lincolnshire, where alternative employment oppor-

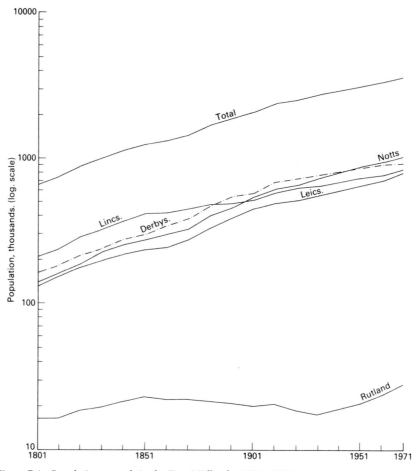

Figure 7.1 Population growth in the East Midlands, 1801–1971

tunities were limited. The fastest expansion took place in the county towns, the textile villages and towns around Derby, Nottingham and Leicester, the coal and iron working areas of the Erewash valley, and the south Derbyshire-Leicestershire coalfield. Gradually, however, the overall rate of increase fell behind the national average, partly as a result of substantial outmigration from rural Leicestershire and Lincolnshire. Between 1841 and 1861 only Derbyshire, with its expanding coalfield, matched the national rate of growth, while the others were increasingly subject to outmigration. Although Lincolnshire grew from 209,000 to 499,000 during the nineteenth century, by the 1820s local people were beginning to look for work outside the county. Between 1851 and 1861 93 per cent of the natural increase of Lincoln migrated beyond the county borders, although this figure fell to 59 per cent as employment

Table 10 Population and physical size of the East Midlands counties

County	% of East Midlands acreage	% of East Midlands population, 1750	% of East Midlands population, 1900
Derbyshire	19	23	29
Leicestershire	15	21	21
Lincolnshire	48	35	24
Nottinghamshire	15	19	25
Rutland	3	3	1

(Sources: Deane and Cole 1969: 103; 1901 Census)

opportunities increased during the following decade (Hill 1974: 126). In the opposite direction a number of Irish labourers settled in several of the towns, almost certainly after participating in the annual migration in search of harvest work (Barber 1982). The migratory trickle became a flood during the flight from the land in the agricultural depression of the final two decades of the century. By 1900 a new population structure had appeared in the East Midlands, with the largest concentration in the major towns of the western part of the region, notably Nottingham, Leicester and Derby, together with their satellites. It was the culmination of a trend which had begun in the medieval period and which produced a distribution pattern which is not dissimilar to the present day.

The pull of the towns was considerable, and their rapid growth could not have been achieved merely by natural increase. Even eighteenth-century Nottingham, which many contemporaries regarded as favourably situated and healthy, could hardly maintain its numbers without considerable migration from the surrounding countryside (Chambers 1960). Tracing the process of migration is rather more difficult than calculating its effect. Migrants usually travelled only short distances unless they were heading for one of the great centres of commerce and industry, but the distances increased as the economy expanded and as transport improved. This general picture seems to hold true for the East Midlands. Although during the twist net boom which took place in the lace industry during the 1820s migrants are thought to have travelled to Nottingham from 80 miles around in search of work, by 1861 half the non-natives of the town had been born in the county. Among framework knitters in the villages of Ruddington, Lambley, Skegby and East Leake those who had migrated into the villages had usually come from other local industrial centres (Turland 1983). The opening up of the concealed Nottingham coalfield during the second half of the nineteenth century offered considerable employment opportunities. Some predominantly agricultural or framework knitting settlements grew rapidly as the result of an influx of miners; between 1841 and 1881 the number at Basford rose from 3 to 444, at Bulwell from 2 to 846, at Kimberley from 133 to 636, and at Nuthall from 66 to 263. Many of these men migrated into the villages from the surrounding area (Table 11), despite the traditional tendency for miners to move between coalfields rather than to be limited to a particular region. This trend helps to explain the number of miners from the south-west Warwickshire, Staffordshire and south Derbyshire coalfields who settled in Hucknall towards the end of the century (Horriben 1985). Longer-distance movement seems to have been associated with the railway. In Nottingham by 1891 only 20 per cent of non-natives had been born in the county (Church 1966: 224).

Table 11   Migration into Nottinghamshire mining villages, 1881

Village	Born in village	Notts/ Derbys/ Leics	Rest of England	Foreign	Total
Bulwell	264 (30.6%)	379 (44.8%)	191 (22.6%)	12 (1.4%)	846
Kimberley	383 (60.2%)	223 (35.1%)	30 (4.7%)	—	636
Nuthall/					
Awsworth	82 (31.2%)	152 (57.8%)	27 (10.3%)	2 (0.8%)	263
Basford	125 (28.2%)	223 (50.2%)	96 (21.6%)	—	444

(Source: Census Enumerators' Returns)

The Nottinghamshire pattern was repeated elsewhere. Migration into Leicester measured by the Register of Apprentices suggests that the average length of movement had increased by the late eighteenth century and that this included a preponderance of incomers from the agricultural east of the county (rather than the west where agricultural employment was supplemented by hosiery). By 1851 45 per cent of Leicester's inhabitants had migrated into the town, and this proportion rose to 62 per cent by 1911. Over the same period a small increase also occurred in the number of migrants coming to the town from beyond the county border, from 20 per cent in the 1850s to 28 per cent by the 1890s (VCH Leics IV 1958: 193, 276). Migrants into Lincoln in the mid-nineteenth century came mainly from the surrounding villages, with groups of twenty to fifty or so from Boston, Gainsborough, Louth, Horncastle and Sleaford. Out of 17,536 people in the city in 1851 47 per cent were born outside of the town and 22 per cent beyond the county boundaries. Those coming from a distance travelled mainly from Nottinghamshire and Yorkshire, and they were going against the normal trend for people to leave the county (Hill 1974: 126).

By the 1850s and 1860s agricultural conditions in Lincolnshire were such that outmigration was on the increase. County and regional boundaries were less important than distance and ease of communication for would-be migrants, and many moved to London and to the northern industrial centres. Within the East Midlands Nottingham was a reasonable centre to make for, although prior to the final quarter of the century, the reluctance to travel long distances, and the restricted number of occupations for which agricultural workers were suited in an urban environment, seems to have limited the numbers moving. Most migrants into Nottingham came from the surrounding area, and often from places with carrier service links, including Newark and Mansfield. Migrants travelled further if they came from east of Nottingham, partly because there were no large towns to divert them. On the other hand these long moves seem to have been less important quantitatively than shorter distance migration from north, west and south of the town (Maude 1974: 270, 340–2, 350–4).

Land and People

In 1750 around one-quarter of the land was controlled by the greater settled estates of either aristocratic provenance or pretension, although it has to be said that many of these were found on the region's poorer land including the Dukeries in Nottinghamshire. There were six dukes with substantial estates in the region, and more than a score of other peers. Families such as the Manners, Cavendishes, Saviles, Cecils and Berties had consolidated their estates into monolithic properties in such a way as to suggest that they were more entrenched by 1750 than they had been a century earlier (Holderness 1979). As symbols of their presence they planned lasting reminders. Kedleston Hall, the most splendid Georgian house in Derbyshire, was started in 1759, two years before Nathaniel Curzon was created Lord Scarsdale. In Nottinghamshire, Welbeck was rebuilt and improved by Lady Oxford during the eighteenth century; work on Clumber House began in 1770; Thoresby, rebuilt in the 1740s by the second Duke of Kingston, was improved early in the nineteenth century at a cost of over £8,000, and completely rebuilt between 1864 and 1875 with an outlay of £171,000. Overall, the passion for building was insatiable in the county; by one estimate thirty gentry families built themselves houses between 1760 and 1800 (Chambers 1957: 49). In Leicestershire the old manor house of Staunton Harold was transformed during the 1760s. The Hon. John Byng commented that it was 'a flaring, lately-built, ill seated house', although recent commentators have been less critical (Andrews 1935, II: 72; Millward 1985: 68). The Gothic revival was represented in Derbyshire by Richard Arkwright's Willersley Castle at Cromford, built 1789–90, and in Leicestershire by Donington Hall (1790–93) (Pevsner and Williamson 1978: 44, 255; 1984: 125). On the other hand, some landowners were in such dire financial straits that they allowed their houses to fall into disrepair. When the sixth Lord Byron, the poet, inherited Newstead Abbey in 1798 it was in a state of total disrepair, and some parts were in ruins (Coope 1979).

Plate 7.1 Thoresby Hall, Nottinghamshire. The Pierreponts, earls and dukes of Kingston, built the first Thoresby Hall in 1683. It was destroyed by fire in 1745, and replaced in 1767–71, but in the mid-nineteenth century the third Earl Manvers decided to erect a new mansion on a scale far more ambitious than any other Victorian house in Nottinghamshire. Built of Steetley stone, it was the work of Anthony Salvin, who had earlier been responsible for another east midlands house, Harlaxton, in Lincolnshire.

The plan follows the formula used by Salvin at Harlaxton, and also at Keele Hall in Staffordshire, with a large internal courtyard, and a room layout reflecting the organization of vast Victorian households.

In the 1880s Manvers owned more than 35,000 acres in the East Midlands, of which nearly 27,000 acres were in Nottinghamshire. He was one of the great landowners in the north of the county for whose vast estates the term 'dukeries' was coined. From these estates he derived the income which enabled him to build on this grand scale; in 1883 the gross annual value of his Nottinghamshire estates was put at nearly £37,000, and of his estate *in toto* at nearly £52,000. Tithe and colliery income was on top of this. The Thoresby accounts show that money was spent on the project every year between 1864 and 1876, by which time £171,015 had gone into the project. Stables, a woodyard, and a new church at the adjoining village of Perlethorpe, consumed a further £52,000.

Building continued in the nineteenth century. The present Belvoir Castle dates from the early years of the century, while in Nottinghamshire Kelham and Kingston Halls were rebuilt, the latter on a new site. Extensive restoration and rebuilding took place at Flintham Hall, Newstead Abbey and Rufford, and, more eccentrically, at Welbeck, where the fifth Duke of Portland's extensions made him one of the chief employers of labour in north Nottinghamshire.

The grandest Lincolnshire house from the Victorian period is Harlaxton, built by Anthony Salvin for Gregory Gregory in the 1830s, and described by Pevsner as 'the wildest and most fanciful mansion of the 1830s' in England (Pevsner and Harris 1964: 561–5).

Nor were landowners content merely with large houses. Formal gardens were laid out in the early eighteenth century including the water gardens at Shireoaks, but as tastes changed Exton, Burley-on-the-Hill, Garendon and Staunton Harold were landscaped on a grand scale, to include artificial lakes, long avenues, summer houses and follies (Millward 1985: 69). Between 1790 and 1820 approximately 1,000 acres were added to the Nottinghamshire parks of the greater owners, bringing the total to a peak of around 23,000 acres (Fowkes 1967). Humphry Repton was consulted at a number of venues including Thoresby and Donington Hall. Gardens were laid out during the nineteenth century. At Elvaston Castle, Derbyshire, where the house was remodelled early in the nineteenth century in a castellated Gothic style, between 1830 and 1850 William Barron's work included landscaping, topiary, a lake and grottoes, and garden buildings. The 1830s also saw Joseph Paxton's work on the grounds at Chatsworth, including the building of the Great Conservatory (1836–40). Elsewhere presence was signalled in a different form, through estate buildings such as those of the dukes of Devonshire at Baslow, Beeley and Edensor, and the Harpur-Crewes of Calke at Ticknall; estate villages including Sudbury in Derbyshire and Bradmore, Bunny and Thrumpton in Nottinghamshire; or, in the case of the dukes of Rutland, by establishing three cadet branches of the family on the periphery of the main estate (Holderness 1979; Pevsner and Williamson 1978: 44–5).

The significance of the greater owners was not all-pervasive. A handful of gentry families turned themselves into greater landowners during this period, including the Pelhams of Brocklesby, while also in Lincolnshire the Benniworths of Toynton progressed by way of piecemeal purchases of property. However, most of those who acquired extensive tracts of land did so on the basis of a fortune made in other pursuits. London merchants and financiers were important purchasers in eighteenth-century Lincolnshire, while elsewhere the *nouveaux riches* of the expanding industrial centres looked to put down roots. The Walkers, Rotherham ironmasters, acquired the Blythe estate in Nottinghamshire by 1806; William Denison of Leeds bought extensively in Lincolnshire; Samuel Shore of Sheffield acquired Norton in north Derbyshire, while the Barnsley grocer, linen-draper and land-jobber John Beckett, acquired extensive properties in Lincolnshire. Nor did all the newcomers emanate from outside the region. Sir John Robinson, who bought what was left of Worksop Manor from the Duke of Newcastle rose from modest beginnings in Arnold, near Nottingham, where he founded the Home Brewery Company at Daybrook. Robinson also bought the Georgian Thurgarton Priory for his son, and a landed estate of about 4,500 acres (Holderness 1974; 1979; Weir 1986: 44–8).

The figures produced in Table 12 provide an indication of the structure of ownership. The dominance of the great landowners is clear in Nottinghamshire and Rutland. Nearly three-quarters of Rutland was owned by just six men, headed by the Earl of Gainsborough; while Nottinghamshire's five largest owners, the dukes of Portland and Newcastle, Earl Manvers, Lord Middleton and A. W. Savile, jointly controlled 137,000 acres, or 27 per cent of the county total. The Duke of Devonshire owned 14 per cent of Derbyshire, and in north Lincolnshire the dominant owner was the Earl of Yarborough with 55,000 acres (Fuller 1974). Elsewhere in Lincolnshire, and in Leicestershire, the influence of individual owners was less obvious. The figures can also be used to reveal the extent of turnover. Of 159 Lincolnshire estates of 1,000 acres or more at least eighty originated in the eighteenth century and another two dozen were of nineteenth century origin (Holderness 1974: 559).

Table 12   Estate sizes as a proportion of total area, 1873

Size (acres)	Derbys	Leics	Lincs	Notts	Rutland
3000+	47.9	38.1	41.7	55.0	71.0
1000–3000	10.3	12.5	9.6	8.4	8.0
300–1000	11.4	15.8	15.4	10.8	4.9
100– 300	10.3	16.0	12.7	9.4	5.8

(Source: Bateman 1971)

Beneath the elite were the lesser owners of land, whose fortunes have long been a source of debate among historians. Evidence drawn from a variety of parishes in the region suggests that many of the occupying owners who farmed their own land were dispossessed in the century or so down to 1780, but that they enjoyed a short-term resurgence in the prosperous years for farming during the Napoleonic wars, 1793–1815 (Davies 1927; Chambers 1940; 1947). Whatever the nature of this resurgence it must have been short-term since by the 1870s less than 25 per cent of the east midlands acreage was held in parcels of 100–1,000 acres, and only 12 per cent in the 100–300 acre category. These of course are crude general figures. More detailed study reveals that the smaller owner-occupiers tended to disappear earliest in the mixed farming areas, but that they resisted more successfully in the areas of pasture farming. In Nottinghamshire on the clay soils a considerable turnover of small owner-occupiers did not produce a reduction in numbers (Chambers 1966: 203–7). In Lincolnshire the small owner survived on the fens and marshes to the end of the nineteenth century; as late as 1881 the north of the county was described by a Royal Commission as 'a district of peasant proprietors', and W. O. Massingberd, a local historian of some note, argued at the beginning of the present century that while small owners may have gone from the Lincolnshire wolds, heath and cliff, they had increased their numbers on the marsh and fen (Thirsk 1957; 1974). Smallholding also remained significant in the Derbyshire mining communities. At Middleton, near Wirksworth, in 1834 nearly all the miners owned their cottages, and some had a few acres of land attached (Millward and Robinson 1975: 199). The pattern was similar in pastoral Leicestershire, where in the later eighteenth century 82 per cent of the land was held in parcels of less than 50 acres, and it is clear that the farmer-grazier operating on the eastern claylands of the county remained an important figure.

Economic conditions and the longer-term result of enclosure drove considerable numbers of smaller owners from the land. When Great Easton in Leicestershire was enclosed in 1804 twenty-five holdings were of 10 acres or less. Eleven of these small proprietors disappeared by the 1820s. A similar picture was true of Wigston Magna, where between 1766 and 1795 the amount of owner-occupied land increased, but the number of owner-occupiers declined from 48 to 34. While some men had sold up, others had increased the size of their holdings and were operating as graziers. By 1851 the large farm and the absentee landlord had finally replaced the older economy in which owner-occupiers had flourished (VCH Leics II 1954: 234–5; Holderness 1979: 40; Hoskins 1957: 264–7).

These differences in the land pattern may have reflected the variety of village types which emerged in the region during this period. In much of Lincolnshire and eastern Leicestershire the village economy was almost entirely dependent on agriculture. In parts of Lindsey, for example, the landscape was full of villages in which agricultural workers far outnumbered independent farmers, while in the Kesteven village of Corby Glen 65 per cent of the population in 1851 was classified as farm labourers, labourers, or servants-in-husbandry, and only 26 per cent were craftsmen and tradesmen (Steel 1979: 169). A second village type was the dual occupation community, found predominantly in areas where small farmers pursued a pastoral economy (Thirsk 1961; Mills 1980). The Derbyshire Peak Distict was just such an area. Although agriculture was the basic form of employment, it was often coupled with lead mining, cotton spinning, hosiery and lace making. The most frequent combination was agriculture and lead mining. In Great Hucklow, a small township in the parish of Hope, eight of the forty-seven households in 1851 were wholly dependent on agriculture, and six on a combination of agriculture and lead mining. Among adult males 43 per cent were lead miners, 27 per cent were farmers, and only 4 per cent were agricultural labourers (Gardiner 1983; Fletcher 1971; Hall 1974; 1978).

Finally, in a number of villages industry became the dominant occupation, particularly in the hosiery areas of Nottinghamshire and Leicestershire. Probably because frame rents were such that machines could not be left idle, the take-over in these areas was often so complete that industrial activity was rarely combined with anything other than small-scale farming (Rogers 1981; Mills 1982). Framework knitting arrived in Shepshed towards the end of the seventeenth century, and during the eighteenth century the village became the most intensively industrialized rural community in the county. By 1812 a population of 3,000 supported 1,000, mainly wide, frames. Wigston Magna went through a similar metamorphosis. The stocking frame arrived late in the seventeenth century, and by 1765 only three families in ten occupied any land. By 1851 the greater part of the village was divorced from the land, and by 1901 only 3 per cent of villagers were involved in farming. On the other hand, a dominant landowner could effectively veto industrial development. Bottesford had not a single craftsman in 1831 because the dukes of Rutland used their influence to exclude all types of industrial pursuits from the village (Levine 1977: 4, 17; Hoskins 1957: 212, 217, 282).

Farming

The coming of industry had important implications for agriculture. Where the dual economy was practised the quality of husbandry was likely to be affected adversely, and it is no surprise to find Thomas Brown reporting from Derbyshire to the Board of Agriculture in 1794 that when the occupation of the soil had fallen into the hands of men engaged in other pursuits the land had been neglected (Brown 1794: 46–7). However, Derbyshire was not typical, and considerable agricultural change and improvement took place in the region during the period. Enclosure, which had begun in the seventeenth century, continued apace, particularly down to 1815, while a change took place in the nature of livestock farming – particularly in Lincolnshire – and new crops and rotations were introduced into the region's arable areas.

Enclosure had probably the most dramatic effect on the region not merely in terms of farming practice but also visually. Following the cattle distemper of the 1750s Leicestershire landowners again began to examine the possibilities of enclosing their land for permanent grass (Hunt 1957–58). In neighbouring Rutland by the 1790s three-fifths of all enclosure resulted in heavy land being put down to grass. However, it was not necessarily the case that following enclosure the whole parish was grassed down. Rutland's lighter soils were retained in tillage (Dury 1963: 124–6), and although when Wigston Magna was enclosed in 1766 about 600 acres were put down to permanent grass, even in 1832 the total had risen only to 2,000 acres, two-thirds of the parish (Hoskins 1957). In Nottinghamshire by 1800 nearly one-third of the best arable remained unenclosed, but a mere 13.5 per cent of prime pastoral had escaped. Even so, as Table 13 reveals, the east midlands counties were all above the national average in their pre-1793 enclosing activities, and if the change was most spectacular in Leicestershire it was also significant elsewhere. Kesteven had 100 open-field parishes in 1750, but only Stamford remained open in 1815 (Grigg 1966: 47). Beyond 1793 enclosure was usually for turning

Table 13 Parliamentary enclosure in the East Midlands. (Total enclosure in specific time periods as a proportion of parliamentary enclosure.)

	Pre-1793	1793–1815	1816–29	Pre-1830
Derbyshire	42.6	45.5	8.4	96.5
Leicestershire	78.2	20.2	0.8	99.2
Lincolnshire	51.0	41.9	2.1	95.0
Nottinghamshire	52.3	35.7	5.7	93.7
Rutland	42.4	42.0	4.8	89.2
England	37.7	42.6	8.6	85.9

(Source: Turner 1980: appendix 10)

open fields into larger cereal farms, a movement spurred on by the high price of grain during the Napoleonic war years.

Visually, the impact of enclosure on the landscape was profound. In place of the great open fields which had been the characteristic feature of the countryside since the early Middle Ages came a quilted pattern of small fields enclosed between hedgerows, or, in Derbyshire, the familiar stone walls. New, brick-built, farmsteads were raised among the open fields to serve a compact holding. Where enclosure was for grass, as in so much of Leicestershire, it is still possible to see the hedges cutting apparently indiscriminately across the ridge and furrow of the old fields, although in fact the pattern was often worked out with the best interests of steeplechasing in mind. Only Laxton in Nottinghamshire remains as a symbol of the traditional landscape, and even here the open fields have been much reduced in size. In 1841 John and Thomas Keyworth, who between them worked 238 acres in the village, held 159 separate parcels of land including forty-one strips in the South Field (31 acres), thirty-eight strips in the Mill Field (33 acres) and fifty-three strips in West and East Fields (43 acres) which were worked as a single unit (Beckett and Foulds 1985: 115). In 1985 just 164 strips survived in the three remaining fields, worked by eighteen farmers (four of whom were part-time). Laxton also has a number of enclosed farms, separated out in the 1720s when the economics of farming the more distant strips became unviable, but this first stage in what for many places was the opening salvo in a process of enclosure beginning long before legislation entered the statute books, was never completed. Elsewhere piecemeal enclosure was reflected in the proportion of parishes enclosed before legislation was obtained. Around Southwell 42 per cent of the parish of Farnsfield was already enclosed when the Enclosure Act was passed in 1777, and at Normanton the proportion was 45 per cent (Lyth 1985). However, piecemeal enclosure by agreement has left a much more irregular pattern of fields and roads than the straighter lines drawn after legislation was obtained. So much is clear from the contrast between the Lindsey heath in Lincolnshire, an area of late-eighteenth-century enclosure, and the outer marsh where

Plate 7.2   Taddington, Derbyshire, the impact of enclosure. Taddington provides a good example of the impact of enclosure on the landscape. In the left foreground are early, pre-parliamentary, enclosures, generally undertaken to facilitate grain production. On the right of the picture, in the upland part of the village, can be seen the geometrically square-shaped field pattern dating from the late-eighteenth-century parliamentary enclosure of what had previously been open moorland. The fields are divided by the dry stone walls which are a characteristic feature of the Peak District.

Taddington still betrays its linear village structure, and the original farms can be seen in this picture, stretching along the main road. The church, unusually for this type of village, is on the outskirts, and was at one time a chapel-of-ease of the large parish of Bakewell. Today Taddington is bypassed by the Bakewell–Buxton section of the A6, which can be seen in the left foreground.

piecemeal agreement proceeded from the Middle Ages onwards (Johnson 1963).

Where enclosure was designed to improve arable output it needed to be combined with new rotations, including turnips and temporary grasses, together with the integration of arable and pastoral farming into 'alternate husbandry'. The turnip enabled what had previously been bare fallow to be used for provisioning livestock, while still allowing the land to rest between grain crops, and even where it was unsuitable, as for example on the claylands, better drainage could help to improve cultivation and enclosure made selective breeding easier. By the end of the eighteenth century considerable progress had been made in the region, although the overall effect was patchy. In Nottinghamshire a positive lead was taken by the greater landowners of the Dukeries. In Sherwood Forest the Duke of Portland's 400 acres of water meadows were widely applauded; indeed James Caird referred to them in 1851 as 'the most gigantic improvement of its time and the pride of Nottinghamshire' (Caird 1852: 206). Similarly William Mellish (d. 1791) was an enthusiastic innovator who introduced the 'Norfolk system' and the Rotherham plough into north Nottinghamshire. Considerable advances were made on the Duke of Newcastle's Clumber Park estate, where 2,000 acres were brought under regular cultivation, using improved rotations, and providing support for several thousand sheep. Robert Lowe, writing of Nottinghamshire in the 1790s, commented that in general the county's agricultural practices had improved over the previous twenty years, although little was done on the claylands before the 1830s (Edwards 1944: 524; Chambers 1966: 222; Pickersgill 1979; Fowkes 1971a).

The wider adoption of root crops and clover in Derbyshire during the last quarter of the eighteenth century failed to improve the county's agricultural practices to any notable extent. Even in the 1840s upland areas with only small amounts of arable land had often failed to evolve regular crop rotations. Evidence for *c*. 1840 from the tithe files points to the continuing occurrence of bare fallows in various parts of the county, which according to one of the commissioners 'are almost wholly without turnips etc', and most of the assistant commissioners were struck by the general backwardness of the county's agriculture. They noted the predominance of grassland in the Peak, where township after township recorded more than 80 per cent of its titheable land in grass. At Castleton, according to the commissioner, 'it is the custom here, as in the whole neighouring district, for the occupiers to take in great quantities of cattle to ley from May to November, from Yorkshire, Lancashire and other counties'. Grain production was particularly important in the Ashbourne-Derby-Uttoxeter area, while enclosure helped to increase the output of cheese and butter in the High Peak (Henstock 1969: 36–7). Perhaps surprisingly in view of the tithe commissioners' strictures, only a decade after their work was completed James Caird found Derbyshire a picturesque and pleasant county 'where the pastures are well managed, the ploughed land neatly cultivated, and the stock suitable to the soil and carefully tended' (Kain 1986: 355–6; Caird 1852: 407).

Progress in Leicestershire and Lincolnshire was less marked. Admittedly the Duke of Rutland transformed the Belvoir ridge by putting the lower claylands to grass and turning the lighter soils which were traditionally the grazing lands into first-rate mixed farming country, and Stilton cheese was made on the enclosed pasture lands. Most eighteenth-century improvement in Leicestershire, however, was geared towards stock breeding. Robert Bakewell's pre-eminence in livestock breeding and farm management at Dishley (near Loughborough) was symptomatic of the county's interests. By 1801 turnips accounted for 11½ per cent of all arable in the county. James Caird was not impressed by progress in the county: 'it is to be regretted that hitherto the large proportion of landlords in Leicestershire have given little attention to the improvement of their estates' (Caird 1852: 220; VCH Leics II 1954). Even so, the evidence of a pilot crop survey of 1854 reveals that whereas in 1801 less than 17 per cent of the county was under the plough, by 1854 arable accounted for 36 per cent, grass for 59 per cent, and rough grazing for a further 16 per cent (Dodd 1980).

Lincolnshire's record in this period was mixed. Evidence compiled by the tithe commissioners suggests that while high farming was practised in a number of places, particularly on the light soils near to Lincoln, dead fallowing was still common, overploughing was found in various places, and both enclosure and drainage were necessary in a great number of parishes (Kain 1986: 85–6). By the late eighteenth century a major problem for much of the area was the declining profitability of wool. Efforts were made by the producers to increase productivity in order to compensate for low prices and to persuade central government to introduce protective measures (Turnor 1782), but economics were against them. With the diffusion of new fodder crops in the uplands the role of sheep farming declined, and the pressures of demand led to new breeding patterns (Perkins 1977a: 19–52). With rising cereal prices in the 1790s heavy investment in more intensive systems of farming became worthwhile, and some of the farming practices adopted were sufficiently advanced to enable the Lindsey uplands to ride out the post-war agricultural depression. By the 1840s this was regarded as one of the most advanced farming regions in England (Perkins 1975a; 1976). In the south of the county progress was slower, partly because the greater landowners took relatively little interest in farming. The stimulus of war led to the widespread cultivation of turnips and artificial grasses, and the period 1815–50 was one of considerable improvement in local husbandry practice. By the mid-nineteenth century the majority of farmers were following some form of improved rotation, and artificial fertilizers came into widespread use during the 1820s and 1830s. Lincolnshire continued to be noted for its animal husbandry; in 1887 one commentator noted that 'it would be difficult to speak too highly of the stock kept on the Lincolnshire farms' (Grigg 1966: 63, 82–3, 144–50, 199; Beastall 1978).

Local farmers were sufficiently involved with arable production to be concerned at any attempt to repeal the Corn Laws, With the expansion of wheat growing in Lincolnshire any threat to the 1815 legislation, which regulated imports and exports according to the prevailing price at home, was viewed with alarm. The return of two Tories for Lincolnshire in 1841 suggested that the county stood solidly behind the Laws (Hill 1974: 23). The Anti Corn Law League, which was established in the 1830s to fight for repeal, gained most of its local support from the towns. Leicester hosiers saw repeal as likely to help them resist foreign competition, and they backed an association founded in the town in 1838. In 1841 4,000 people attended a meeting in the market place. The following year 8,000 people turned out for a similar meeting in Nottingham, although opinion in the town was divided on the issue (VCH Leics IV 1958: 206–7; Fraser 1966). Sir Robert Peel's government repealed the legislation in 1846 but the decision was not accepted without a struggle in the countryside. It dominated the by-elections of 1846 and 1851 in the largely rural south Nottinghamshire constituency, while in Lincolnshire a campaign to restore the laws culminated in the adoption of James Banks Stanhope of Revesby as an independent in the 1852 election. In the longer term, however, it proved impossible to swim against the tide (Fisher 1981; Olney 1979: 153).

Partly as a sop to the landowners Peel introduced government loans for funding underdrainage. In the nineteenth century improved drainage enabled farmers on the claylands and on the marsh and fen of Lincolnshire to compete with the lighter soils. Tile drainage was introduced from the 1820s, and by 1851 the whole of west Kesteven had been drained. During the 1840s extenive underdrainage also took place on the fens. Two bad outbreaks of sheep rot in the 1820s highlighted the need for draining the clays (Grigg 1966: 142–4; Beastall 1978: 177, 180). In the north of the county underdraining began in 1831 on the Earl of Scarbrough's 11,000-acre estate, but overall progress should not be exaggerated since Caird found Lincolnshire insufficiently drained (Caird 1852: 217; Phillips 1979).

On the surface, efforts to drain the fens were taken up with renewed vigour after 1750, and in 1790 the Hon. John Byng was impressed with the fens,

> these are now so drained and cultivated as to deceive my expectation,
> which fancied an infinity of canals, causeways, reeds and rushes;
> instead of which I travelled on fine gravelly roads, and the country was
> tilled for grain.
>   (Andrews 1935, II: 226)

The cost was enormous – around £400,000 was needed to drain the north Holland fens – and great numbers of windmill pumps were installed. By the 1820s the main drainage lines stretched across virtually the whole of the fenlands. Unfortunately windmills could not stop flooding, but a crucial development came when steam pumps were introduced in the 1830s and 1840s. As with all fenland improvements opposition was fierce; residents of the northern fenland held out against pumps until 1866. They were eventually won over by the obvious effectiveness of the pumps, and although final improvements were not completed until towards the end of the century the risk of flooding had ceased to be a prime concern of the fen farmers by the 1850s (Fuller 1957: Grigg 1966: 138–41; Darby 1983). As a result, the techniques of the agricultural revolution could be introduced into the fens, and corn production grew so rapidly that within two generations the Spalding region became a net exporter of wheat (Beastall 1978: 70–1).

The second half of the nineteenth century saw first the era of 'high farming' between 1846 and 1873, and then the prolonged and debilitating depression which overtook agriculture during the last quarter of the century. During the 'high farming' years the proportion of permanent pasture to arable

---

Plate 7.3 Grimsthorpe, Lincolnshire, 1905. Lincolnshire suffered considerably in the agricultural depression of the final quarter of the nineteenth century, and one of the few local success stories related to the production of powered mechanical implements for agriculture, including steam engines and pumps for drainage. From about 1850 portable threshing machines and engines were produced in considerable numbers.

The success of the Lincolnshire firms was largely derived from their conquest of overseas markets. By the 1850s they were selling to Russia and the Austro-Hungarian empire. The trade was threatened by the agricultural depression, but local firms redoubled their efforts to sell abroad, and exports to South America and Russia peaked in the 1890s. Several firms also responded to the depression by diversifying their output; Marshalls of Gainsborough, for example, began producing machinery for the Indian tea plantations from the early 1870s.

Overall, between about 1845 and the end of the nineteenth century the engineering industry in Lincolnshire developed from a network of small family concerns into an industry which dominated the economies of the three towns most closely associated with it, Lincoln, Grantham and Gainsborough.

declined in Nottinghamshire and Leicestershire, although not elsewhere in the region (VCH Leics II 1954: 245). New types of fertilizer and farm machinery – including the mechanical reaper – were introduced into north Nottinghamshire, and drainage schemes forged ahead. Irish migrant labourers flooded into Lincolnshire – 50,000 of them in 1851 – to help with the harvest (Barber 1982), and landlords were encouraged to invest both in improved machinery and in drainage schemes. Between 1862 and 1877 £5,590 was spent draining the earls of Scarbrough's Lincolnshire estates, more than had been laid out during the whole of the previous thirty years (Phillips 1979: 176). However, few of the drainage schemes turned out to be financially profitable, largely because they were overtaken by the agricultural depression.

The depression brought severe problems to the region's agriculture during the last quarter of the nineteenth century, particularly in areas most heavily dependent on arable production. On the Lincolnshire wolds Cornelius Stovin complained that his 600-acre mixed farm was not making sufficient profit in 1872 to permit improvements to furniture and house. Three years later the depression was biting hard:

> My flock is anything but satisfactory. My corn crop is not superabundant, though the quantity and quality fair, but the price of wheat is low. The low price of wheat and the small number of sheep for sale next Spring will constitute our agricultural year one of singularly small profit.
>
> (Stovin 1982: 111, 183)

On the fens the depression brought a remodelling of local agriculture towards horticulture and market gardening. A number of people in south Holland entered the bulb trade, and directory evidence shows that the number of growers and merchants increased during the depression (Eagle 1950). Elsewhere in the region areas with a high proportion of permanent grass, including Leicestershire and south Derbyshire, were partially protected; indeed, since pastoral farming remained profitable as a result of increasing demand from urban areas (which the railway made it possible to supply) it is hardly surprising that the amount of land in permanent pasture increased in Leicestershire – by 61,157 acres over the period 1880–1910 (VCH Leics II 1954: 245–52). A similar trend took place throughout the region (Table 14). The most significant

Table 14   Land utilization in the East Midlands 1870–1900

Year	Crops and grass	%	Arable	%	Permanent grass	%
1870	2,913,505		1,728,755		1,204,750	
1880	3,017,281	+ 3.6	1,667,713	− 3.7	1,349,568	+ 12.0
1890	3,053,188	+ 1.2	1,559,681	− 6.9	1,495,506	+ 10.8
1900	3,022,656	+ 1.0	1,505,279	− 3.6	1,520,388	+ 1.7

(Source: Land Utilization Surveys)

changes were in Derbyshire, where the proportion of arable fell by 68 per cent between 1870 and 1900, and Leicestershire (54 per cent); while permanent grass increased in all the counties by more than 20 per cent over these thirty years.

Labour in the Countryside

For those who worked on the land conditions varied between different parts of the region and across time. During the eighteenth century Lincolnshire appears to have been a prosperous county for labourers, and Arthur Young was impressed by the comparative comfort in which the work-force lived. The myth that enclosure reduced employment opportunities on the land and forced agricultural workers into the towns was long ago exposed by J. D. Chambers, who showed that the demand for labour actually increased. Men were needed for attending to road upkeep, for building fences, digging drains, and for building bridges, gates, farm buildings and outhouses (Beastall 1978: 59–60, 108). As a result the absolute size of the Lincolnshire labour force grew from the later eighteenth until the mid-nineteenth century. Improved farming on the Lindsey uplands helped the trend, and Chartist leader Thomas Cooper, looking back on his childhood, described how 'we never knew what poverty was – we never saw it – in Lincolnshire. Nobody knows what real poverty is in that happy country' (Obelkevich 1976: 71; Perkins 1976, 1977b).

These favourable conditions were not necessarily found elsewhere. The appearance of closed villages, and the post-enclosure loss of squatters' rights on the commons, seems to have had a detrimental effect on day labourers in Nottinghamshire towards the end of the eighteenth century, while periodic food riots in Derbyshire also pointed towards discontent with existing conditions (Chambers 1966: 288–90; Thomas 1975). 'Closed' villages occurred when landlords sought to keep down the poor rate by excluding all but a bare minimum of wage-dependent families. In nineteenth-century Leicestershire 134 villages were 'closed', by comparison with 174 which remained open (Mills 1980: 76–7). In closed villages the population remained stable or even declined, hence the fact that in twenty-six Lincolnshire settlements the population was lower in 1851 than half a century earlier. The corollary was that large numbers of labourers were forced into 'open' villages, and between 1801 and 1851 twenty-one Lincolnshire market towns and 158 rural parishes doubled in size. Labourers lost their cows and their common rights to become an agricultural proletariat. Many were faced with the extra expense and fatigue of having to walk long distances to and from work, and the evidence of wills is that as labourers found security increasingly difficult to attain they became more concerned with the welfare of their wives and families (Johnson 1979; Obelkevich 1976: 90–102). In some areas labour gangs were formed to help relieve the shortage which occurred; one contemporary account relates to a gang of children, the eldest a girl of eight, which worked its way from farm to farm in the fens between Crowland and Peterborough working for fourteen hours a day. Migrant Irish labourers also helped to fill the gap at harvest time (Beastall 1978: 114–19: Holderness 1972b; Barley 1972: 178).

As conditions of employment deteriorated discontent increased throughout the region. Problems occurred in Lincolnshire during the Swing riots of 1830, and outbreaks of incendiarism took place in Lindsey in 1834–35, 1837 and 1844–45. Arson was also reported during the bad winter of 1850–51. Conditions for agricultural labourers seem to have been reasonable in the Newark area in the 1830s (Marshall 1960), but to have been worsening, albeit temporarily, in Leicestershire. Few problems appear to have arisen during the years of high farming, but the situation changed again when depression set in. The agricultural depression hit the region hard, and brought with it considerable movement off the land. From the 1870s the rural population was in decline virtually everywhere. Rutland, almost wholly rural in its occupational structure, suffered severe decline from 1861, and with it a significant fall in the number of rural craftsmen (Table 15). Laxton's population increased from 573 in 1801 to 659 in 1831. A decade later the number had declined slightly at 641, but it then began to slip noticeably, to 534 in 1851 and to 394 by 1901. The decline began slightly later in the Derbyshire Peak where most of the villages increased in size down to the early 1870s. Tideswell, Eyam and Youlgrave were among those to suffer significant depopulation between then and 1901 (Hall 1978: 72). In Leicestershire an agricultural labour force of 25,000 in 1851 fell to just under 6,000 by 1939 (VCH Leics II 1954). Occasional efforts were made to stem the tide. In Lincolnshire allotments were regarded as a possible cure for rural depopulation, but while they helped to supplement wages they

Table 15   Numbers of (male) rural craftsmen in Rutland 1851–1931

Craft	1851	1871	1891	1911	1931
Millers	63	43	26	22	2
Brick makers	38	37	24	15	4
Sawyers	33	37	20	10	13
Cabinet makers	31	24	17	10	5
Coopers and turners	15	8	4	2	—
Wheelwrights	74	69	44	42	22
Blacksmiths	116	114	102	83	49
Building trades	514	494	493	415	311
Saddlers	31	34	25	24	12
Tailors	173	114	81	63	20
Shoemakers	236	183	189	138	63

(Source: Saville 1957: 74)

seem to have offered 'no real and effective cure for rural depopulation' (Hare-sign 1983: 33).

Lincolnshire was prominent during the spring and summer of 1872 in the 'revolt of the field', a farmworkers' trade union movement designed to protect labourers against their employers. On 13 July the Lincolnshire Labourers' League was established, and by the early months of 1873 branches had been established throughout the county as well as in Norfolk, Nottinghamshire and Yorkshire. A union was also set up in Leicestershire, which claimed 4,000 members by the beginning of 1873, but it lacked finance and was poorly led (Horn 1967–70). By 1874 the Lincolnshire-based union had more than 12,000 members. A struggle took place, predominantly in Lindsey, between the employers and the work-force in an attempt to secure better wages. A compromise was reached on this occasion, but the union could not survive the ravages of the agricultural depression, and it collapsed at the end of the decade (Russell 1956; Obelkevich 1976: 77–8; Beastall 1978: 233–4).

For those who stayed in the countryside changing conditions were producing a new and harsher environment. Traditional holidays and pastimes such as parish feasts and hiring fairs declined. In the eighteenth century Shrove Tuesday was a general holiday. At Messingham in Lincolnshire 'cock fights were held at the public house in the morning. In the afternoon foot-ball was played and the day was concluded with dancing and cards', while Easter Monday at Hallaton in Leicestershire was commemorated with a 'scrambling' for ale and meat pies, 'the ringing of bells, fighting of cocks, quoits, and such like exercises' (Malcolmson 1973: 29). Enclosure put an end to some pastimes, but the most obvious example of an attack on traditional celebrations was in terms of the harvest celebrations. The old harvest-home had often been a spontaneous and rowdy occasion. From the 1860s it was increasingly replaced by orderly harvest suppers, often associated with a church service and a collection for some worthy cause such as the county hospital. This change came about for a number of reasons, including the growing social divide between the new capitalist farmers and their employees, the damage to relations caused by resentment towards mechanized harvesting, moral arguments about excessive drinking, and unionization (Ambler 1976). Along with the harvest-homes, maypole dancing and traditional 'plough' plays came under attack, although Plough Monday plays survived until 1914 (Barley 1953). Fairs were reduced in length and hiring fairs disappeared almost completely. Where they survived greater sobriety was expected, so that from Louth it was reported after the 1870 fair that drunks were fewer and that most visitors were on their way home by 8 p.m. (Obelkevich 1976: 83, 158–60; Olney 1979: 91, 176–7).

Housing conditions also left much to be desired. Mud and stud cottages were still being built in Lincolnshire after 1815 (and survivals of thatched mud and stud can still be seen at Thimbleby 2 miles from Horncastle). J. A. Clarke,

Plate 7.4 Harlaxton, Lincolnshire, a nineteenth-century estate village. The village was rebuilt in the early nineteenth century, and now contains quite a number of crazily detailed cottages, resulting at least partly from advice offered by the landscape-gardener-cum-architect J. C. Loudon (1783–1843). Loudon's principles included spending money in features such as the porch, the chimney pots and the gardens; making sure that there was some architectural feature in or about the gardens as well as in the cottage; never employing two styles of architecture in the same cottage; not omitting objects purely ornamental; and indicating the occupation of the inhabitant.

writing of Lincolnshire in 1852, provided a graphic description of the construction of such buildings:

> a common mode of building hovels, barns, etc, on a small scale, is to fix up a framework of wood, and cover it with plaster. This plaster is the white marl mixed with water, having straw well chopped up amongst it; and after standing a week before use, makes a hard and cheap walling for light buildings. This style of architecture is called 'mud and stud', and formerly the cottages of the poor were universally erected after the same rude and miserable model.
>
> (Clarke 1852: 98)

Mud and stud building continued largely because the county had little suitable stone and no slate. Brick and slate houses began to appear on the fenland in the later eighteenth century, but elsewhere these materials were mainly confined to farm houses and outbuildings. It was only after 1815 that they started to replace mud and stud more widely, and then the cost was such that the buildings erected were small. At Revesby in the early years of the nineteenth century Arthur Young found that brick cottages cost one-third more to build than mud and stud (Young 1813: 40–1). Clarke noted in the 1850s that newer cottages in the marsh and fen districts were generally constructed of brick, tile and slate, but cost ensured that they were 'small, low and incommodious . . . badly ventilated' (Clarke 1852: 153–4).

Inadequate housing conditions also reflected the decline of paternalism before the forces of supply and demand. In closed villages houses were allowed to decay in order that undesirables might be excluded, with the result that the majority of the work-force lived in open villages, or overcrowded market towns. Since rural employers shelved the question of responsibility for housing, labourers were often to be found living in insanitary, ugly tenements, and housing conditions in rural Lincolnshire remained deplorable throughout the nineteenth century. Supply and demand was also responsible for poor conditions in the upland pastures which were converted to permanent tillage. Landlords were not short of capital, but while farm improvements were a high priority, cottage building came low on their list of interests. The majority of casual and day labourers had to compete for limited village accommodation; the result was a level of overcrowding which bore comparison with the worst contemporary urban slums. By the 1860s there were calls for state aid to provide housing for the agricultural labouring class, but a solution – of a sort – to the problem, came in the 1870s with the flight from the land (Perkins 1975b).

In an attempt to provide some tolerable housing for agricultural workers poor law officials in various parts of Lincolnshire erected cottages. Prior to 1834 it was the responsibility of the parish to provide families with individual dwellings, whether they were on relief or in employment. Parish cottages provided minimal accommodation and were often built in inconvenient places or on sites which posed a serious health risk. Usually they were small and badly constructed. On occasion, poor law officials also paid the rents of cottages owned by private landlords but occupied by labourers and paupers. This practice was popular between 1815 and the reorganization of relief after 1834. Louth, for example, was spending as much as £500 annually on rents during the 1830s, largely because little waste land was available on which to build cottages for the poor. Rent subsidization and the provision of pauper cottages declined after 1834 and had disappeared by the 1850s, although the maintenance of existing parish cottages continued in some areas. Even so, by the mid-nineteenth century what had once been an extensive public commitment to housing the poor had come to an end, and in the absence of adequate private or public schemes inadequate accommodation was inevitable (Perkins 1977b).

The decline of paternalism in the countryside was also reflected in church attendance. As the Church of England failed to provide sufficient places for would-be worshippers, nonconformity was allowed a foothold, which soon proved to be permanent. Methodism spread rapidly in Derbyshire. In 1811 John Farey pointed out that in the north and east of the county

> where the large parishes are situate, the number of dissenting and Methodist meeting houses seem very numerous and are appropriated to most, if not all, of the prevailing religious sects . . . the chapels of the Methodists seem the most rapidly increasing, in the manufacturing districts of this and the adjoining counties.

He found 'several intelligent gentlemen' who believed that the exertions of dissenting and methodist preachers had brought about 'visible improvements in the sobriety and orderly conduct of their labourers in general' (Farey 1811, I: 93–4). Nor was this surprising; although the size and number of parish churches is a crude measure of religious habits and interest, in 1835 the Anglican churches offered accommodation for only 30 per cent of the population, and were the least well-equipped of the denominations to serve the industrial villages of the north and east of the county. In fifteen cases in Derbyshire a population of over 400 was settled more than 2 miles from an Anglican church or chapel, a situation the archdeacon of Derby described as 'unquestionably the most powerful and efficient cause of dissent'. Even though considerable efforts were poured into improving the Anglican position between 1772 and 1832 it was only after 1835 that the need to provide free sittings for the working class was recognized. Over the following twelve years twenty new churches were built and forty-one others enlarged, but by then the battle had been lost (Austin 1973, 1982).

The situation in Lincolnshire was in many ways similar. Between 1760 and 1845 few Anglican churches were built, and in south Lindsey many had fallen into disrepair both internally and externally. In the 1840s Broxholme church was described by the archdeacon as 'a small ruinous old building held together by the lead', while Hammeringham was 'a miserable remnant of a church', and Ashby Puerorum was 'in a sad state'. Attempts at rectification began at the end of the 1820s, although it was still necessary to use the railway waiting-room in the new village of New Holland as temporary accommodation until a church was opened in 1851. Meantime forty Methodist chapels had been built in the county by 1800, and the number increased fivefold during the early decades of the nineteenth century; in some villages the Methodist chapel became the dominant building. Wesleyan strength was concentrated in the north of the county – Epworth, where the Wesley brothers grew up, became something of a pilgrimage centre – and south Lindsey where it represented 'the most important event in the religious life of the poor since the Reformation'. Methodist aggression and the Anglican counter-attack probably produced a rise in church attendance prior to 1851, but it also corresponded with a favourable set of social conditions including the gradual emergence of a class society (Obelkevich 1976: 108, 319, 325; Wright 1982: 107, 201). However, while the weakness of the Anglican church in Lincolnshire appears to parallel the situation in Derbyshire, the number of churches per head of population was greater than any other place except Rutland, a timely reminder that it was not merely the inability of the Anglican establishment to provide church places which accounts for the growth of Methodism. The importance of nonconformity in the countryside is also clear elsewhere. Among Nottinghamshire villages Methodist chapels were built at Gotham, Oxton and Calverton (1790), Bingham (1792), Bulwell (1793), Epperstone (1795), Farnsfield (1796) and Normanton (1797), while in Leicestershire the number of nonconformist chapels increased sixfold between 1800 and 1850, especially in the agricultural villages (Swift 1982: 19–28; Thompson 1972).

The result of Anglican inertia became clear in the 1851 religious census. This revealed that in Derbyshire one in six of the population attended nonconformist services in the south of the county and one in eight in the east; the least support, not unnaturally, was found in 'closed' villages. Methodism was strongest in the agricultural parishes of the Trent valley, particularly in parishes with large numbers of freeholders (Tranter 1981). On the coalfield in the south of the county more than 70 per cent of worshippers on the evening of census Sunday were to be found in Methodist and Baptist chapels (Griffin 1969). Church attendance was below average in the industrial villages, and in villages with 600 or more people, while only six of the county's one hundred open villages lacked any nonconformists (Thompson 1972). In Lincolnshire 46 per cent of those attending were at the county's 705 Methodist chapels, but in south Lindsey church attendance was customary only for a large minority of the village population (Wright 1982: 238; Obelkevich 1976: 157).

In the countryside Methodism clearly represented a form of revolt against the established order. While attendance at Anglican churches remained high in closed and small villages, the opposite was the case in open and large ones; indeed, the vigour of nonconformity during this period, which partly reflected the role of the chapel as an outlet for personal ability and social ambition among the labouring classes, also ensured it a place in the forefront of protest movements. In south Lindsey religious dissent played an important role in the transformation of social relationships which eventually produced a class society. More overtly, dissenters were prominent in the farm workers' revolt of the 1870s. When the union was established in 1872 Primitive Methodists made up a high proportion of union officials, especially at district level. Many were active preachers, including Tom Willmore, who put his pulpit eloquence at the service of the Amalgamated Labour League, appeared on platforms with Joseph Arch, its leader, and became district secretary for north Lincolnshire. Others were trustees and circuit stewards. As a result the Revolt of the Field even had union camp meetings and union love feasts, as well as a revivalist and even millenarian atmosphere (Scotland 1981: Russell 1956; *ex info.* M. W. Barley). The failure of the union and the onset of agricultural depression may help to account for the loss of momentum among the nonconformists towards the end of the century. The Primitive Methodists were unable to sustain their membership in Nottinghamshire villages during the 1890s (Morris 1968 85–6), and a similar picture was true of south Lindsey (Obelkevich 1976: 217, 253).

Local Government in the Countryside

Until the passing of the County Councils Act of 1888 local government in the English countryside remained very largely as it had been since the close of the Middle Ages, except perhaps at the parish level. Changes did occur; responsibilities grew; central government intervention increased; but quarter sessions proved remarkably resilient, and quite effective in practice. The gentry were reluctant to give up power, but they were ill-equipped to deal with the problems which built up through time, particularly since many small settlements grew into large towns while remaining under quarter sessions oversight. Although eighteenth-century literature often suggests that justices acted in an arbitrary fashion the traditional country bumpkin image is not entirely accurate. In Nottinghamshire during the last quarter of the century the fifty-three justices who have been identified included two aristocrats, six baronets, thirty-two gentry and twelve clergy. Of these around twenty were active on the bench, although it was unusual for more than two to four JPs to sit at any one meeting. These men also played an important role away from sessions, sitting alone or in pairs, and attending the monthly meetings which prepared the groundwork for quarter sessions. While the range of duties was considerable, in Nottinghamshire they were carried out carefully with no clear evidence of serious abuse of power (Welby 1974; Chambers 1966: 48–51). What brought the justices' work into clearer focus was the growing cost of local government; between 1792 and 1832 the annual county rate for England and Wales rose from £315,806 to £783,442, while over the period 1784–1832 the poor rate increased from £2 million to £7 million. Local government was becoming more expensive and contemporaries wanted to know why.

The rise in the county rate was attributed to an increase in crime, and to inadequate provision for dealing with criminals. Quarter sessions were concerned with crime in both their administrative and judicial roles, and at the end of the eighteenth century it was the state of the prisons and the supposed increase in crime which most concerned contemporaries. John Howard's detailed study of prison conditions, which was published in 1777, revealed a depressing catalogue. The county gaols in both Nottinghamshire and Leicestershire were found to be damp and unhygienic, while in the Derbyshire county bridewell food was put through a hole in the floor 6 in. square, and prisoners were in danger of drowning when the water level rose. At Folkingham he found the bridewell to be 'under the keeper's house . . . five damp rooms, two of which are used for a lunatic, who has been confined here some years' (Howard 1777: 204–7, 279, 289). As a result of Howard's report, national spending on gaols rose from £92,000 in 1792 to £177,000 by 1832. At Lincoln work on a new gaol began in 1786, and five years later a new prison and court-house was completed for Lindsey, with thirty-two cells and accommodation for a further eighty-four people. A new gaol to serve Kesteven was built in 1808, the same year as Holland enlarged the gaol at Spalding and authorized the building of another on the outskirts of Boston. All three divisions of Lincolnshire embarked on prison-building programmes in the 1820s (Olney 1979: 104–14). More difficult to demonstrate is the supposed rise in the level of crime. In late eighteenth-century Nottingham a press campaign was launched against crime in the county, with the justices attempting to meet the criticisms levelled against them by regulating the sale of spirits (Chambers 1966: 70). However, the only clear evidence is from Lincolnshire, where a county rate of £60 1s. 2d.

Plate 7.5   Lincoln, the prison chapel. Lincoln gaol (now the Archives Office) was built in 1787, inside the castle. It was enlarged in 1845–46, and the chapel almost certainly dates from this period. The chapel was designed to ensure that when attending services the convicts could see the preacher but not see – and therefore not communicate with – each other. To this end tiers of head-high cubicles were built, in which the prisoners stood for the period of the service. Because the side walls of each cubicle hinge to form the doorway into the next one, the system is self-locking. This also ensured that the prisoners could only be released one at a time.

The chapel remains as a monument to a brilliant design, although today it is only sightseers who stand in the cubicles.

was sufficient for justice and policing for a whole year in the 1770s, but only for a single quarter by 1802 (Hill 1966: 20–1, 187).

Expenditure on the poor was certainly increasing. In Lincolnshire poor rates averaged £43,024 1783–85, but £230,191 annually 1813–15 (Beastall 1978: 127). In the village of Corby Glen poor rates rose from £88 in 1776 to £309 in 1803 – when one-twentieth of the population was receiving some sort of aid – to £640 in 1819 (Steel 1979: 178). Under the terms of legislation in 1723 and 1782 a number of parishes joined together to set up workhouses. Nottinghamshire had eighteen by 1776, and Derbyshire thirty by 1811 including Tissington (1753), Winster (1774) and Shardlow (1811). Some workhouse schemes were not a success. The parishes around Ilkeston erected a workhouse in 1738, but it was pulled down in 1779 at which point it was uninhabited, and the various parishes were 'sick of sending boarders to the house and repent the money spent on it' (Heath 1982: 168; Chambers 1966: 237–42). In Lincoln a former glue manufactory was turned into a house of industry for the poor of subscribing parishes, and by 1789 it was full, chiefly from the rural parishes. By the early nineteenth century it cost £4,800 annually to run, and had 175 inmates (Hill 1966: 206–10). In the county as a whole about a hundred of the 705 parishes came together to form voluntary unions after 1782 and workhouses were established at Caistor, Lincoln and Claypole.

One attempt to tackle the problem of cost came in the shape of the 1834 New Poor Law, passed in an attempt to deal with the problems of rising rates but rather incongruously retained as a separate local government function operated by the parishes. By utilizing the principle of less eligibility and the practice of the workhouse test, it was hoped to reduce poor relief by persuading the able-bodied of the benefits of self-reliance. Parishes were grouped into unions, each of which was to build a workhouse. Lincolnshire's parishes were divided between fourteen unions. Twelve new workhouses, designed to accommodate 3,400 paupers, were built in the county 1834–38, at a cost of £72,760. Heavy expenditure could be avoided where provision still existed, and the existing houses at Caistor and Gainsborough continued in service (Brocklebank 1962). Similarly forty Nottinghamshire and Derbyshire parishes had formed the Basford Incorporation in 1814, and another forty-nine around Southwell set up the Thurgarton Incorporation in 1823–24. Although both groups were dissolved in 1836 their successors, the Southwell and Basford unions, utilized the existing workhouses (Caplan 1970: 85–6).

Lincolnshire unions were usually based on a market town and encompassed the surrounding parishes within a radius of 7–10 miles. This was not a popular move. At Gainsborough a mob set fire to a workhouse under construction in 1837. Corby Glen was one of thirty-seven parishes which formed the Bourne union, where a £9,000 workhouse was built to accommodate 300 inmates. The villagers, who had previously had little to do with Bourne, greatly resented having to foot their proportion of the bill, and while £188 was spent by the village overseers on in-relief in 1838, £1,698 went on outdoor relief, a figure criticized by the poor law commissioners (Steel 1979: 179–80). In any case, the workhouse test was a blunt instrument for dealing with seasonal unemployment among the county's agricultural workers. The guardians refused to implement the test in full, and by 1842 the new workhouses were barely half full, since it was cheaper to maintain paupers on parish relief rather than to pay the cost of sending them to a distant union workhouse and in the process risk reducing them to permanent poverty. As a result, recipients of outdoor relief in south Lindsey usually outnumbered the inmates by ten to one (Brocklebank 1962: 32; Obelkevich 1976: 74–5). This particular experiment in bringing the countryside under the wing of the local towns proved less than wholly successful, even if the cost per head of population was reduced in the wake of the legislation.

Although initially resented, the unions set a precedent for rural parish groupings designed to tackle particular problems for which the existing structure of rural local government was inadequate, including lighting and watching, baths and washhouses, burial grounds and highway repairs. Often the boards and councils which were established in this fashion had overlapping boundaries and forms of election, and their effectiveness was severely limited. When, during the middle decades of the nineteenth century, the boroughs became increasingly progressive in the provision of welfare, the rural areas remained in a state of chaos. This is clear from the problems associated with policing. In Lincolnshire Holland declared itself in favour of a police force in 1836 and Lindsey in 1839, but when in the latter year legislation was passed permitting the establishment of professional county police forces only south Holland showed any inclination to act. The county magistrates decided not to implement the legislation, but legislation of 1842 made it possible to build up a police force on a piecemeal basis and as a result by the early 1850s police stations with cells and magistrates courts appeared in various parts of Lindsey. A county force was established only as a result of an Act passed in 1856 (Olney 1979: 122–4). A similar situation occurred in Derbyshire where considerable debate took place in 1839–40 on the merits of establishing a county force, but after a motion to quarter sessions was withdrawn in October 1840 the county followed Lincolnshire in postponing further measures until the passing of the 1856 Police Act (Heath 1980). Derbyshire landowners opposed a police force for fear of having their traditional powers undermined, but the gradual encroachment on the powers of quarter sessions could not be prevented. Although the justices continued to shoulder the burden of rural responsibility through the middle decades of the nineteenth century they finally gave way with the election of the first county councils in 1889.

The County Councils Act of 1888 established a dual system of local government. Large towns had their own councils, whereas elsewhere local government powers were shared between county councils, and urban and rural district councils within county areas (Table 16). By 1894 most unincorporated towns in Lincolnshire obtained a board and so turned themselves into urban districts, which were really miniature versions of municipal boroughs. Rural districts were sub-divided into a number of parishes, and in 1894 parish councils were set up with responsibility for appointing overseers, for lighting and roads, and for the provision of baths, burial grounds, washhouses and playgrounds. However, the changes of 1888 served not so much to revolutionize government in the countryside as more effectively to divorce town and county government while leaving the latter firmly in the hands of the landed magnates. The result was continued lack of appreciation of some of the problems commonly associated with the towns but also present in the countryside (Olney 1979: 138–41).

Table 16 Local government in 1900

County councils	Derbyshire, Leicestershire, Lincolnshire Lindsey, Lincolnshire Kesteven, Lincolnshire Holland, Nottinghamshire, Rutland
County boroughs	Derby, Leicester, Lincoln, Nottingham, Grimsby
Municipal boroughs	Buxton, Chesterfield, Ilkeston, Glossop, Loughborough, Boston, Grantham, Louth, Stamford, Mansfield, East Retford, Newark
Rural districts	Derbyshire 9, Leicestershire 13, Lindsey 10, Kesteven 6, Holland 4, Nottinghamshire 10, Rutland 3
Urban districts	Derbyshire 16, Leicestershire 10, Lindsey 16, Kesteven 4, Holland 4, Nottinghamshire 12

(Source: Census Returns 1901)

Education

Under the terms of Forster's Education Act of 1870 elementary education was provided for all children. It was a landmark in English education, particularly in the rural areas since these had always been less well provided with schools than their urban counterparts. Country children living close enough to small towns could often benefit from the available facilities, since many had grammar schools, among them Ashbourne and Dronfield in Derbyshire, and East Retford and Tuxford in Nottinghamshire. Prosperous and ambitious farmers might send their sons and daughters to private day and boarding schools in nearby market towns or even smaller settlements; by 1841 in north Nottinghamshire, for example, there were eighteen private academies and a variety of day schools, so that almost every settlement in the area had provision for elementary education at some point during the week (Biggs 1977). However, throughout the region the majority of rural children who received an education did so at charity schools. Many of these schools dated from the eighteenth

219

century; Derbyshire, for example, had seventy-four by 1800 (Johnson 1970: 15–29). In the early nineteenth century the founding of the British and Foreign Schools Society (1808) to promote nonconformist principles, and of the National Society (1811) to do the same for the Church of England, coupled with government school grants between 1833 and 1870 helped to improve the available facilities. In Lincolnshire 200 grants were made to 148 separate schools, totalling £33,172. Even so, in 1862 637 of the county's parishes had no annual grant, and the number of schools built without government aid greatly outnumbered those which were helped (Russell 1960). Despite these provisions, many children had to be content with the education offered by Sunday schools. By 1851 in Lincolnshire there were more children in Methodist Sunday schools than in those of Anglicans (Wright 1982: 238), although in south Lindsey Wesleyan Sunday schools were greatly outnumbered by church schools, prompting the suggestion that the Church of England 'was closer to being a majority institution among children aged 5 to 12 than in any other segment of the population' (Obelkevich 1976: 193, 166–7).

The aim of the 1870 Education Act was to augment the voluntary schools by providing rate-supported local facilities. Central government accepted the basic principles of a national responsibility for elementary education, and it also agreed to monitor the new system in order to make alterations when inadequacies came to light. Legislation in 1880 imposed a fine on parents whose children failed to attend school, and in 1902 the school boards set up under the 1870 legislation were replaced by local education authorities, and provision was made for all elementary schools to be rate-financed. In 1870 the number of school places had to be counted, and the voluntary bodies were given six months to fill the gap. If they failed, a school board was to be elected with power to build and run new schools by levying a rate. Derbyshire was found to have a deficiency of 8,828 places, and by 1882 forty-two school boards were operating in the county, with 53 per cent of the population living in a school board area. In Lincolnshire Church of England and nonconformists alike set out to provide sufficient places. By the end of 1873 thirty-four new schools had been built and fifty-five enlarged, but it was not enough; although Lindsey had just five boards at the end of 1872 another thirty-two were elected during the following six years, and by 1895 the county had 119 board schools (Russell 1965, III: 57–69; IV: 43–62).

Although elementary education was provided, facilities for secondary and higher education occurred on only a random basis in the countryside. The need for scientific and technical education became apparent after the Great Exhibition. The Department of Science and Art which was founded by Lord Aberdeen's government in 1853 introduced classes six years later which were designed to educate the labour force and to maintain industrial prosperity. Inevitably most of these classes were held in towns, but towards the end of the century a number took place in smaller rural centres. By 1890 most villages in Nottinghamshire had access to classes organized in conjunction with this scheme, although facilities in Leicestershire were poor until towards the end of the century. By 1902 the county had eighty-three evening schools (Tolley 1982; Simon 1968: 183ff.). Some places also organized adult self-help groups, among them the village philosophical societies in Castle Donington and Melbourne.

Before 1750 the great majority of the populace lived in the countryside and depended for their living on working the land. This situation was transformed during the Industrial Revolution. Population increase was no longer accommodated in the countryside and migration to the towns was an outstanding feature of the period, but this did not mean that rural England was untouched by the stresses and strains of the period. The small owner-occupier gradually declined as land was increasingly owned in larger blocks, and cultivated by wealthy tenant farmers ready to introduce the latest husbandry and breeding techniques. To keep such tenants, landlords were forced to invest in their property, particularly in improved drainage. Land use changed, especially on the claylands, as breeding and rearing replaced the old and often unprofitable mixed husbandry. Parliamentary enclosure, the agent behind much of this transformation, altered the landscape of the region almost out of recognition. Even the villages were changing. Architecturally, a number were rebuilt as estate villages in the nineteenth century, among them Sudbury, Harlaxton and, in Nottinghamshire, Kingston on Soar where Edward Strutt was responsible for a symmetrical group of semi-detached gabled brick cottages, with each pair built to a slightly different design. In terms of occupation, while agriculture was still the primary function of villages throughout the region, in addition to the dual-occupation settlements commonly found in the Peak District, a number of places, particularly in the west of the region, were coming to depend almost entirely for employment on industry.

For those who remained on the land the prosperous conditions of the eighteenth century disappeared after 1815. Paternalism fell victim to the market economy. 'Closed' villages deprived labourers of their old privileges and rights; the new Poor Law offered a harsh alternative to its predecessor, particularly in times of economic depression; employers often found it convenient to ignore the housing problems of their labourers; and the Church lost its way before the rise of noncomformity. On top of all this the structure of local government was inadequate for the tasks involved, particularly in the larger settlements, and the many local boards tended only to complicate matters. It is hardly surprising as a result that the conditions under which many people lived were harsh, but efforts to organize the labourers in the 1870s collapsed as a result of the agricultural depression, and by the 1880s and 1890s large numbers were fleeing the countryside in search of salvation in the towns. Moreover, the towns looked attractive, and were gradually adopting functions for which the country was inadequate. Poor Law unions were usually centred on towns; educational provision was often better in the larger settlements; and cultural, sporting and employment prospects all seemed brighter in an urban environment. For young, and sometimes not so young people, in the depressed agricultural conditions of the later nineteenth century, the limited facilities of a local market town had fewer advantages than larger places. By 1900 the traditional dispersion of interests was fast disappearing, and the countryside was looking to the towns through the extensive carrier network, and increasingly to a few large centres.

Chapter 8

Towns

Towns had always been important for their marketing, manufacturing and service activities, but in an agrarian economy they played second fiddle to the basic task of coaxing a living out of the countryside. In the eighteenth and nineteenth centuries this changed. In mid-eighteenth century England about 23 per cent of the population lived in towns of 2,500 or more people. A century later the population was slightly more urban than rural, and by 1900 the urban orientation was firmly established. Even allowing for distortions caused by boundary changes it was a staggering development, and it was almost entirely as a result of improved technology. Developments in agricultural practice broke the syndrome whereby low levels of productivity restricted urban growth. Industry evolved beyond its earlier dependence on the land for raw materials. The net result was that economic growth in the towns and economic growth itself became synonymous: individual regions continued to centre their activities on the most important town, but the satellite region surrounding it grew in size. Overall, the period 1750–1900 marked a fundamental change in the balance between town and country.

Urban Growth

The spectacular urban growth of this period is apparent from Table 17. Rutland is omitted since even its county town, Oakham, was little more than a small market centre throughout the period, and the county's population figures make little difference to the overall numbers. Even when allowance is made for boundary changes this is a remarkable picture, and the overall proportion would be higher if some of the lesser settlements were added. On the other hand growth was not uniform. It was relatively limited in Derbyshire, for example, where even the first nine towns accounted for just 37 per cent of the population, and the figures for Lincolnshire appear to reflect the county's continuing preoccupation with agriculture. Growth took place on existing sites – only Coalville in Leicestershire, and to a lesser extent Scunthorpe in Lincolnshire, can be regarded as wholly new creations. The location of industry, proximity to improved communications, and the capacity to develop trading and leisure functions were among the factors which determined which towns expanded during these years.

Table 17   Proportion of population living in the five largest towns of each county

County	1801	1901
Derbyshire	17	29
Leicestershire	24	62
Lincolnshire	13	34
Nottinghamshire	34	61

(Source: Census Returns)

In general terms the most significant growth occurred in the county towns, and those with a firm industrial base. The latter included Ilkeston, Loughborough and Mansfield, but also smaller places like Long Eaton, which was no more than a village even in the mid-nineteenth century, and Clay Cross. Some towns experienced rejuvenation after a period of stagnation, including Newark and Grimsby, while towards the end of the nineteenth century the east coast resorts started to grow. By contrast, in a number of towns growth was either slow or non-existent. Some of the centres which were in the forefront of early industrial growth failed to make significant later progress, including Hinckley, Belper and Cromford, while older market centres which were left behind included Stamford, Oakham and Southwell, and most of the smaller Lincolnshire towns. Many of these suffered from stagnant or even declining population in the second half of the nineteenth century (Wright 1982: 224).

Without doubt it was the county towns which benefited most from urban growth in this period. Derby, Leicester, Lincoln and Nottingham were the largest towns in the region in 1750, with the latter's 12,000 people making it by far the most substantial. At that time, however, their joint populations represented only 7 per cent of the overall east midlands population; by contrast, in 1900 this figure was 28 per cent. As major administrative, commercial, professional and cultural centres, they dominated their counties. Both Leicester and Nottingham grew to a point by 1901 where nearly half the total county poulation lived within their confines. In addition, while in 1801 Leicester was three times the size of the next largest town, Hinckley, and Nottingham was five times larger than Newark, by 1901 Leicester was ten times the size of

Loughborough (now the second largest town) and Nottingham was eleven times larger than Mansfield (even without taking into account rapidly expanding suburban villages such as Beeston). Derby's position was less dominant since in the north of the county the Chesterfield area looked towards Sheffield, and Buxton towards Manchester, while in the south-east Ilkeston and Long Eaton looked to Nottingham. As a result, Derby tended to take second place to Nottingham as the regional capital of the middle Trent basin (Vollans 1949: 97–102). Even so, Derby was 48 per cent larger than Chesterfield in 1801, and 73 per cent greater in 1901. Although by 1900 Lincoln had yielded first position to Grimsby, it was still very much larger than Gainsborough, the third town in the county. Even allowing for the distortions of boundary changes these figures are impressive. What is perhaps most surprising is that none of these towns developed into a regional capital, although Nottingham has the clearest claim to such a position, dominating Derby if not Leicester. In the 1840s the *Nottingham Review* was sold in much of the area eastwards from the town to the Lincolnshire coast.

The County Towns

Nottingham, so beloved of Celia Fiennes, was still a genteel town in 1800 judging by the lifestyle of the diarist Abigail Gawthern (Henstock 1980). After 1815, however, the towns's respectable inhabitants began to vacate their mansions in favour of fashionable villages nearby, and by the 1840s the town was a notorious slum described in a government report as 'hardly to be surpassed in misery by anything to be found within the entire range of our manufacturing cities'. In the later eighteenth century it was restricted to a site of 876 acres because of the proximity of private estates and 1,400 acres of land vested in the corporation. The failure to enclose this land ensured that a site which had been adequate for 12,000 people in 1750 was overgrown with 50,000 inhabitants by 1831. Growth had been possible only by infilling and by splitting of tenements, and even then four-fifths of the town's population lived in 8,000 courts or back-to-back houses. Conditions in the worst areas of the town, the Broad Marsh, were so bad that the average lifespan was just eighteen years (Brazier *et al.* 1984: 28). Since further growth was almost impossible by the 1830s the new industrial villages beyond the common fields generally benefited, including New Basford, New Lenton, New Sneinton, New Radford, Carrington and Hyson Green. Pressure on space within the town produced high rents, and according to William Felkin this had the effect of driving the hosiery and lace industries out towards the villages (Church 1966: 8, 164–5, 169). After the enclosure of 1845 the town expanded again. Between 1851 and

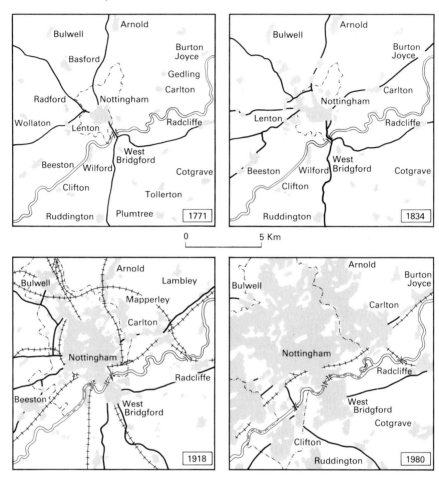

Figure 8.1 The growth of Nottingham, 1771–1980 (based on Brazier *et al.* 1985: 32)

1858 3,522 new houses and sixty-seven warehouses (often replacing genteel houses) were built, and between 1849 and 1856 £250,000 was spent on building work. During the 1870s the town reached out towards the industrial satellites, while a remarkably successful private development by the fifth Duke of Newcastle produced the middle-class Park estate on the town's west side (Brand 1985). In 1877 the borough was extended to include Sneinton, Basford, Bulwell, Radford and Lenton, and these areas were welded onto the town by the construction of a network of boulevards in 1883–84. Finally, in 1897 Nottingham was created a city. Without doubt, however, an opportunity had been missed over the previous half century. The enclosure act had laid down building standards and the width of roads, as well as outlawing back-to-back housing, but it proved less than easy to implement such ideas, particularly on the low-lying meadows – although few back-to-back houses were built whereas they were still being constructed in large numbers in major provincial cities such as Leeds. Although the phrase 'new Nottingham' was used of the post-enclosure town, it turned out to be a drab and depressing place in which to live (Chambers 1952: 11, 13; Church 1966: 183–7).

Leicester, the second largest town in the region in 1750, had none of Nottingham's land restrictions, and consequently grew much more rapidly in the first half of the nineteenth century. Much of the town had been rebuilt in brick during the eighteenth century. The Hon. John Byng referred to it as a 'long town, whose streets are wide, but, generally of low houses', and even in 1800 it was still not densely built (Andrews 1935, II: 84; Pye 1972: 283, 287; Simmons 1974, I: 99–101). Expansion was easiest to the east of the town, and as a result a shift took place in the centre of gravity; in 1801 St Margaret's parish contained approximately one-third of the town's inhabitants, but this rose to two-thirds by 1851. Space ensured that Leicester developed relatively few slums; by 1901 the town enjoyed one of the lowest proportions of population living in overcrowded conditions (Elliott 1979: 102–7). The conversion of the racecourse into Victoria Park in 1882, and the formation of a park from Abbey Meadows and St Margaret's Pastures in 1877 ensured that Leicester had extensive tracts of open ground adjacent to the town centre. By then considerable numbers of people were moving into the suburbs of Belgrave, Humberstone and Aylestone, a process speeded by the coming of horse-drawn buses in 1874. All three areas were incorporated when the town boundaries were extended in 1892 (Brown 1970). However, none of these developments produced particularly profound results. Leicester was, and is, undistinguished, never having been able to develop the genteel urbanity of neighbouring Nottingham.

Derby grew more slowly than Nottingham and Leicester, but this did not relieve it of some of the same problems. St Mary's bridge was rebuilt in 1788–89, and by the end of the eighteenth century the town was one mile long and half a mile wide. Population growth brought an increase in the number of houses from 1,637 in 1788 to 2,644 by 1811, although even at the latter date it was still possible to see town houses with neat gardens (Heath 1979), and even in the 1840s Derby was described as 'a most comfortable town'. The traveller Dr Granville noted that Derby

> exhibits strong marks of general improvement, by an extension as well as renovation of its principal buildings. The range of edifices consisting of the royal hotel, a new post-office, and the bank in the corn-market, is a mass creditable to the town.
>
> (Granville 1841: 121)

But closed courts and slum dwellings, together with an inadequate water supply, ensured that the town had its black-spots. Expansion in the nineteenth century was largely associated with the railway. The largest railway works in Europe were built in Litchurch, beyond the town boundary to the south, and with them came a new community. As in Leicester, the effect was to alter the town's axis, bringing a 'slow slide southwards' as Derby moved towards the railway (Heath and Christian 1985: 32–4). Many of the newcomers travelled considerable distances. In 1851 43 per cent of Derby's inhabitants aged twenty and over were born outside the county, a much higher proportion than Nottingham's 35.5 and Leicester's 28 per cent. In 1877 the borough was expanded to incorporate 'railway Derby', and the town's physical limits grew from 1,793 to 3,445 acres (Standen 1958; Vollens 1949: 107).

In the course of the eighteenth century Lincoln at last emerged from the prolonged decline which had marked its history since the Middle Ages, although until the 1840s the town did not really expand beyond its medieval boundaries. In the second half of the nineteenth century growth took place on all sides of the medieval site, but especially on low-lying land to the south and south-east of the town. Houses were also built in the parishes of St Swithin and St Martin near the new engineering works. Much of this was small and of poor quality. Long drab rows of housing did not help to improve the scenery, but Lincoln did not suffer the overcrowding which bedevilled Nottingham (Hill 1974: 128, 290; Wright 1982: 226–7).

The county towns grew for a variety of reasons, not the least important of which was their role as cultural and service centres, although Lincoln suffered in this respect from the social divisions between those on and those below the hill. As one contemporary put it:

> if there was a playhouse in Lincoln, it must be in one of the following predicaments. If it was situated on a hill it would be all boxes; if under the hill all gallery, and if in the midway all pit; and, therefore, as a playhouse cannot subsist but by the union of boxes, pit and gallery, I should apprehend fortunes are not acquired by theatrical performances at Lincoln.
>
> (Dibdin 1801, I: 377)

From the mid-eighteenth century county towns had assembly rooms where balls, dinners and plays put on by touring companies, took place for the benefit of the local gentry and wealthy townsfolk. These were exclusive institutions; at Derby, for example, attorneys' clerks and shopkeepers were just two groups who were not permitted to be members (Heape 1948: 32). Lincoln had a theatre in 1732, and its assembly rooms date from 1757. Leicester's date from about the same time (Hill 1966: 58). The New Subscription Assembly in Derby became the centre of glittering social events during the 1770s (Sturges 1978), while in 1836 a splendid new suite of rooms built in Grecian style replaced Nottingham's old assembly rooms. Although plays sometimes took place in the assembly rooms, purpose-built theatres were also built from new or set up in buildings converted from other uses. The first in Nottingham, which was later described as 'a very dull looking building' was opened in 1760. According to White's *Directory* it was not particularly successful 'owing to the greater part of the middle classes being now dissenters, and averse to theatrical performances' (White 1844: 176–7). It was replaced by the Theatre Royal in 1866, which seated 2,200 patrons. New theatres were built at Leicester in 1836 and 1840, but the town could not support them both and the latter was demolished in 1848. An opera house was opened in 1877, although as with the surviving theatre it enjoyed only limited success (Simmons 1974, II: 39–40).

Classical concerts were a feature of cultural life in eighteenth-century Derby, reaching a peak with the town's first music festival in September 1788. The first season attracted 1,000 people including most of the Derbyshire gentry. It was a brilliant social occasion but an attempt at repetition in 1791 had to be cancelled and the 1793 season passed off quietly. During the 1820s the festival became a triennial event, and the town also had a flourishing choral society (Sturges 1978: 190–4; Taylor 1947). As a result of the demand for classical music St George's Hall in Nottingham was opened in the mid-nineteenth century to provide a venue for concerts, although this was not a success and the building eventually became a music hall. Sometimes, however, more could be done to promote interest by the activities of individuals, and the Farmer family (three generations of singers, instrumentalists and composers) were prominent in promoting glee clubs and classical concerts in mid-Victorian Nottingham (Barker 1985: 72).

Intellectual and debating societies were usually found in the county towns. The most famous literary and philosophical society in the region was in Derby, founded in 1782–83 by Dr Erasmus Darwin, (Sturgess 1977–78; Robinson 1969), but there were others in Leicester – where the society helped to bring together members of the middle class who differed in religious and political matters, as well as contributing to the museum keeper's salary and giving money to acquire specimens – and Nottingham, where the group was formed in 1869 out of earlier societies including the Literary and Science Society (1824) and the Literary and Debating Club (1837). County towns were the focal point of the archaeological and antiquarian societies established during the nineteenth century (Simmons 1974, II: 30, Church 1966: 214, 379).

The county towns also tended to be recreation centres. Horse-racing took place annually in Leicester's Victoria Park until the opening of a new course at Oadby in 1880 (Simmons 1974, II: 36), while in Nottingham races were held on the Forest immediately after Goose Fair, and in Derby racing was revived in 1845 when the annual football match was transferred to the Shrovetide wakes despite opposition from the participants (Delves 1981). Cricket grounds were laid out during the nineteenth century. Wharf Street, Leicester, hosted some of the principal matches in England 1825–60, and the present county ground at Grace Road dates from 1878. Nottingham had two cricket grounds in 1844, one adjoining the Forest 'now allowed to be one of the

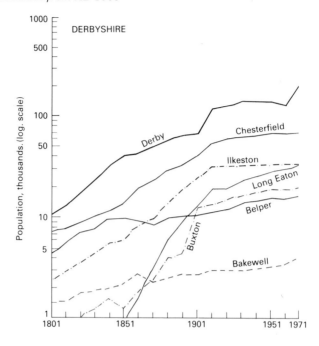

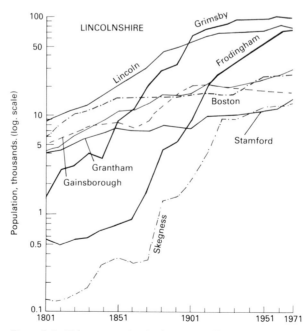

Figure 8.2 Urban expansion in the East Midlands, 1771–1980

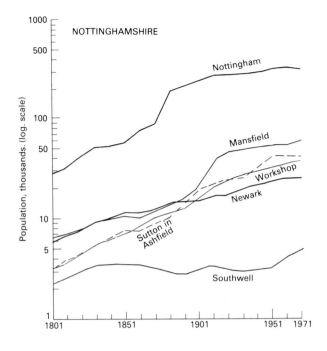

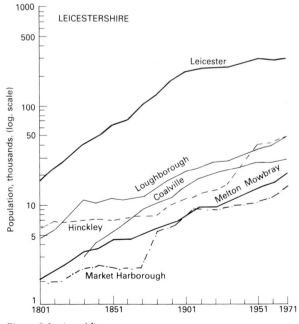

Figure 8.2   (cont'd)

best grounds in England', and the other at Trent Bridge. The latter was established by William Clarke following his marriage to the proprietress of the Trent Bridge Inn, and by the 1880s the county cricket team held almost a monopoly of the championship (Church 1966: 211–12; White 1844: 177). Football was also organized in the county towns. By 1880 the Leicester Football Club took charge of both rugby and association football, but the two clubs moved to different grounds in 1891–92 (Simmons 1974, II: 37). In Nottingham, Notts County was founded in 1862 and Nottingham Forest three years later, while Lincoln City dates from 1884. Also in Nottingham the Trent was a focus of activity including an Aquatic Club, rowing clubs and in 1887 a sailing club, while similar activities took place on the Derwent in Derby. Bicycle sports were established in both Nottingham and Lincoln towards the end of the century (Meller 1971: 67; Hill 1974: 12–13).

Among the services provided by county towns were hospitals. During the 1760s decisions were taken to establish county infirmaries in Lincoln and Leicester, while at Nottingham the general hospital was founded in 1781 on a 2-acre site provided jointly by the Duke of Newcastle and the corporation, and Derby's infirmary opened in 1810 (Heath 1979: 190–3). In most cases the inspiration came from the county gentry, and financial support was usually provided by annual subscription concerts (in the assembly rooms) and sermons. In Lincoln the sermon was preached in the cathedral, and a charitable assembly took place during race week (Hill 1966: 70–1), while assembly-room concerts were held to celebrate the infirmary openings in both Nottingham and Leicester. Finance was always a problem, however, because these hospitals were inevitably found wanting for space as towns increased in size. Lunatic asylums and fever hospitals were also opened to supplement the available health care. Financial help often came from legacies, including the £10,000 which enabled Leicester in 1860 to build an extension increasing the number of beds to 200 (Frizelle and Martin 1972).

Other Towns

Outside the county towns the places which developed important industrial functions were usually those which grew most rapidly. In percentage terms Derby grew much less rapidly than Ilkeston, Alfreton and Heanor, although they all began from a lower base. Across the border in Nottinghamshire the fastest-growing towns were in the textile–coal belt around Mansfield, while in Leicestershire Loughborough grew by nearly 400 per cent in the course of the nineteenth century. Among the most spectacular examples of growth were Coalville in Leicestershire, the iron-making town of Scunthorpe in north

Lincolnshire, and Clay Cross, little more than a small Derbyshire farming community in the 1830s, but a thriving iron-producing and coal-mining community with more than 6,000 inhabitants by 1860. On the other hand, industry was no guarantee of growth. Hinckley, the second town in Leicestershire in 1801, and one of the earliest centres of framework knitting, was overtaken by both Loughborough and Coalville, and grew by just 35 per cent between 1801 and 1881. Power-driven machinery finally rescued the town from prolonged depression during the final decades of the century. In Derbyshire, Cromford, famous as the site of Arkwright's first mill, had a smaller population in 1901 than in 1801, while Belper, also a centre of cotton manufacturing and hosiery at the end of the eighteenth century, declined from being the third largest town in the county in 1801 to ninth a century later, with the demise of the nail-making industry.

While in general terms industry usually had a positive impact on town growth it was by no means dependent on an urban environment. Textile production was originally located in the villages of south Nottinghamshire and north Leicestershire. Indeed, the application of steam power to the hosiery industry in the mid-nineteenth century produced a further devolution, since employers welcomed the possibility of retreating to the countryside to side-step higher wage rates imposed by strong unions in the towns. The effect was to bring growth to some of the villages and small towns. Beeston, just to the west of Nottingham, grew by 185 per cent 1871–1901 as the lace industry decentralized from Nottingham, and most spectacularly of all Long Eaton expanded from a population of less than 1,000 in 1851 to over 13,000 in 1901, making it probably the fastest-growing town in the region during the second half of the nineteenth century. The region's extractive industries inevitably located wherever the resources were to be found, but again this was often in the countryside. Chesterfield was associated with the revival of the Derbyshire iron industry from the opening of the appropriately named Chesterfield canal in 1777, but the ironworks were found predominantly outside the town. As a result, it was still a small market town in the 1830s. In 1835 it was 'said to be thriving and improving in its trade' (PP 1835 (116), xxv, p.1792) but its population topped 7,000 only in 1851. Contemporary descriptions during the eighteenth and nineteenth centuries all emphasized the town's role as a marketing centre, and during the 1830s questions were asked as to why it was not more prosperous given its favourable position for industrial development. It was only after 1840 that rapid industrial development began in the town rather than in the surrounding countryside, partly reflecting the coming of the railway (Bestall and Fowkes 1978: 2, 8, 39–47).

Trade brought prosperity back to the long-declining medieval ports of Boston and Grimsby, but although both grew during this period it was Grimsby which experienced the most spectacular transformation. Between 1789 and 1792 no goods were landed in the town, and when Christopher Clayton died in the latter year the town was left without a merchant of any stature. When the

Hon. John Byng visited in 1791 he found 'a wretched borough, existing only by venality; and with such an alehouse as could not have been slept in' (Andrews 1935, II: 389). Even so, following legislation in 1796 a new dock was completed in 1801, at which point Grimsby was a town of 1,524 people. Trade did pick up a little, aided by the setting up of rope making in 1803 and whaling between 1807 and 1821, and the population topped 4,000 in 1831. This was hardly the revival which had been planned, and overall the new dock was not a success, largely because the developers had failed to realize the importance of easy communications with the hinterland. Considerable criticism was levelled at the absence of 'back carriage' in the form, for example, of a link with the Trent. With little hinterland of its own to call upon Grimsby was unattractive as a port of call. In 1843–44, forty-three foreign ships cleared the port, but only four carried an outward cargo. The town's roperies failed in the 1830s and by 1841 125 houses were standing empty. All this changed in the mid-1840s. In 1844 a group was formed to promote the Great Grimsby and Sheffield Junction Railway Company, and at the same time a new Grimsby Docks Company acquired the assets of the old Haven Company. In 1845 the dock and railway companies merged. Almost immediately it was decided to build a new dock on reclaimed land stretching out into the Humber. Trains began to run in 1848, and the dock was opened in 1852. From 3,700 in 1841 population increased to 8,860 in 1851, and to 63,000 by 1901. Its staple trade became the import of Baltic timber, and the export of coal and other goods from south Yorkshire and agricultural machinery from Lincoln. By 1865 it ranked as the fifth port in the kingdom, and although little industry or manufacturing developed an important fishing industry was built up in the second half of the century (Gillett 1970; Jackson 1971: Sigsworth 1981).

Boston did not plumb the depths experienced by Grimsby but neither did it share in its nineteenth-century growth. Although in 1751 a traveller described Boston as being 'worse than it was ever known to be', it was still the second largest town in Lincolnshire with a population of 3,300. The draining of the Witham fens in the 1760s and subsequent improvements to the river link between Boston, Lincoln and the Trent all proved to be to Boston's advantage. Between the 1760s and the 1780s the Grand Sluice was built to help flush mud from the haven, and to stimulate trade. In 1811 Boston sent more than one-quarter of the total import of oats into London that year, and throughout the first half of the nineteenth century it remained the premier commercial town in Lincolnshire. By 1851 its population had reached 15,000, but fifty years later it was only 16,000. Boston lost out after 1850 to King's Lynn, where new docks were built in the 1860s, and to competition from the railway. A line reached Boston in 1848, and by 1859 it was directly connected to Nottingham. The intention was that Erewash coal should be exported through Boston, but in practice the line proved much more effective in diverting the grain trade away from the coast. Trade slumped after 1848 and the town stagnated. It was not until the 1880s that an attempt was made to break out of this depression, with the building of a dock on the south side of the town, and the deepening of approaches to the Wash in order to permit larger vessels to reach the town, and to replace the lost coastal trade with overseas concerns (Fuller 1954: Lewis and Wright 1973).

Few of these places developed the cultural and service functions of the county towns. Sixteen provincial theatres were built in the smaller towns of Lincolnshire, including two at Boston, and another at Grantham – the latter designed to emphasize the town's role as a staging post (Plumb 1972). A few towns were actually designed for cultural and leisure purposes. Buxton, arguably the region's only real resort in 1750, was developed to compete with aristocratic watering places of the calibre of Bath. In the 1780s the fifth Duke of Devonshire employed John Carr of York, the best-known architect in the north of England, to design and lay out a crescent, at a cost of £120,000. The Hon. John Byng was not impressed. He found Buxton 'a most uncomfortable, dreary place', and he was particularly offended by the grand crescent which he described as a 'huge mausoleum' (Andrews 1935, II: 167, 186). In 1841, however, Buxton was said to have 'a fragrance of aristocracy in the very air', although as the nineteenth century progressed it became predominantly a retreat for the new millionaire capitalist aristocracy (Heape 1948). Other local spas neither aspired to, nor achieved, the pretensions of Buxton. Matlock Bath was described in the 1840s as an 'inferior' watering place, and its main claim to fame in the nineteenth century came from Smedley's hydropathic cures. Day trippers were brought in by the railway. Woodhall Spa in Lincolnshire was discovered by accident during an abortive search for coal. In the 1840s it was reported to be a resort for 'farmers and people belonging to the industrious classes', although it was later turned into a more select resort (Granville 1841; 24, 68, 115). By 1892 its reputation was rising, whereas Ashby de la Zouch – which depended on its waters being transported from the pits at Moira – was one of the many putative spas which failed to achieve fashionable status (Wright 1982: 197–8; Hillier 1983). By this time the trend was towards sea bathing, an interest which owed much to the coming of the railway (see pp. 268–70). In the course of the nineteenth century the railway also helped to turn the market town of Melton Mowbray into a 'metropolis' for fox-hunting. More than half of the town's working population in 1851 was engaged in service industries, and less than two-thirds of household heads had manual occupations (Royle 1979–80).

As service centres the smaller towns were no match for the county towns. Hospitals generally developed later. Loughborough had a general hospital as early as 1819, and by 1845 Stamford had a hospital and six other Lincolnshire towns had dispensaries. It was the 1860s, however, and in the light of Florence Nightingale's work in the Crimean War, before a surge of building took place. Cottage hospitals were provided in several Lincolnshire towns, including one with nine beds in Grimsby (1866), and others with up to six beds in Louth, Boston and Market Rasen (1869–71). Grantham's twenty-eight-bed hospital

Plate 8.1 Buxton, Derbyshire. A sketch of the interior of John Barker's bath, 1712, as it was in 1807.

Buxton developed as a spa in the course of the eighteenth century, and this drawing depicts one of the early improvements made under the patronage of the second Duke of Devonshire. In the opening years of the century Devonshire commissioned John Barker of Rowsley (1668–1727) to reconstruct the baths, and other buildings adjacent to the hall. Barker was a talented minor architect who had worked at Belvoir and Chatsworth, and this is a sketch plan of the stone vault he built over the hot bath. The antiquarian, Dr William Stukeley, wrote that 'the bath room is arched overhead and the whole made handsome convenient and delightful', although this seems to have flattered what was in fact a rather modest development, of which the façade had much in common with country-house stable blocks.

Buxton's importance as a spa grew under the influence of the fifth Duke of Devonshire who hoped to develop it in such a way as to create a Peak District rival to Bath. In the process Barker's developments were overtaken. Even today, however, his baths are marked by three wide, semi-circular windows in the eastern third of the Old Hall Hotel.

---

was built 1874–75, and Spalding's twenty-six-bed hospital in 1881. Other towns to acquire similar facilities before 1914 included Woodhall Spa, Bourne, Spilsby and Gainsborough (Wright 1982: 235). Hinckley, Melton Mowbray and Market Harborough were among Leicestershire towns to open hospitals towards the end of the nineteenth century (Pye 1972: 559–60).

The Market Towns

Despite the growing importance of the larger towns the restrictions on personal mobility ensured that for many people the local market remained the centre of interest. In Lincolnshire during the eighteenth and nineteenth centuries smaller markets tended to decline, but new ones were opened up and others revived. Existing centres added extra market days, and increased the volume of goods exchanged. Lincoln, Gainsborough and Barton-upon-Humber opened fatstock markets, while sheep markets commenced at Louth in 1805 and Boston the following year. These developments reflected an increase in animal marketing for local consumption and for sales into Nottinghamshire and Yorkshire, and towards London (Reynolds 1982). Nottinghamshire, which had more than thirty markets in the medieval period, could boast just ten in 1780, and of these Bingham, Blyth, Ollerton, Southwell and Tuxford were considerably reduced in importance by the nineteenth century (Weir 1986: 49). Tuxford, according to the Hon. John Byng, was 'a mean, dirty place' (Andrews 1935, III: 23). Derbyshire also had fewer; John Farey found seventeen surviving markets in early nineteenth-century Derbyshire (Farey 1811, III: 459). The number of fairs declined slightly between the late eighteenth and late nineteenth centuries (Table 18). These figures hide some turnover in places holding fairs – in Derbyshire, for example, a total of thirty places held fairs at one or other of the two dates – but the most notable trend is the decline of fairs in smaller Lincolnshire settlements.

Table 18 East Midlands fairs

County	1792	1888
Derbyshire	24	24
Leicestershire	15	14
Lincolnshire	52	39
Nottinghamshire	16	19
Rutland	2	1
Total	109	97

(Source: *Royal Commission on Market Rights and Tolls* (PP [*c.* 5550] 1888, liii, 156–200)

The decline of smaller markets and fairs was often brought about by improved communications. Bingham, in Nottinghamshire, gained the right to hold a market in 1314, but by the nineteenth century it was overshadowed by Nottingham and Newark, and White's *Directory* described its market in 1832 as of 'trifling importance'. Southwell failed to develop beyond its function as a market, growing by less than 1,000 people during the nineteenth century, despite the fact that in 1884 its minster became the cathedral church for a new Anglican diocese based on Nottinghamshire. In the eighteenth century Southwell served as the centre of trade in one of Nottinghamshire's most prosperous arable areas, and its handsome red brick houses bear testimony to its prosperity. According to the Hon. John Byng, passing through in 1789, 'Southwell is a well built, clean town, such a one as a quiet distressed family ought to retire to' (Andrews 1935, IV: 140). By the nineteenth century the town found itself too close to Newark (8 miles) and Mansfield (12 miles) both of which were served by good communications and developed over time into industrial centres while retaining their market functions. Southwell served only a limited clientele, and the provision of railway communication in 1871 – on the Mansfield–Newark line – made little difference (Edwards 1966a).

Some of the region's other market towns also failed to make much progress. In Lincolnshire these included Horncastle – 'only famous for its horse fair' according to Byng – and Sleaford. Spalding was 'large, clean, well built', but Tattershall 'a small market town, with a mean market-place' (Andrews 1935, II: 221, 354, 377). Byng also visited Castle Donington, another market town which made little progress in the nineteenth century. In 1789 he found it 'a large, well-built village, with many creditable Houses, in a dry soil, and lofty situation'. He was so well received at the Turk's Head that he returned the following year to find new buildings in the village and 'the comfort of coals' (Andrews 1935, II: 74, 160). Hosiery, lace and basket making aided development, and by 1841 the population had reached 3,508. However, this turned out to be the high point, from which numbers decreased to 2,662 in 1881. Despite being described in 1868 as 'one of the most beautiful of Midland towns of its class', Castle Donington suffered from the migration of textile workers into the larger towns, the failure to secure a railway until the end of the 1860s, and eventually the loss of its marketing functions to the larger settlements of Derby, Leicester and Nottingham, Loughborough and Ashby (Lee 1956).

On the other hand, conditions across the region were by no means uniform. In the Peak District viable market towns were much smaller than in north Nottinghamshire and the Trent valley, while the traditional idea of a market town drawing its clientele from a small radius round about was increasingly divorced from reality. Places like Nottingham, Derby, Chesterfield and Mansfield, as well as some of the smaller centres including Newark and East Retford, Bakewell and Ashbourne, drew their market-day users from far afield. Improved communications ensured that by the end of the nineteenth century a greater proportion of the population using a particular market centre was able to visit the place regularly, and not merely on market days. One result, which is perhaps reflected in the decline of fairs in smaller Lincolnshire villages, was that the more remote markets suffered as their original small population declined or grew only slowly, and their hinterlands lacked regular access to the market. By 1900 they were losing out to the more accessible larger towns (Hill 1972).

The Reform of the Corporations

Town growth was not accomplished without considerable growing pains, particularly in local government. Until towards the end of the nineteenth century unincorporated towns were assumed to be part of the countryside for judicial and administrative purposes, which produced immense problems for settlements like Mansfield, which at the beginning of the nineteenth century was still governed by churchwardens and overseers appointed by the vestry. Legislation was obtained for an improvement commission which began its work in 1823. However, it met behind closed doors, and while its achievements were considerable this secrecy became a matter of great dissatisfaction. Under the 1848 Public Health Act a local board could be created in any locality, and a number of towns petitioned for such boards. In Lincolnshire these included Gainsborough – where the board took over the powers of lighting, watching and improvement – Market Rasen, Cleethorpes and Scunthorpe. However, at Spalding, Lincolnshire's largest unincorporated town in 1851, a private improvement Act was promoted in preference to adopting the terms of the 1848 legislation, and this in itself points to some of the confusion which crept into local government during the middle decades of the century (Wright 1982: 236–7). Elsewhere Ilkeston acquired a local government board in 1864, but some places preferred to go it alone. Mansfield's improvement commission was reformed as a result of private legislation in the 1870s, but that merely served to increase the calls for incorporation, which was finally achieved in 1890 (Williams 1955; Buxton 1932).

Events in Horncastle also point to the problems which occurred in a growing town without an appropriate structure of local government. Population more than doubled between 1801 when it stood at 2,000 and 1841, at which point it had risen to 4,500. It remained under the government of a vestry, with limited powers and resources. To deal with crime, for example, two constables were appointed annually, but while they were adequate to deal with general problems of vagrancy few powers existed to deal with minor criminal acts. In October 1838 sixty-one ratepayers, the town's 'leading inhabitants' resolved to adopt the provisions of the 1833 Lighting and Watching Act and set up a seven-man committee with responsibility for a police force in the town. Despite opposition, which partly reflected the absence of a formal means of taking such decisions within the town, a police force was established, which succeeded during the next thirty years in greatly reducing the level of crime (Davey 1983).

The situation was different for the municipal corporations, which from 1835 had an increasingly formal and structured government. In the eighteenth century several of them were largely moribund, including Louth, Stamford and Grimsby in Lincolnshire. The corporations were never intended to be democratic organs of local government. Rather they were corporate bodies concerned with managing the corporate property, the town's rents and income. They owned and managed the property and charities of a town, and they spent its rents and other traditional incomes. As private bodies whose prime responsibility was to the constituent members of the corporation they were not expected to render accounts, and little control existed over their powers. Naturally they were not averse to a little self-indulgence. To celebrate George III's birthday in 1761 Nottingham corporation feasted on backloin of beef, lamb, chickens, hams, tongues, salmon, lobsters, cheese cakes, tarts and puffs, gooseberry pies, custards, soft cheese and old cheese, ale and punch (Gray 1960: 124). Any public functions for the good of the town were merely coincidental, and the scope for corruption was considerable.

Urban growth presented the corporations with problems for which they were wholly ill-equipped. Nottingham became notorious for disorder, riotous behaviour and other forms of popular discontent. In July 1794 Abigail Gawthern noted 'a mob in the market place; they went to Mr Dennison's cotton mill and set fire to the workshops', and six years later she commented on 'a riot in the market place on account of the high price of provisions' (Henstock 1980: 61, 82). Several historians have gone so far as to argue that unrest in the town sometimes verged on revolution, although the point remains in contention (Thomis 1969: 169; Wells 1984). In 1754 the corporation employed twenty-nine constables – whose duties included clearing small boys from the church-yards during the time of divine service – and four blue-coated watchmen who were armed with staves and a handbell. Such an *ad hoc* system clearly did not meet with the approval of the townspeople and in 1788 a number of people combined to establish a rotary system of night watching (Chambers 1966: 66, 71). This would not seem to have been particularly effective since in 1803 Charles James Fox asked the House of Commons if they knew of any other town of Nottingham's population with so high a crime rate (Thomis 1968: 75). Between 1811 and 1816 the town was seriously affected by machine breaking during the Luddite disturbances, and in June 1815 the town clerk feared that law and order could not be maintained without a substantial body of troops. Nottingham was also connected with the abortive Pentrich rising of 1817 (Thomis 1969: 207, 209; 1974; Stevens 1977: 154) and was at the centre of unrest during the Reform Bill disturbances of 1831 and 1832. Following the House of Lord's rejection of the first bill in October 1831 a mob attacked Colwick Hall, the home of a prominent Tory magistrate John Musters, set fire to the Duke of Newcastle's castle, and burnt down a silk mill in Beeston belonging to another well-known Tory, William Lowe (Thomis 1969: 225–35). These outbreaks of violence were supplemented by regular disturbances on Saturdays, which was not only market day but also the day on which framework knitters brought their work into the town, swelling the resident population according to a traffic census of 1819 by nearly 40 per cent. This was more than the hundred or so constables guarding the town by day and the forty to fifty watchmen taking over at night could deal with. By 1835 there seems to have been little chance of criminals being caught (Henstock 1986; Church 1966: 177).

Municipal corporations were not equipped or able to meet the demands of industrial society, and improvements usually took place outside their authority, often through the medium of Improvement Commissions estab-lished by Act of Parliament. Such a commission was set up in Derby in 1792 (Heath 1979: 187–90), and its powers were extended in 1825 to include responsibility for repair of the footpaths and roads, the construction of sewers, the cleansing and lighting of the street, a third-share in the waterworks, and the power to levy a rate to bring about improvements (Standen 1958: 161). By the early 1830s the reputation of the corporations had reached an all-time low, and the Whig government appointed a Royal Commission to enquire into their activities. The commissioners were encouraged to see conditions in the worst possible light, and the picture they painted was of corruption and nepotism among closed corporations in the disposal of their income and in the neglect of the legitimate rights of the burgesses. Leicester came out worst of all, partly because the town clerk, Thomas Burbidge, refused to comply with what he called 'Star Chamber tyranny', and did not supply the necessary documentation

Plate 8.2 Mansfield Town Hall. The town hall, which stands in the Market Place, was erected in 1836 by W. A. Nicholson of Lincoln in a heavy neo-classical style with a four-column Tuscan porch. It is a good example of a small English town hall, and not dissimilar in style to the Exchange Building in Nottingham which was pulled down in the 1920s to make way for the present Council House.

The building of the new town hall in Mansfield was accompanied by an enlargement and alteration to the market square which was turned from a north–south to an east–west axis, with the hall as its *point-de-vue*.

The date is interesting, a year after the Municipal Corporations Act, which did not affect Mansfield. The town continued to be inadequately governed by a combination of churchwardens, overseers, and an improvement commission. The problems of local government were only finally resolved when the town was incorporated in 1890.

(Patterson 1954: 202). The commissioners, understandably piqued, concluded that

> this corporation has been shown to be a self-elected, close and irresponsible body. The results of this system have been highly unsatisfactory, and altogether incompatible with the legitimate objects of municipal government.
>
> (PP 1835 (116), xxv, p. 1909)

Overall the Royal Commission's findings were a damning indictment of the corporations, even if they exaggerated the reality. Leicester corporation was blatantly corrupt, having involved itself in parliamentary politics to the extent of running up a debt of £10,000 in 1826 (Fraser 1979: 122). By contrast, some

242

corporations, including Nottingham and Boston, evidently ran their town estates with considerable skill, and with a sense of public responsibility (Clark 1984: 38).

Reform was inevitable, and the Municipal Corporations Act of 1835 abolished over 200 corporations and replaced them with 178 municipal boroughs governed by elected councils. A further sixty-two boroughs were incorporated down to 1876, and the Municipal Corporations Act of 1882 applied the system to a further twenty-five boroughs. For the towns affected, the legislation was of considerable significance. Quite apart from the political blood-letting which took place in the ensuing elections – particularly in Leicester where the old Tory-Anglican elite was replaced by Whig, dissenting business families (Freer 1977–78) – the principle of individually conferred charters was superseded by a uniform constitution and a greater dependence on future legislation to extend local authority. The only compulsory function bestowed upon the new councils was in relation to policing, and in the wake of the legislation Derby's force was found to be adequate, Leicester established a police force in 1836, and changes were made to the existing arrangements in Nottingham. Boston and Lincoln appointed new watch committees, and Stamford, Grantham and Louth established police forces from scratch. Grimsby was rather slow off the mark, appointing twelve part-time constables in 1838 but no full-time equivalents until 1846 (Standen 1958: 202–3; Simmons 1974, I: 149–52; Church 1966: 177; Wright 1982: 116).

The lack of real powers granted to the corporations in 1835 proved to be a handicap, but the extension of responsibilities during the course of the nineteenth century served to tighten the grip of central government on the localities. Treasury sanction was required for raising loans or alienating corporate property; the privy council could allow or disallow by-laws; and watch committees had to report quarterly to the Home Office. The acquisition of additional powers largely depended on obtaining local Acts of Parliament, at least until the value of statutory powers had been tested, and Public General Acts were passed in their place. Each extension of authority to deal with a practical problem was a step along the road to municipal welfare, and from the sewers and reservoirs built by the early councils the vision extended beyond the terminology of sanitation to encompass recreational and cultural requirements so that later councils – sometimes aided by sponsorship from wealthy businessmen – built swimming pools and opened libraries. Increasing awareness of the problems of rapid urban expansion brought with it a desire for civic pride. This included exhibitions and festivals, and the erection of new civic buildings. Leicester's new town hall was completed in 1876, and plans were drawn but not executed for a new guild-hall in Nottingham. Eventually these laudable aims were encouraged by central government through the introduction of compulsory elementary education and public health legislation designed to ensure adequate standards of building construction, ventilation and sanitation.

The Corporations and the Drive for Improvement

The rapid urban growth of the later eighteenth and early nineteenth centuries confronted the Victorians with problems of environmental control on a scale not previously encountered. The cholera outbreak of 1832 which killed 50,000 people nationwide first highlighted the sanitation problems which beset the new towns. More than 300 cholera deaths occurred in Nottingham that year, mainly in the lower-lying areas of the town which were badly drained and lacked adequate sanitation. To cope with the crisis emergency boards of health were set up in Nottingham and Lincoln. This enthusiasm could not be sustained, although further attention was paid to urban health in the Poor Law legislation of 1834 which empowered unions to appoint medical officers. In Leicester, both districts of the town appointed an official (at an annual salary of £150). It was the publication in 1842 of Edwin Chadwick's *Report on the Sanitary Conditions of the Working Classes*, and a further series of investigations during the 1840s which highlighted the problems. In 1841 Leicester and Derby had a death rate of 30 and 28 per 1,000 respectively, both well above the national average of 22 per 1,000. Nottingham, described by a local surgeon in 1842 as basically 'a healthy town', contained some of the worst slums in the country (Church 1966: 162–3). Leicester's problems arose from the fact that much of the town was low-lying and difficult to drain. Inundations from the river Soar were frequent, and flooding was often followed by outbreaks of fever. Typhus, measles, scarlet fever, smallpox, and 'summer diarrhoea' – which was particularly rife among the under-fives – frequently occurred in epidemic form in the town (Heydon 1979–80).

It was easy to highlight the problems but to provide solutions presented the fledgling corporations with considerable difficulties. Edwin Chadwick pointed out that Leicester's death rate was one of the highest among the large towns of England, and that life expectancy for all classes was a mere twenty-five years. Extracts from the report were published in the *Leicester Chronicle*, but rifts within the council, the continuing irritation of the borough debt bequeathed as a result of the old council's political machinations during the 1820s, and the lack of any codified powers, ensured that little was done for almost a decade (Fraser 1979: 125–8). A report into the state of large towns in 1844–45 commented on Derby's high death rate, and on the confusion of authority over street cleaning and sewer construction. The problem here was that the new corporation had come into conflict with the improvement commissioners, who were spurred by the report to renewed action and spent £63,000 on drainage, footpaths and roads over the period 1838–48. Even so, their efforts could not keep pace with the growth of problems in the town, which in 1849 had 352 enclosed courts with no drainage, privies or running water (Richardson 1949: 200). Two enquiries in the early 1840s pointed to the problems in Nottingham, and in 1847 a committee was appointed to conduct a broad general survey of the town's public health. It was a necessary move since 900 cases of typhoid were under care at the time.

These various reports pointed to the inadequate powers conveyed by the Municipal Corporations Act, but central government proved incapable of action until the passing of the 1848 Public Health Act. A board of health was established with powers to set up local boards on petition from the ratepayers where the local death rate exceeded 23 per 1,000. The central board was dissolved under the terms of the 1858 Public Health Act. By this time 670 local boards had been set up, and more followed so that by the time the Royal Sanitary Commission reported in 1871 there were over 700 urban sanitary districts nationwide. Following this report the Local Government Board was set up as a separate government department, the first competent department for the control of local government and sanitation. The Public Health Act of 1872 made borough councils, local boards of health and improvement commissions into urban sanitary authorities and for other places the boards of guardians became rural sanitary authorities. The Public Health Act of 1875 consolidated the relevant legislation, and thereafter the number of provisions relating to public health gradually increased. The 1875 legislation made standards of adequate construction, ventilation and sanitation and access enforceable for all new houses. As a result, local authorities had the powers – if they were willing to use them – to control future housing developments.

The reaction to these innovations varied. Leicester established a local board of health in 1849, and obtained a Sewage Act in 1851 which sanctioned a scheme to spend £40,000 replacing the antiquated drains with main sewers. The work, which finally cost £45,000, was completed by 1855. An improved water supply was also introduced during the decade and by 1874 Leicester had a death rate of 23.3 per 1,000, the lowest rate for any major manufacturing town in the country. Even so, deficiencies in the system remained. In 1880 Joseph Gordon was appointed borough surveyor, and he drew up a £300,000 scheme for building new main sewers and preventing floods. This was completed during the 1890s and the death rate fell to 14.6 per 1,000 by the first decade of the twentieth century (Elliott 1979: 41–85; Simmons 1974, II: 10–20; Brown 1970: 71–7).

In 1850 the Derby improvement commissioners finally surrendered their powers to the corporation, following a critical report on their work prepared by a government inspector appointed following the 1848 legislation. The Local Government Act of 1858 was adopted in order to give the council powers relating to the streets, buildings, smoke and slaughter houses. New waterworks, opened in 1851, and extended in 1868 and 1873, were purchased outright by the council in 1880, after which steps were taken to ensure that all new-built houses were provided with a water supply. Improvement Acts of 1879 and 1881 strengthened the council's powers, and together with a new sewage system more or less completed in the 1860s, helped to reduce the death rate to 18.1 by 1885 (Standen 1958: 161–97). In Nottingham lodging houses were brought under the sanitary committee's control in 1851, and the committee ordered the removal of sixty-three houses or sets of dwellings built over privies, the modification or complete destruction of seventy-three sets of privies, and the erection of thirty-seven other sets. Enclosed courts were ordered to be paved and drained, public lavatories to be built, and manure to be properly removed. The council turned itself into a local board of health in 1858, and appointed the country's first full-time borough surveyor – Marriott Ogle Tarbotton. Improvement Acts were obtained in 1874 and 1878, the waterworks company was taken over in 1879, and the general efforts of the corporation reduced the death rate to 18.5 per 1,000 by the end of the century (Church 1966).

By 1900 Derby, Leicester and Nottingham represented one of the most comfortable urban areas of the country, but where corporations were less active the picture was rather less favourable. This was the case in Lincoln. By the 1850s progress had been made in only two areas: burial grounds, resulting from a local scandal when a widow was witness in 1847 to the removal of her ten-years' dead husband's remains to make way for further interments; and water supply, under the terms of private legislation in 1846. As a result of the 1848 Public Health Act a plan was prepared for building main sewers through the town, but turned down on the grounds of cost. The 1858 Public Health Act was not adopted, and so putrid was the river that in 1863 the corporation agreed to allow 50 tons of lime to be thrown into it. A Home Office inspector visited Lincoln in 1870. He reported that the river was a foul, stagnant sewer, and that 'there is not a town in England that offers a more flagrant instance of the dereliction of this duty than the city of Lincoln'. The council continued to prevaricate until, following a High Court order, a contract for a new drainage system was signed in September 1876. As a result, most houses – except those in the Bracebridge area – were connected to the main sewer by 1881, but complaints were raised about the water supply, which was eventually held responsible for an outbreak of typhoid in the town in 1905 after which the council was forced to take improvement measures (Hill 1974).

Housing was a second problem with which the corporations had to deal. Town growth put pressure on the existing housing stock, and in Nottingham, which was restricted to a small site before 1845, large gardens were overbuilt and people were packed into closed courts and back-to-back houses. Most of the property was constructed by speculative builders in search of a quick profit. By contrast with the early mill towns, few entrepreneurs in the larger settlements found it necessary to provide housing. Thomas North built Napoleon Square in Basford, consisting of superior working-class houses with two upstairs and two downstairs rooms, in order to attract workers to what at the time was an undesirable location. Further out, the Hucknall Collieries Company built good-quality houses in 1873 (Horriben 1985: 10–11). For private builders the objective was to construct houses which they could let at a reasonable rent. The problem arose with families who could not afford a rent of 3s. a week. This was the group which migrated to the old enclosed courts and back-to-backs in the lowest-lying parts of the town, the Broad and Narrow Marsh areas. By 1845 there were cases of thirty to forty houses using a single privy and a single standpipe at a time when in terms of overall housing the number of persons per house in the town was 4.1 (Wilson 1970: 71–6, 82–4). Where land was not a problem, as in Leicester, these difficulties were less likely to occur. Although in 1848 the borough medical officer found 347 courts containing 2,000 dwellings with no proper ventilation arrangements, in terms of density Leicester was well housed by contemporary standards (Pritchard 1976: 36–7). A similar situation existed in Lincoln (Hill 1974: 127–30).

In Nottingham, enclosure was seen as the necessary first step to improvement, and encouragingly the Enclosure Act of 1845 contained a building code designed to cover houses constructed on newly enclosed land within the borough limits. Unfortunately, of 2,101 houses built between 1851 and 1856 just 4 per cent were rented at 3s. or less, and because the building regulations were only nominally adhered to some back-to-backs were still erected (Wilson 1970: 93–4, 117, 119). In fact, it was not until the 1860s that corporations began to accept that there was a problem. A local Act of 1868 was designed to improve the standard of new building in Leicester, and some success was achieved in raising the quality of new construction. The local board of health was able to insist on seeing copies of all plans for new domestic and industrial buildings, and over the forty years 1871–1911 around 35,000 houses were constructed in the town under a set of controls which ensured that it became one of the least overcrowded of major English cities (Pritchard 1976: 34–5; Elliott 1979). The Nottingham Improvement Act of 1874 included provisions to enforce building regulations and to build artisans' dwellings, while the Artisan's Dwelling Act of 1875 enabled local authorities to prepare reconstruction schemes for areas of insanitary property. A problem, however, remained. While the town's lace workers were usually well enough off to move into five-roomed houses in the suburbs, with separate sculleries, living accommodation and bedrooms (Chapman 1963), the hosiery workers were always likely – even in the improved conditions for the industry after 1860 – to sink into poverty in the slum areas. A possible solution was for local councils to clear the areas, and to provide housing for the people displaced at a price they could afford. This was an option which was fiercely resisted.

The corporations first began to recognize a responsibility to provide housing during the 1870s. In Nottingham the industrial dwellings committee recommended the erection of dwellings for corporation employees, and as a result Victoria Dwellings (three-storey tenements) were built on Bath Street at a cost of £11,000. Seaton, the medical officer of health, designated Broad Marsh as an unhealthy area, as well as other parts of St Anne's Street, and the area between Long Row and Upper Parliament Street. To rehouse those displaced the council built homes on Ortzen Street and on land near the

Plate 8.3 Nottingham, Victoria Dwellings, Bath Street, an early example of municipal housing. Under the terms of the Artisan's Dwelling Act of 1875, Nottingham Corporation agreed to build two blocks of workmen's dwellings to be leased to council employees. A competition for the design was won by the local architects Bakewell and Bromley, and building work began in the second half of 1875. The name, Victoria Dwellings, was agreed in November 1876, and in January 1877 it was decided that the apartments should be made available to any local working people, not merely council employees. The building was completed in August 1877, and provided 82 separate dwellings.

Victoria Dwellings were not the success for which the corporation had hoped. Initially the rents were set too high, and within a few years of the project being completed the dwellings were reported to be overcrowded. On a number of occasions the police were called to keep order and to quell disturbances. Moreover, they failed to pay their way as model housing was supposed to do in late-nineteenth-century England.

Victoria Dwellings were renovated and remodelled in the 1970s when they were renamed Victoria Park View.

Hunger Hills Road. During the 1880s the council was concerned with its own debts, and refused to take further action, effectively ignoring the 7,000 working-class houses which constituted 13 per cent of the town's housing stock but occupied a mere 7 per cent of the original borough. An occasional lead was taken, as when working-class dwellings were erected on Coppice Road in 1899, but the major rebuilding in the town during the 1890s came as a result of the destruction of 5,000–6,000 houses to make way for the Great Central railway. With an inadequate replacement policy pressure on the existing stock simply increased (Church 1966: 344–5; Wilson 1970: 162–4, 236–8). Nottingham was not alone. The suggestion that the council provide subsidized housing was first put forward in Leicester in 1888, but resistance was fierce. The estates committee put forward a similar scheme in 1897, as a result of which flats were built in Winifred Street, but costs rose, and by the time the flats were let in 1900 the rents were more than the really poor could afford (Elliott 1979: 121–2). A scheme whereby Lincoln corporation would have built fifty houses at New Boultham in the 1890s was defeated on a similar argument that the rents would be too high to support the people most in need (Hill 1974: 238–9). It was not until the twentieth century that councils at last began to recognize a social duty with regard to housing.

Municipal Socialism

If public health preoccupied the corporations in the middle decades of the nineteenth century, by the closing years a significant shift had taken place towards ideas of civic pride and municipal socialism. The urban middle classes were able to use the corporations to suppress some of the more notorious working-class pursuits, usually on the grounds that they interrupted trade. Bull running in Stamford was finally outlawed in 1840 (Malcolmson 1973: 126–35), the annual Shrove Tuesday football match at Derby was moved in 1845, and the Humberstone Gate Fairs were ended in Leicester in 1904 after twenty years of campaigning (Boase 1980). In their place the working classes were offered libraries and museums, parks, municipal baths and organized sport. The Town and County Library in Derby, founded in 1835, was taken over by the corporation in 1869, and reopened two years later in conjunction with a museum. New facilities were provided as the result of generous sponsorship from the town's MP Michael Bass in 1879, and in 1882 he also funded an adjoining art gallery (Standen 1958: 216–20). Nottingham's city library was founded in 1868 following various petitions from ratepayers and school-teachers. By 1900 six branch libraries and a children's library had been established. Museums, and the Castle Art Gallery followed in the 1870s (Church 1966: 352–4). In Leicester the council decided in 1862 to set up a free library on the rates, although no action was taken until 1869–70 when the Mechanics Institute was purchased to provide facilities and the library was part of the deal. Newark corporation bought the castle in the 1880s, and a local maltster financed a library which was built in the grounds. Lincoln set up a library in the 1890s, while smaller boroughs which were beginning to establish them by the first decades of the twentieth century included Boston, Stamford, and Ilkeston (Wright 1982: 245–6).

Alternative facilities were provided in the light of the 1833 Select Committee on Public Walks, which deplored the absence of open spaces in which the middle and lower classes could take exercise. Probably the first public park was the 11-acre Derby arboretum, which was given to the town by Joseph Strutt and opened in 1840 with restricted access to the general public. It later came under corporation control as, during the 1860s, did another recreation ground and a swimming pool in the town provided by Michael Bass (Standen 1958: 213–15). Leicester corporation laid out Victoria Park to the south of the town, although contemporaries claimed that it was a wasteland and not a proper park, Abbey Park to the north, and several smaller recreation grounds (Simmons 1974, II: 38). In Nottingham the castle grounds, the arboretum, the forest, and Queen's Walk in the Meadows, were all laid out for public use. The arboretum (1852), consisted of 17 acres of parkland with botanical specimens and an artificial lake. Although initially it had an admission charge of 6*d*. for adults and 3*d*. for children this was soon abandoned. Swimming baths also opened in the town towards the end of the century (Meller 1971: 63; Church 1966: 210, 377). Boston corporation provided the first People's Park in Lincolnshire, when a 33½-acre site with pleasant walks and a bandstand was opened in 1871; Bishop Wordsworth opened the 13-acre arboretum on the eastern edge of Lincoln in 1872; and in 1883 a People's Park was opened in Grimsby (Wright 1982: 243). By the end of the century councils were also providing sports facilities including football and cricket pitches.

The Relief of Poverty

The municipal corporations had to build up their powers gradually as the nineteenth century progressed, but some of the responsibilities of local government were never entrusted to them, in particular the administration of the poor law and the provision of educational facilities. In both cases separate authorities were empowered to act, and this may have been of most benefit to the smaller towns, which were not hampered by the inconveniences arising from quarter sessions. Poor Law unions were established in the main towns within a couple of years or so of the new legislation, but the workhouse accommodation usually proved to be inadequate. Leicester established a union in 1836, and a 600-place workhouse was erected costing £10,500. It was rebuilt in 1850 at a cost of more than £20,000 to hold 1,000 inmates (Thompson 1980). Each of Derby's five parishes had its own workhouse prior to 1834, but when they were joined in the new union which was formed in 1837 by several outlying townships, among them Litchurch (which the council did not control until the borough extension of 1877), some rationalization was obviously in order. A new workhouse was built at a cost of £8,000, but it had to be replaced by a larger building in the 1870s which cost £40,000 (Lindsay 1980: 96; Standen 1958: 231; Styles 1971–3). The cost was less daunting at Nottingham where two of the existing workhouses were closed on the formation of the union in 1836. However, this simply led to overcrowding, with 600 people in the 500-place building in 1837. Nassau Senior, one of the poor law commissioners, visited Nottingham in 1841 and declared the workhouse to be the worst he had ever seen. After this, work began on a new workhouse designed to accommodate 1,000 paupers, and costing over £18,000. It opened in 1843 (Church 1966: 114–21; White 1853: 68). Nor was it merely the county towns which saw the opening of new workhouses after 1834. The Chesterfield Board of Guardians decided on such a policy almost immediately after their inaugural

---

Plate 8.4   Derby, the Porcelain Factory. The building dates from 1839 when it was constructed at a cost of £8,000 to become the new Derby Poor Law Union Workhouse. Known as the bastille, it fulfilled this role until a new workhouse was opened on the west side of the town in 1878. The building was then converted for porcelain manufacture.

Porcelain was first made in Derby in the mid-eighteenth century, and under Royal patronage it acquired the title Crown Derby in 1773. The first factory, dating from 1756, came to an end in 1848. The following year William Locke, the last manager at the 'Old Derby Factory' opened new premises on King Street, which were eventually acquired by the Royal Crown Derby Porcelain Company Ltd in 1935.

This company had originated in 1876 with a subscribed capital of nearly £68,000, and had acquired the workhouse premises to begin porcelain manufacture. It originally traded under the title 'Derby Crown Porcelain Company'. In 1891 it become the Royal Crown Derby Porcelain Company.

meeting in October 1837, despite the fact that the town had had a workhouse for a hundred years. The new workhouse was to house 300 inmates (Watson 1981).

Workhouses or no workhouses, enforcing the workhouse test proved almost impossible, largely because it was a blunt instrument when dealing with seasonal unemployment. In both Nottingham and Derby the rules were bent to allow for the seasonal problems of the framework knitters. At Basford in 1837 the Poor Law board was overwhelmed with applications for relief from able-bodied men. The chairman requested permission from the Poor Law commissioners to consent to relief in kind. This was eventually conceded because of the plight of the knitters. Five years later in Nottingham the Guardians waived the test and extended outdoor relief, with the result that 4,500 people immediately qualified. When the test was in force individuals went to extraordinary lengths to avoid the workhouse. At Basford between 1840 and 1870 not more than 7 per cent of all inmates were able-bodied (Caplan 1970: 93), and while 1,500 people were reputed to have begged Mayor William Rowarth to provide work in Nottingham in 1839 few families applied to the workhouse for relief (Church 1966: 117–19, 139). On the other hand, the rules may have been tightened up periodically. In 1842 outdoor relief was given to framework knitters in the Mansfield union when the workhouse was only two-thirds full, but four years later when 900 were out of work and 101 applied for relief all were offered the workhouse (Caplan 1984; 30). Poverty had, in practice, been partially shifted off the rates, which was a major aim of the reformers in 1834.

If poverty did not disappear, how did people manage? The better-off provided for themselves through friendly societies. In 1801 about 7 per cent of Nottingham's population belonged to such groups. By 1839 the annual revenue of the town's endowed charities exclusively devoted to the relief of poverty was £2,272, divided between £1,392 given direct to the poor and £880 used for the support of fifteen almshouses. But this was a drop in the ocean when compared with the £20,000 being spent annually by the Guardians during the 1840s. All it could do was to offer limited relief to individual families falling on hard times in a period of general prosperity (Smith 1974). Other forms of support were organized on a random basis. In 1839 work was provided for more than 500 able-bodied Nottingham men on Mapperley Plains; and the Derby Guardians put able-bodied paupers to work for thirteen hours a day breaking Quorn Blue stone into gravel (Styles 1971–3: 61). However, the provision of road work and stone breaking for the under-employed framework knitters merely led to their fingers hardening and this handicapped them on returning to their trade. Two years later a public subscription was raised for the relief of the framework knitters, and 2,000 destitute people who had refused to apply to the workhouse were fed on soup and bread (Church 1966: 117, 119: Caplan 1970: 91). Nor was Nottingham alone. At Lincoln, where the workhouse test was rigidly enforced, soup kitchens were regularly set up during the winter months to feed the poor. A Charity Organization Society was formed in the town during the 1870s to offer relief, but only in kind after a home visit (Hill 1974: 134, 296). Similar organizations were also started in Nottingham during the 1880s (Meller 1971: 21–8).

Education

Prior to Forster's Education Act of 1870 it was normally the case that the larger towns had the best provision for children, with an amalgam of free grammar schools, private academies, writing schools and common day schools. Many of these were run by clergy, and the great majority were private establishments catering for the better-off social groups who could afford to pay for education. The poor were forced to rely on charity schools, of which Nottingham's most successful was the Bluecoat, founded in 1707 after an appeal had produced donations totalling £110 3s. Similar schools were opened in Lincoln, Boston and Leicester during the eighteenth century (Hill 1966: 71–3; Wright 1982: 17). Sunday schools became popular in the wake of the evangelical revival, and by 1803 in Nottingham one-quarter of all children five to fifteen years old, were registered with a Sunday school. This total rose to 60 per cent of the town's children by the 1830s (Chapman 1962). With the founding of the British and Foreign Schools Society and the National Society, provision increased. Nottingham's first BFSS school was opened in 1810, and the first church school the following year. Educational facilities in the town were such that by 1830 there appears to have been no shortage of places, and this happy situation continued down to 1870 at which point 12,000 places were available in the town. The deficiency of 307 places meant that Nottingham had a far better record on educational provision than other major industrial towns (Wardle 1967: 47–50).

Conditions in the other large towns were less favourable. Leicester had provision for only 500 children in 1814, but by 1851 the town had twelve Anglican, four nonconformist and three Roman Catholic schools, providing for 2,965 scholars. Between 1846 and 1870 twenty-three elementary schools were opened, offering 3,000 places, and by 1870 the town had 10,355 places on offer altogether (Rimmington 1978: 46, 61). In Derby by 1871 5,000 children were regularly attending school, but 9,490 were in need of education (Standen 1958: 221–5), while among Lincolnshire towns relatively good coverage seems to have existed in Lincoln, Boston, Gainsborough and Stamford (Hill 1974: 141–2; Wright 1982: 238–9).

From 1870 school boards were set up in many of the region's towns. This was not always achieved without a struggle. In Ilkeston, for example, new National Schools were built 'to prevent a School Board' (Johnson 1970: 118ff.), but this was exceptional, and in any case boards usually turned out to be far more powerful in the towns than they were in rural areas. Derby elected a board in January 1871, which immediately set about remedying the deficiencies in school provision, and by 1882 the town had six board schools. In 1888 41 per cent of the town's children were being educated in board schools (Heath 1978; Standen 1958: 225–7). Leicester's board schools were efficiently run, and consistently earned a high level of grant on the results of examinations. The compulsory leaving age was raised to eleven in 1891, two years ahead of government provision; in 1892 special facilities were introduced for the mentally disabled; and Leicester was also the first place to have separate classrooms (Simon 1968: 170). Among Lincolnshire towns Horncastle already had adequate provision in 1870 (Clarke 1976: 9), but while boards were established at Grimsby (1874) and Boston (1894) Lincoln resisted. In 1870 the county town had a deficiency of 1,000 places, but all attempts to introduce a board failed and in 1902 Lincoln was one of only seven county boroughs in England which had avoided a board. Although the Anglicans opened or enlarged a school nearly every year down to 1907 the deficiency continued to rise, and Lincoln's average attendance was worse than that of any town of equal size in the country (Hill 1974: 273–6). A board was elected in Nottingham in 1870, but its first real test came in 1877 when, with the passing of the Borough Extension Act, it was faced with a deficiency of 4,600 places. As a result, and despite the continued efforts of voluntary schools, the board was for ever struggling to find sufficient places. However, the success of the board can be seen from the fact that by 1903 all Nottingham's children were placed, compulsory attendance was enforced for five to eleven – and often thirteen year olds – and average attendance was 90 per cent (Wardle 1971: 115–16).

Secondary education was less well provided by 1900. Until the nineteenth century few schools offered education beyond the elementary level. In Nottingham these included the Free Grammar School (now the Nottingham Boys' High School), the Bluecoat School and High Pavement (1788), as well as a number of private academies. Until the need for scientific and technical education was highlighted by the Great Exhibition little more was available, but from 1859 classes sponsored by the Department of Science and Art were established across the region, and as interest grew, voluntary schools began to open in the evenings as science classes under the auspices of the Department of Science and Art (Tolley 1982). School boards began to take an interest in secondary education during the 1870s, again looking to forge links with the Department. From 1880 boards began to set up higher-grade schools for older children; the first in Derby was established in 1888, and the introduction of science was aided by the appointment of a science class organizer the following year (Heath 1978: 134). During the 1890s the Nottingham board took charge of scientifically and commercially based courses, and by 1889 two schools had been opened to offer a genuine secondary education. During the 1890s the town's Free Grammar School, which had declined during the century to be little more than a writing school, was revived, and a Girls' High School and a number of higher-grade schools were founded. In 1895 nearly 8,000 students enrolled in six higher-grade schools, known at the time as 'commercial and technical centres' (Wardle 1971: 117–24, 131–7). Leicester was ill-provided with higher-grade schools before the 1890s, although the Chamber of Commerce had sponsored a technical school to teach the techniques of hosiery manufacture, dyeing and boot making to artisans' and manufacturers' sons (Simon 1968: 178–81).

Demand for post-school education was initially met by the establishment of libraries, but as these usually employed the subscription principle they were frequented by the middle classes. In 1816 the banker John Wright was prominent in setting up the Nottingham Subscription Library at Bromley House, which became the cultural centre for town luminaries, while the Leicester Permanent Library (1791) with its annual subscription of 25s. was also exclusive. Efforts to help the working class included Nottingham's Artisan Library (1824), and a number of small working-class libraries founded during the 1830s and 1840s. Mechanics Institutes were the real breakthrough. They were set up in Leicester and Lincoln (1833), Nottingham (1837), Derby (1839), Chesterfield (1840) and later in a number of other places. Most provided lecture programmes and libraries. In Nottingham the library ran to 2,400 volumes by the 1830s (Inkster 1978) and in Lincoln a collection of 12,000 books was assembled by 1899 (Hill 1974: 147, 276). In most places, however, the impetus was lost by the end of the century, with the exception of Nottingham, where membership gradually increased to nearly 3,000 in 1881 (Wardle 1971: 139–40, 177–82). In many places the institutes lost their educational function and became social centres, although occasionally, as in Lincoln, Newark and Mansfield, this function was rescued by the introduction of science and art classes after 1859 (Tolley 1982).

In general terms the Mechanics Institutes were unsuccessful as educational establishments, and only in Leicester and Nottingham were efforts made to rectify the situation. In 1864 David James Vaughan, vicar of St Martins in Leicester, began a working men's reading room and discussion group. Vaughan College, as it later became, began by offering elementary education, but it soon began to include scientific and technical classes, and by 1900 it was catering for 2,225 students (Pye 1972: 516–17). To build on this beginning, in 1880 the Rev. Joseph Wood, president of the Literary and Philosophical Society, urged members to consider the possibility of a university in the town. It was a call repeated periodically throughout the century, but Leicester could never work up quite enough enthusiasm. In 1873–74, for example, it proved difficult to muster 200 people for university extension courses (Rimmington 1978: 194). These classes were the direct result of a request from Nottingham that Cambridge University should organize a series of lectures in the town. As a result, the country's first university extension classes were delivered in the Nottingham–Derby–Leicester area during 1873, and in contrast to Leicester Nottingham raised audiences of 2,000. With this beginning, and an anonymous £10,000 donation (from W. H. Heymann, a wealthy lace manufacturer), the foundation stone was laid in 1877 of the Shakespeare Street building which became known as University College. It was a municipal project, completely controlled by the council, and designed to provide facilities which would be useful to Nottingham and the East Midlands, such as the teaching of technology for the hosiery and lace trades (Tolley 1981; 1983).

Religion

The Church of England never succeeded in coming to terms with industrialization. It was assaulted by the Methodists, the shock troops of the evangelical revival; it failed to provide new accommodation for a growing population; and it had no answer to the spread of apathy, particularly in the industrial towns. Both Nottingham and Derby already had a tradition of dissent, centred primarily on the High Pavement chapel in Nottingham and the Presbyterian meeting-house erected in 1698 in Friar Gate, Derby. A sermon preached at Nottingham's Malt Cross in 1740 introduced Methodism into the town, and John Wesley was a visitor the following year. In 1743 Charles Wesley established a society in the town, and by 1764 Methodists were said to be meeting in several private houses. The first chapel was built in the 1760s, but this was soon too small, and in 1783 John Wesley opened a new one on Hockley, designed to accommodate 800 people. By 1851 the Wesleyans had two congregations in the town, including 2,000 hearers in the Broad Street chapel opened in 1839, while 500 New Connexion Methodists were meeting in a chapel on Parliament Street. The old Hockley chapel, together with another on Canaan Street opened in the Broad Marsh in 1823, accommodated the town's Primitive Methodists, while the Wesleyan Reformers who split from the main movement in 1849 were meeting in the Corn Exchange. Also in Nottingham the various Baptist groups, and the Independents enjoyed a resurgence during the first half of the nineteenth century (Swift 1982: 19–28, 89–96; Weller 1957: 22–7; Morris 1968: 81–5; Rogers 1972: 82). A survey of religious observance in Nottingham carried out by Richard Hopper in 1833 revealed that dissenters outnumbered Anglicans by 12,000 to 5,800 in the congregations, and by 4,530 to 330 in terms of membership. Nottingham was a well-known centre of dissent, but this was still a far cry from the 1720s when dissenters represented only one in four of the town's population (Chapman 1962: 40–1).

While the nonconformists built and rebuilt their chapels the Church of England looked on. Nottingham's three parish churches could accommodate 2,300 people in 1780 – although less than 800 attended Easter communions – but the combined parishes totalled 17,000. New churches were opened in 1809 and 1822, but nothing more was done until the 1840s by which time only 6,200 seats were available in a town of more than 50,000. The 1840s, a decade of church reform nationally, saw the opening of six new churches in the town, few of them memorable – with the exception of St John's Leenside (bombed 1941) by Sir Gilbert Scott – and the gathering together of congregations for a further three (Weller 1957: 9, 11, 47–58). Lincoln had similar problems, with seating – including the cathedral – for just 28 per cent of the population in 1831. The 1851 religious census revealed the full measure of the growth of dissent. Half of Nottingham's churches and chapels had more than three-quarters of their pews occupied on census Sunday for at least one service, but only one-third of attenders were in an Anglican church. The proportion was higher in both Leicester and Lincoln, but it was still only 41 per cent (Elliott 1980–1; Hill 1974: 177–8, 311).

The religious census revealed a third feature, to which again the Anglican establishment had little answer: apathy. Just 39 per cent of the total population attended a church or chapel on census Sunday, and the towns tended to return the lowest figures, even though Leicester with 62 per cent and Nottingham with nearly 58 per cent achieved the highest figures among the major industrial towns (Church 1966: 315). The Anglican response was to build churches. Several were erected in Leicester between 1860 and 1885 including two built entirely at private expense (Thompson 1979: 429–34, 439). A spate of building in the 1850s and 1860s, and again during the 1880s and 1890s, produced twenty-three new or rebuilt churches in Nottingham and its adjoining villages. Among these was St Stephen's, Hyson Green (1897) by Christian, Caroe and Purday, which included various artifacts from a church in the town centre demolished to make way for the new Victoria Station. In Lincoln seven new churches were built during Bishop Wordsworth's episcopate, 1869–85. Dissent too was on the march. During the second half of the nineteenth century nearly a hundred chapels were built or rebuilt on the Nottingham circuits of the four main branches of Methodism (Swift 1982: 157–8). In Lincoln Bishop King complained in his 1886 Visitation returns about 'Dissent, Dissent, Dissent', for which he had good reason since the city itself had seen new chapels for the Wesleyans in 1875 (replaced 1878), the United Methodists and the Primitives, the Congregationalists (1876), the Particular Baptists (1871), the General Baptists (1886), and Methodist and Congregational chapels on the outskirts (Hill 1974: 242–3, 250). A similar picture could also be drawn for Leicester (Thompson 1972, 1979).

For all this effort the spiritual battle was being lost. Various religious surveys in Lincoln between the 1870s and 1903 were interpreted as showing that all denominations were losing ground relative to overall population (Hill

1974: 253–5). Leicester opened a secular hall in the town in 1881 (Elliott 1980–1: 91–4), the same year as a survey of attendance in Nottingham revealed that just 26 per cent of the townspeople went to church on the appointed Sunday. The nonconformists were also losing their vigour. Although the Primitives formed new Nottingham circuits in 1877 and 1883, by the 1890s chapel membership was beginning to wane, a trend which continued into the twentieth century (Morris 1968: 85–6). It was increasingly clear, in fact, that urbanization had taken a heavy toll of church attendance, and that the decline revealed in 1851 simply continued thereafter. By the end of the century this was forcing urban evangelicals to adopt new lines of action. In Nottingham, for example, the emphasis moved to work of a socio-religious nature, such as the Temperance Movement and William Booth's Salvation Army (Meller 1971, Ch. 3).

The physical growth of towns in this period was remarkable, and it reflected their growing significance as local centres. Nottingham and Leicester saw probably the most sustained growth, although the figures are distorted by boundary changes, while the rejuvenation of Grimsby and the rapid growth of a number of smaller towns were out of all proportion to anything which had gone before. Industry (Ch. 9) was one of the major forces behind growth, although the case of Chesterfield shows how the extractive industries could be centred around but not in a town. At the same time industry alone does not explain the remarkable expansion of the county towns, whose dominance was partly a reflection of their roles as cultural and service centres. These facilities were not as fully developed elsewhere, although the smaller towns in turn became local service centres with their workhouses and their cottage hospitals. At the same time, town growth was not guaranteed. Many of the smaller market towns lost out to larger neighbours with the result that by the end of the nineteenth century trade and services were concentrated in a relatively small number of places. The picture was quite different from the network of marketing centres which had emerged in the twelfth and thirteenth centuries. Growth produced enormous problems. The reform of the municipal corporations, and the addition of legislation through the nineteenth century eventually made it possible for the major towns to tackle the sanitation problems confronting them, and although these were by no means solved by 1900, sufficient progress had been made for the corporations to begin the task of turning their towns into attractive centres. Poverty and education were tackled by separate authorities, although in the case of Nottingham's university much of the initiative and sponsorship came from the council in the nineteenth century. Overall, the shift in the balance of population into the towns may have produced considerable public health problems, but it also produced a society which was predominantly orientated around a few large towns. By 1894 in Nottinghamshire 143 and 136 settlements respectively were connected with the markets at Nottingham and Newark, but the other three functioning markets in the county at Mansfield, East Retford and Worksop, were connected to thirty-eight, forty-six and thirty-three settlements each (Cracknell 1984: 77). As the economy grew it was the county and other large towns which generally stood to benefit the most. Small market centres and other settlements which failed to develop or sustain an industrial base, almost always lost out. The significance of these economic forces will become clearer in Chapter 9.

Chapter 9

Communications, Trade and Industry

Improvements in the road and water networks prior to 1750 had been designed for the easier movement of men and goods, but they seem paltry in comparison with the changes which took place between 1750 and 1900. Road, water and – from the later 1830s – rail transport, cut travelling times and costs, and boosted trade. The mining and movement of coal provided the major incentive behind transport improvements, and the coalfield helped to determine the location of industry in the Mansfield–Leicester belt, although by the mid-nineteenth century it was spreading to all parts of the region. Many projects were designed in this period, of which a great number failed or were aborted, but the overall result was first a strengthening of the intra-regional links and with it a growth of local trade; and second, with the coming of the railway an inter-regional network of communications which made possible the expansion of industry on a scale previously inconceivable. At the same time this cut through the economic ties which had been built up within the region, and while it had a profound effect on most branches of the local economy it also broke down the remaining regional constraints.

Transport

In 1750 only the major roads passing through the East Midlands had been turnpiked, and they were not necessarily in prime condition; indeed, in 1766 the route of the Great North Road was altered and a new road made from Markham Moor through Retford to Barnby Moor to replace the old sandy track which had previously been thought sufficient (West 1956?). Over the next two decades 1750–70 the region was caught up in the mania which swept the country, and no fewer than 51 of the 103 turnpike Acts relating directly to East Midlands roads went through Parliament 1753–66. By 1765 all the major

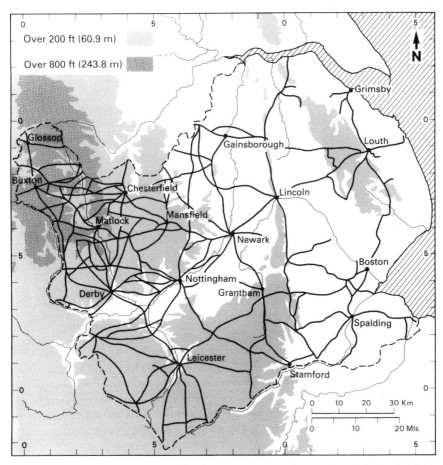

Figure 9.1 Turnpikes in the East Midlands, *c.* 1700–1830 (after Wright 1982; Heath 1982)

roads in Leicestershire, and 159 miles of Nottinghamshire's roads had been turnpiked (Cossons 1934). Nottingham itself was linked by turnpike or firm roads on the Bunter sandstone in all directions, and Leicester established good communications with Uppingham, Narborough, Coventry, Hinckley and Ashby (VCH Leics III 1955: 81). Twenty-eight new turnpike trusts involving Derbyshire roads were brought into existence during the 1750s and 1760s, (Scott 1971–3: 198) and in the space of less than ten years (1756–1764) almost all the cross-country routes through the county were turnpiked. By 1791 no fewer than eight turnpiked roads led into Derby (Heath 1982: 110; Hopkinson 1979: 19). Even Lincolnshire was brought within the network. Thirteen trusts were set up between 1756 and 1765, and by the end of the 1760s most of the roads into Lincoln, Louth and Stamford were turnpiked (Wright 1982: 33–9).

From about 1770 the passion for turnpikes eased, partly because the major roads had been improved, partly because of competition from water transport, and partly because of the difficulty of turning the intentions expressed in the relevant legislation into practice. When the Bakewell–Chesterfield–Worksop Act of 1739 was renewed in 1758 no attempt had been made to turnpike the section between Bakewell and Chesterfield, and despite an outlay of £5,225 only six miles of the Worksop road had been repaired. When work did take place roads were usually straightened and sometimes realigned, but improving the surfaces proved to be much more difficult. Between 1759 and 1780 £4,000 was spent turnpiking the Chesterfield–Mansfield road, but it was still found to be in a wretched condition (Hopkinson 1979: 19). In 1770 Arthur Young wrote of one of the Kesteven roads turnpiked since 1756: 'we were every moment either buried in quagmires of mud or racked to dislocation over pieces of rock which they term mending' (Wright 1982: 35–6). William Marshall described the Trent Bridge–Bunny Hill section of the Nottingham–Loughborough turnpike as one of the worst kept roads in the kingdom when he passed that way in 1790. On the other hand that same year the Hon. John Byng noted that 'the road from Mansfield to Chesterfield, now so broad, beaten and frequented by mail coaches' had required a guide before it was turnpiked (Andrews 1935, II: 151). According to John Farey Derbyshire turnpikes were above average, but this did not prevent the Derby–Wakefield route from being 'reckoned one of the worst roads in England by travellers and coachmen' (Hopkinson 1979: 29). Granite from Charnwood Forest was used in Leicestershire from 1787 in an attempt to improve the quality of road surfaces (VCH Leics III 1955: 81; Palmer 1983: 39), but even with the general improvement in construction techniques by the early nineteenth century White's Nottinghamshire *Directory* for 1832 noted that 'in some of the lanes and bye-roads, the traveller has still to contend with a deep sand, and in some places with an adhesive clay, which latter he finds as fatiguing in wet weather as the former is in dry' (White 1832: 54).

By the time turnpike fever blew itself out attention was turning towards water as the most economical form of transport for the movement of goods, and particularly of coal. In the 1750s the Don navigation scheme improved the waterways of south Yorkshire to the extent that in 1769 the colliery proprietors sold 30,000 tons of coal along the Trent between Gainsborough and Newark. Clearly this posed a threat to the Erewash valley coal owners, and the first successful response was the 1769 scheme to construct a canal running from Chesterfield through Worksop and East Retford to the Trent. The canal was opened in 1777 (Hopkinson 1957: 237–46), and it provided an example which was soon followed at the southern end of the coalfield. The Loughborough navigation, completed in 1778, linked Loughborough along the river Soar and a newly built 1½-mile stretch of canal to the Trent. Coal prices in the town immediately fell by 40 per cent. Linked to this navigation was the Erewash canal, which followed the natural route of the Erewash valley from its junction with the Trent at Sawley, to Langley Mill (Schofield 1981: Hadfield 1966: 39–41). The Loughborough and Erewash connections to the Trent, together with the Grand Trunk which provided a link from 1777 with the Bridgewater canal near Runcorn, opened the river to a variety of new trades, but for part of its course it could still be navigated by vessels of only 10 or 12 tons. Despite considerable opposition legislation of 1783 established the 'Company of Proprietors of the Trent Navigation', with powers to improve and maintain the river from Cavendish Bridge to Gainsborough. Under William Jessop's guidance ten years' work produced a depth of 3 ft or more along 65 of the 70 miles placed in the company's care (Wood 1950).

The early 1790s were the years of canal 'mania' in England, between 1792 and 1795 fifty-one canal acts passed through Parliament, and the East Midlands was a leader of fashion because of the need to move its landlocked coal and iron. Between 1794 and 1797 five canals were opened in the Nottingham–Derby area. The Cromford canal was a 14½-mile stretch linking Cromford and Pinxton to the Erewash canal (Schofield 1981); the Nutbrook canal was an independent branch of the Erewash canal built to serve the collieries at West Hallam and Shipley (Stevenson 1970); the Derby canal was designed to supersede the old Derwent navigation; the Nottingham canal – first proposed by the Trent Navigation Company because of problems achieving a suitable draught of water around the town – linked the Trent to the Cromford canal at Langley Mill and provided a waterway to Beeston and to Trent Bridge avoiding the more treacherous stretches of the river; and the Grantham canal linked Nottingham along a 33-mile cut to Grantham in Lincolnshire (Wood 1950: Wright 1982: 46–7). South of the Trent the Leicester navigation extended the Loughborough navigation to the county town, and its sister project, the Charnwood Forest canal, linked Leicester to the south Derbyshire–Leicestershire coalfield. Legislation was also obtained for the Wreak and Eye navigation, for a canal to link this with Oakham, for a canal between Leicester and Market Harborough (which eventually became the Leicestershire and Northamptonshire Union canal), and for the Ashby canal, which provided a link towards Coventry and the west. Improved waterways also permitted Erewash valley coal to penetrate the Lincolnshire market. The river Witham was improved during the 1760s, and Lincolnshire trade was boosted by the opening in 1794 of the Slea navigation to link the river to Sleaford, and in 1802 by the Horncastle navigation which did the same for Horncastle. By 1830 most of Lincolnshire's market towns were served by navigable waterways (Acton 1980).

For every canal constructed there were any number of putative proposals which made no progress, and the level of success enjoyed by the schemes which were carried into practice also varied. Projects abounded; in Lincolnshire, for example, proposals were advanced for canals affecting Market Rasen, Alford, Stamford, Wragby and Holbeach, and in 1833 a proposed route would have linked Grantham and Sleaford in order to provide a direct waterway from the

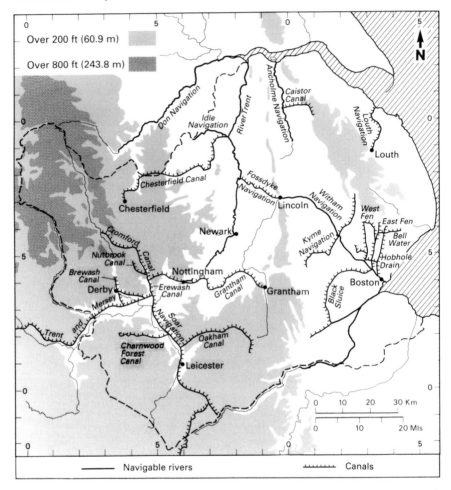

Figure 9.2 The principal waterways in the East Midlands, *c.* 1830 (after Wright 1982; Aldcroft and Freeman 1983)

Erewash valley to Boston (Acton 1982; Wright 1982: 50–1). Most ambitious of all was the Grand Commercial canal, a project designed at an estimated cost of £366,000 to provide a waterway through Derbyshire into south Yorkshire. Fortunately for the projectors it was still on the drawing-board when the railway intervened (Hopkinson 1957). Among those canals which were completed some had a relatively short life. The Charnwood Forest canal was designed to allow coal owners on the Leicestershire coalfield to supply the Leicester market (Griffin 1977–78). The canal soon fell into disuse, but since this meant that most of Leicestershire's coal came from the Erewash valley, the Leicester Navigation Company enjoyed considerable prosperity and paid dividends of 8 or 9 per cent down to the 1820s (VCH Leics III 1955: 97–101).

Water transport was particularly important for the coal industry, and where collieries were not immediately adjacent to a river or canal tram-roads were constructed as feeders. Sixteen such links were made into the Cromford canal, and between 1813 and 1815 a tram-road was built to supply Belvoir Castle (which had the largest private brewery in the country) with coal carried along the Grantham canal. From tram-roads it was one short step to railways, a transport revolution which swept the country leaving road and water improvements as casualties in its wake. In terms of routes, as with roads so with railways. With one exception the first routes were constructed to link the East Midlands north into Yorkshire and south towards London. They were followed by connections between the major towns, by lines linking the lesser and newer centres of population, and finally by infillers which criss-crossed the region during the 1870s and 1880s.

The first railway in the East Midlands was the Leicester–Swannington line, laid out in 1832 ostensibly to fill the gap left by the failed Charnwood Forest canal by allowing the Leicestershire coal owners to sell in the county town and thereby to make it profitable for them to reopen some of their larger collieries (Griffin 1977–78; Hopkinson 1959). The Erewash valley coal owners were not slow to recognize this threat to their monopoly, and at a meeting in the Sun Inn, Eastwood, on 16 August 1832, they agreed to fund the extension of the tram-road linking Mansfield with Pinxton, south across the Trent to Leicester. By the time legislation was obtained in 1836 this particular project had been overtaken. By then the Midland Counties Railway Company had been formed with the intention of opening routes between Nottingham, Derby and Leicester. The first section of the new railway linked Nottingham and Derby, and it was opened in 1839 with, according to the *Derby Mercury*, great ceremony, large crowds, and much celebration. The journey took just forty-four minutes (*Derby Mercury*, 12 June 1839). The following year a further link connected Derby to Leicester and onwards via Rugby to London. By this time the Erewash valley route had been rejected, partly because of opposition from the North Midland Railway Company, which obtained legislation in 1836 to build a line between Derby and Leeds through Chesterfield and Rotherham. This line, built by the entrepreneur George Stephenson, was opened in 1840, a year after Derby had also been linked by rail to Birmingham and London. Derby became the headquarters of the three companies, which amalgamated in 1844 as the Midland Counties Railway, under the chairmanship of the railway king George Hudson (Heath and Christian 1985: 32–3).

By the mid-1840s the Erewash valley coalfield was linked south through Leicestershire – where its coal was again competitive – towards London, and west across the Midlands. Although Derby was the best served of the county towns, the significance of the railway was such that for the whole area it made possible the widening of the market for manufactured goods and consequently

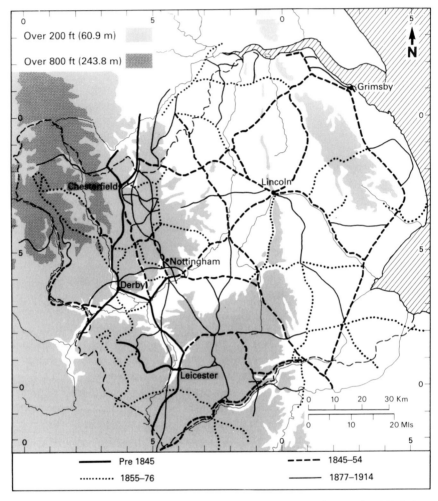

Figure 9.3 Railways in the East Midlands in the nineteenth century (after Wright 1982; Leleux 1984)

the mechanization of the hosiery and footwear industries became economic. For the coal industry it was possible to exploit some of the richest seams which had previously been landlocked, hence the opening of the Clay Cross colliery and the initial exploitation of the western part of the concealed Nottinghamshire coalfield (Hopkinson 1959). At the same time the Midland Counties Railway was successful in opposing schemes to connect London to the north through Lincolnshire, so that by 1840 the county was surrounded by railways but none came closer than Nottingham or Hull; indeed, it was another six years before the county enjoyed its first line, a 33-mile route between Lincoln and Stamford. By 1850, however, the Nottingham–Grantham line, the Nottingham–Lincoln line through Newark, and the Sheffield and Lincolnshire Junction line connecting Sheffield to Gainsborough through Worksop, East Retford and Lincoln, brought the county into the east midlands network (Hopkinson 1969; Wright 1982: 16–22). Once the major network had been completed it only remained to fill the gaps. The 1850s and 1860s saw west Leicestershire drawn into the network as well as the building of a series of lines to link the smaller Lincolnshire towns. Among the latter were the lines from Stamford to Essendine and from Horncastle to the loop at Kirkstead. However, some areas, notably west Derbyshire, east Leicestershire and the Lincolnshire coast, had to wait until the final quarter of the century for a regular service (VCH Leics III 1955: 120–4).

The Movement of People

The network of communications which developed between 1750 and 1900 affected the movement of both people and goods. With improved roads people were able to move about more quickly and more frequently. In 1757 the journey from Derby to London took three days by coach, but this had been reduced to one day by 1764 (Heath 1982: 112). A regular coach service from Leicestershire to London was established in 1753, and the county's first stage-coach followed six years later. By 1764 two coaches a day were leaving for London, and the earliest mail coaches were introduced in 1785 (Pye 1972: 314–15). This made an immediate difference to business; it was reported from Hinckley in 1789 that before the changes

> the letters only arrived from Coventry three times a week; the same from Leicester, which occasioned a very great delay and detriment to business. The mail now accommodates the market towns of Lutterworth, Hinckley, Atherstone and Tamworth which had no regular post before.
>
> (Gomme 1896: 26)

Competition was fierce. White's 1832 Nottinghamshire *Directory* listed thirty-four regular services from four different inns in the county town; coaching towns such as Market Harborough, Stamford, Grantham and Newark flourished. In 1830, the peak year for the coaching trade, forty mail and thirty stage-coaches passed through Stamford every day (Wright 1982: 56). Long-distance road services could not compete with the railway but

throughout the nineteenth century village carriers retained an important position carrying local people to market and acting as a shopping 'agent' for those
unwilling or unable to travel. Between 1861 and 1891 the number of carters
and carriers in Lincolnshire increased from 439 to 1,153, while in the 1880s at
least 220 of Leicestershire's 350 villages were served by a carrier travelling
direct to the county town, and many more were linked through subsidiary
centres (Wright 1982: 202; Odell 1957; Everitt 1973). Between 1853 and
1894 the number of Nottinghamshire villages linked by carrier to the county
town increased from 81 to 113, and the total number of connections to the
county's five market towns rose from 190 to 309 (Cracknell 1984).

It was the railway which opened up new vistas in the movement of
people. In July 1840 the Nottingham Mechanics Institute hired a special train
to take its members to Leicester. The visit was returned a week later, and the
following month the Midland Counties Railway started running excursions
between Nottingham and Leicester. Even more portentiously, in 1841 Mr
Thomas Cook, a wood-turner and temperance preacher from Melbourne in
Derbyshire, privately organized a return trip from Leicester to Loughborough
at the cost of one shilling (VCH Leics III 1955: 117). The excursion had been
born. The annual festival held at Derby arboretum attracted 16,000 people in
1847, many of them travelling by train from Nottingham, Birmingham, Leicester and Sheffield; and for the opening of the People's Park in Grimsby in 1883
excursions ran from Boston, Sheffield, Bradford and Doncaster (Metcalf
1984). When Nottingham shop assistants were granted a half-day holiday in
1883 a Thursday Half-Day Holiday Association was immediately formed to
organize excursions (Meller 1971; 63). The holiday also became possible, even
if for many people this meant staying with relations rather than visiting a
resort; Levi Barley was brought up in Gainsborough at the end of the
nineteenth century, and spent holidays with his uncles at Peterborough and
Mexborough. His most distant holiday was in 1905 when he stayed with his
eldest brother in Kent (*ex info.* M. W. Barley).

Above all it was the spas and resorts which benefited from the movement
of people by train. Matlock Bath was crowded on bank holidays in the
nineteenth century with visitors pouring in from half a dozen counties (Heath
1975: 121–3). These were also the occasions on which visits to the coast
became possible. In 1848 the Manchester and Sheffield line reached Grimsby,
and although it was a 2-mile walk to the tiny resort of Cleethorpes day
excursions began. The Lincolnshire resorts had enjoyed little business before
the 1840s. The Hon. John Byng described Cleethorpes as 'a bathing place of a
better complexion than the 2 others we have seen upon this coast', but it was
still 'a place to be avoided by tourists' (Andrews 1935, II: 372, 387). In 1829
the accommodation was said to have been much improved in recent years, 'and
the salubrity of the air . . . will always render it a desirable summer retreat for
the valetudinarian or the invalid' (Gomme 1896: 117). The railway changed all
this. In 1850, two years after the line reached Grimsby, cheap trains were

running from Nottingham to Grimsby (Sigsworth 1980: 181), and despite considerable opposition a single line was finally built from Grimsby docks to Cleethorpes in 1863. The line was doubled in 1874 as a result of the success of the town in attracting day-trippers, and the town itself was developed into a sizeable resort.

Further south Skegness and Mablethorpe were only just recognizable as resorts in the eighteenth century; indeed, the Hon. John Byng described Skegness in 1791 as a 'vile, shabby bathing place'. Alfred Tennyson was a regular visitor to Mablethorpe between 1813 and 1843, while in 1866 Skegness was still 'a retired watering place . . . free from bustle'. Seven years later the railway was brought the 5 miles from Wainfleet and Skegness was transformed. For the August bank holiday gala of 1874 10,000 trippers arrived in the town, and eight years later 20,000 visitors came for the same event. The Earl of Scarbrough used his position as landlord to set about planning Skegness as a new

---

Plate 9.1 Skegness, the ninth Earl of Scarbrough's development plan for the resort, 1873. The plan, drawn in the same year as the railway reached the town, shows the gridiron plan Scarbrough laid down for residential development at Skegness.

    The Skegness project was not the success Scarbrough anticipated. Although 787 houses had been built by 1878, only the southern half of the scheme was ever put into effect. Population grew from 349 people in 1871 to 1,332 a decade later, but it took until 1921 to reach 5,000. Many of the newcomers were people with building trade skills, and people connected with the holiday trades (Hewson 1986).

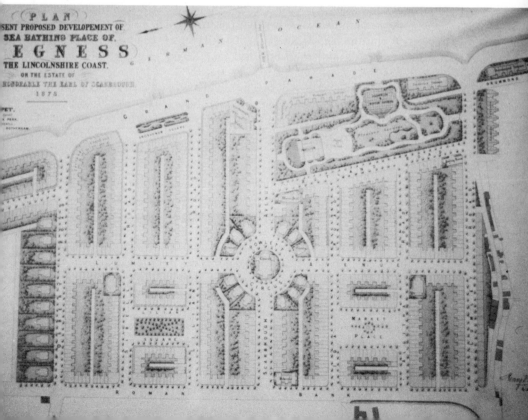

town, with pleasure grounds, a pier and a cricket ground. A gridiron plan shows that he planned a town of 787 houses, and although this proved over-ambitious he himself laid out more than £5,000 on roads, £2,000 on a cattle market, and £2,000 on the town's water supply. When Lizzie Lamb, a farmer's daughter from Wilford near Nottingham, visited the town in the 1890s, she walked on the sands stopping to watch a ventriloquist perform before taking a ride on the switchback, patronizing the spiral railway, and strolling on the pier (*The Guardian*, 21 June 1986). However, resorts depended on business elsewhere, and this is nowhere clearer than in the relationship between Skegness and Nottingham. During the 1882 season 230,000 visitors passed through Skegness, but three years later numbers were down to 118,000 as a consequence of depression in Nottingham. Such figures are a vivid reminder of how the town's fortunes were inextricably linked with industrial conditions 80 miles away (Gurnham 1972; Aspinall 1976; Pearson 1968; Robinson 1981).

The Movement of Goods

The initial movement of people was later matched by the movement of goods. Improvements in transport were usually seen in terms of their trading returns: as one Lincolnshire land agent explained in 1766 when suggesting support for a turnpike from Wainfleet to Boston.

> Sheep may always be sent to Smithfield market which sometimes are greatly impeded by bad roads in the Spring . . . That wool may at all time be sent either to southern or northern markets for that article which can now only be effected in the summer.
>
> (Aldcroft and Freeman 1983: 57–8)

Coal was of particular importance. Both the coal and lead industries were encouraged to use turnpike roads by reduced tolls (Cossons 1934: 23), and the proprietors of the Chesterfield canal deliberately set out to enable Derbyshire coal to undercut Yorkshire coal in the Trent valley. The price at East Retford fell from 15s. 6d. to 10s. 6d. a ton when the canal opened (Hopkinson 1957). If the facilities came about because of coal this did not limit their uses. In 1755 large quantities of corn were sent from Lincolnshire along the Foss Dyke, the Trent and the Derwent, to relieve the grain shortage in Derbyshire, and the traffic in agricultural produce increased with the provision of facilities. By 1804 Lincolnshire corn was being sold via the waterways in Lancashire, and the serviceable link which existed with the Derby–Leicester–Nottingham area enabled the county to look westwards for markets when in the past coastal sales through Boston might have been preferred. In 1824 James Dixon of Caistor had factors in Wakefield and Leeds with whom he exchanged coal along the Ancholme and the Aire and Calder navigations. By that date Lindsey farmers had weekly information on market prices at Wakefield and Leeds, Hull and Nottingham. As a result of these developments Lincoln was rejuvenated and Horncastle was able to build a new corn market and butchery as well as to expand its internationally known horse fair (Wright 1982: 60).

At the centre of this network of waterborne trade was the river Trent. In 1770 alone lead, copper, iron, coal, cheese, salt, beer and pottery passed downstream, while up river came Norwegian timber, Swedish iron, hemp, flax, groceries and various London goods. From the 1790s the Butterley Company was supplying London waterworks companies with piping; in 1815 it shipped the new Vauxhall Bridge through Gainsborough in twenty-seven vessels, and during the 1820s cast-iron bridges, water and gas pipes, steam engines and sugar mills from the company all passed down the river. Even so, 60 per cent of the company's customers between 1790 and 1830 were from Nottinghamshire and Derbyshire, while London accounted for just 13 per cent (Riden 1973: 42). Coal sales were considerable. In the early 1770s the principal article of trade to Lincoln was coal carried along the Trent and Foss Dyke (Quincey 1775: 41); in 1794 300 vessels were said to have loaded or delivered at Gainsborough; and in 1808 270,000 tons were shipped from Derbyshire. In 1816 it was calculated that of 5½ million tons of coal reaching the east coast by inland navigation annually, Derbyshire supplied 942,218 and Nottinghamshire 494,665 tons. But waterborne carriage was not sufficient to break into the lucrative London market; between 1821 and 1828 only 5 per cent of Erewash coal went to the capital. Possibly the 1830s and 1840s were the heyday of the river. It was estimated in 1834 that 30,000 tons of coal, lime and stone were brought into Gainsborough annually, and a further 50,000 tons passed along the river. During the course of the year 158,000 tons of goods were transhipped to London, and two years later 4,000 tons of coal were passing through Gainsborough weekly. In the heady atmosphere induced by the prosperity this brought to the town it was made a port in 1841, just at the point where it began to decline. It lasted in this capacity until 1881 (Beckwith 1967a).

These impressive statistics pale into insignificance when the impact of the railway is considered. Water transport, which had cut costs so effectively in the past, now appeared to be expensive. The Butterley Company calculated in 1843 that whereas selling a ton of coal by water in Derby, Leicester or Nottingham cost between 2*s*. 10*d*. and 4*s*. 6*d*., by rail it fell to between 1*s*. 6*d*. and 2*s*. 10*d*. (Chapman 1981: 40). Even more important to the producers was the impact on sales to London. The price barrier was at last broken and it became possible during the 1850s for coal from the East Midlands and south Yorkshire to compete on equal terms with Northumberland and Durham, although aggressive rate fixing enabled Derbyshire coal sales in the capital to double during a period when sales from south Yorkshire fell. With the opening of the St Pancras terminus in 1868 the Midland Railway Company was able to ignore agreements with the GNR on carriage rates in order to dominate coal supplies to London and the south-east, and in the process to facilitate the rapid expansion of coal production in the East Midlands (Church 1986: 42). The Clay Cross Company's London sales rose from 45,000 tons in 1850 to nearly 400,000 tons in 1870 with the extension north of the Erewash valley line, and Midland Railway sales to the capital from the principal coal producers in Derbyshire reached 1,069,000 tons in 1870 and 1,763,000 tons in 1890 (Chapman 1981: 66, 82).

London cheesemongers controlled warehouses on the Trent at Burton, Willington and Shardlow. By 1789 they were using the river to import 2,000 tons annually into the capital, a figure which rose to 5,000 tons annually by 1809 partly because of army requirements during the Napoleonic wars. With the coming of the railway the figure reached 8,000 tons in 1846, and 10,000 tons by 1857, at which point cheese was being sent to all parts of the kingdom. During the 1870s demand was so great that factory production commenced, and local dairy farmers were able to move from their dependence on cheese and butter manufacture to producing liquid milk for distant markets. The sale of fresh milk to London was facilitated by the extension of the Ashbourne–Uttoxeter line to Buxton in the 1890s (Henstock 1969; Heath 1982: 128). Lincolnshire farmers also benefited. By the 1840s large numbers of pigs and cattle were carried into Lancashire on the Manchester–Sheffield line, but more significantly the county became the biggest wheat producer in the kingdom. By 1865 it had a surplus of 5,725,000 bushels a year, much of which went to London by rail. So important was the connection that a number of farms were named after London districts such as Pimlico and Stepney (Beastall 1978).

The railway moved people and goods on a scale never before considered possible, but it also left casualties in its wake. Long-distance road carriage rapidly disappeared. Whereas thirty-four regular carriers left Nottingham in 1832 only the Royal Mail survived in 1853. The *Lincoln Gazette* carried an obituary in 1841 for 'the London and Leeds Mail-Coach, in the 5th year of its age. . . . The immediate cause of its dissolution is the *spread of Railways*'. The waterways were similarly affected. Some Lincolnshire waterways lost all their traffic within twenty or thirty years. The minute book of the Trent and Mersey Canal Company recorded in 1874 how

> the canal has been unfavourably affected by the declining trade in potters' raw materials and earthenware, and also because traffic is more and more being transferred from the water to the railway.

Takings on the Grantham canal reached a maximum of £13,079 in 1841, but fell to £242 in 1905. While there is little doubt that short-distance traffic increased with the railway, thus actually pushing up the income of a number of turnpike trusts, the longer-term impact was detrimental to both roads and canals (Wright 1982: 185–6; Rogers 1970: 77).

Nor was it merely the transport facilities which suffered, since several towns were forced to adjust to a change of circumstances. A year after Gainsborough lost its port status in 1881 the town was described as having been 'among those river ports which have been much injured by the railways' (Beckwith 1967a: 11). Newark was a flourishing coaching town and river port prior to 1830. Passing through in 1789 the Hon. John Byng noted that it was a 'clean, well-built town, and newly paved . . . The market-place is of much good building, and beauty' (Andrews 1935, IV: 140). Seventy-seven carriers operated in a 10–15 mile radius of the town, and seven operated regular long-distance services. In 1832 thirty coaches called at the town each day. Newark had three wharfinger yards, and from 1772 when the course of the river Trent

---

Plate 9.2   Melton Mowbray, Leicestershire. A Stilton cheese fair. The famous cheese was originally made in the dairy farms of the surrounding district. Tradition has it that a Mrs Elizabeth Orton of Little Dalby learned how to make Stilton cheeses when she held the position of housekeeper to the Ashby family at Quenby, where it was being made in the late seventeenth century. From about 1730 she is reputed to have begun making the cheese in quantity, largely to supply the Bell Inn at Stilton, hence the name.

The coming of the railway provided a considerable boost to Melton Mowbray, which became famous during the nineteenth century as a centre for the making of Stilton cheese and pork pies. By 1850 1,500 tons of Stilton were being sent out of the county annually. Cheese making was a considerable asset during the agricultural depression of the late nineteenth century, when local smallholders found it a particularly profitable sideline.

Originally it took eighteen months for a Stilton to mature, but modern techniques have considerably shortened this period. Seventeen gallons of milk are required to make a 14 lb cheese.

was altered, all water transport had to pass through the town. Prosperity was reflected in the growth of population, up 18.2 per cent in the 1820s. After 1830 the position changed. Railways destroyed the long-distance coal and waggon traffic, as well as reducing the carriage of coal and grain on the river, although the picture was not entirely gloomy since the malting capacity of the town increased. Newark remained a significant marketing centre, but whereas population increased by 42 per cent between 1801–31, it rose by only a further 57 per cent down to 1901 (Cooper 1970, 1971).

Further south Grantham offset the loss of coaching traffic through the manufacture of agricultural implements during the nineteenth century, while Stamford's growth was artificially constricted by the Marquesses of Exeter (Elliott 1969). However, it was not merely towns on the Great North Road that ran into difficulties. Market Harborough was an important centre on the Leicester–Northampton road, and the Leicester–Market Harborough–Northampton canal, both of which gave it links towards London. It became a distribution centre for the 'export' of Leicestershire coal, and the 'import' of grain, which was required in greater quantities as the county was put down to grass. However, in 1840 the Rugby–Leicester railway line cut out the coaching business. A bank failed in 1843, and other businesses struggled. Between 1831 and 1871 the town hardly developed at all (Davies 1964). On the other hand Derby's position on the rail network was reflected in its transformation from a textile to an engineering centre, and a 72 per cent increase in population between 1831 and 1851. Nottingham, away from the main line, and cursed by enclosure problems, grew by a mere 5.7 per cent over the same period.

Industry

Around the turn of the eighteenth century the county reports prepared for the Board of Agriculture, although primarily concerned with farming, provide an interesting contemporary view of local industry. Derbyshire was said in 1794 to abound with mines and manufactures sometimes at the expense of agriculture, while in a later report John Farey enumerated a total of 163 separate trades in the county. If some of these were 'of small importance', he considered the whole to present 'a most flattering picture of the varied and great manufacturing industry of the county' (Brown 1794: 38–9; Farey 1811, III: 476–97). Robert Lowe, reporting on Nottinghamshire in 1798, drew specific attention to hosiery manufacture, cotton mills, a mill for combing wool and another for spinning worsted, silk and lace making, and work with marble, stone, white lead, iron, pottery and even sail cloth (Lowe 1798: 138–9). The contrast with Lincolnshire was striking. Lincoln was described in the 1770s as having 'an air of ancient greatness . . . but little trade in proportion to the size of the place, and no other manufacture than a small one of camblets' (Quincey 1775: 39–41); and this sense of glory passed was reflected in Thomas Stone's report on the county to the Board of Agriculture in 1794. In his view opportunities for diversification had been wasted, and only a few minor textile interests had survived. Nor could Arthur Young, who prepared a later report, improve on this verdict; he dismissed Lincolnshire's manufacturing interests in little more than one page out of 500 (Stone 1794: 95–6; Young 1813: 455–7).

These were the views of a number of individuals primarily interested in the state of agriculture, but the picture they painted was not unfair. In the second half of the eighteenth century the introduction of mechanization and power into a number of industries was predominantly associated with the textile districts of the Derby–Leicester–Nottingham area. Although as a result these areas can boast some sort of primacy in the introduction of factory textile production the movement was not sustained (Chapman 1967). Power was employed in the hosiery industry only from the mid-nineteenth century. Even so, the area made more rapid progress than Lincolnshire. The rise of the cotton industry put the county's wool producers at a disadvantage, and despite the efforts they made to promote the wearing and manufacturing of woollen garments, it can be argued that the absence of cheap fuel condemned their interests to a slow death once steam power and mechanization were applied to the West Riding wool textile industry. In addition, local farmers resisted the establishment of industry for fear that it would reduce the labour supply. Consequently textile manufacture failed in the county, and the industrial void did not begin to be filled until engineering was established in the 1840s (Perkins 1977a: 26–7).

Taken together, the abortive nature of early factory employment, and the failure of textile production in Lincolnshire, suggest that the East Midlands did not enjoy the full benefits of the Industrial Revolution. Perhaps a more significant period for progress was the third quarter of the nineteenth century. In the wake of the railway, the hosiery and lace industries introduced powered machinery, the coal industry adopted the full range of technological innovation and moved on to the concealed Nottinghamshire coalfield, the iron industry reached a peak in output, and the potential loss of male jobs with the spread of power in the textile industries was offset by industrial diversification including footwear manufacture in the Leicester area and engineering throughout the region. This latter development was crucial. It incorporated the engineering requirements of the railway, the machinery required in the newly powered hosiery and footwear industries, precision engineering including rising concerns such as bicycle making, and in Lincolnshire the manufacture of agricultural machinery.

Coal

The importance of the railway for industrial production in the region is nowhere clearer than in the coal and iron industries. Since coal was found near the surface in both the Erewash Valley and the Leicestershire–south Derbyshire fields the industry remained small-scale and technologically backward. John Farey listed eighty-six active mines in the Erewash valley and a further thirteen in Leicestershire around 1806. This compared with twenty-eight pits on the smaller coalfield in 1780. Shafts were still of a moderate depth, and more than a hundred lay abandoned, reflecting the technique of sinking on a new site rather than mining to greater depths. Glover's *Directory* for 1829 lists 108 active mines, 92 of them on the Erewash and 9 on the Leicestershire field. Such a scatter did not prevent a considerable rise in output. Recent estimates suggest that the coalfields produced about 140,000 tons of coal in 1750, 384,000 in 1799 and 1.6 million tons in 1816. This rapid rise, which took east midlands output from less than 3 per cent to more than 6 per cent of national production, almost certainly reflected the importance of the canals, but it was by no means uniform since much of the Leicestershire and south Derbyshire coalfield experienced mixed fortunes between 1760 and 1790; indeed, in the years down to 1830 mining in Leicestershire was in some danger of dying out altogether (Owen 1984: 135, 141, 160, 187). Moreover, since the industry was largely dependent on expanding its sales within the region the growth of output 1816–30 was probably not considerable and output fell below 6 per cent of national output by 1830 (Pollard 1980: 216; Flinn 1984: 26).

The railway changed the locus of the industry and raised output beyond all expectation. Cheap transport made it possible for entrepreneurs to risk investing in large-scale, deep collieries. Deeper pits were sunk from the 1820s in the Selston and Pinxton areas, partly in response to growing demand from Mansfield, but from the 1830s the picture was transformed. Mining in the Derbyshire–Nottinghamshire area took place predominantly in the exposed western section of the coalfield, the 900 or so square miles mainly in Derbyshire, but from the 1830s it began to expand on to the 2,000 square miles of the Nottinghamshire section. During and beyond the 1850s collieries were opened in the Langley Mill, Eastwood and Ilkeston areas, and the 1870s saw no fewer than sixteen new collieries brought into production, a larger number than in any other decade either before or since. These, together with a further twenty-five opened between 1880 and 1910, were mostly situated along the Nottingham–Mansfield axis, except for Clifton and Gedling. Considerable injections of capital were required, and this had the effect of transforming the nature of the industry (Griffin 1971). The results were impressive. Production stood at 3.1 million tons in 1854–55, but the coalfield enjoyed above average rates of growth in the second half of the nineteenth century, partly as a result of the introduction of steam power into the hosiery, lace and engineering industries; indeed, demand from local industry increased from around one-fifth of production in 1869 to perhaps one-half by 1913. By 1880 more than 12 million tons were being raised annually, and by 1900 production probably exceeded 24 million tons. From 5.6 per cent of national output in 1830, east midlands coal had risen to 10.4 per cent by 1890, at which point the coalfield had overtaken the West Midlands and Lancashire and Cheshire. What this meant for individual proprietors is clear from the case of the Staveley Coal and Iron Company. Coal production stood at 50,000 tons in 1845, but rose to 337,000 tons in 1860, 800,000 tons in 1870 and 1 million tons by about 1890 (Chapman 1981: 76). Simultaneously, deeper mining began on the Leicestershire coalfield, where production rose from 432,000 tons in 1854–55 to over 1 million tons in 1880, and to more than double that by the end of the century (Royal Commission on Coal 1871, vol. III App. p. 82; Gibson 1922: 23–5; Church 1986: 3, 10, 29; Owen 1984: 236–91).

The impact of coal mining on the community was considerable. Coalville in Leicestershire, the one example of a new town in the region during the nineteenth century, owed its existence to coal. In 1822 William Stenson began mining in the concealed part of the Leicestershire–south Derbyshire coalfield, and the Long Lane colliery was opened two years later. Without improved transport Stenson's project was not likely to have prospered, and it is hardly surprising that he played an active role in promoting the Leicester–Swannington railway in 1832. As a result of this development the hamlet of Long Lane, soon to be known as Coalville, grew from about 100 people in 1830 to 800 in 1836, to 1,200 in 1846, and to 1,449 by 1851. At this point it was a colliery village, in which even the houses and facilities were owned by the company, but during the second half of the century the growth of population was matched by the expansion of economic opportunities. Women found work in domestic textile manufacture, and later in elastic web making, while for men brick and tile manufacture began in the 1850s, and engineering in the 1860s. By 1901 these secondary industries were rivalling coal in importance, enabling Coalville to mature into a sizeable town (Royle 1978; Baker 1983).

In complete contrast, Mansfield had enjoyed the position of marketing centre for western Nottinghamshire and adjoining parts of Derbyshire since the Middle Ages. Towards the end of the eighteenth century and in the first half of the nineteenth it came to be dominated by domestic hosiery manufacturing, iron foundries and two water-powered cotton mills. By the 1860s hosiery provided work for 4,000 people in the Mansfield Poor Law union, the nine water-powered cotton mills employed a further 800, and the domestic clothing and footwear industries another 1,200. Mansfield was already a town of 12,000 people in 1871, but the opening of the concealed Nottinghamshire coalfield produced further rapid growth. Small-scale mining had taken place in and around Kirkby since the 1820s, and Annesley colliery opened in 1865. From that time onwards the dye was cast, and Mansfield, Sutton-in-Ashfield

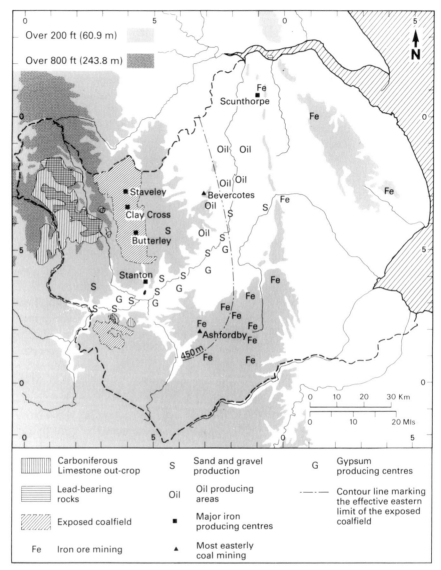

Figure 9.4 Mineral deposits in the East Midlands

and Kirkby-in-Ashfield developed into an urban sprawl largely dictated by the location of the mines (Edward 1966a: 472–5; Law 1962–5).

More often than not collieries were sunk in out of the way places. On the Erewash coalfield a number of colliery companies provided housing, including the Worswicke Company at Annesley, and the Hucknall Colliery Company in Beardall and Watnall Streets in Hucknall. The Butterley Company undertook to provide housing in thinly populated districts. Between 1797 and 1813 over a hundred cottages were erected, including twenty at Codnor Green, and the company also built Portland Row at Selston. Usually the company built in long terraces of twenty to fifty houses, all with a generous garden, and from the beginning they thought in terms of several hundreds and possibly thousands of houses (Griffin 1971; Horriben 1985: 9; Riden 1973: 31). A tradition of housebuilding by colliery owners dated from the early eighteenth century on the Leicestershire and south Derbyshire coalfield. John Wilkins erected 'cottage rows' to house part of the work-force at the Swannington and Measham collieries. Housing, including two stone-built terraces of twenty-five houses each, was erected at Moira in 1811 in conjunction with the opening of several mines, and further additions were made in 1868. Much of the inspiration came from the earls of Moira who saw themselves as responsible employers providing the work-force with a decent living in return for appropriate deference (Griffin 1977). Housing was also provided at Coalville, together with a church, chapel, public house and hotel (Royle 1978).

Paternalism could not prevent labour from organizing, and the first trade union on the Erewash valley coalfield was founded in 1844 as an offshoot of the Miners Association of Great Britain and Ireland. This lasted less than a year (Griffin 1955: 7–11), and apart from one or two small and isolated unions the next major development did not come until 1865 with the formation of the Derbyshire and Nottinghamshire Miners' Association, as an offshoot of the National Association of Miners. Membership reached 300 in 1866, and rose to more than 7,000 when an organizer was sent from the national union. The employers refused to recognize the union on the south Derbyshire coalfield, and a struggle began in February 1867. Members were locked out and in September all miners were called out on strike in an attempt to close the collieries. The employers brought in labour from elsewhere and the coalfield was convulsed with violence until the union was finally broken in the spring of 1868 (Griffin 1981).

In the years which followed, labour shortage tended to ensure reasonable conditions. The Barber Walker Company, one of the largest in the Erewash valley by the late nineteenth century, made improvements designed to ensure a good safety record in their pits. Compensation was offered to injured miners, and the company built a number of houses in Eastwood as well as subsidizing fares on a train running between Ilkeston and the collieries (Griffin 1978). Unions flourished in these conditions but the economic cycle tended to dictate both their effectiveness and their survival. The DNMA became increasingly moribund, and in 1881 the Derbyshire and Nottinghamshire coalfields decided to found their own unions, which proved durable despite having to accept fluctuating conditions for their members, depending on the trade cycle. Occasionally they resisted, as in 1893 when economic conditions led to the closure of many collieries and short-time working elsewhere. The Nottinghamshire owners suggested a 25 per cent wage reduction, and when the union resisted the workers were locked out from July until September. Derbyshire miners were also locked out from late July, and a settlement was found only in November (Griffin 1955; Williams 1962).

Iron and Steel

Iron production was at a standstill by the mid-eighteenth century but improved communications turned out to be the spur to future development. On the Ashby coalfield Joseph Wilkes's ironworks at Measham in 1783 included a forge for producing boilers and chains, and a steam-powered blast furnace operated for a few years at Moira 1800–11 (Palmer 1984: 87–96). Ironstone mining continued through the nineteenth century in the area (Cranstone 1985). On the Erewash valley coalfield apart from a coke furnace erected at Morley Park near Ripley in 1780, the breakthrough was predominantly associated with the Chesterfield canal. Figures for the early nineteenth century suggest that seventeen or eighteen furnaces had been built in Derbyshire, and that they were turning out somewhere between 9,000 and 10,000 tons of pig-iron annually. Production depended heavily on the Chesterfield canal, since 60 per cent of output came from around the town (Heath 1982: 86; Farey 1811, I: 397; Chapman 1981: 14). In the south of the county the most important organization was the Butterley Company, formed in 1790. Its first furnace was in blast in 1791, and the prosperity arising during the Napoleonic wars permitted diversification into coal mining, and brick and tile making (Riden 1973; Lindsay 1965). Its iron output in 1806 was the largest from a single company in the county.

The early decades of the nineteenth century were not kind to the Derbyshire iron industry, and by 1830 even Smiths of Chesterfield, the most successful of the local firms, was in financial difficulties. Whereas 13 per cent of all English blast furnaces were in Derbyshire in 1806 the proportion was just 5.4 per cent in 1830. Only the Butterley Company flourished in these decades, but such was its confidence that in 1811 it began to build a new town on 67 acres of meadowland in Alfreton parish. This was Ironville, the earliest planned settlement on the east midlands coalfield, although until 1830 it consisted merely of two rows of cottages. With the expansion of Codnor Park ironworks the nucleus of the model village was built in the years 1834–40. Houses were brick built, and of standard four-room type costing £63 15s. or £65 15s. each. Of these 126 were built, plus six three-storey houses in 1842–43. A National School was erected in 1840–41, and a mechanics institute in 1843, by which time the model village was complete. With the building of a church in 1852, and some further additions, the village reached by the 1860s what is substantially its present form, although in 1875 a number of houses were demolished to make way for a railway line (Fowkes 1971b; Pevsner and Williamson 1978: 253).

The Butterley Company was to some extent unusual since in general terms prosperity did not return to the local iron industry until the railway arrived. Production rose from 18,000 tons in 1830 to 95,000 in 1848, when twenty furnaces were in blast, and to 185,000 tons in 1869, by which time forty-three blast furnaces were operating in the county. Innovation was encouraged. At Butterley Sir John Alleyne perfected a revolutionary method of forge welding in 1862, which made possible the construction of the roof of St Pancras station in London. At 240 ft, this was the longest free metal span in the world at the time. By 1900 output had reached a level 75 times greater than equivalent figures for a century earlier. The railway permitted two further developments within the county's iron industry. It became possible for Derbyshire iron to be 'finished' outside the county – particularly in the Birmingham area – and for supplies of ore to be brought into Derbyshire as local resources dwindled. Between 1855 and 1870 350,000–400,000 tons of local ore were mined annually from among the coal measures, but by the end of the 1870s iron production from local ores was almost entirely confined to Butterley. Only 150,000 tons – 16 per cent – of the ore used in Derbyshire furnaces in 1880 was locally mined, and just 3,000 tons by 1900. To ensure supplies local companies acquired interests elsewhere. The Wingerworth Company started to work ore at Stamford in the 1870s, and the Staveley Coal and Iron Company began mining at Scunthorpe in the early 1880s (Warren 1961).

These interests in the Jurassic ore found in a belt running south through Lincolnshire and Rutland also help to explain the growth of Scunthorpe. Ore was discovered on the estates of Rowland Winn at Frodingham in north Lincolnshire in 1858–59, a community of less than 1,300 people at the beginning of the decade. He initially leased the resources which were carried to Elsecar in Yorkshire for smelting, but by the mid-1860s three companies had established blast furnaces in the area. By 1880 twenty-one furnaces had been built, of which fifteen were then in blast, and from 790,819 tons of ore and 481,807 tons of coal 207,704 tons of pig-iron was produced. Meantime the population rose to nearly 6,000 in 1881 and to 7,500 in 1891 (Daff 1973; Armstrong 1981: 31–8). Further south on the same belt of ore, extraction began around Melton Mowbray in 1874, and by 1900 Leicestershire had become one of the largest producers of ore in the country, mining 700,000 tons annually. A number of furnaces were also built in the area (Pye 1972: 353).

Nationally, by the final quarter of the nineteenth century steel production was gradually replacing the traditional iron industry, but this trend was not reflected in Derbyshire. It continued to supply the surviving Staffordshire forges, and it came to specialize in the making of cast-iron goods (especially pipes). Several inefficient iron smelting plants were built towards the end of the century in the Ilkeston area, but these failed soon after 1918. The Butterley Company tried steel making in the 1870s, but gave up by 1902, and no major steel works was established in Derbyshire (Warren 1961). In north Lincoln-shire the Frodingham Iron Company started making steel in 1890. The initial aim was to produce 400 tons weekly, but by 1895 670 tons were being produced, and this rose to 1,473 tons in 1900 when seven furnaces were operating (Pocock 1962–65).

Lead and other Extractive Industries

With the Derbyshire lead industry the situation was rather different. The 1750s and 1760s and the years from the late 1780s to 1796 saw boom conditions. Production may have reached 10,000 tons a year in the 1760s, while firmer figures suggest just under 6,000 tons were raised annually in the 1780s, making Derbyshire the most productive lead field in England at the time (Burt 1969). Capital flowed into the industry, and by 1778 thirteen Newcomen engines had been set up in the Derwent valley. From 1796, by contrast, the industry entered forty years of crisis. Farey, writing in about 1809, listed 292 mines, and eighteen reverbatory furnaces (cupolas), but he found several smelters who had relatively little business 'and some have their works shut up occasionally, owing to the supply of ore being now so greatly inferior to what it was about twenty years ago'. In addition, in his view the mining laws were being misap-plied in such a way that

> on the whole, I cannot but recommend a speedy revisal and alteration
> of these mining laws . . . which can henceforth, in their present form,
> tend only to the injury and vexation of the farmer . . . and to the
> material injury of the interests which the Crown has in the lead mines of
> Derbyshire.
> (Farey 1811, I: 252–70, 364, 385–6)

The root problem was that as readily accessible ore was mined out confidence was lost in the capacity of the Derbyshire industry to retain its position as a major producer (Willies 1979: 139–44). When prices fell after 1815 the situation became serious. Innovation after 1800 was scarce, and sometimes misguided. However, all was not lost since the years after 1835 saw three relatively short-lived improvements which checked the downward trend in lead prices. The first, lasting from 1836 to 1842, produced a marked upsurge in activity; the second, 1853–57, was associated with the introduction of limited liability; and the third was in 1873. Between 1845 and 1881 168,477 tons was raised, over 6,000 tons annually, but this represented only 7.3 per cent of the national total (Burt and Atkinson 1976). Moreover, the failure to sustain output was reflected in the numbers employed in the industry. From 2,333 in 1861 the figure fell to 871 in 1881 and to 285 by 1901 (Fuller 1965: 385). In the longer term the exhaustion of ore which could be exploited at the prevailing price levels ensured the demise of the industry. By the end of the eighteenth century it was no longer possible to justify looking for new deposits, and during the nineteenth century the task of exploiting known resources became increasingly unrewarding. With the exception of Mill Close, lead mining in Derbyshire had effectively come to an end in 1885 (Willies 1986).

A number of other extractive industries prospered in the East Midlands. The Duke of Devonshire had a copper mine under Ecton Hill, just over the Derbyshire border into Staffordshire, which was the deepest in England and a marvel to visitors, including the Hon. John Byng in 1789:

> One of the managers of the mine conducted us up the shaft to the water engine, which drains the mine; and a dirty and tedious walk it was. . . . In this infernal region one cart of ore passed by us. At the water engine we were stunned by the noise, and astonished at the body of water; one river flowing above, and one below us. Next, we were carried to the smeltings of the copper, and lead, saw several siftings, and the many children employed in the laborious pounding of the stone, by which hand work they *may* gain 6*d*. a day. The women wash the ore. In the several branches are employed many hundred labourers.
>
> (Andrews 1935, II: 58)

Devonshire built smelting works in 1769, and by 1817 his mines had yielded 66,000 tons of high-grade copper ore, worth £852,000, much of which was used to pay for building the Crescent in Buxton (Cooper 1982: 122–3). Millstones were made in the Peak District (Tucker 1985) and gypsum, used for plaster of paris, cement and alabaster, was mined around Gotham, Newark, East Retford, Chellaston and Tetbury, and in the Isle of Axholme. Large-scale extraction of limestone began at Dove Holes near Buxton, while significant quantities were raised at Marple, Ashover, Crich, Cromford and Wirksworth, and during the nineteenth century at Ticknall, Barrow-on-Soar and Breedon. The lime was used in agriculture, as flux in iron smelting, as road metal, as ballast for the railways, and for decorative purposes. Fireplaces, usually designed for the more substantial houses, were made from Hopton Wood limestone (Harris 1968: 60–74; Pye 1972: 354–5). Granite-type rock was worked at Mountsorrel, largely for road making. By 1877 the companies involved employed 600 hands and processed 100,000 tons of granite annually. The Swithland slate industry prospered until the 1840s when it fell victim to cheaper and lighter Welsh slate brought in by train. The last slate pits closed late in the 1880s (Palmer 1983: 38–9).

From the 1790s fire clay was raised in the Alfreton area of mid-Derbyshire and from the south Derbyshire and Leicestershire mines to serve the earthenware works established at Gresley. By 1811 seven potteries were active in the area, and a further sixteen began business before 1840. Nineteenth-century public health legislation gave a significant boost to the sanitary pottery industry (Spavold 1981). Pottery making is recorded at Wirksworth from 1787, and from around the turn of the century at Ironville, Shipley, West Hallam, Ilkeston and Eastwood. The 'slack' coal used in the kilns, which encouraged the industry in some of these places, also helped Derby to become famous for its 'Crown Derby' pottery. These works were founded by William Duesbury in 1755, while the world-renowned works at Denby were set up in 1819 (Nixon 1969: 87–92). Stamford enjoyed temporary fame for its terracotta between 1858 and 1875 (Wright 1982: 206).

Hosiery

Textile production was largely confined to an area bounded by Mansfield to the north and Hinckley to the south. Much of the capacity was found in the major centres of Nottingham, Leicester and Derby, together with secondary centres, among them Mansfield, Sutton-in-Ashfield, Loughborough and Hinckley. By the mid-nineteenth century more than half of Nottingham's working population and 75 per cent of the industrially employed in Leicester worked in textile production (Head 1962). In Hinckley 68 per cent of the work-force were involved in some branch of textiles. Such a heavy dependence on textiles was to have severe long-term repercussions, but this was not clear during the years when framework knitting grew beyond all expectation. Spurred on by its success, silk weaving, cotton, lace and elastic-web manufacture all developed in the same area. Elsewhere the picture was less bright. In Lincolnshire, no noticeable progress was made in textile production through this period (Wright 1982: 70–4).

By the middle of the eighteenth century the framework knitting industry was concentrated in and around Derby, which specialized in silk hose, Nottingham (cotton hose), and Leicester (worsted hose). Of 14,000 frames in England in 1753 10,000 were in the area, and through time the concentration increased; 88 per cent of all frames were in the three counties in 1812 and 91 per cent by 1844. A mature organization had already evolved by 1750. Nottingham had around fifty merchant houses by 1740, most of them employing knitters direct, rather than through middlemen. This total rose to around a hundred in the 1770s, and perhaps 200 by the end of the century. Firms developed more slowly in Leicester, but the town had ten 'principal manufacturers' in 1750, and eighty-five firms in 1794. Expansion on this scale was possible because of what has sometimes been called the golden age for hosiery between 1781 and 1811. The mechanization of the production of cotton and worsted yarns had the effect of cheapening hosiery yarns, which forced the remaining hand knitters out of the market without seriously affecting the framework knitters. The success of Jedediah Strutt's 'Derby rib' hose (1758) stimulated the knitters to extend the use of the frame from stockings to underwear, breeches, gloves, handkerchiefs and a number of other goods, so that by 1812 forty distinct fabrics were being knitted on the frame (Chapman 1967: 19). New meshes, designs and garments partly reflected alterations in fashion, as in 1797–98 when long-arm gloves of 22 in. replaced the 18–19 in. gloves which had been fashionable for the previous seventy years.

The structure of the industry also changed in response to these developments. The status of the stockinger declined as he became increasingly dependent on the bag-hosier (or putter out), renting from the hosier rather than owning his own frame. Companies grew larger. By 1813 one Nottingham hosier reportedly had £24,000 invested in frames, another employed 300 workers, and a third paid wages exceeding £200 a week (Wells 1972: 61, 71). By 1824 several manufacturers owned more than 1,000 frames. However, this pattern of growth proved in the longer term to be an albatross around the industry's neck. Larger firms were able to impose a stranglehold, and as a result frame renting, truck, stinting and price cutting all came to feature in the organization of the industry, forcing knitters to take on additional frames and to employ child labour. Employers also opposed technical improvements, since the frames had little depreciation value and while labour remained plentiful it was in the owners' interest to resist change. As a result, while technology was altering the face of British textile production in the first half of the nineteenth century, hosiery manufacture was in a trough of depression. This was the direct result of several related factors. One was overmanning; the industry was open to unskilled labour which helped to keep wages depressed. Second, the introduction of the wide frame at the end of the eighteenth century made possible the knitting of wider pieces of fabric for shirts and underwear, and the making of stockings which were cut from the fabric and then seamed up ('cut ups') rather than being fully fashioned at greater expense on the narrow frame. This was the chief grievance of the knitters who petitioned Parliament in 1812, and the wide frame was a particular object of the Luddites' wrath. Third, the industry suffered from the loss of government contract work when the Napoleonic wars ended in 1815; and fourth, a change of fashion at roughly the same time from breeches to trousers further exacerbated the situation (Wells 1972: 80–4).

The knitters took matters into their own hands. Riotous behaviour was frequent in Nottingham from the 1780s, and disturbances were reported from Hinckley in 1816, 1818, 1819, 1826 and 1829. Luddite troubles were reported from many hosiery villages particularly in 1811–12. Problems were severe when individual communities became overreliant on hosiery. A classic case was Hinckley were, in 1829, two-thirds of the population of 6,000 were in receipt of poor relief, but the town had a mere 400 ratepayers (Royle 1978–79). The government did finally respond to this situation with a commission of enquiry in 1844 which found that capacity had increased while demand had remained stationary. One-third of Leicester's frames were not being used, and several thousand more were underemployed. Consequently no incentives had existed for manufacturers to improve working conditions, or to introduce new technology, and the knitters suffered. Many of them lived in overcrowded conditions; at Hinckley, for example, several cases were found of more than one family living in a single room (Pye 1972: 365; Chapman 1974a).

By the time the commission reported the first steps had already been taken towards pulling the industry out of depression. In 1839 Pagets of Loughborough opened the first power-operated factory, setting an important precedent which was soon followed. From 1844 Pagets were using the circular frame, and in 1847 Matthew Townsend of Leicester invented the tumbler, or latch needle, which simplified the knitting mechanism. These precedents were quickly taken up elsewhere. Nottingham's first power-operated factory was opened by Hine and Mundella in 1851, and similar enterprises had been set up in the town by the time Thomas Corah's St Margaret's factory became the first such undertaking in Leicester. In 1864 William Cotton's flat frame, driven by rotary mechanism, made it possible to produce a dozen hose simultaneously. It still took time to redirect the industry, but by 1871 there were seventy-four steam-driven hosiery factories in Leicestershire and forty-five in Nottinghamshire. The 1870s, with a combination of compulsory elementary education and the abolition of frame rents, saw a rapid extension of the use of power, and by 1890 95 per cent of output was from powered machines. At that date just 5,000 hand frames still operated. Nor were factories limited to the main towns. Hinckley had twenty factories by 1894, and a number were opened in Mansfield. Moreover, by 1912 all the framework knitting centres which had 500 machines in 1844 had attracted manufacturers, as had two-thirds of those with 100–500 machines (Wells 1972: 119; Edwards 1966a: 304–5).

Silk and Cotton

Silk production was mainly centred on Derby, and the town had twelve spinning mills in 1789 providing work for 1,200 employees. Traditionally the industry concentrated on producing silk yarn for the framework knitters, but in the early nineteenth century subsidiary ventures were started using locally produced silk. Among these were the weaving of tapes, and by the 1820s the manufacture of silk piece goods and ribbons. At Derby in 1789 the Hon. John Byng reported himself to be 'bewildered' by the silk mills: 'such rattlings and twistings! Such heat and stinks! that I was glad to get out: we should be full as happy, if silk worms had never been' (Andrews 1935, II: 62). By 1833 Derby had 233 powered silk ribbon looms, and the 1847 factory returns placed Derbyshire third in a country ranking of workers in silk factories, with nearly 12 per cent of the national total. However, these figures could not be sustained, and from forty-two in 1862 the number of factories declined to just fourteen in 1890. Correspondingly the number of employees declined from 4,732 to 1,664. Only two manufacturers survived in 1912 (Smith, D. M. 1962).

Cotton manufacture also grew out of links with hosiery. James Hargreaves and Richard Arkwright were attracted to Nottingham in 1769 by the

---

Plate 9.3 Cromford Mill, *c.* 1783. Arkwright built his first mill at Cromford in 1771, and his cotton spinning activities were largely responsible for creating the village for his workforce. Although Cromford did not in the end develop into a major industrial centre, the mill attracted considerable interest from passing visitors. Among these was Joseph Wright of Derby, who painted several versions of his 'View of Cromford, near Matlock', a romantic view of the great cotton mill, its windows ablaze with light, with the moon emerging from behind a bank of clouds.

Wright (1734–97) was the first professional painter directly to express the spirit of the industrial revolution. The son of a Derby lawyer, he began his career as a portrait painter, and from an early stage one of his major preoccupations was with the study of light. This was a subject with which he experimented for much of his career; hence the concern in this particular picture with two of his major preoccupations as a painter, industry and light.

The original mill of 1771 is still to be seen, but now with three rather than five storeys. The top two were removed after a fire in 1930.

town's demand for cotton yarn in the hosiery industry, the availability of capital, the experience of the local labour force in operating textile machinery, and the fact that attempts had already been made to spin cotton yarn with machinery in Nottingham. Arkwright finally opted for Cromford, where he built his first mill in 1771, a second in 1777 and a third in 1780 (Swindell 1964–65). The impact on Cromford was considerable. Writing in 1790 the Hon. John Byng noted that

> these vales have lost all their beauties; the rural cot has given place to the lofty red mill, and the grand houses of overseers; the stream perverted from its course by sluices, and aqueducts, will no longer ripple and cascade. Every rural sound is sunk in the clamours of cotton works . . . the vales are every way blocked up by mills. I saw the workers issue forth at 7 o'clock a wonderful crowd of young people, made as familiar as eternal intercourse can make them; a new set then goes in for the night, for the mills never leave off working.
>
> (Andrews 1935, II: 195)

Between 1771 and 1789 thirteen further mills using Arkwright's spinning frame were sited along the river Derwent and its tributaries. By 1788 Derbyshire had twenty-seven mills and Nottinghamshire nineteen, including the first steam-driven mill in England which was opened at Papplewick in 1786 using a Boulton and Watt engine. The Strutts' mills at Belper and Milford represented a turning-point in industrial architecture; the North Mill at Belper, erected in 1804, pioneered iron-framed fireproof buildings, and it replaced a conventional mill built in 1786 which burnt down in 1803.

The decision to move into the relatively thinly populated Derwent valley placed a burden of responsibility on the entrepreneur to provide housing and other facilities. Arkwright and Strutt chose Cromford and Belper, which as centres of lead smelting and nail making had no immediate housing problem. This situation did not continue for long. Arkwright built his first houses when the second mill was opened in 1777 – 'the bold rock opposite this house is now disfigured by a row of new houses built under it', wrote Byng in 1790 – and Strutt followed suit at Belper and Milford. Arkwright's houses were on three storeys with a cellar and a living room, a bedroom, and an attic weaving room. Strutt's houses were stone built, and hardware was made in Strutt's foundry which was established primarily to cast columns and window frames for the mills. At Darley Abbey the Evans family built fifty-six three-storey houses at a cost of £60 apiece, to complement the mills completed in 1783. Like the Strutts, they built workers' homes of high quality for the period. Nor were houses the only priority. At Cromford Arkwright was responsible for the inn (1779) and the market place (1790). The Strutts probably planned Belper and Milford as model villages; they provided their work-force with coal and milk, meat, fruit and vegetables, and John Strutt started a works band of musicians and designed 'an orchestra, with the desks and boxes containing the instruments, to fold and pack up so that with the addition of a pair of wheels the whole forms a carriage (for moving) the *corps de musique* to Derby or the surrounding villages'. The Evanses offered housing, wages above the level of those earned by agricultural workers, medical and educational facilities, in return for moral oversight enforced by fines for lateness, absence, swearing and failure to attend day and Sunday schools (Chambers and Barley 1961; Chapman 1967: 162; Cooper 1982: 238–47; Lindsay 1960).

Altogether ninety-five cotton mills were established in the Nottinghamshire–Derbyshire area between 1769 and 1800, but by then the industry was moving firmly in the direction of Lancashire, partly due to physical limitations in relation to imports and exports, and partly through depression in the hosiery industry. As a market for cotton yarn hosiery was no substitute for the flourishing Lancashire weaving industry (Chapman 1982). However, enough demand remained to sustain the water-powered cotton industry of the area through the first half of the nineteenth century. In 1838 steam represented only 20 per cent of the power used in the local industry, and Dr Granville considered this to be no bad thing:

> It is a curious fact that all the cotton mills on the Derwent whether
> belonging to the Strutts or the Arkwrights, continue to be worked by
> water. This is wonderfully fortunate circumstances for the industrious
> classes engaged in the works, and equally so for the inhabitants
> generally of the places where such cotton mills are established. Their
> health and comforts are not bartered away by a heartless manufacturer,
> in a dense and smoky atmosphere or in moist and heated rooms.
>
> (Granville 1841)

In 1850 there were still ninety-three mills in the Derbyshire–Nottinghamshire area, but they represented a mere 5.3 per cent of the national total, and many of the water-driven mills were put out of operation by depression in the American Civil War years (Smith 1960: 260). By 1876 the largest concentration of cotton manufacturers, thirteen, was in and around Nottingham. Almost all were involved in doubling yarn to meet the demands of the lace and factory hosiery industries. Mansfield, Leicester and Chesterfield were also prominent centres. However, the scale of the industry gradually declined leaving thirty-seven manufacturers still in business in 1912 (Smith, D. M. 1962).

Lace and Elastic Web

Machine-made lace making, which originated in Nottingham in the later eighteenth century, was another branch which grew from the great tree of hosiery as framework knitters adapted the frame for lace production. The invention of the point net frame in 1778 helped to promote the production of cheap lace, and to plug a gap in the market which the hand knitters were unable to fill. Nottingham stood to benefit because of local expertise in working with cotton, but the crucial development which brought the industry firmly into the town was John Heathcote's invention of the bobbin net machine in 1808. Heathcote, a framesmith, effectively mechanized the hand lace making processes, and his work was further developed in 1813 with John Leavers' invention of the bobbin and carriage machine. Once Heathcote's patent expired in 1823 the industry passed through what was known as the twist net boom, and people poured into the town and its satellite villages from as far as 80 miles away. By 1826 Nottingham and its surrounding areas had 1,400 bobbin net machines – of which 567 were located in Radford, Sneinton, Hyson Green and Basford – and this increased to 2,160 by 1833. By then the boom had passed. Between 1831 and 1836 more than 500 owners of one to three machines became journeymen or left the trade altogether, and many of those who survived did so because, as with hosiery, power-driven machinery came late to the industry. In 1833 there were just four powered lace factories in the Nottingham area, and it was not until the 1850s that the situation changed greatly. In the years 1851–77 seventy-one factories and forty-one warehouses were built in the town, and the Lace Market began to develop as residential areas around St Mary's church were cleared (Oldfield 1984). High wages, however, forced the industry out of the town, and by 1911, of 46,000 full-time lace workers in England and Scotland about half were in Nottingham and a further quarter in Beeston, Long Eaton, Sandiacre and Derby. Long Eaton had grown from a tiny village to a thriving industrial town with the migration of the fancy lace trade from Nottingham (Smith 1960; Honeyman 1982), but efforts to establish the industry further afield, including Boston and Stamford, did not succeed (Wright 1982: 74).

A final development arising from hosiery was elastic web manufacture which started in Leicester during the second quarter of the nineteenth century. It originated during the 1830s and really took off in 1839 when Caleb Bedells of Leicester devised a new type of webbing which could be used for the cuffs of gloves as well as stockings. The real importance of the industry derived from its relationship to the growing footwear industry, particularly with the increase in demand for web to make elastic-sided boots. Two manufacturers were operating in Leicester in 1855, but the number rose to seventeen in 1864 and to forty-six in 1876, by which time it had also spread to Derby – partly as a result of depression in the silk industry during the 1860s – and to Nottingham, where it was manufactured for elastic hosiery and surgical appliances. By 1872 elastic web ranked third behind hosiery and footwear in Leicester's economy, but this was the peak of achievement. With changes in fashion the demand for elastic-sided boots fell away, and the number of operative factories declined from fifty in 1879 to thirty in 1890. By 1899 just thirty-eight manufacturers were still left in the region (Smith, D. M. 1964).

Footwear and Engineering

The introduction of power into the hosiery and lace industries after 1850 may have pulled them clear of depression, but it also posed a threat to employment. In Leicester by 1881 five women worked in the hosiery industry for every three men, while by 1901 in Nottingham 14,701 women worked in the lace industry and 6,925 men. The potential threat posed to male employment was offset by the availability of new opportunities, particularly the footwear industry in Leicester and a number of other towns including Hinckley and Mansfield; and in engineering, which came to the region partly as a result of the demand for machinery in the newly mechanized textile and footwear industries, and partly because the process of mechanization released on to the labour market large numbers of men skilled in working machinery.

Until the mid-nineteenth century Leicestershire's interest in footwear manufacture was unremarkable. In 1841 11.2 persons per 1,000 were involved in the trade, which was slightly below the national average of 11.6, and in a different league from neighbouring Northamptonshire (35.2). During the 1850s Thomas Crick – a master shoe manufacturer employing twenty-two men and twelve women in 1851 – perfected a riveting method for joining the soles of shoes to their upper and inner parts. It was a revolutionary development requiring less skilled labour than even the cheapest hand-sewn shoes, and it came at a point when plenty of low-cost labour was available in the town and skilled workers from Northamptonshire sought work to avoid the strikes and lock-outs which occurred in the county from opposition to the introduction of machinery. Crick's turnover increased from £3,500 in 1853 to £100,000 in 1868, and over the same period the number of footwear factories in Leicester increased from four to seventy. By 1871 Leicester had overtaken Northampton as a centre of footwear manufacture, and importantly it was predominantly a male industry with nine men to every four women (Simmons 1974, II: 2–4). During the 1860s factories were established in smaller centres near Leicester including Anstey (1863), Sileby and Earl Shilton (1870), and Bar-well (1877). Numbers employed in the industry rose from 5,000 in 1861 to

17,000 in 1881 and to 30,000 by 1891 (Mounfield 1964–65; Pye 1972: 366–70).

Engineering grew in importance from the 1830s and affected the whole region. Derby came to be almost dominated by engineering because of its connection with the railway. A number of companies moved to the town during the nineteenth century, while the most important incomer – Rolls-Royce – came in 1908 (Lloyd 1978). In Leicester, iron founders operated in the town from the late eighteenth century, but it was the demand for hosiery and footwear machinery which helped to make engineering the town's third largest employer of labour by 1900 (Brown 1970: 65). One of Nottingham's earliest and most important engineering interests was in bicycle manufacturing, for which the mechanical skills were similar to those needed in the construction of lace and hosiery machinery. By 1897 more than 5,000 people were employed in the industry (Church 1966: 247). Engineering works were established at Coalville during the 1860s, and slightly later in Loughborough. The attraction of the latter was the availability of labour, good rail communications, and an adequately drained floodplain. The British Company moved from Lambeth in 1889, and Herbert Morris from Sheffield in 1906. The companies supplemented the earlier development of bell founding in the town during the 1840s.

Much of the engineering which developed in the Derby–Leicester–Nottingham area was light engineering, with precision work such as telegraph instruments, clocks, lenses and optical goods. As with Nottingham's bicycles, it reflected the available skills. By contrast, in the east of the region engineering developed to take advantage of the mechanical revolution in agriculture of which Lincolnshire was in the forefront. The railway made it possible to bring cheap coal and iron into Lincolnshire and to improve market access for entrepreneurs, with the result that the county 'was quite exceptional in the number of [iron foundries] which made the grade to national and indeed worldwide renown' (Wright 1982: 137). Between the 1840s, when the railways first reached Lincolnshire, and the 1890s, Lincoln, Grantham and Gainsborough developed extensive engineering interests in powered mechanical implements for agriculture. The initial impetus, particularly in Lincoln, came between 1849 and 1857 with the establishment of firms manufacturing steam engines and drainage pumps. From about 1850 portable threshing machines and engines were produced in the county. By 1851 Clayton and Shuttleworth of Lincoln had produced 126 portable engines, and as a consequence of their prominent place in the Great Exhibition they built another 209 engines during that year. By 1890 the company had produced 26,000 portable engines and 24,000 threshing machines. Such levels of output were sustained by overseas exports. Clayton and Shuttleworth were selling to Russia and Austria-Hungary in the 1850s, while by 1857 Richard Hornsby of Grantham was looking beyond Europe to South America, Australia and New Zealand. The agricultural depression of the 1870s and overseas competition threatened to halt this rapid progress, but positive marketing pushed up exports to South America and Russia to record levels in the 1890s, and diversification saw a number of firms move into the market for mining, electric lighting, and tea processing machinery, and gold-dredging plant. By the end of the century Lincolnshire's engineering industry supported a large proportion of the county's urban population (Wright 1982: 140–57).

As the nineteenth century progressed the scale and variety of industrial interests in the region grew. Nottingham, traditionally a textile town, developed new interests in mining and engineering, food and drink, transport, tobacco processing and pharmaceuticals. It was a sign of things to come when, in 1877, Jesse Boot opened his first shop in Goose Gate, Nottingham under the banner 'J. Boot: Drugs and Proprietary Articles at Reduced Rates' (Church 1966: 236–42; Chapman 1974b). In Lincolnshire Boston became the headquarters of GNR lines in the county, with a locomotive depot, civil engineers' yard, and a gas-making plant for carriage lighting. Chemical manure works were set up in Lincoln during the 1850s, and by 1882 the county directory included at least twenty-five chemical manufacturers (Hill 1974: 118–19, 210–11). Across the county as a whole a range of opportunities became available for female labour in pipe tobacco production, railway luggage labels, steam laundries, and various other concerns. Many were small-scale and short-lived, but a reporter of 1900 could not have dismissed industry in the county with the disdain of Arthur Young, and across the region in general the diversity of Derbyshire noticed by John Farey had been developed onto a much firmer base. By 1900 industry had supplanted agriculture as the major economic interest.

Industrial Relations

The growth and development of industry inevitably produced tensions between employers and employees. The framework knitters were prone to take direct action in the form of frame breaking, and this took on a particularly serious form in the Luddite troubles between 1811 and 1817. In 1811–12 most of the troubles occurred in Nottinghamshire, but the outbreak of 1816 was rather different. It began with a night attack on Heathcoat and Boden's lace factory in Loughborough. A reward of 500 guineas was offered for the apprehension of the guilty parties, and from this it became clear that gangs of machine breakers were available to carry out breaking for hire. James Towle, the leader of this particular outbreak, was tried at Leicester and executed along with five others while another three were transported (VCH Leics II 1954: 126–7).

Next week we shall publish AN ENLARG-
ED SHEET, with the proceedings of the
PUBLIC MEETING at full length, together with the PEOPLE'S CHARTER,
if our limits will allow it; and other intelligence highly interesting to the public.
Our country agents will forward their or
ders in the course of the week. As we are
sure to print more than 2000 Reviews of
our next impression, it affords a very fa-
vorable opportunity for Advertisers, and
we respectfully entreat them to send their
advertisements early.

—>>◉<<—

NOTTINGHAM REVIEW.

—▸▸◄◄—

THE NOTTINGHAM RADICAL
DEMONSTRATION

A few remarks upon this topic will be expected
from us, especially as the intended public meeting, is
to be held on Nottingham forest, on Monday next.
Large assemblies of the people have been convened
in Birmingham, Manchester, Leeds, Glasgow, Sheffield, and other places, to express the opinions of the
non-represented part of the community, as to the
necessity of an organic change in the constitution
of the electoral and legislative bodies. The leaders
of this movement for a radical change, insist that the
present system has worked ill for the masses—that
the benefits promised from Earl Grey's Reform
Bill have not been realized—that as to the people
at large, those promises have only been illusory—that
the boasted Reform Bill did not go far enough—that
in fact it was based on a wrong principle, that it
only emancipated *property*, instead of emancipating
persons, and that it left the great majority of the
nation, every one not possessed of a certain amount
of property—it left all these without political rights,
without privileges or votes, and in fact in a situation
very little different from that of slaves and helots of
the system.

It is well known that we **are** strenuous advocates
for an EXTENSION OF THE SUFFRAGE. We hold
that the suffrage is the right of every man; that
abstractedly considered, no man can, without in-
justice, deny to his fellow man the right of a vote,
if he be not incapacitated by nature for want of
reason, or by law, for the commission of crime.—
We know however there are others who argue differ-
ently, who say the *people* do not want the vote, that
only a *few* of them are sensible of its worth—that
the people are so ignorant that they do not under-
stand the value of a vote, nor have they any desire
for the attainment of it.—Is this so?—Radical Re-

formers of Nottingham and its neighborhood, *we
appeal to* YOU—YOU can determine this, as far as this
part of the country is concerned—if you are so
ignorant as not to know the value of the elective
franchise—that it is this, and this alone, that can
peaceably, quietly, and effectively, work a nation's
weal or woe—if you are so ignorant as this, STAY
AWAY FROM THE MEETING, AND DESERVE ALL YOUR
ENEMIES SAY OF YOU—if you are so careless that
you regard not the privelege of a vote, STAY AWAY
*from the meeting, and your friends will cease to urge
that you have intelligence and virtue sufficient to en-
title you to the franchise.*—The question can alone
be determined by YOU, and we leave the issue of
Monday next to decide it.

Others say that the masses are not to be trusted,
that they would use force to effect their object—that
universal suffrage would be dangerous to property,
and that you know not yet how to respect the rights
of others. Can this be true? WE say that it is a
calumny; your friends every where declare the same;
let your conduct on Monday show that you are peace-
able and orderly, that you know how to respect the
rights of others, while you uphold your own, and let
not the poignant feeling of your wrongs, lead you to
utter a word which shall give reasonable cause of
alarm or dissatisfaction to any who would desire to
uphold your righteous cause. Be firm, be peacea-
ble, be united, and by this conduct you will gain the
support of the wise and the good, by which, and by
which alone, you will, you must, at no distant day,
gain " a full, a free, and fair representation of the
people in Parliament." But if you do not attend
the meeting, if the working men of this populous
district, manifest so much apathy in the cause, that
they will not even cross their own thresholds, to ask
for their rights, then it will be demonstrated to all,
that the time is not yet come, and you will be held
up to the scorn and derision of your political enemies.
If you desert your own cause, blame not the middle
classes for not coming to your rescue. The middle
classes know they are powerless, without you to aid
them; and they are anxiously awaiting to see, whether you are alive to your own interests, to assist in
working out your own deliverance.

We know there are many who will be ready to
reply, that wages are small, that the wants of the
family are large, that a day's work can ill be spared,
that a few hours will make a difference in the figure
on Saturday night. Granted—we know it; we feel
your difficulties, we commiserate your situation—
but remember, the object in view is *a display of
numbers, to show you are in earnest*—to prove that
you are aware of the value of the working man having a voice in Parliament, where at present he is
only virtually represented and really misrepresented—
if you think this is not worth the sacrifice, that this is
not worth striving for, stay away from the meeting, and
proclaim to all the world, that you are ready, like
Esau, to sell your birthright for a mess of pottage.

Plate 9.4   Chartism, an editorial from the *Nottingham Review*, 2 November 1838. Opinions in the press regarding the Chartist movement in Nottingham were deeply divided: the *Nottingham Journal* was published in the conservative interest; the *Nottingham Mercury* was a whig paper in decline by the 1840s; and the *Nottingham Review*, from which this extract is taken, was a radical paper.

Reports on Chartist activity in the three newspapers tended to reflect the political position of the proprietor, and the *Nottingham Review* , founded by Charles Sutton in 1808, consistently supported the Chartist cause. It printed the national petition in full on two separate occasions, and carried many editorials on the subject of franchise reform. One of the movement's leaders, the Nottingham MP Feargus O'Connor, once described the *Review* as 'the best supporter of our cause of all the provincial papers' (*Nottingham Review*, 29 October 1847). Despite this, the *Review* was less of a Chartist paper than a middle-class journal with radical views, largely as a result of the influence of its editor, Richard Sutton. This middle-class radicalism was also reflected in its strong support for the repeal of the Corn Laws.

A more peaceful, though potentially troublesome manifestation of tension among the textile workers came in the Chartist movement of the 1830s and 1840s. The Chartists sought political reform, including male suffrage and the secret ballot, as a means towards ameliorating the economic and social problems of the poor, and to this end they presented mass petitions to Parliament in 1839, 1842 and 1848. Although all three failed, the movement elicited considerable sympathy in the east midlands industrial towns. The first major Chartist meeting in Nottingham was chaired by a prominent member of an early framework knitters union, and 'in the Nottingham area Chartists *en masse* tended to be equated with framework knitters' (Church 1966: 128, 153). The early leaders in Loughborough were both framework knitters, and the trade also provided leadership in Leicestershire (Harrison 1959).

The first phase of the movement was in 1838–39, and an early initiative in Leicestershire came at Loughborough in August 1838 with the formation of 'The Loughborough District of the National Union', and during the autumn interest spread to Nottingham with a mass meeting on the Forest. By February 1839 the Loughborough Chartists were reported to be arming, and rumours spread that pikes were being made in Shepshed and Loughborough and that firearms had been acquired. A second mass meeting was held in Nottingham in March 1839, and from May regular Sunday meetings were held at different venues around the town. Through July the Chartists held evening meetings in the Market Square, occasionally attracting up to 3,000 people, while trouble was threatened in Hinckley, and the Home Secretary was asked to send troops to Loughborough. After the national holidays called for mid-August, however, the movement lost much of its momentum.

A second phase opened in 1841, and in a period of adverse economic conditions Feargus O'Connor, a national leader of the movement, received a tumultuous welcome when he spoke in Nottingham in February 1842. Leicester could muster 3,000 Chartists by July 1842, while regular meetings in Loughborough attracted crowds of up to 7,000. Special constables were sworn in and 1,500 arrests were made at an evening meeting during June. Leicester was the venue for strikes and riots during August 1842. The movement also gathered momentum in Nottingham when a by-election was held in the town in August. Leading Chartists lent their support to Joseph Sturge, a Quaker reformer whose programme included five of the six points of the Charter. Sturge was not elected, and efforts to use industrial disruption in support of Chartism were frustrated because the magistrates took measures to prevent a crowd of 5,000 Chartists marching on the town from Mapperley Hill. The second Chartist petition was rejected in 1842, and the movement again lost impetus, but it revived with O'Connor's election as one of Nottingham's MPs in 1847, which coincided with a further period of economic depression. In April 1848 10,000 Chartists assembled on the Forest, and the movement was also revived in Loughborough and Leicester (Smith 1975; VCH Leics II 1954: 14; Church 1966: 128–47; Wyncoll 1966).

Ultimately the movement failed, even if most of the points of the charter were later achieved. What it revealed was the willingness of industrial workers to rally around a cause if they considered it likely to ease their economic difficulties. To this end the agitation was also firmly linked to anti-Poor Law sentiments after 1834. Leicester Chartism was stiffened by the opening of the town's new workhouse in 1837, and similar connections between the two movements have been demonstrated for agitation at the Basford Union Workhouse in 1844 (Griffin 1974), and for Chartist rioting at Leicester in the summer of 1848 (when new regulations were introduced by the Guardians) (VCH Leics IV 1958: 217). Chartist activities in Nottingham in 1848 coincided with a trade depression which saw 1,600 people packed into the workhouse (Church 1966: 146). Chartism was in fact a substitute for union organization in these years. Embryonic organizations seldom survived a downswing in the economic cycle, and the textile industries were beset with the additional problems of a dispersed and predominantly female labour force. Hundreds of women had full-time jobs, often putting their children out to child minders – who might be girls of no more than six to eight years old – or dosing them with 'Godfrey's Cordial' (laudanum dissolved in treacle) in order to keep them quiet.

The conditions under which textile workers operated were often appalling. In the lace trade boys began as threaders, which was not particularly arduous work, but which could involve them working all hours of day or night. Lace finishing usually took place in small workshops where in the 1840s women often worked twelve or thirteen hours a day. Wages were poor. Girls usually started at 1s. or 1s. 6d. a week, rising to perhaps 3s. by the age of twelve. This was lace, and conditions were marginally worse in the hosiery trade, where children started younger, worked longer hours, and earned relatively less. Such conditions were possible because factory legislation did not touch the workshops at the heart of the two trades, and it was only with the introduction of compulsory elementary education that some of the worst abuses of child labour were eradicated (Wardle 1966).

Attempts to organize the framework knitters began before the end of the eighteenth century, but apart from ambitious schemes such as those of Gravenor Henson in the opening years of the nineteenth century, economic conditions, the dispersal of a large proportion of the work-force and the fragmentation of early unions, all helped to prevent effective union activity before the 1850s. When it eventually arrived this tended to be among the skilled workers, including the Rotary Union and the Circular Union in Nottingham. As the industry moved into factories it was possible for the unions to exercise some discipline over their members and to force up earnings and reduce hours when economic conditions were favourable. In the gloom of the 1880s it was still difficult for unions to survive, especially as many employers moved their businesses into the countryside to escape the restrictions which were being imposed in the towns. But progress was possible. In 1884 the Leicester and Leicestershire Amalgamated Hosiery Union was formed with the intention of recruiting among women and in the countryside. A major strike in 1886 led to firms leaving the town, and to strengthen interests the Nottingham, Leicester and Ilkeston workers were brought together in 1888 in the Midland Counties Hosiery Federation. Recruitment was attempted in some of the more difficult centres including Belper and Hinckley, but the problems of recruiting in the villages proved almost insuperable (Gurnham 1976: 8–17, 31–42, 45–56).

The picture was similar in the lace industry where unions only became successful in the prosperity which followed the Great Exhibition. As demand for lace spread across the globe, twisthands sought to set up associations for their mutual benefit, and the curtain, lace and plain net branches of the trade all established craft unions to monopolize skilled labour. The employers' response was to move into the countryside leaving Nottingham as the commercial centre. The craft unions came together in the 1870s as the Amalgamated Society of Operative Lace Makers, but the new organization made the mistake of looking leniently upon, and sometimes even helping, men who became part or full owners of machines. This facilitated fragmentation and enhanced the trend for Nottingham wages to be 30–50 per cent higher than those in Long Eaton, Beeston and Derby. In the 1890s the union had to accept lower wages in Nottingham, while its restrictive practices encouraged employers to move into the villages. But the Amalgamated Society remained as the pre-eminent union in the industry down to 1914, despite the establishment of other unions within the trade, and despite its inability to control abuses of the Factory Acts outside of Nottingham. As late as 1905 it was still possible for a man to work from 4 a.m. to 10 p.m. seven days a week in Long Eaton (Cuthbert 1960).

Between 1750 and 1900 the transformation of communications in the East Midlands had incalculable repercussions. Goods and people could move faster and more cheaply than ever before, and the knock-on effect in terms of trade and industry was immense. Change was already beginning in 1750 but turnpike roads and canals together increased the movement of goods in the region on a scale not previously considered practical. The economic significance which this gave to the region proved short-lived. From the 1830s the railway not only transformed the movement of goods, it altered the basic economics of whole industries. The concealed Nottinghamshire coalfield was opened up; the Derbyshire iron industry was kept in production by bringing in ore from elsewhere; the hosiery and lace industries were mechanized; engineering grew to become a major interest; and a variety of new ventures commenced. It may even be argued that the railway unlocked the resources which made it possible for the East Midlands to enjoy the full benefits of the Industrial Revolution, at last breaking down the stifling communications barriers, and creating opportunities which made mechanization viable. The railway also did much more, protecting the dairying concerns of south Derbyshire against the worst ravages of the agricultural depression, for example, or enabling thousands of people to pay regular visits to the seaside or to visit relations. By 1900 some of the fundamental problems confronting the region's economy had been overcome: coal sales were no longer restricted to local markets, and the lost Lincolnshire wool industry had been adequately replaced. Town growth, rapid before 1830, had proceeded remorselessly until the balance of population was firmly in the urban communities. While some places and industries suffered in this transformation, the great majority benefited.

Local insularity could not survive in these circumstances; the debate over relations between the locality and the nation simply faded from view as enclosure, turnpike, canal and railway Bills brought parliamentary legislation into the everyday lives of local people, and as the benefits of local government reform became apparent in the towns just as the evils arising from the absence of reform were being exposed in the countryside. With the Poor Law coming under the auspices of a central board of commissioners, and with educational provision moving from the voluntary societies into the hands of school boards elected according to central government rules, the concept of the nation became ever more real. Moreover, the breakdown of insularity was not merely in terms of the locality and the nation. The multitude of small communities served by separate market towns disappeared. Since the Middle Ages the size of the market region had gradually been increasing, until improved communications made it possible for a few large towns to become local capitals with strong links across a broad hinterland. The county towns were the clearest example of this process. A downturn in the Nottingham economy, for example, affected the number of daytrippers and holidaymakers visiting Skegness, with severe repercussions for lodging house keepers in the resort. By 1900 much of the East Midlands had come under the influence of a few large towns, particularly those in the industrial belt, and this was a trend which continued into the present century.

Part four

The East Midlands in the Twentieth Century

Chapter 10

Town and Country

Since 1900 the East Midlands has experienced changes which have been in many ways more profound and far-reaching than during any previous period, and in economic terms the region has been one of the most dynamic outside the south-east. Some of the changes have extended trends already well under way in Victorian England. Thus population has continued to grow, and the dominance of the urban centres has become more marked. Just 23 per cent of the region's population lived in Lincolnshire by 1971, a far cry from the county's medieval ascendancy. On the other hand, in the course of the present century many of the old remaining communications barriers have disappeared. Travel, already made easier by the railway, has been further transformed by the internal-combustion engine; energy, dictated for so long by the location of the coal-fields, now comes from electricity, natural gas and oil (the last two being brought into the region). Transport costs have been cut to a point where they no longer dictate the location of industry, and this in turn has ensured that almost all goods pass out of the region by road or railway. New technology has affected virtually every activity of the region. Even in agriculture the changes have been marked. Leicestershire, for example, is no longer predominantly a pastoral county because modern farming techniques, together with price and subsidy incentives, have made it profitable to plough up the clays once again.

Population

The majority of East Midlanders reside today in the urban belt stretching south from the Yorkshire border and bounded on the west by a line from Chesterfield to Derby, and on the east by a line from Worksop to Nottingham, with an outward advance into the new colliery villages created in the 1920s. In the south of the region the boundary is formed by Leicester and Hinckley (Osborne

1954). This urban belt largely coincides with east Derbyshire and the Nottinghamshire concealed coalfield. Some 30 per cent of the total population reside in
the three largest towns and their fringes, and about 18 per cent on the
industrialized section of the main coalfield. Overall numbers have continued to
follow an upward movement. From 2 million in 1901 population passed 3
million and reached 3.47 million in 1971, a rise of 69 per cent in seventy years.
Structurally the changes of the nineteenth century have not been repeated, and
the distribution of population remains much the same as in 1901 (Table 19).
Some further relative decline has occurred in Lincolnshire, but Nottinghamshire and Leicestershire have continued to increase their overall proportion. A
slight reduction in Derbyshire's numbers can probably be explained in terms of
boundary changes, particularly in regard to suburban areas in the north of the
county which have become part of Sheffield. Eastern Leicestershire has continued to decline, and in 1951 70 per cent of the county's population was
concentrated in Leicester, Loughborough and their surrounding urban districts. In the first half of the century Nottinghamshire was gaining by migration
from the northern industrial counties, but losing to London and the south-east.
A pronounced inflow has also taken place from Derbyshire. In the decades
before 1901 Lincolnshire was the chief single source of migrants into Nottinghamshire, but while numbers from Derbyshire increased down to 1951 the
flow from Lincolnshire diminished.

Table 19   The structure of population in the twentieth century (%)*

County	1911	1921	1931	1951	1961	1971	1981
Derbyshire	29	29	28	27	27	26	28
Leicestershire	20	20	20	21	21	22	26
Lincolnshire	24	24	24	23	23	23	17
Nottinghamshire	26	26	27	28	28	28	30
Rutland	1	1	1	1	1	1	—

* The figures relate to county totals as given in the census, and are not adjusted for
boundary changes. The consequent distortion is most obvious in relation to the 1981
figures, following the local government reorganization of 1974 in which the county of
Rutland became part of Leicestershire, and part of north Lincolnshire was subsumed
into the new county of Humberside.

(Source: Census Population Tables)

Migratory trends in Derbyshire for 1931–51 show that urban industry
tended to determine population trends. Much of the county experienced
outward movement, particularly from the coalfield and the Peak area. Virtually all of Nottinghamshire south of the Trent (including Nottingham) increased
through migration, while areas north of the river were characterized either by
emigration or rates of immigration well below the county average. The broad
picture is of movement into Greater Nottingham and migration away from the

coalfield as the exposed seams were worked out. The outstanding feature of population change in the county 1931–51 was the continuous and rapid expansion of the urban industrial areas as compared with relatively small increases in the more rural areas of eastern Nottinghamshire. It also highlighted Nottingham's links with the Erewash valley towns of Derbyshire and the urban belt of Leicestershire, as well as the concentration of the coalfield population in the towns between Nottingham and Worksop (Powell 1955b).

The expanding dormitories for Nottingham, Leicester and Derby had a considerable impact on surrounding parishes. The spread of urban influence was particularly marked in Leicestershire where industry had been widely distributed in both towns and villages (Powell 1955a). Parts of the Peak District and Sherwood Forest are still sparsely populated, and along the Trent and the foot of the Lincoln Edge agricultural villages persist. By 1931 many Derbyshire and Nottinghamshire parishes had smaller populations than a century earlier, and the same was true of Leicestershire. In the north-west of the county industrial development brought marked growth, especially around Coalville. With Hinckley and Loughborough it constituted one of the three largest towns in the county (outside Leicester), each of which had grown as a result of industrial development. The rural-urban balance was slightly adjusted during the Second World War as military camps and other war establishments temporarily increased rural population. After 1945 rural growth was inhibited by the housing shortage and the lack of public transport provision, but although population decline again occurred in the countryside during the 1950s it did so on a scale much less widespread than in the nineteenth century.

Between 1951 and 1961 all the east midlands counties experienced natural increase either equal to or exceeding the national rate. Except for Holland and Kesteven they not only retained the equivalent of the whole of their natural increase, but also gained further population by net inward migration. For the region as a whole between 1951 and 1961 the increase was 6.8 per cent, with Leicestershire, Nottinghamshire and Rutland above, and Derbyshire and the three divisions of Lincolnshire below this figure. The largest increase was in Rutland (14.4%) and the smallest in Holland (1.7%). Absolute decline in numbers occurred in the surrounds of Market Harborough and Ashbourne and in the High Peak, with the greatest losses of all coming from the centres of Derby and Leicester. Areas of substantial increase included the Soar valley around Leicester, the middle Trent valley, and parts of the concealed coalfield.

The redistribution of the region's population, as a result of migration and differential rates of natural increase, has led to an impressive growth of towns and industrial, mining and suburbanized villages. Few agricultural villages have grown since the mid-nineteenth century, apart from a number connected with quarrying and with RAF stations, and many have declined. The built-up areas have spread outwards, most notably in the Nottingham and Derby districts, and on the coalfield stretching northwards. Continuous urban, or suburban, development extends west of Nottingham into Derbyshire, and very nearly one-half of the total population of the region lives within a 20-mile radius of central Nottingham, including Derby and the conurbation of Mansfield, Mansfield Woodhouse, Kirkby-in-Ashfield and Sutton-in-Ashfield (Edwards 1966a: 354–7). In 1961 Nottingham was the eighth largest city in England (though it slipped to eleventh in 1981 and lost its position as the largest city in the region to Leicester), but its official population of over 300,000 in 1961 was just part of approximately 700,000 people living within a 10-mile radius of the Old Market Square. Leicestershire also has its urban sprawl. Leicester, Lough-borough and Hinckley were the focus of population growth down to 1971, with the result that the county's population is heavily concentrated in an unbroken urban area stretching from Kegworth in the north to Hinckley in the south-west.

The most recent structural changes have seen population movement out of the city centres and into the suburbs, thereby reducing the size of some of the major towns and leading to the growth of villages around them. Leicester declined in population during the 1950s, but this was amply offset by the growth of numbers in the adjoining urban districts of Oadby and Wigston and in rapidly growing parishes in the rural districts of Barrow-on-Soar, Billesdon and Blaby. Birstall, Thurmaston, Newtown Linford, Glenfield, Glenfield Frith, Kirby Muxloe, Leicester Forest East, Braunstone, Enderby, Narborough, Croft, Countesthorpe, Glen Parva, Evington, Sileby, Scraptoft, Queniborough and Syston have all increased since 1945 as a direct result of proximity to Leicester. On the other hand, although by 1970 the administrative unit of the county borough of Leicester contained only 37.1 per cent of the county's population compared with 45.2 per cent in 1951, its suburban development had spread to a point where its local dominance was greater than ever before (Pye 1972: 443, 449).

Towns

In regional terms, the twentieth century has witnessed a trend towards town-based sub-regions within the East Midlands. Although the county towns are the clearest cases of this phenomenon they are not alone; Mansfield, for example, stands at the centre of an urban complex in west Nottinghamshire, as does Chesterfield in north Derbyshire, while some of the smaller Lincolnshire towns, including Market Rasen, Horncastle, Sleaford and Louth, are recogniz-able as regional urban centres. Perhaps surprisingly, none of the individual towns has emerged as a regional 'capital'. Twentieth-century regions often pivot on a capital town: the south-west is seen to hinge on Bristol, the West

Midlands on Birmingham and the north-east on Newcastle. However, distinctions of this nature are not always straightforward, and just as the north-west has no obvious capital because of the proximity of Manchester and Liverpool, so the rivalry between Nottingham and Leicester in the East Midlands has had the same effect. Nottingham, which enjoys the status of being a leading provincial town, is often taken to be the capital, but the position of Leicester ensures that neither city plays a role parallel to that of Birmingham in the West Midlands (Fawcett 1960: 114; Law 1980: 26–7). At the same time Leicestershire is arguably the best English example of a 'city region', since the county is dominated by a centrally located county town with its suburbs and satellites, and further out a ring of market towns near the edge of the county. Parts of north Leicestershire look towards Loughborough, Derby and Nottingham, while the Ashby area has links with Burton on Trent, and in the south-west attention is focussed on Hinckley, Rugby and Coventry (Pye 1972: 472–8).

Urban regions have grown out of town development in the nineteenth century, but since 1900 the emphasis has changed. Physically, boundary changes mean that the major towns are now much larger than they were in the past. Medieval Nottingham measured approximately 1,250 yards by 800 yards; today, after a series of extensions, the town is roughly 9 miles north–south and 5½ miles west–east. The area covered by the city of Leicester doubled in 1935 when a newly defined boundary took in a number of suburbs including Humberstone and part of Braunstone. A borough extension of the 1960s raised Derby's physical area from 8,100 to 19,100 acres. A boundary extension in Grimsby during the 1920s increased the extent of the borough from 3,260 to nearly 6,000 acres. Such changes partly explain the growth of town populations during the twentieth century, which has otherwise been rather less impressive than during the nineteenth century. They have also left Nottingham, Leicester and Derby at the centre of a vast urban sprawl through the western portion of the region. As smaller places have grown the effect has been of a long line of urban settlement, typified by the countryside west of Nottingham towards Derby and along the Erewash valley, and around Mansfield.

Meanwhile in the town centres the ravages of the planners, particularly during the 1960s, have led to the destruction of much of Victorian Leicester, and the construction of at least one major city centre road in Nottingham which bears no relationship to earlier patterns. Traffic schemes in both Nottingham and Mansfield are said by one of the most eminent of recent commentators to 'have involved the destruction of a number of good buildings and the disruption, to no aesthetic advantage, of the old street patterns . . . the redevelopment of parts of Nottingham has promoted very little architecture of merit' (Pevsner and Williamson 1979: 37–8). Churches and railway stations have disappeared; modern shopping centres have taken their places. The results have not always been very flattering. Derby's architectural heritage has been all but destroyed by post-war development. The whole of twentieth-century architecture in Lincolnshire (town and country) was dismissed by Pevsner in 1964 as not worth commenting upon (Pevsner and Harris 1964: 79–80) – a far cry from the pages he devoted to the county's medieval limestone churches – and neither Derbyshire nor Leicestershire fared much better in his opinion.

Within this east midlands urban sprawl are to be found the majority of economic activities other than agriculture, even though it covers barely one-eighth of the total area (Edwards 1966b: 63). It is a region characterized by a well-diversified industrial and employment structure. As a result, it was spared the worst deficiencies of the inter-war years, and was well-placed to capitalize on opportunities which abounded in the two decades after 1945 (Edwards 1966a). Nottingham, Derby and Lincoln all grew in numbers at or above the national rate in nearly all the intercensal periods to 1961. In Nottingham and Derby continuous growth was possible because staple industries were prosperous for long periods, and because eventual stagnation or contraction was offset by the growth of new kinds of manufacturing. Thus by the time the lace industry went into decline during the 1920s Nottingham had established bicycle, pharmaceutical, telephone and tobacco industries, and when railway engineering stagnated in Derby it was more than compensated by aero-engines and artificial fibres. Where replacement industries failed to materialize urban stagnation was likely, as in Lincoln when the engineering industry languished during the inter-war period. Mansfield, Worksop and Hucknall are among smaller towns to benefit from the eastward movement of population on the coalfield. The spectacular growth of Long Eaton came to an end after 1911 when the lace industry contracted, and further development came only with the subsequent expansion of other industries.

Some smaller towns, particularly market towns, have found growth difficult to generate. East Retford stagnated 1911–21, and since then growth, though smooth, has been undistinguished. Wirksworth was virtually static from 1841–1961, reflecting the decline of its lead mining and marketing interest. Southwell has registered little growth, but Ashbourne and Bakewell in Derbyshire have both experienced steady growth in the twentieth century, although in the 1950s this was entirely through migration since both recorded a natural decrease, and little significant population growth has taken place in their hinterlands during the twentieth century. They are, however, very much smaller than what might be regarded as their counterparts in the east of the region, such as Newark, Grantham, Stamford and Melton Mowbray (Edwards 1966a: 347–53).

The County Capitals

Nottingham, 'Queen of the Midlands' and proverbially famous for its pretty girls, has enjoyed considerable prestige throughout the twentieth century as it has grown out into its suburbs, particularly those north of the river. The face of the city centre has been greatly changed. J. B. Priestley found 'some very rough quarters still' in the 1930s (Priestley 1977: 130), but shortly after the war it was possible for one local writer to describe the town as

> an important, beautiful and progressive City. . . . We have seen, in the last 25 years, a splendid city begin to arise around us, a thing of beauty and design, a city for living in (not merely for getting a living in).
>
> (Chambers 1952: 8)

In 1929 the old Exchange Building in the market square was replaced by the neo-baroque Council House, but elsewhere in the city centre the influence of the planners has been all-pervasive. Maid Marian Way, laid out during the 1960s to relieve modern traffic pressures, cut diametrically across the fan of Norman streets leading from the Market Square to the Castle and created a discordant mixture of architectural styles and road alignments. The Victoria and Broad Marsh shopping centres are perhaps the most significant reminders of the demands of modern shopping and the motor car. More impressive has been the vast slum-clearance schemes of the 1920s and 1930s and, in more recent years replacement of dilapidated nineteenth-century housing in the Meadows and St Ann's, Sneinton, Lenton, Radford and Hyson Green, although the consequence has often been the dispersal of historic communities (Brazier *et al.* 1984).

At the beginning of the century Nottingham was a town of nearly 240,000 people but the rapid growth of the nineteenth century did not continue at the same level after 1900. Population climbed steadily to a peak of nearly 312,000 in 1961, since which time it has slipped to 277,203 in 1981. The reorganization of residential land, and population dispersal to outlying suburbs, and the creation of dormitory towns outside the city boundary, has been largely responsible for this trend. Although it is characteristic of English conurbations the speed of decline has been faster than in comparable towns, and it is the more remarkable in view of the influx of ethnic minorities from the new commonwealth countries (Husain 1975). Nottingham's rapid decline has been sufficient to ensure that Greater Nottingham, which reached almost 500,000 in 1971, slipped by 4.5 per cent during the 1970s even though only one of the six suburbs, West Bridgford, experienced a reduction in numbers, and Arnold grew by 11.4 per cent.

Modern Nottingham has a variety of industrial interests which give it a

Plate 10.1 Beeston, Nottingham, the Boots industrial site. Jesse Boot was one of the foremost entrepreneurs of the region in the late-nineteenth and early-twentieth centuries. He opened his first retail pharmacy in Nottingham in 1877, and used his astute business sense to build up an empire running to over 1,000 outlets by the early 1930s. Today, *Boots* is a household name countrywide.

The Company has various sites in Nottingham, of which the most significant is the massive industrial complex between the railway and the canal in Beeston (which lies west of the city). In 1927 a Works Planning Committee was established to organize the movement of the company's operations to the Beeston site, and a year later the earliest plant was opened, the soap factory in the south-east corner of the site. Building has continued since that date and two of the factory buildings, together with the office building, have been described by Pevsner as among 'the most important twentieth-century work in the county' (Pevsner and Williamson 1979: 70). The massive glass and concrete building for the wet and dry goods, which was opened in 1933, did much to change the Boots image by erasing the local picture of a firm operating from out of a jumble of old factories on the edge of Nottingham's slums. It also helped to raise the company's productivity.

Boot was also a considerable philanthropist, and one of his most lasting memorials is the University of Nottingham's campus on the Highfields site between Nottingham and Beeston. Boot acquired the estate in 1920, and the following year he devised a scheme for a public pleasure park and a 60-acre University College campus on the property. After the University building was opened in 1928 by King George V, Boot was created Lord Trent.

well-balanced economic structure. The dominance of textiles, particularly hosiery, lace and clothing before the First World War is less marked. Lace, in particular, has declined in importance, and in recent years employment in the tobacco industry has also fallen. By contrast, the pharmaceutical industry has seen considerable growth. Jesse Boot's pioneering shop of the 1870s had become 1,000 branches nationwide by 1933, and for Nottingham the retail outlets are no less significant than Boots' enormous industrial complex west of the town. These developments, along with the manufacture of bicycles and telephone equipment, and together with the expansion of engineering and the rapid growth of service industries, have helped to maintain Nottingham's industrial position in the twentieth century. Broadly speaking industry has concentrated in the Leen and Trent valleys to the north-west and south of the city centre, while the major business district has been located around the Old Market Square. The market place was itself transformed in the 1920s when stalls were removed to a covered building on Parliament Street, the new Council House was built, and the annual Goose Fair transferred to its present site on the Forest (Edwards 1966a: 242; 374–86).

Leicester has continued to grow for much of the twentieth century, with an increase of population from 212,000 in 1901 to 284,208 in 1971. In 1981 the city's population stood at 328,835. Leicester became a city in 1919; in 1928 the title of Lord Mayor was conferred upon its chief magistrate; and in 1926 the see of Leicester was carved out of the diocese of Peterborough. For all that it has remained an unimpressive town. J. B. Priestley wrote in the 1930s of its centre that it was 'neither dignified nor very extensive, indeed hardly worthy of the excellent residential quarters outside it' (Priestley 1977: 115). The most striking change in the town's community life since 1945 has arisen as a result of the influx of immigrants from the Commonwealth. Abundant employment opportunities initially attracted migrants from the West Indies during the 1950s, followed by a further influx from India and some from Pakistan. From the late 1960s immigrants began to arrive in the town from Kenya, of whom three-quarters were Asians. The Kenyans made up nearly 40 per cent of Leicester's immigrant total by 1971 when Leicester had the highest concentration of East African Asians anywhere in Britain. Their numbers were further swelled in 1972–73 when Asians were expelled from Uganda. As a consequence of these trends, by 1983 Commonwealth immigrants accounted for 24.1 per cent of the city's population, and over 75 per cent in two areas, Highfields and Belgrave (Simmons 1974, II: 104–5; Millward 1985: 117–19). Industrially Leicester has moved during the twentieth century away from an emphasis on hosiery and footwear towards other industries, particularly engineering. In 1901 nearly 45 per cent of the city's labour force was in hosiery, 35 per cent in boots and shoes, and 4 per cent in engineering. By 1925 the proportions had changed to 40 per cent, 25 per cent, and 14 per cent respectively. By 1951 the respective figures were 30, 20 and 22 per cent.

Derby has grown steadily through the twentieth century, partly aided by boundary changes, to reach 220,000 in 1981. In 1927 the Anglican diocese of Derby was formed out of the existing diocese of Southwell and the parish church of All Saints Church became Derby Cathedral. In 1977 the town was granted city status. The major industrial developments of the twentieth century have included the opening of the British Celanese works at Spondon, and the further growth of engineering. In 1938 three major industries characterized the town; the manufacture of railway rolling stock, of motor cars and aero-engines, and of artificial silk. These groups, coupled with engineering and electrical and mechanical engineering, occupied 48 per cent of the registered employed, while

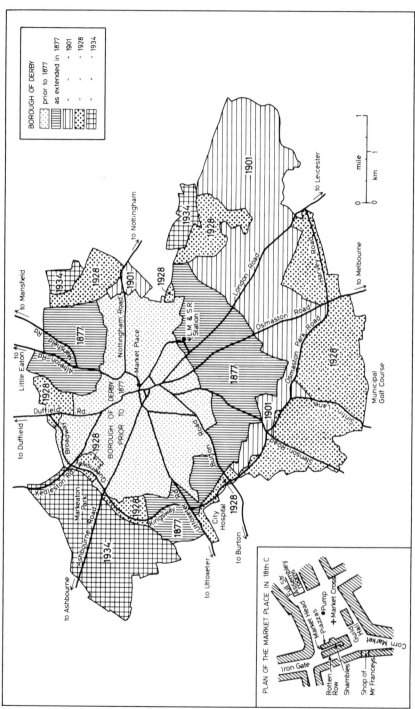

Figure 10.1 The growth of Derby, 1877–1934 (after Heath and Christian 1985)

three major firms stood out, the LMS railway company, Rolls-Royce and British Celanese, which turned towards synthetic fibres and chemical products after beginning with cellulostic fibres, in addition to fabrics. Late twentieth-century Derby is still an engineering town, particularly with regard to the railways and aero-engines at Rolls-Royce. By contrast with Nottingham, Derby has not diversified its industrial structure, and it has been much slower to build up service industries. It has been replaced by Matlock as the administrative centre of the county, and in general terms its influence extends little further than Matlock to the north, Ashbourne to the west and Burton on Trent to the south-west. To the east, as has always been the case historically, its influence has been severely curtailed by the role of Nottingham, the larger centre (Vollans 1949; Edwards 1966a: 242–4; 457–67).

Lincoln, with 81,000 people in 1981 is by far the smallest of the major county towns in the region. The social division brought about by the 'hill' retains its fascination for outsiders; hence J. B. Priestley's vivid description dating from 1933:

> To be anybody in Lincoln you must live 'uphill', like my host and his friend, who nearly sent themselves to social oblivion, in their innocence, by first considering residence on the mere plain. Maids wanting a job point out that they have 'uphill experience' and so demand 'uphill' mistresses. In short, a successful social life in Lincoln is essentially uphill work. You labour down below, in the clanging twentieth century, and spend your leisure by the side of the Cathedral, in the twelfth century.
>
> (Priestley 1977: 343)

During the twentieth century much of Lincoln's prosperity has been derived from the engineering industry. In 1961 81 per cent of males employed in manufacturing were in engineering, and much of the work was then provided by Ruston and Hornsby. In recent years the cattle market, and the horse, sheep and cattle fairs have gone, and agricultural implement making has declined (Hill 1979). By 1961 60 per cent of all those in employment worked in the service industries, reflecting the town's role as a commercial and administrative centre for an extensive agricultural hinterland. The commercial centre lies in the southern part of the old city (Edwards 1966a: 248–9; 467–72).

Other Towns

Beyond the county towns the major growth areas have been related to industrial development. Mansfield enjoyed a second period of rapid growth associated with coal mining between 1891 and 1921, when the population rose from 16,000 to 45,000. Mining, in turn, was supplemented by the growth of factory hosiery production. As coal mining migrated eastwards Mansfield grew rapidly and housing estates were built near to each colliery, producing the urban sprawl in the area today which stretches in effect from Annesley to New Clipstone and embraces Mansfield itself (57,644 in 1971), Mansfield Woodhouse (24,805), Sutton-in-Ashfield (40,716) and Kirkby-in-Ashfield (23,628). Mansfield remains the predominant service centre for the area, and since 1945 metalworking and engineering have become significant in the town. By the 1960s Mansfield had six foundries (Law 1962–5). Chesterfield has also become the centre of a heavily industrialized region, and with a population of 74,000 in 1981 it was easily the largest Derbyshire town outside of Derby itself. Coal, iron making, chemicals and heavy engineering have become its dominant interests, although the decline of the Staveley and Sheepbridge companies has led to some diversification of the town's industrial structure with, among others, the Post Office becoming a major employer as a result of the devolution of its administration from London.

Loughborough's population had reached 46,000 by 1981 largely as a result of the twentieth-century influence of Herbert Morris (cranes) and Brush (electrical engineering), both of which offered considerable employment opportunities for men, as women became the dominant part of the hosiery labour force (Wedlock 1954). Loughborough grew as a result of broadening its industrial base, whereas Hinckley, which remained predominantly a hosiery town (although the footwear villages of Barwell and Earl Shilton were both within its urban district), grew less quickly. Scunthorpe experienced a large net inward movement during the 1950s and also registered a high rate of natural increase. Its population grew by nearly one-quarter during 1951–61 and reached nearly 80,000 by 1981, while several of its neighbouring parishes were affected by suburban growth. Ilkeston has gradually adapted to the demise of coal mining, and become increasingly dependent on textiles. It is also a commercial centre, with 40 per cent of the locally occupied population employed in various types of services in 1961 (Edwards 1966a).

East of the industrial area the towns have depended heavily on engineering, which has not always been in their best interests. Gainsborough died in the 1930s because of its rather narrow commitment to heavy engineering. In the 1960s two new firms accounted for nearly three-quarters of manufacturing employment, one of which was predominantly concerned with agricultural machinery. Grantham grew to 31,000 by 1981 largely as a centre for the production of farm machinery. However, in the 1960s manufacturing accounted for little more than one-third of the town's employment, the majority of the town's population being predominantly concerned with the construction trades and services. Newark is still a thriving market town, with some significant industrial interests including the manufacture of ball-bearings, but it also relies heavily on the service industries. Southwell, although a diocesan and administrative centre, has not expanded beyond its country-town status, and had a population of just over 6,000 in 1981 (Edwards 1966a).

It was by no means inevitable that smaller towns would fail to make progress. Stamford enjoyed significant municipal enterprise in the opening decades of the twentieth century, and the borough council has carried out an extensive programme of rehousing slum dwellers. By the 1960s one-third of the town had been rebuilt by the council (Rogers 1965: 109–110. Louth has developed as a regional centre for north Lincolnshire. In the 1950s its Friday stock market was one of the largest in the East Midlands, with no serious rival in a 45-mile radius. As a shopping centre it was able to compete successfully with Grimsby and Lincoln, while the *Louth and North Lincolnshire Advertizer*, and the Lough General Hospital, both served a considerable – if relatively thinly populated – hinterland. The town has developed a number of industries concerned with agricultural products, including food processing and preparation. Malting, canning and milling were the main interests of the 1950s, while a Leicester firm established glove making in an old canal warehouse (Goulding 1957). But this may not have been typical; in the mid-1950s no firms existed at

---

Plate 10.2   Grimsby, the docks. The revival of Grimsby in the nineteenth century was remarkable in view of the sad condition into which it had sunk by about 1700 from the former glory it enjoyed in the twelfth and thirteenth centuries. In the twentieth century its name has become synonymous with fishing, and the picture shows steam trawlers along the North Wall of the Fish Dock.
   Since 1945, trawling has offered fewer job opportunities, and Grimsby has diversified into food processing and alternative industries.

all in some of Lincolnshire's smaller country towns, while relatively few people enjoyed an industrial occupation in places such as Sleaford and Spilsby. After 1945 industrial expansion in the smaller country towns partly depended on the role of larger centres, particularly Leicester (Weekley 1957).

The fortunes of the ports and resorts of the east coast have varied. Grimsby grew steadily down to the 1930s but its population of 92,429 in 1981 was almost exactly the same as the 1931 figure. A housing shortage in the 1920s led to a borough extension in 1927 to provide building land. This did not produce a comparable increase in population because of the movement into the suburbs. Even so, by the 1960s the council had built more than 5,000 houses. Trawling was the town's major interest through the twentieth century, and until the 1960s the only industrial report to appear weekly in the local paper was concerned with fishing. As the industry became more efficient the number of fishermen declined. In 1881 5,000 or more fishermen caught under 1,000,000 cwt of fish; by 1951 3,200 fishermen landed 3,970,000 cwt. Meantime the town had grown, and more and more people were finding employment in food processing and freezing, chemicals and heavy engineering, as well as the distributive and service trades. Even this was not to last; Grimsby lost population in the 1960s partly because cod fishing declined, and the trend has continued into the 1980s, partly as a result of the Icelandic cod war (Gillett 1970).

Immingham, situated 6 miles to the north, was built as an adjunct to Grimsby in 1912, but until 1945 it was a relative failure with great areas laid out for a development which did not materialize. The coal, iron and steel industries were of particular significance to the port during the years to 1939, and after 1945 petrol and chemicals became important. By the 1960s Immingham was one of Britain's fifteen major ports, and during that decade its population increased by 50 per cent (Leave 1967). Among goods exported through Immingham in the 1960s were coal from central Nottinghamshire and north-east Derbyshire. Today it imports massive quantities of iron ore for processing at Scunthorpe. Boston hardly grew at all over the first three decades of the century. J. B. Priestley described it as having 'a very pleasant quality', and a vitality on market day which suggested prosperity in the countryside around (Priestley 1977: 349–50). After 1945 population increased as timber, foodstuffs and fertilizers became significant local industries. Agricultural employment associated with the immediate hinterland declined, although the town remained a minor regional centre for the intensively farmed fenland and for the southern wolds (Molyneux 1962–65). Its port still enjoyed a little trade, including the export of coal from the East Midlands during the 1960s (Edwards 1966a: 282).

The coming of the railway enabled the east coast resorts to develop a substantial holiday trade during the twentieth century. In 1901 Skegness had a population of 2,140 and Cleethorpes 12,578, but growth thereafter was spectacular in terms of national trends, Skegness reaching 13,580 and

Cleethorpes 35,837 by 1971, from which point they had both declined slightly by 1981. In a league drawn up in 1911 of 135 resorts classified according to population size Cleethorpes stood twenty-first and Skegness seventy-sixth (Walton 1983: 65). Skegness is a good example of how proper planning could enable a resort to develop. In 1871 Mablethorpe's population was nearly twice the size of Skegness, and in 1876 it had eighteen boarding houses to its rival's ten. With the coming of the railway it developed as a resort; during the 1880s pavilions were erected in the sandhills (Wright 1982: 189). But the town was uncoordinated and poorly planned, with the result that by 1920 Skegness was twice the size of Mablethorpe, which has continued to compare unfavourably with its southern neighbour ever since.

Despite the apparent success of the resorts from the 1870s, their relatively late development was to prove a permanent handicap in terms of expansion, and they have remained in the second division of seaside resorts. More recently Sutton, Ingoldmells and Chapel St Leonards have also grown. Ingoldmells, immediately north of the Skegness urban district boundary, was the site of Billy Butlin's first self-contained holiday camp in 1937, while along with the other two settlements it has become an area dominated by its static caravans. The sandy beaches hardly offset the colourless and featureless coastline which greets visitors, but one of the surviving regional links is provided by the relationship between this part of the coast and the inland industrial towns. In 1964 53 per cent of visitors to Skegness came from the counties of Nottinghamshire, Derbyshire and Leicestershire, and a further 25 per cent from the West Riding of Yorkshire, with 72 per cent of all day-trippers to Skegness on the August bank holiday Monday coming from the East Midlands. Even today Skegness can be regarded as 'Nottingham-by-the-Sea'. It contains branches of Nottingham shops, including the Greater Nottingham Cooperative Society, and the Nottingham *Evening Post* still circulates in the town. The coast remains an attractive retirement centre for people from the Nottingham area. The relationship survives despite the tedious 84-mile journey which still takes over two hours by road (Gurnham 1972: 73–4; Robinson 1981).

Local Government

The demands on local urban authorities during the twentieth century have been considerable, particularly in regard to house building. If the 'homes fit for heroes' promised to returning soldiers after the First World War were to materialize, a great deal depended on local government. Lloyd George's coalition administration promised in 1919 to build 500,000 houses over the following three years, thus laying down a challenge which local authorities had little option but to take up. Under the Housing and Town Planning Act (1919), and further legislation in 1923 and 1924, a massive programme of house building commenced. Nottingham corporation was particularly active. Twenty municipal estates were built during the 1920s and 1930s, mainly on the northern and western fringes of the city, while forty smaller schemes of less than a hundred dwellings each were erected in the older parts of the city, often on slum clearance sites. Between 1919 and 1965 33,178 out of 48,296 new dwellings were provided by the council, while private housing was more heavily concentrated in the surrouding suburban districts of Beeston, West Bridgford, Carlton and Arnold. The council also acquired Wollaton Hall and its 800-acre park for £200,000 in 1924, but immediately recouped the outlay by selling building plots for private houses, while leaving the house and 50 acres intact. The housing programme was accompanied by the construction of the ring road – Middleton Boulevard was built on former parkland – and by the promotion for recreational purposes of open spaces to the west of the city, including Wollaton Park. After 1945 house building resumed in the Bulwell and Bilborough areas of the city, and during the 1950s the municipal boundary was pushed out beyond the Trent into Clifton. The last major estates resulting from the 1919 principle were Clifton (1957–73). and Bestwood Park (1958–68).

Leicester City Council also took up the housing challenge after the First World War. A survey in 1919 found 1,455 households (2.6 per cent of the total) wanting to be rehoused by the authority, and a housing scheme instituted under the 1919 Act was drawn up to meet this need. The plan was to build 1,500 new dwellings, but it was only half completed by 1923 when further legislation permitted the erection of 800 more houses. Another 4,700 houses were built under the terms of legislation passed in 1924, and altogether over 9,000 houses were built by the corporation and another 3,000 were erected as a result of private enterprise with the aid of subsidies. Municipal housing estates were developed on the periphery of the city, at Braunstone, Aylestone and New Humberstone (Pritchard 1976). Slum clearance took place, particularly in the area south of St Margaret's Church. However, the council's chief contribution to municipal housing has come since 1945 as the result of plans drawn up between the wars – with municipal schemes on the east, south and north-west of the centre. Suburban development, particularly in areas such as Oadby, which grew from 6,200 to 16,300 between 1951 and 1966 almost entirely as a result of speculative building, Wigston, Blaby, Thurmaston and Birstall, has helped to produce a town which covers both a greater area of land, and is also socially divided. Expansion has involved the drastic clearance and rebuilding of parts of the inner city which has seen the disappearance of much of Victorian Leicester. A mid-Victorian industrial district of hosiery factories and terraced housing, which stretched from the Newarke south towards the Royal Infirmary, and west to the river, has been replaced, largely by the polytechnic and the much expanded infirmary. The commercial heart of

Leicester lies in the city centre, particularly the focal point around the Galow-tree Gate–Humberstone Gate apex, and the adjacent market.

Derby's built-up area increased considerably in the inter-war period as both the council and private builders erected low-density residential housing. The council was initially reluctant to become involved, proposing to build only 446 houses under the terms of the 1919 legislation. Pressure from the Ministry of Health led to a new plan for 1,000 houses, but the rate of building soon fell behind schedule. In an attempt to catch up, a delegation went to Sheffield in 1925 to inspect the cast-iron houses built in the town. They were attractive to the council not merely because of their durability, but because five could be built weekly, and the houses would not interfere with the existing programme. As a result work started in 1926 to erect 250 such houses, and such was the success of the scheme that 500 cast-iron houses were built in the town by the end of 1927. Thereafter conventional methods were sufficient to keep the building programme in being, but the 500 houses were part of 6,852 council properties built in the town between the wars (Nolan 1984). Despite borough extensions in 1927 and 1934 ribbon development meant that by 1939 the borough boundaries fell considerably short of the built-up area. Clearance took place within the town, and municipal enterprise was responsible for schools, hospitals, a technical college, and the acquisition of Markeaton and Darley Parks, quite apart from the bus station which was one of the most advanced to be completed in the 1930s. Since 1945 industrial estates have been developed, and pre-war housing plans have been fulfilled with the building of the Mackworth estate in the north-western part of the borough, and the Chaddesden estate to the north-east. An outer ring road was built in the 1920s and 1930s, but a major development of the 1970s was the realignment of the A52 from Nottingham as a dual carriageway almost to the centre of the town, part of a massive redevelopment – including the completion of an inner ring road – which has changed the face of the modern town.

In Lincoln council-house building commenced in the 1920s, and by the 1970s between one-third and one-half of Lincoln households occupied council houses. These new estates have been built on land beyond the old core of the town, towards the city boundary on the north of the town, and beyond the boundaries to the south, thereby diluting the old tensions and jealousies. A boundary extension in 1959 took in 1,390 acres of open land, largely for building, and congestion in Lincoln has been reduced by the recent opening of a new ring road.

Housing was not the only problem faced by local government in the twentieth century. Most authorities kept up their earlier concern with civic pride by attempting to ensure that towns had adequate open spaces. Leicester council purchased a 20-acre site at Aylestone in the southern suburbs of the town as an open space for local people, but this was the only such area established in the first two decades of the twentieth century in the town. The council also hoped to establish small open sites in the older parts of the built-up area, but here the problem was a difficulty in acquiring the sites, and only three small ornamental gardens (Castle, Westcotes and St George's Church) as well as two playgrounds were set up. As the suburban districts expanded from the 1920s onwards, the council embarked on a rapid programme which ensured the location of a major park or recreation ground within or adjacent to the newly emerging suburban districts. The largest was Braunstone Park, opened in 1925 on a 157-acre site. Between 1950 and 1975 a further twenty-seven parks and recreation grounds were opened forming a suburban ring of open spaces around the city. Altogether the council had established fifty-five park sites by 1975 (Strachan and Bowler 1976).

As local education authorities, councils also found themselves responsible for schooling. Since 1902 the local education authorities have controlled and directed education. Independent schooling continues; indeed, it has increased since the end of the direct grant system. Both Loughborough and Nottingham have flourishing high schools, but Derby's caters only for girls and Leicester has no large independent school. The Leicester LEA took over in 1902 what was at the time a very efficient system of schooling, the major new developments being required in secondary rather than elementary education, but it was the 1920s before any marked advance took place. The number of places in secondary education increased to 3,800 by 1939, and of these 300 were free places. The elementary system was also reorganized in the town during the decade. Educational provision was not always made available without difficulty during the inter-war period, as is clear from the problems encountered in setting up new schools in the expanding Dukeries villages of Nottinghamshire (Waller 1983: Ch. 7).

With the 1944 Education Act a considerable expansion of education facilities has taken place. Leicester's school population rose from 36,000 in 1945 to over 50,000 by 1970, partly because of the birth rate, but also because children were staying on longer at school. Leicestershire was at the forefront of educational experiment; in 1969, for example, it became the first county in England to eliminate selection at age eleven, partly as a result of the 'Leicestershire experiment' of 1957 which pioneered the use of 11–14 and 14–18 schools. The transition was generally smooth, partly because the majority of secondary schools were maintained, rather than denominational. Only the Loughborough endowed schools refused to join. The leaving age was raised to sixteen in 1972. Nottingham in the 1960s had 125 primary schools with places for over 31,000 children, while a further 20,000 pupils were to be found in the city's secondary schools, eighteen of which were developed along bilateral lines to accommodate intelligent children who failed the eleven-plus, by enabling them to take O-levels. It was replaced by the comprehensive system during the 1970s. The town's first comprehensive school, Fairham, on the Clifton estate, was opened in the mid-1960s.

Further and higher education took longer to establish, but it grew steadily after the Second World War. Leicester established a teacher training college, and both the colleges of art and technology (which later became the polytechnic) expanded. Nottingham developed similar facilities in the post-war period including People's College, Clarendon College and Basford Hall as further education colleges. The College of Education was opened at Clifton in 1960, and during the 1970s merged with the Regional College of Technology to form Trent Polytechnic. Other colleges of education were opened in Lincoln and Leicester, Derby and Matlock (both now combined with the Derby College of Technology), and Eaton Hall near East Retford (now closed). Adult education gained momentum from the early years of the century as a result of Workers' Educational Association classes. By 1911 branches had been established in Nottingham, Derby, Mansfield and Sutton-in-Ashfield. In 1919 the local branches of the organization were combined to form the East Midlands district, while in 1920 Nottingham University founded the first Department of Adult Education in the country, with centres in Matlock, Derby, Loughborough, Lincoln, Grantham, Stamford and Boston. Since that time Leicester University's department of Adult Education has become responsible for the south of the region, while the University of Hull has interests in north Lincolnshire, and the universities of Manchester and Sheffield in northern Derbyshire.

The region has three universities, one in Nottingham already established by 1900; the second, in Leicester, though much discussed in the 1880s, a product of the 1920s; and the third the former College of Technology in Loughborough. University College, Nottingham, dates from the 1870s. After the First World War plans were drawn up for an East Midlands University, which would have incorporated the technical schools at Derby, Lincoln, Northampton and the technical college at Loughborough, the agricultural college at Sutton Bonington, and the proposed Leicester university college. In the end Leicester refused to cooperate, leaving Nottingham on its own. Financial problems dogged the university until the 1920s when Sir Jesse Boot made available money and land for a new campus, as a result of which the university moved most of its departments away from the original city centre site. The Trent Building at Highfields was built in 1928, the same year as Florence Boot Hall, which was for women students, and was named after Boot's (or, as he had now become, Lord Trent's) wife. The Midland Agricultural College at Sutton Bonington was incorporated into the College in 1947, and an independent charter was obtained in 1948 when the city council finally relinquished control. There was a spate of building during the 1960s and 1970s including the Portland Building, the new library and a number of halls of residence. The new teaching hospital was opened during the 1970s.

Leicester University dates from the 1920s, after a long gestation period from its first mooting in the 1880s. It grew out of the Leicester, Leicestershire and Rutland College, which was funded by an appeal designed to commemorate the war service of the men of Leicestershire, and was partly designed for its own sake and partly to emulate Nottingham. With a successful appeal, and a munificent gift of the old county asylum, the new college admitted its first students in October 1921. During that decade it began to prepare students for London University BA and BSc degrees, and despite acute financial problems it took over Vaughan College in 1929, and also started training teachers. In 1945 University College, Leicester, was placed on the University Grant Commission's grant list, and student numbers immediately began to rise, from 200 in 1946 to 800 in 1957, the year it received its charter as an independent university. Thereafter the university grew rapidly in terms of numbers, departments and buildings. Among the latter is the engineering building (1963), a ten-storey glass tower which has been widely acclaimed by architects and critics in Britain and America, and is regarded as one of the most important buildings to be erected in Britain during the 1960s. Over its first fifty years Leicester University was 'quiet, undemonstrative and unemphatic', but from the 1960s it grew into a major provincial university, with 3,750 students in 1975 (Pye 1972: Ellis 1976: 132–4, 137).

Loughborough University has a much shorter history. At its establishment in 1966 it was the first of the Colleges of Advanced Technology to receive a charter, and it thus became first technological university in England. The university can trace its history back to one of the earliest technical colleges in the country, which came into being in 1909, and which grew to become the internationally recognized Loughborough College. After 1945 the old College broke up, to be succeeded by the College of Education, the College of Art and Design, and a technical college. In turn the university and the college of education were amalgamated in 1976, with a student population of over 4,000 (Cantor and Matthews 1977).

The Countryside

The dominance of the town in the twentieth century has obscured considerable changes in the countryside which have generally meant declining numbers, changing land use, and more efficient farming. Occasional increases in the rural population have reflected changes in structure – particularly the rise of the commuter village – since everywhere the proportion of agricultural employment has declined. The rural exodus of the nineteenth century slowed down early in the twentieth century, partly as a result of temporary prosperity in agriculture, and partly as a result of suburbanization. Smaller market towns such as Market Harborough and Melton Mowbray, which lost numbers during the nineteenth century, benefited from the expansion of light industry in the twentieth (VCH Leics III 1955). In the remoter villages, however, numbers have continued to fall. Laxton declined from 659 in 1831 to 394 in 1901 and to 264 by 1971. Numbers in Corby Glen, Lincolnshire, fell from 710 in 1911 to

664 a decade later, and this downward trend proceeded in the inter-war period as a result of continued mechanization of agriculture and the amalgamation of holdings (Steel 1979: 18). The picture was the same elsewhere. In 1931 112 parishes in Derbyshire (with more than fifty people) had declined during the previous fifty years. In Nottinghamshire about 150 parishes contracted, with the result that whereas the declining areas of both counties held about 23 per cent of the population in 1831 the figure was only 6 per cent a century later. They constituted about half the respective area of each county, lying in the rural west of Derbyshire and the rural east of Nottinghamshire, outside the mining area, into which migrants from the rural districts had moved. By 1951 only a few enclaves with a high commitment to farming remained, including Ashbourne RD in Derbyshire, where 46 per cent of the employed population worked in agriculture, and the Melton and Belvoir RD, where the proportion was 35 per cent (Smith 1959).

Between 1951 and 1961 the heaviest concentration of agricultural employment was still in the east of the region, in Lincolnshire and Rutland, leaving the three industrial counties with only a tiny minority of agricultural workers (Table 20). By contrast the weight of employment in industry was almost exactly reversed. In both Derbyshire and Leicestershire 54 per cent of the occupied population in 1961 was in mining and quarrying or industry, while the proportion was 49 per cent in Nottinghamshire but 33 per cent in Lindsey, and only 19 per cent in Rutland and Kesteven and 13 per cent in Holland. Rural areas have continued to lose population. In south-east Lincolnshire during the 1950s there were widespread rural declines and negligible town growth. At Corby Glen numbers were about 550 in the late 1970s, and the whole nature of the community had changed. The village now has far more old people and many fewer young people than in the past (Steel 1979: 18). In the Southwell RD of Nottinghamshire during the 1950s increases took place in a number of settlements associated with coal mining, but numbers fell in parishes in the east which were mainly agricultural (Osborne 1966). Laxton has only just sufficient tenants to maintain the open fields, but that at least means it has an above average proportion of farmers living within the village. If the system collapsed it would almost certainly become a commuter village, providing housing within easy reach of Newark. In Leicestershire Charnwood Forest is relatively sparsely populated, and the eastern half of the county also has much lower densities, reflecting the continued role of agriculture, particularly in the Melton and Belvoir district (Pye 1972: 444).

Significant changes have taken place in the landscape during the present century, some of them arising from the demand for leisure pursuits. In the 1930s the Council for the Preservation of Rural England took upon itself the special care of the Peak District, and as an indirect result in 1951 this became the first British National Park. It is surrounded by urban areas with a total population of about 18 million people, but some of the wear and tear that this has predictably brought to the paths and trackways of the area has been relieved since 1968 by the creation of country parks. By 1981 there were five of these in Derbyshire, including Elvaston, Shipley and Hardwick, six – with one more under construction – in Nottinghamshire, among them Clumber, Sherwood Forest and Holme Pierrepont, two in Leicestershire and one in Lincolnshire (Countryside Commission 1981: Wheeler 1982). Other places have been designated Nature Reserves, including Gibraltar Point in Lincolnshire (Robinson 1981).

Table 20 The proportion of the occupied population engaged in agriculture, 1951–61 (%)

County	1951	1961
Derbyshire	4.3	2.9
Leicestershire	4.3	2.8
Lincolnshire – Holland	40.3	32.9
– Kesteven	22.5	17.4
– Lindsey	13.2	8.9
Nottinghamshire	3.3	2.4
Rutland	22.9	14.2

(Source: Osborne 1966)

Country parks partly reflect another twentieth-century change, the decline of the great estates built up by the late nineteenth century. Lord Howe sold his 10,000-acre estate at Gopsall in Leicestershire in 1919; the Caves of Stanford sold 3,700 acres in 1924, and by 1940 the Duke of Rutland's holdings had declined from the 70,000 acres he owned in 1883 to just 18,000. The Hastings sold up altogether after the Second World War (VCH Leics II 1954: 247–52). Several of the country parks have been created from parkland associated with large estates in the region, as at Elvaston Castle, Rufford and Clumber. At Elvaston, which was opened in 1970 as a contribution to European Conservation Year, the house has become a countryside museum and field studies centre operated in conjunction with the park. Other estates were sold to institutions. At Corby Glen the southern half of the heath was sold in 1968 to become part of the farming interests of the Norwich Union Insurance Company, while other farms in the parish were put into the hands of a trust company. Large acreages have been parcelled and sold to tenants. By the 1970s Leicestershire had few large landowners, and more than half of all farm holdings in the county were in the hands of owner-occupiers (Pye 1972: 328). From this change has come both an alteration in the pattern of ownership, and also a surplus of country houses.

Many of these houses have survived by means of transfer to alternative uses, although a number have disappeared. Several have been transferred to educational purposes: Welbeck is now an army college; Harlaxton is an overseas campus of an American university: Clifton Hall, after being a girl's school for a time, became part of Nottingham's Trent Polytechnic; Stoke Rochford and Eaton Hall became Colleges of Education; and Caythorpe, Riseholme and Brackenhurst, Colleges of Agriculture. Stanford Hall is now a Co-operative College. Wollaton Hall was purchased by Nottinghamshire County Council and converted into a natural history museum. Rufford was also purchased by the council, but they could find no use for it and it is now mostly demolished. Derby City Corporation acquired Allestree Hall and 325 acres of park in 1944. Much of the land was turned into a public recreational area and golf course (Pye 1972: 338; Clemenson 1982). A number of houses have been saved for the nation, and come under the auspices of the National Trust, among them Belton House in Lincolnshire and, most recently, Kedleston Hall and Calke Abbey near Derby. Not all the surplus could be absorbed, and many houses have been demolished, or allowed to deteriorate. Fourteen have gone in Nottinghamshire since 1900 (Pevsner and Williamson 1979: 39–40). Scrivelsby Court in Lincolnshire was abandoned after the Second World War, and eventually levelled in 1956. Garendon Park in Leicestershire and Easton Hall in Lincolnshire were demolished as a result of damage incurred while they were requisitioned for war service between 1940 and 1945 (Clemenson 1982: 138). Others have been drastically reduced in size, including Brocklesby Hall in Lincolnshire during the 1950s. An indication of usage is given in Table 21.

Table 21   The fate of a sample of East Midlands country houses, 1880–1980

County	Sample number	Demolished	Private ownership	Public/Institutional ownership
Derbyshire	10	2	5	2
Leicestershire	8	4	3	1
Lincolnshire	16	7	6	3
Nottinghamshire	9	2	3	4
Rutland	3	0	3	0

(Source: Clemenson 1982: 143, 152–3, 232–3)

Relatively few country houses have been started from new in the twentieth century. Among new houses erected since the 1890s are the Queen Anne style country house Ednaston Manor in Derbyshire (for W. G. Player, chairman of Imperial Tobacco 1912–14), Barnsdale Hill in Rutland, Burrough Court in Leicestershire, and Caythorpe Court in Lincolnshire. Not that newness has saved such houses from the ravages of time. Barnsdale has become flats and Caythorpe is an agricultural college, while Papillon Hall in Leicestershire, remodelled 1903–04 for Frank Belville, has since been demolished (Aslet 1982).

Farming

The transformation of the countryside which began before the end of the nineteenth century as a result of the agricultural depression has continued into the twentieth century. Most important has been the decline of land under permanent grass since the late 1930s, and with it an extension of the arable which in recent years has led to the removal of hedgerows – with obvious consequences for the landscape – and large-scale mechanization. In 1866 60 per cent of Leicestershire lay under permanent grass, and this trend towards pasture continued into the present century. More than 61,000 acres were put down to permanent grass 1880–1910, with dairying and milking expanding at the expense of grazing. The trend was temporarily reversed during the First World War as government powers were used to persuade farmers to plough up 40,000 acres (10.7 per cent of the permanent pasture), but it gathered pace again during the agricultural difficulties of the 1920s to reach a maximum of nearly 86 per cent in 1938. The pattern was then drastically reversed. By 1943 the 'plough-up' campaign of the Second World War had cut the total to 49 per cent, and although it rose slightly in the 1950s the proportion of permanent grassland (including Rutland) was 38.4 per cent in 1979, almost exactly equivalent to the national average. By the 1950s dairying was dominant in the Vale of Belvoir, while around Market Harborough graziers continued to concentrate on prime beef products. Grazing has been superseded by dairying in the west of the county, with the result that over the period 1874–1939 dairy cattle increased from 23 to 38 per cent of all cattle in the county. Cereal crops are now grown in rotation with intensively managed temporary grassland, while machinery and the swallowing of small farms into larger units has changed the external appearance of the landscape. Hedgerows have been ripped out to make larger fields, and deep-ploughing has eradicated much of the ridge and furrow which characterized the county at the beginning of the century (Bowler 1981). Moreover, the change of routine which involves ploughing and sowing immediately after harvest so that the fields are green with young corn or rape before the end of the year means that there are no more stubbles, and the countryside has taken on a rather different visual appearance. Leicestershire today is a county of mixed farming. Land use changes of a different kind resulted from the establishment of military aerodromes, at Cottesmore and Luffenham in Rutland; and in Leicestershire at Castle Donington (which is now the East Midlands airport), Ratcliffe, Rearsby and Bitteswell (Millward 1985: 120–2).

Many of the features found in Leicestershire were also common elsewhere. Both Nottinghamshire and Derbyshire experienced a decline in acreage under the plough between 1870 and 1913. The tillage area rose to a peak during the First World War, but shrank again in the depression of the 1920s. It began to rise again late in the 1930s, reaching a high point well above that recorded in 1914 during the Second World War. Since then Nottinghamshire's wartime level has been maintained, although in Derbyshire the area in tillage declined again after the war. Barley production increased substantially in both counties, largely as a substitute for wheat and oats. Bare fallow has disappeared, even in Laxton where the fallow has been replaced by a grass crop. However, traditional local distinctions remain. In the 1960s Derbyshire was still primarily dependent on livestock enterprise, notably dairying and sheep, while Nottinghamshire farming was organized in larger farm units and was predominantly arable. Livestock tended to be integrated within arable farming systems, and productivity has usually been higher than Derbyshire in terms of both land and labour. On the other hand, Nottinghamshire has contributed little to milk sales out of the region whereas both Derbyshire and Leicestershire have sent considerable quantities to London during the twentieth century. The size of holdings has also varied. Between 1910 and 1950 the number of holdings of 1–50 acres in Leicestershire declined by 79 per cent, while between 1914 and 1962 in Derbyshire and Nottinghamshire the number of holdings with more than 1 acre of crops and grass fell by roughly one-third in both counties. The result was an increase in the average size of holdings from 43 to 56 acres in Derbyshire and from 65 to 83 acres in Nottinghamshire (Dury 1963: 150; VCH Leics II 1954: 251; Edwards 1966a: 253–70; Hopkins 1955).

Comparison of farming practice within the region is not easy. A survey carried out in 1947 revealed the importance of livestock in Leicestershire and Rutland, and the much greater importance of poultry and market gardening in Nottinghamshire, Leicestershire and Derbyshire than in Rutland, Lindsey and Kesteven. Holland was not included in this survey, but otherwise 84 per cent of all dairy farms were in Leicestershire and Derbyshire, while the majority of the farms which combined arable and cropping with livestock were in Lindsey and Kesteven (Jones 1954: 46–58). By 1935 3,400 acres in Holland were devoted to growing bulbs and outdoor flowers, mainly on the light siltlands around Spalding. Daffodils and narcissi accounted for two-thirds of the total area while tulips were the main crop in the other third (Smith 1937: 59). Upland farms on the Derbyshire limestone have been able to increase the number of dairy cows since piped water was installed in the late 1960s.

Nor, finally, has agriculture been able to escape the all-pervasive impact of urban development. This has been particularly true of horticulture, which has traditionally been located on the periphery of urban settlements. In the 1960s highly intensive and specialized market gardens at Melbourne in south Derbyshire depended largely on Derby for a market, while at Borrowash, between Nottingham and Derby, the long-established nurseries on medium-light Keuper soils were adequate testimony to the importance of urban markets. Rose cultivation has been of particular importance to the Nottingham district, and the principal growers sited their operations to the east, south and

Plate 10.3   Spalding, Lincolnshire, in the heart of bulb growing on the Fens. This picture shows blooms being sent away from Spalding station before the First World War.

John Thomas White pioneered the collection and sale of snowdrops to London retailers in the late 1880s. The original demand for snowdrop bulbs reflected their medicinal use, but White soon began planting and sending flowers to London, among them tulips, daffodils and narcissi.

The industry developed rapidly and during the inter-war years, 'flower specials' left Spalding every night for London, the Midlands and the north of England. At the peak of the season 40,000 boxes of tulips and daffodils were despatched weekly. Since 1945 the emphasis has tended to be on bulb production rather than cut flowers.

---

south-west of the city. Other important locations for horticulture around Nottingham were Arnold, Chilwell, Ruddington and West Bridgford on the suburban fringe, and a peripheral area slightly further out including Woodborough, Lambley, Lowdham and East Bridgford. By 1981 the predominant area was the north-eastern parishes, Bestwood, Arnold, Calverton, Lambley and Woodborough. The last of these, grade two land on gentle slopes, has a long tradition of market gardening. A high proportion of produce is sold in Nottingham's markets. Hilltop Farm, Woodborough, produces enough mixed vegetables from its 32 hectares to maintain its own wholesale premises in Sneinton Market throughout the year (Edwards 1966a: 271–3; Brazier *et al.* 1984: 133–44).

Chapter 11

Transport and Industry

Before the twentieth century the physical location of manufacturing industry depended on a number of factors including the position of the energy supply (particularly the coalfields) and the market. The significance of coal mining for industrialization had the added effect of concentrating manufacturing industry on to the coalfields and their surrounding areas, as was the case in the Erewash valley. As a result the coalfields surpassed earlier manufacturing areas in importance. Little change took place until the inter-war period when heavy industry and coalmining went into prolonged recession just as power and transport were ensuring that lighter industries no longer found coalfield locations economically advantageous. The age of coal specialization had passed, and many of the coalfields and their associated industrial areas seemed unattractive environments for establishing new plant. As electricity replaced coal and as the costs of power and transport have risen less quickly than other costs, proximity to markets has become the major consideration, while the location of raw materials is no longer so significant. One consequence has been that the Erewash coalfield, which has gradually been run down since 1945, offered fewer attractions to entrepreneurs than in the past, although a number of companies have moved there from the larger towns. A second result is that industry has diversified, particularly in engineering and the service industries. However, the continuing significance of coal and textiles has meant that the region has enjoyed less change than other areas. On the other hand, industries long associated with the East Midlands have been able to broaden their geographical base. Thus the hosiery industry is now more widely dispersed across the country than it was in 1900 although the East Midlands remains the major centre of production and decision-making.

Transport

The twentieth century has seen individuals and local authorities trying to come to grips with the changing problems of transport provision, and the results of their efforts have affected business and personal movement alike. Rail, the great innovation of the nineteenth century, has gradually been superseded by road traffic, which has had profound repercussions for the landscape. The apparently insatiable demand for more and wider roads has seen older routes tarmacked and turned into dual carriageways; while a major motorway, the M1, has taken a completely new route by being cut through Charnwood Forest and along the Erewash valley through the old coalfield. Water transport has effectively disappeared from the region, and the movement of goods by rail is now much less significant. The real headache facing the planners has been the road transport system; new roads have had to be constructed, older roads upgraded, bus services planned and large-scale traffic management instituted. It has not always worked, as, for example, in the ill-fated Nottingham zone-and-collar experiment of 1975 which was designed to discourage private motorists from entering the town centre in peak periods partly by diverting them on to buses known as 'lilac leopards'. Nottingham people chose to ignore the buses, and the scheme collapsed in sixteen months (Brazier *et al.* 1984: 119–31).

Although the river Trent never regained its former glory after the railway arrived, this did not mean to say it was wholly superseded for trade purposes. Traffic amounted to 418,027 tons in 1898, but thereafter the trend was downwards, to 349,511 tons in 1905, to 289,794 tons in 1915, and by 1921 to 251,909 tons. The Trent Navigation Company paid a 5 per cent dividend in 1898 but by 1905 this had been discontinued. The change in fortunes was largely as a result of the state of the river. Although 70- to 80-ton vessels could use it to its junction with the Trent and Mersey canal near Shardlow, the shallower stretches ensured that this could seldom be done without interruption, sometimes including delays of days or weeks. Legislation was obtained in 1906 to try to improve the river by allowing the Trent Navigation Company to dredge, and to construct new locks in order to create a waterway of 6 ft depth between Hull and Nottingham. Progress was delayed by the Great War and the cost, but in 1914 Nottingham corporation took over the river between Nottingham and Newark, and after 1918 this move was reflected in a reversal of the downward trade spiral. In the 1920s traffic began to increase, to reach 539,172 tons in 1930 and in 1939 650,377 tons. The competition of rail and, by the twentieth century, road transport, ensured that the river was always a second-rate method of transport, but gravel and oil-carrying tankers found it still financially viable to move goods by water. Dredging has continued in order to maintain the river, with the result that in the 1960s oil, grain and flour, fertilizers, sand, gravel and stone, and chalk were among the products carried along the Trent (Beckwith 1967a: 11; Wood 1950: 42–3). An industrial dispute during the 1970s had the effect of decreasing the tonnage on the river, but 363,866 tons of sand and gravel were moved along the river between Gainsborough and Nottingham during the year 1985–6 (*ex info*. British Waterways Board).

Although most of the railway network was completed by the end of the nineteenth century, additional lines had to be provided in Nottinghamshire to accommodate the expansion of the coal industry. Various lines were constructed into Sherwood Forest to coincide with the opening up of the Dukeries coalfield in the 1920s, some of them joining the Mansfield–Newark, and others the Mansfield–Lincoln line. As late as 1961 a branch line was laid to link the Bevercotes colliery to the Lancashire, Derbyshire and east coast line, while a line opened the following year connected Cotgrave colliery east of Nottingham to the Nottingham–Grantham line. Over time many lines proved uneconomic and a major pruning of the service took place during the 1960s in accordance with the Beeching plan. Nottingham lost its Victoria Station, which had only opened at the end of the nineteenth century, while a considerable number of services were closed down throughout the region. Whereas 191 trains left Nottingham each weekday for other towns in 1958, the total had fallen to eighty-two in 1984, a reduction of 57 per cent (Brazier *et al.* 1984: 119). With the closure of the Matlock–Manchester line Derby's importance as a railway junction diminished, but travellers from Nottingham, who once had to link with the Derby–London trains at Trent Junction now have to go to Derby. In large parts of the region the railway has almost disappeared, including most of Leicestershire east of the Soar valley, and the western half of the county except for the coalfield. All that is left in Leicestershire is the main line from London through to Derby, lines to Nuneaton and Peterborough, and the main line through the Erewash valley towards Sheffield. The reduction in freight traffic through the region means that Toton sidings, designed in the 1960s as one of the largest locomotive servicing areas in Europe, is today a container plant using only half the available space. In 1900 the region had ninety railway stations; by 1972 the number was seven.

In some places industry saved the railway. As the number of blast furnaces in the region declined during the twentieth century iron ore had to be moved greater distances to be smelted, and since firms from outside the region developed an interest in the Jurassic orefields the demand for rail transport increased. The later nineteenth-century pattern continued whereby considerable quantities were moved from Lincolnshire and Rutland to the Derbyshire centres of Clay Cross, Renishaw, Sheepbridge, and Staveley and Stanton (one of the largest pig-iron producers in western Europe in the 1950s). However, as furnaces were closed, and the ore was less in demand, the railway network also contracted. Even so, in 1971 50 million tons of iron and steel industry traffic was still carried on the national rail network, much of it to and from terminals in the East Midlands. At that time almost all the 5.5 million tons of home-produced iron ore carried by British Rail originated in the east midlands region (including Northamptonshire), and considerable quantities of coking coal also reached blast furnaces by rail. Since then much of the trade has been superseded by the import of iron ore through Immingham to replace ores from the Grantham and Melton Mowbray areas (Siviour 1974).

During the 1870s most turnpike trusts were closed down, and the supervision of roads and bridges passed in 1888 to the new county councils. These took over the principal or 'main' roads, while urban and rural district councils remained responsible for the mass of secondary roads. For all practical purposes main roads tended to be the old turnpikes. By the close of the nineteenth century the signs of a re-emergence of road transport, this time not as a consequence of improved roads but of the internal combustion engine, was preparing the way for what in the twentieth century would be a massive programme of investment (VCH Leics III 1955: 84). Horse trams began to run into Leicester as early as 1874, into Nottingham four years later, and into Derby in 1879. Nearly 11 million passenger journeys were made on Leicester trams in 1903, and nearly 10 million on Derby's trams in 1910. Nottingham's system was electrified in 1901, and those of Leicester and Derby in 1904. In Leicester, as a result, passenger journeys leapt to nearly 26 million in 1905. Many of the tram cars were made by Brush in Loughborough, where even today electric engines are constructed, although more often for overseas than for British customers. A series of tram routes were opened in Nottingham during the first quarter of the century, but by the time the extension along Derby Road to Wollaton Park became operational in 1927 the corporation was already considering converting to trolley-bus service. This change was completed by 1936, while trams disappeared in Leicester 1947–49. Trolleybuses in turn disappeared from Nottingham's streets in 1966.

The great leap forward, however, was given by the internal combustion engine. Up to the end of 1903 182 motor vehicles had been registered in Leicestershire, and from then on – despite the unreliability of many of the vehicles – there could be no turning back. The influence of road transport since that time has been paramount. Towns such as Louth in Lincolnshire, which had never really benefited from the railway, experienced rejuvenation as a result of road haulage (Goulding 1957: 34). Hardly surprisingly, existing roads soon proved inadequate in both maintenance and design. In towns, new roads were built, such as Charles Street in Leicester (1931), and Nottingham's ring road – Valley Road (1925), Western Boulevard (1932), Middleton Boulevard (1928), and Clifton Boulevard (1938). Outside the towns routes of the old turnpikes were the first to be remade and widened, as the road network has been gradually improved since the 1920s. Some new roads were built on old routes, as in the case of the A614 which runs north from Nottingham through Sherwood Forest to join the Great North Road near Bawtry. Many miles of dual carriageway have appeared, particularly along major roads such as the A52 (Nottingham and Derby), the A46 (Leicester towards Nottingham), the A50 between Leicester and the Leicestershire coalfield, and parts of the A6. Improvements of this nature have been noticeably less prominent in Lincolnshire.

From the late 1950s came the motorways. The M1, opened in 1964 to Lutterworth, and then on towards Nottingham and Sheffield the following year, cut a fresh route across Charnwood Forest. Together with the improvement of the Great North Road to motorway standards this has recreated the eighteenth century pattern of two major roads passing north–south through the region (with the M1 arguably replacing the A6 in this role). Improvements to east–west travel came later. Leicester's traditional links to the south-west were strengthened by the opening of the M69 to Coventry, while the M18 has linked Grimsby and Scunthorpe to the major motorway network. Motorways also encouraged local authorities to expand the existing road network. Nottinghamshire County Council's major achievements in the past two decades, while including additional bridging of the Trent and better traffic flow in and around the city, have also included improving roads giving access to the M1. The city's link to the motorway at junction 24 has benefited from a new road providing access to Ratcliffe power station and the East Midlands airport, while roads to junctions 25 and 26 have included by-passes for Stapleford and Sandiacre, Kimberley and Eastwood (Brazier *et al.* 1984: 123–4).

Finally, air transport reached the region in the 1920s. Nottingham's municipal airport at Tollerton was opened in 1928, the second in the country to receive a licence for this purpose. However, a major step forward in the provision of air services came in 1965 with the opening of the East Midlands airport on the RAF aerodrome at Castle Donington. This was a combined project sponsored by a group comprising the corporations of Nottingham and Derby, and the county councils of Nottinghamshire, Derbyshire and Leicestershire. The airport was designed to offer regular services within the British Isles (which has helped to make it a key link in the postal system) as well as to many holiday resorts.

Industry

The changing pattern of industry during the present century has left its mark on the landscape. Debris from the iron and lead industries of Derbyshire can still be seen on the ground, while the evidence of gypsum working is unmistakeable against the predominantly rural scenery around Gotham in Nottinghamshire. The efforts of the National Coal Board in east Leicestershire are now having an impact, particularly at Asfordby, just beyond the boundary of the Vale of Belvoir. The eight power stations along the Trent valley which provide a considerable proportion of the energy requirements of both the region and the nation, and also keep the local coal industry buoyant, are a distinctive feature on the landscape, especially in winter when they create their own clouds. The eight cooling towers and the chimney at Ratcliffe, for example, dominate the countryside for miles around with their plume of steam and smoke, and no

Plate 11.1   Ratcliffe-on-Soar power station. The village of Ratcliffe, a few miles south-west of Nottingham, enjoyed a relatively untroubled existence until a giant new power station was built in the 1960s, together with a new road connecting Nottingham to the M1 at Kegworth. The power station covers 384 acres of land, with 8 cooling towers (each 375 ft high and 169 ft in diameter at the top) and a 654 ft high main chimney. Up to 2,000 megawatts of electricity are generated here, enough for the domestic and industrial needs of about 1 million people. To create this power the station consumes 20,000 tons of coal – equivalent to 65 per cent of all production in the south Nottinghamshire coalfield in 1981–82 – and evaporates 13 million gallons of water each day.

traveller through the Trent valley from Newark to Burton can be unaware of their presence. However, industry has not always scarred the landscape. Coal mining in west Leicestershire has had relatively little impact, with many of the villages retaining a predominantly rural atmosphere, and the county's quarrying works have also tended to be less obtrusive than might perhaps have been expected.

The region escaped relatively lightly in the inter-war depression. The reasons are not easy to disentangle, but they must have included favourable mining conditions on the concealed coalfield which permitted expansion to continue through the 1920s at a time of national contraction in output and employment; the continued growth of hosiery and knitwear; and the buoyancy of footwear and a diversified engineering industry. Further benefit accrued from the expansion of iron and steel making at Scunthorpe, and at Corby in Northamptonshire. In these circumstances diversification took place slowly, without provoking the high unemployment which affected other parts of the country. By contrast with the period 1750–1900 no change took place in the basic location of industry. In 1951 the pattern of manufacturing employment in the region continued to reflect the picture which could have been drawn in the late nineteenth century. Lincolnshire and eastern Leicestershire remained predominantly agricultural, with only Scunthorpe providing a major focus of industry outside the Nottingham–Leicester–Derby triangle (Rawstron 1964).

Since 1945 the regional manufacturing specializations which character-ized the nineteenth century have been substituted by a more clearly diverse pattern. Newer industries have not been constrained by power and transport costs, and so there has been less geographical concentration. Leicestershire had a significant engineering industry at the beginning of the century but it was small in comparison with hosiery and footwear. In 1911 engineering had 7,000 workers, while more than 50,000 worked in hosiery and footwear. Between the wars the growth of machine production in hosiery and footwear stimulated engineering, even as the number of footwear factories, and the number of employees, was decreasing. Hosiery survived, still with 46,000 workers in 1931, but was adversely affected by government policies during the Second World War, precisely the policies from which engineering benefited. By 1967 engineering was the major employer in Leicestershire and Rutland (67,960), followed by textiles and clothing (55,970), and footwear (16,500). Since 1948 employment in textiles had remained steady, but engineering had increased, and footwear had slipped. This kind of change was taking place everywhere; indeed by 1971 every region of Britain had become more diversified (Pye 1972: 373–4).

Pockets of specialization remained, and the East Midlands was no exception because of the continued importance of coal and textiles in the local economy. This did not prevent change, particularly the growth of service industries during the twentieth century. By 1951 they accounted for 41 per cent of the total employed population of Derbyshire, Leicestershire and Nottinghamshire, and they were the fastest growing branch of employment over the following decade. The 1950s witnessed a significant fall in textile workers in the region, but overall an increase in manufacturing employment as a result of developments in engineering, and the food, drink and tobacco industries (Smith 1959; 1962–5). A further significant structural development saw industrial growth in Lincolnshire. In the years down to 1953 the Grimsby–Immingham area benefited from the establishment of chemical and allied trades, while industrial developments took place in some of the less notable places of the region including Melton Mowbray, Market Harborough, Grantham, Stamford, Brigg, Skegness and Oakham (Johnston 1955).

For most of the present century the East Midlands' industrial history was characterized by a tendency to perform better than the national average despite considerable disadvantages. For example, net in-movement of employment from other areas was negligible. There is evidence of considerable outward movement eastwards into Lindsey, or across the Yorkshire border; and of a number of moves into the region from south Yorkshire and the south-east. Firms moved into Lindsey, but movement in the opposite direction was virtually non-existent. Moreover, the region lacked government assistance, and enjoyed or endured a high rate of turnover among firms. Half of the establishments in production in 1947 had closed by 1967, but they had been replaced by a similar number of plants, mostly operated by new firms. Employment was generated almost entirely by locally based firms or local entrepreneurs, and 28 per cent came from completely new firms, without which the region's growth rates would have been less than half that of the country as a whole. Almost 3,000 firms were established in the East Midlands (including Northamptonshire), and although most were small their aggregate contribution to jobs was considerable. Even the short-lived firms which opened and closed between 1947 and 1970 provided up to 20,000 jobs at any one time. Since many of them were in new, expanding industries, they helped to consolidate the trend away from textiles, clothing and footwear. By 1971, for example, there were over sixty plastics firms employing 3,000 or more people (Gudgin 1978: 297–9).

On the other hand differences within the region were considerable. The dominance of large plant has discouraged newcomers, particularly in parts of Derbyshire and Lincolnshire, although in these counties the size of new firms has tended to be larger than elsewhere. At the local level, employment in new firms in 1970 as a proportion of total employment in 1947 in Leicestershire and Rutland was 12.4 per cent, with Loughborough and Melton substantially below, and Leicester and Hinckley slightly above the average. Oakham enjoyed considerable growth (Gudgin 1978: 215–17). Local variations within the region have also been significant. Over the period 1948–67 the number of operatives employed in manufacturing in Leicester declined, as was also the case in Loughborough and Market Harborough. By contrast, smaller settlements including Coalville, Shepshed, Ashby, Melton and Oakham, have experienced increases (Pye 1972: 385–90).

The region has also developed problem employment areas. In the Erewash valley for many years female employment was in short supply, while with the decline of the coal industry male jobs have disappeared. The special needs of the area were officially recognized in 1969. Between 1945 and 1953 moves into the region tended to be to the Nottinghamshire–Derbyshire coalfield and to Derby, with lesser centres in Grantham, Melton Mowbray and Stamford. In the late 1960s the coalfield attracted small firms with a variety of interests to the industrial estates of Alfreton, Ilkeston, Pinxton and Ripley (Rake 1974a). Only a handful of firms have moved into Leicestershire and Rutland, including the English Electric Company's factory at Whetstone, south of Leicester, which was established early in the 1950s. Developments by local firms tended to concentrate in Leicester, south-west and north-west Leicestershire.

Coal

The eastward movement of coal mining into Nottinghamshire during the nineteenth century and the increase of activity on the south-Derbyshire coalfield produced considerable expansion in the industry between 1870 and 1914. Output rose from 26 million tons in 1900 to 29 million in 1920 and to 48 million in 1965. At the same time the proportion of coal raised in the Nottinghamshire part of the coalfield continued to increase. It had reached 46 per cent by 1920, and the trend proved irreversible. The Staveley Coal and Iron Company intensified the development of its collieries near Chesterfield in the 1920s (Turner 1978), but since then the Nottinghamshire section's lead has accelerated. Employment figures give a rough indication of the balance in 1986, when nearly 24,000 industrial workers were employed by British Coal in Nottinghamshire (not including Manton and Shireoaks/Steetly collieries which belong to the south Yorkshire area), and less than 8,000 men were employed in the north Derbyshire collieries (including Bolsover and Warsop for British Coal purposes). Some open-cast mining continues at Bennerley, south and west of Eastwood, and near Clay Cross. Little growth has taken place in Erewash valley towns such as Alfreton, Heanor and Ripley 1921–61 (Edwards 1966a: 345–6). The colliery buildings have gone, the pit heaps have been reshaped, and the open-cast sites have been landscaped, producing, in the case for example of Shipley Hall, a country park.

This shift in production reflected the working out of Derbyshire seams, the continued expansion of the concealed Nottinghamshire coalfield, and above all the development of deep mining in the Dukeries. Production in the south Nottinghamshire area rose from 7.46 million tonnes at the time of nationalization in 1947 – when the industry passed into the hands of the National Coal Board – to a peak of 14.37 million in 1963, reflecting the standing of the south Nottinghamshire coalfield during the 1960s as the largest and most productive field in the country with the greatest proven resources. Calverton became an independent colliery in 1952 (coal having previously been moved underground to Bestwood in the Leen valley), and in the 1960s Bevercotes – the world's first fully-automated colliery – and Cotgrave were opened. In the post-war years the East Midlands was a major supplier of almost all the consumer regions in England serving the domestic and industrial needs of the London market, the south and east, as well as south Lancashire and Cheshire (Estall 1957). But this trend did not continue, partly because from the later 1950s the effects of cheap crude oil imports first began to impinge on the industry. By the 1960s production was increasingly geared towards the electricity industry, nearly 40 per cent of the coal went to the power stations, making the East Midlands the largest supplier of coal in the country for electricity production, a proportion which has continued upwards ever since. Production on the south Nottinghamshire coalfield as a whole was 8.54 million tonnes in 1981–82, and the proportion of coal acquired by the Central Electricity Generating Board had risen to 79 per cent of output, with Ratcliffe-on-Soar power station alone consuming 65 per cent of the output of south Nottinghamshire mines. This has not prevented the smaller uneconomic pits from being closed. Since 1947 sixteen collieries have ceased production, nine of them during the 1960s. No coal is now produced in the Erewash valley, once the hub of the industry in the East Midlands, and the south Nottingham-shire coalfield as a whole is in terminal decline. Only three of the eleven collieries operating in the 1980s are likely to continue in production by the year 2000.

The most spectacular development of coal mining in the region began immediately after the First World War, with the opening up of the Dukeries coalfield. Several of the larger mining companies began to exploit the reserves in mid-Nottinghamshire, and this led to the development of new mining villages in an area predominantly between Worksop and Mansfield. The tiny rural villages of Edwinstowe, Clipstone, Ollerton, Bilsthorpe and Harworth, were subject to rapid expansion and an invasion of workers from other areas. Among the new collieries opened as a result of this initiative were Rufford (1915), Clipstone (1922), Ollerton (1925), Blidworth (1926), Bilsthorpe

(1927) and Thoresby (1928). The *New Statesman* waxed lyrical in 1927 at the opening of Bilsthorpe:

> the latest, but far from the last, of the long line of pits which have transformed the glades and villages of Sherwood Forest, and the Dukeries, into one of the greatest coalfields in the whole of Great Britain. Steadily, quietly, till we stumble on their existence with a shocked surprise, pit after pit has been sunk and worked in the beautiful stretch of country which covers the eastern half of the county of Nottingham. It is one of the romances and revolutions of modern industrialism.
>
> (Waller 1983: 56)

The forest scene was inevitably transformed, as mines, mineral lines and spoil heaps joined farms, woods and stretches of heath. Population grew rapidly. Between 1921 and 1931 Ollerton expanded from 676 to 3,912, Bilsthorpe from 134 to 1,972, Edwinstowe from 963 to 2,818, and Clipstone from 592 to 3,443. Most of the incomers were miners, but many travelled only a short distance. At Ollerton, for example, between 1922 and 1932 48 per cent of those moving into the village came from within Nottinghamshire, 25 per cent from Derbyshire and 27 per cent from more distant coalfields. Many came from mining towns suffering pit closures, including Heanor, Ripley, Codnor and Alfreton in Derbyshire (Waller 1983: 38). Some of the older inhabitants resented the change; an Ollerton man who made monumental tombstones wished

> the pit hadn't come, I've nothing against it in a sense, but we were a very happy community without it. There wasn't nearly so much competition as there is today . . . I myself pay six times as much in rates as I used to before this pit came.
>
> (Waller 1980)

The reluctance of the rural district councils to provide adequate services was a further reflection of antagonism between incoming miners and the settled rural population. On the other hand, the new pits were prosperous in an era when the coal industry in general was depressed, and they attracted considerable investment, £1 million for Ollerton colliery for example.

On the smaller Leicestershire–south Derbyshire coalfield production reached a record 3½ million tons in 1917, but thereafter the coalfield was faced with contracting output and labour problems. By 1933 only 2¼ million tons were being produced, and there was little evidence of recovery until the later 1930s. Output was just over 4 million tons in 1939, but it grew during the war and reached nearly 8 million tons by 1954, as a result of national demand and local efficiency. Production reached over 6 million tons in 1957, only to fall back to 5½ million by 1970–71. As domestic demand slumped the major customer became the electricity industry, and by 1970–71 more than half the output went to power stations. Largely as a result the mines remained relatively healthy (Pye 1972: 354–7; Holmes 1958), although only two or three are still operating today. In 1986 3,700 men were employed in the south Derbyshire and Leicestershire collieries (*ex info*. A. R. Griffin). The most significant recent development in coal mining has been the opening up of the east Leicestershire coalfield. This, the largest coal find in western Europe since 1945, lies in a 90-square-mile area north of Melton Mowbray. The first mine has already been sunk at Asfordby, and by the end of the century the focus of coal mining in Leicestershire will have shifted to the county's eastern quarter (Millward 1985: 122).

Conditions in the coal industry continued to fluctuate down to 1914, and the years 1911–14 saw mounting unrest on the Nottinghamshire and Derbyshire coalfields (Griffin 1955, I: 150, 162). A series of disputes included minimum wage negotiations, and led to a major strike in February 1912. This was conducted in an orderly fashion without the bitterness and conflict with the non-unionists which had marked 1893. The collieries were kept in working order. In an attempt to ameliorate the situation Parliament passed a Minimum Wage Act. The Derbyshire miners were not placated; when a vote took place 13,000 of the 22,000 miners were against a return to work, but nationally the strike was called off on 9 April 1912 amid criticism of the union leaders (Williams 1962: 393, 423–37).

After 1918 the industry suffered considerable depression, particularly in the traditional mining areas, with the worst conditions at the time of the 1926 General Strike in the coal mining centres of Mansfield and Coalville. Preparation for the General Strike was minimal among trade unionists, but the response was overwhelming. The TUC noted that in Nottingham it was 'unexpectedly fine' on the opening day, while 6,000 workers walked out in Leicestershire. Pit villages and towns, including Coalville, Hucknall and Alfreton, were solidly behind the strike from the beginning. The miners were not alone at the beginning. Derby's railwaymen were solidly behind the strike; in Loughborough, the Brush works came to a standstill; hosiery workers came out in Hinckley; and even market towns like Melton Mowbray were affected. But it was the miners who stayed out the longest and endured the greatest deprivation. They combed 'slag' heaps, and outcropped for fuel. One Ripley man sank a 12-ft shaft in his own back garden in order to bring up a few bags of coal (Skelley 1976). The strike was, ultimately, a failure, but long after most groups of workers had capitulated, the mining community held out, with, in the longer term, divisive effects.

Nottinghamshire was fertile ground for the non-political trade union movement. During the lock-out of 1921 many miners recognized that their wages were depressed because they were grouped with less prosperous districts. In the depression which followed the lock-out the Nottinghamshire

Miners Association was weakened by the loss of membership, and in the 1926 lock-out one of those favouring a compromise settlement was George Spencer, a man who was to play a significant role in industrial relations over the following decade. By early October 1926 70 per cent of the Nottinghamshire Miners Association's 34,000 members were back at work in the county, but a group headed by Spencer decided to form a separate union because they were reluctant to remain on strike for the sake of less prosperous coalfields. By December breakaway unions on the Spencer pattern had been formed in several districts among men who had returned to work before the lock-out ended. Spencer's own view was that non-political trade unionism was a return to conditions before 1914 when the industrial weapon was used for industrial and not for political ends, but in fact the union also eschewed the conventional strike weapon, preferring negotiation and cooperation in an effort to achieve its aims. The Spencer union (the Nottinghamshire Miners Industrial Union) remained independent of the NMA until an amalgamation took place as the Nottinghamshire Miners Federated Union in 1937. However, the willingness of the county's miners to form a separate organization rather than to be dictated to by larger organizations was again demonstrated in 1984 with the formation of the Union of Democratic Mineworkers.

The success of Spencerism in Nottinghamshire was largely for historic reasons. In its heyday the Erewash valley coalfield had been perhaps the most prosperous mining area in Britain, and Spencer was determined that earnings in each district ought to be according to local profitability. Since Nottingham-shire miners stood to gain from such an agreement it is not surprising that many of them supported this stand; indeed, even in 1974 Nottinghamshire was the only large area which returned a majority for reintroducing incentive payments (A. R. Griffin and C. P. Griffin 1977: 133–62), while in the 1984 strike the Nottinghamshire decision to stay at work was determined not merely by a desire to maintain the union's democratic tradition, but also by the acknowledged benefits that the miners had received as a result of the reintro-duction of incentive schemes in 1977–78. The Dukeries coal faces are easier to work, and the rewards correspondingly great (Griffin 1984; *The Guardian*, 4 May 1984).

The attitudes displayed by the Dukeries miners are a classic example of self-interest at work. The new pits of the 1920s, which remain among the most profitable in Britain even today and which were the centre of some of the most violent picketing in 1984, were also citadels of Spencerism in the 1920s and 1930s. The new villages posed a problem for organized labour; because they were built and controlled by the companies unionization was almost imposs-ible. During the 1920s the Butterley Company continued a tradition of welfare spending dating from their activities at Ironville and Codnor Park in the 1850s by investing £320,000 on housing in New Ollerton, as well as financing churches and pubs, attracting female employment, and taking an interest in schools, sport, and other forms of recreation. Amenities were obviously seen as

Plate 11.2 Nottinghamshire, the face of battle during the 1984 coal strike. It was in the new Nottinghamshire pits of the 1920s that the 1984 coal strike was fought out with most vehemence.

The Nottinghamshire miners opposed the National Union of Mineworkers' strike call, and violent scenes ensued. Police reinforcements were called in from other parts of the country to help miners get into their pits while pickets tried to persuade them to strike. As a result, parts of Nottinghamshire witnessed a massive police presence during the dispute. In the end the unwillingness of the miners to be dictated to by the national union left their NUM leaders isolated, and led to the formation of the Union of Democratic Mineworkers.

a means of attracting and keeping labour, but the employers' policy also had a negative side. Any deviance from the company line was followed by immediate eviction; the company provided policemen to patrol the villages; and they fined men for failing to keep up their gardens. Partly as a result of this regime the migrants who came to live in the Dukeries, although mainly from Yorkshire and Nottinghamshire, failed to impose a distinctive culture on the area. D. H. Lawrence wrote that they were 'in a sense an accident in the landscape and Robin Hood and his merry men were not very far away'. Both at Ollerton, and in some of the other villages, the Labour Party made no headway until the 1940s as the villagers regularly returned conservative or liberal local councillors until 1945. In terms of labour organization the situation was bizarre. A closed shop was operated against the Nottinghamshire Miners Association in favour of the non-political Spencer union – in 1934 among pits sunk after 1918 less than 10 per cent of miners were members of the NMA – while large numbers of miners remained outside the union (Waller 1979; 1983: Ch. 5).

Iron, Steel and Lead

Although the Clay Cross and Staveley companies both went in for major new works early in the twentieth century the smaller ironworks could not survive the competition, partly because the demand for wrought iron was contracting. On the eve of the First World War the Staveley works were flourishing, with blast furnaces and pipe shops as modern as any in the country. Stanton, an undistinguished company producing pig-iron in the later nineteenth century, had become the country's leading pipe manufacturer by 1914. After 1918 the contraction of the industry had considerable repercussions. In two and a half years from June 1928 seventeen of the thirty-five furnaces in Derbyshire were demolished or went out of production. This rapid contraction reflected both the uneconomic fashion in which the furnaces had been constructed, with the intention of using local coal, and the loss of the crucial Midland Railway links with the Jurassic ores in Northamptonshire. Even the companies which continued to enjoy prosperity recognized the need to rationalize production.

Alfreton (Riddings), owned by Stanton, closed in 1926, and the old works at Staveley by 1930. Butterley abandoned its blast furnace plant in 1926. After 1930 the raw material sources and the product range of Derbyshire ironworks remained much the same down to 1960. Clay Cross closed down its blast furnaces in the 1950s, while by 1959 Staveley was operating the county's four smallest furnaces. In 1960 iron production was concentrated in three firms around Chesterfield (Staveley, four furnaces; Sheepbridge and Renishaw two furnaces each), and at Stanton (five furnaces in the lower Erewash valley). That same year Stanton and Staveley were united into a single organization while in 1961 the Sheepbridge works were closed, and the Stanton furnaces went out of blast in 1974. Today neither pig-iron nor wrought iron is produced in Derbyshire, although iron pipe making remains important, but the county still has the legacy of ironworking in the form of waste heaps, old mineral lines and derelict plant, and the sprawling industrial buildings at Stanton (Warren 1961; Chapman 1981).

The five townships on which the north Lincolnshire iron industry was centred in the later nineteenth century were united in 1919 to form Scunthorpe, as the new conglomeration became known, one of Lincolnshire's largest urban areas (Wright 1982: 167–78). In 1918 the town had a population of 26,000 of which 4,000 were iron and steel workers, and production amounted to half a million tons of pig-iron and nearly 300,000 tons of steel. Growth during the twentieth century continued apace, with population topping 67,000 by 1961, and output rising to 2.3 million tons of pig-iron and nearly 2.5 million tons of steel. In the inter-war years Scunthorpe's proportion of national pig-iron output increased from 6 to 14 per cent, and of steel from 3 to 10 per cent. In the latter case relatively low production costs were a major advantage, and this helped to attract capital. During the period 1945–65 £175 million was invested and pig-iron and steel outputs were raised from 1 million to nearly 4 million tons (Pocock 1963). By 1974 Scunthorpe accounted for almost 24 per cent of English pig-iron and 16 per cent of steel output (Armstrong 1981: 115–17), but like other steel-producing areas it ran into difficulty as a result of the rapid decline in demand for the product. Rationalization in order to adjust to the changing conditions involved the closure of Normanby Park and the rebuilding of the other two surviving plants into a single complex.

Ironworking began in Rutland with the opening of the Cottesmore works in 1882, but only expanded when work began at Pilton and Burley after 1914. Output of inferior oolite ironstone topped 313,000 tons in 1922 and 475,000 tons in 1930. After a slump in the early 1930s recovery set in during the war and 1.3 million tons were raised in 1942. Production declined again after 1945, but gradually recovered to 1,353,000 tons in 1968. However, the location of the industry was moving, and with the closure of the Exton Park works in 1973 iron mining in the county came to an end (Beaver 1982–83). Meanwhile in Leicestershire between 1958 and 1965 the older centres at

Eaton, Eastwell, Holwell and Tilton were abandoned, while new quarries were opened at Harston and Buckminster, which were linked with larger deposits in Lincolnshire. Despite redistribution output rose from under 750,000 tons of ore in 1949 to more than one million by 1965, only to decline again to under 500,000 tons by 1970 (Pye 1972: 357). In part this is because changing technology had reduced the demand for marlstone, which is the most common type of ore found in the county, and ore is no longer raised in the area.

In the twentieth century lead mining has more or less come to an end. The Mill Close mine in Darley Dale, which was abandoned in 1764 and lay dormant for a century until Edward Wass reopened it and installed a 50-in. Cornish engine in 1859, became the richest lead mine in the country. Between 1861 and 1939 nearly half a million tons of ore were produced, containing an average of over 80 per cent lead content. Of the 29,000 tons of lead raised in Britain in 1931, no less than 26,000 tons came from this single mine. It remained in production until just before the Second World War, aided by a revival of the industry between the wars. By 1938 the workings had sunk to a level of over 1,000 ft. In that year, however, 2 miles from the shaft, and nearly 900 ft below the level of the Derwent, shot-firing breached the wall of an underground lake with the result that the workings were drowned out. The mine was abandoned the following year and the industry is now little more than a pale shadow of its former greatness, although the spoil heaps and workings of the lead mines are being re-worked for fluorspar, barytes and lead concentrates (Cooper 1982: 159–60; Ford and Rieuwerts 1983: 28; Edwards 1966a: 231: Heath 1982: 177).

Other Heavy Industries

The twentieth century has also witnessed the development of new industries. In 1939 there were two electricity generating stations on the banks of the Trent between Burton and the Humber, established to supply Burton and Nottingham respectively. At that point the Trent valley was still of little importance in the provision of electricity, but the situation was transformed after the Second World War. Eight power stations were built in Nottinghamshire and Derbyshire as part of a programme which ended in the late 1960s with the completion of Ratcliffe, Cottam and West Burton. Total expenditure topped £500 million, and helped to preserve the viability of local coal mining as well as to encourage the sand and gravel industry. This expansion reflected the region's importance as an economic area for electricity export by transmission, largely because cheap coal of the right kind is mined locally. It is no coincidence that the stations were located on the Trent – from which 5,200 million gallons are drawn daily for cooling – at convenient points for rail transport from the coalfields (Rawstron 1954; Brazier *et al.* 1984).

Other significant extractions in the twentieth century have included hard-stone in Leicestershire. Although established in the nineteenth century the industry developed after the Second World War first to maintain existing roads, and then to supply demand when a major new road building programme began during the 1950s. Leicestershire in the 1970s was the leading source of igneous-type rock in Britain. Production was also buoyant in the county's sand and gravel industry during the 1960s, while fire clay has continued to be worked in the north-west of the county (Pye 1972: 359–60). Sand and gravel are worked along the entire length of the Trent in the East Midlands. Gravel workings in Derbyshire have moved steadily westwards along the Derwent valley, and similar works are to be found in the vicinity of Lincoln. The needs of the building trade gave a new impetus to gypsum production in the Nottingham–Derby area after 1945, and today it is the most important production area in the country providing around 40 per cent of national production. The industry has flourished around Gotham in south Nottinghamshire, and Newark. Limestone working has continued in Derbyshire throughout the present century, particularly around Buxton, Wirksworth and Matlock, areas which were excluded from the Peak District National Park when it was laid out in 1950. The Earles Cement works in the Hope Valley are a reflection of the need to provide employment in a National Park, though the conflict of interests between the demands of industry and the wishes of conservationists continues to the present day. In Nottinghamshire oil exploration around Easkring, where production began in 1939, Egmanton and Bothamsall, had almost ceased by 1980. In that year just 49,000 tonnes were raised. Oil has also been sought in the Gainsborough area and at Plungar in north Leicestershire. In the 1960s British Petroleum had sunk more than 600 oil wells in the region (Edwards 1966a: 283–302; Brazier *et al.* 1984: 39).

Textiles

In the early years of the century hosiery continued to disperse into the smaller towns and villages of Leicestershire, Nottinghamshire and Derbyshire, sometimes to provide female employment. By 1914 the transition from domestic to factory production was virtually complete. Initially this brought a decline in employment, but by 1912 70,086 people worked in the industry, and far less work was put out than in the past. Women provided a considerable proportion of the labour; as a proportion of the work-force in hosiery factories they increased from 62 to 75 per cent over the period 1886–1906. As a result of the hosiery industry the number of girls in employment in Nottingham was well above the national average. However, the division of labour within the industry seems always to have been determined by the desire to prevent any threat to male jobs. Women were poorly paid and entrusted with the most menial tasks. In 1909 their average weekly pay was 13*s*. 11*d*., whereas men earned 34*s*. 7*d*. (Wyncoll 1985: 427–8). On moral and humanitarian grounds most women were dismissed when they married (as was also the case with other leading employers in Nottingham including Players and Boots); although J. B. Priestley formed the view during the 1930s that 'nine out of every ten of those girls working at the long rows of machines only see their factory life as a busy but dreamy interlude between childhood and marriage'. One consequence, however, was that married women were sometimes forced to look for domestic work to supplement the family income (Priestley 1977: 128; Taylor 1977).

The hosiery industry expanded after the First World War, unlike other branches of textile manufacturing with the exception of artificial silk, and in the face of competition from Japan, Germany and the United States. Despite a brief recession after 1921 employment had increased by 1924 to 97,468. Female workers constituted about 80 per cent of the work-force. J. B. Priestley commented of the Leicester factories that 'except among the vats of dye where men do the work, there were enormous rooms filled with women and girls'. He stopped to watch one particular girl:

> She was a pleasant-looking girl, and quite bright. She explained that she was on piece-work, had to do so many pairs of socks, hundreds and hundreds a day, and was generally able to make between two and three pounds a week. The manager had been telling me that, in his experience, girls preferred purely routine and monotonous jobs because once they had learned the fairly simple necessary movements they could then work all day and think about something else while they were working . . . I said that it seemed to me impossible that the girl who did the conjuring trick with the socks and the transfers could possibly think about anything else; but she assured us that she could, and though it looked all wrong that she should be performing such a task at such a speed all day, truth compels me to add that she showed no signs of being anything but a cheerful, healthy young woman.
>
> (Priestley 1977: 125–6)

In 1924 hose exports accounted for some 20 per cent of output. By the time of the 1935 Census of Production the hosiery industry employed 130,000 workers, and of that number roughly two-thirds were in the three east midlands counties. Nearly half the firms listed at that date were also in the region (Wells 1972). Despite severe contraction during the Second World War, the industry recovered thereafter, and even in 1964 128,000 people were employed, 60 per cent of them in the East Midlands. Some dispersion had taken place since 1931 as the external economies offered by the East Midlands became gradually less significant (Rawstron 1958). By the early 1960s Leicester was producing about 30 per cent of national output, with more than 25 per cent of the county's produce going for export.

On the other hand, increases in production had come about through automatic machinery replacing outwork rather than by an expansion of the labour force. The industry has become more dispersed since 1945, with little expansion in some of the older areas including Arnold, Heanor, Hinckley and Loughborough, some decline in Leicester and Derby, but expansion in Mansfield and Sutton-in-Ashfield, in most of the towns of the Erewash valley, Ollerton and Worksop. Minor centres of the industry appeared in Coalville, Lincoln, Melton Mowbray and Oakham. In 1966 5.1 per cent of all people employed in the region worked in hosiery. Even so, the industry has remained predominantly small-scale. Of 604 firms recorded in the 1958 Census of Production, one-third employed twenty-five to fifty workers, while only fifteen employed 1,000–4,000 workers. The variety of goods produced, the opportunities for specialization in particular lines, and technical conditions all tended to favour the small firm, but in the 1960s a number of larger firms, most notably Courtaulds, began to buy up their lesser neighbours. By 1968 this one firm controlled about 25 per cent of United Kingdom hosiery production (Wells 1968). The industry diversified in the 1960s, and concentration in the East Midlands lessened as a number of local firms began to operate factories in other parts of the country. This trend was partly reversed in the 1970s, and in any case much of the high-level decision-making has remained in the East Midlands (Dury 1963: 164–5; Rake 1974b).

Organizing the female part of the labour force proved almost impossible during the nineteenth century, and not much easier in the twentieth. A severe blow was dealt to the industry in 1911 when the long-serving secretary of the Hosiery Federation and the Leicester Hosiery Union was found to have been embezzling the funds, and the main outcome was a break-up of the Federation. By 1914 there were five separate union districts. Between the wars the number of employees peaked at 120,800 in 1939, but it was not merely numbers that were important, but regularity of work in contrast to the fluctuations of earlier years. The problem of attracting women workers remained, and in the 1930s only about 20 per cent were trade unionists. The proportion was twice as great among men. Labour organization was strongest in Leicester and Nottingham while union members were also found in Hinckley and Loughborough. In the villages it remained as difficult as ever to recruit to the unions. Moreover, the sectional nature of unionism remained. In 1897 there were fourteen unions in the industry in the East Midlands, a number which was reduced to six by 1925. The power of the work-force increased when in 1946 the National Union of Hosiery and Knitwear Workers was formed. With over 58,000 members by 1968 the national union was in a strong position, particularly as by that time something like 50 per cent of all women workers were members (Gurnham 1976: 65–9; Wells 1972).

The lace industry peaked during the first decade of the twentieth century, and in 1911 46,000 people were employed full-time in lace manufacture, nearly half of them in Nottingham and a further quarter in Long Eaton, Beeston, Sandiacre and Derby. Lace making generally took place in tenement factories. The machines were built in Nottingham, but because they were large and expensive, many were acquired on hire-purchase terms, and shift working made for intensive usage. In the 1920s demand for lace collapsed, and within ten years the industry shrunk to half its former size. Little lace was produced during the Second World War, but the industry survived. By the 1960s well over half the total output of lace and net was produced by twenty-five firms, each employing 100 or more workers, and although the industry was reduced to a mere 5,000 employees it remained prosperous at that scale (Edwards 1966a: 308–9). By 1971 less than 1 per cent of Nottingham's employed population worked in the industry out of a total of nearly 9 per cent in textiles (Brazier *et al.* 1984: 62).

Cotton manufacture, having gradually declined during the nineteenth century, has been of relatively limited significance in the region during the twentieth century. In 1951 6,580 people were employed in the three counties of Derbyshire (4,254), Nottinghamshire (2,019) and Leicestershire (307), just over 2 per cent of the total work-force for England and Wales. At that date the major concentration was in the Derwent valley between Derby and Matlock, where nearly one-quarter of all East Midlands cotton employees were involved with four main plants manufacturing sewing cotton. Other significant works were to be found in Nottingham, Leicester and Mansfield. The contraction of cotton firms is given in Table 22, and with the closure of the Belper works the industry has now all but disappeared from the area. Only synthetic fibres are now manufactured at Belper.

Table 22   Cotton manufacturers in the East Midlands

	Derbyshire*	Leicestershire	Nottinghamshire
1912	17	8	11
1922	16	10	13
1936	11	10	11
1958	10	9	11

* Not including the Glossop and New Mills area.

(Source: D. M. Smith 1962: 266)

Narrow fabrics production in the Leicester region, which is largely synonymous with elastic web manufacture, mainly supplied the corset factories of Leicester and Market Harborough by the 1970s. Since 1945 ownership has been increasingly concentrated, and the bulk of productive capacity brought under Courtauld's wing, while Coalville – which acquired its first elastic web factory only in 1918, has replaced Leicester as the main centre of production (Pye 1972: 381).

Footwear and Engineering

Little change took place in the footwear industry over the first half of the twentieth century, but it became relatively much less important in the economy of Leicestershire than it had been in 1900. Whereas in 1901 8 per cent of the occupied population worked in footwear, this number had been cut by half in 1951. At the latter date Earl Shilton, Barwell and Sileby all had more than 1,300 people employed in making footwear. Since 1950 the situation has changed. Traditionally, Leicestershire manufacturers concentrated on womens' and children's shoes of medium quality, but this has proved to be a disadvantage as plastic and synthetic uppers replaced leather. Production of the latter often requires mass production for economic reasons, with the result that many of Leicester's traditionally small family firms have closed or been taken over. This has not affected the region's dominance of the industry nationally, although it has produced local changes, including a movement away from specialization in order to cater for changing demands. Employment in the industry fell by over 11,000 between 1945 and 1970, with a particularly severe decline in Leicester, Barwell and Earl Shilton. Leicester remains important in the trade, while new centres have also been established at Clay Cross and Swadlincote in Derbyshire, Grantham and Sleaford in Lincolnshire and Worksop in Nottinghamshire. Melton Mowbray and Measham have also developed a significant interest in the industry (Mounfield 1964–65, 1967, Mounfield, Unwin and Guy 1984; Pye 1972: 381–2; Rake 1975).

Since 1945 the region has enjoyed a considerable expansion and diversification of its engineering interests, particularly in electrical engineering and machine tools. In addition, new activities have greatly increased the local product base. Leicestershire has been predominantly concerned with the more complex and lighter branches of metal using. In 1967 engineering was the leading industrial employer in Leicestershire, with two-thirds of the jobs being located in Leicester and its immediately adjacent industrial satellites. Loughborough is dominated by its engineering firms, while Melton Mowbray is the only place to have suffered an absolute decline in engineering and metalworking employment in the post-war period. Engineering employment in the county increased by 67 per cent 1948–67. Nottinghamshire and Derbyshire tend to be dominated by the heavier and more basic engineering and metalworking industries. Lincolnshire's specialism is in mechanical engineering, particularly agricultural and constructional machinery. Small-scale, light engineering is found in many parts of the region. Among the region's more notable interests are the manufacture of hosiery, lace and footwear machinery, bicycles, aero-engines (Rolls-Royce), and cranes (Herbert Morris in Loughborough). The overall result has been a considerable diversification of the region's engineering interests (Rake 1976).

Finally, a number of less easily classifiable industrial interests have become established in the region. These include food processing and plastics. Of the former, Petfoods Ltd employed nearly half of the industrial population of Melton Mowbray in 1970, while Meredith and Drew were established in Ashby and Nabisco Frears and Walkers Crisps in Leicester. However, the most significant development of the twentieth century has been in the service industries; around Nottingham by 1981 more than 50 per cent of the total workforce in the urban and rural suburbs extending from Arnold to West Bridgford consisted of service workers (Pye 1972: 384; Brazier *et al.* 1984: 69).

Epilogue

The East Midlands Today

In the course of the twentieth century the old county boundaries became increasingly anachronistic and for planning purposes down to 1979 central government showed considerable interest in the use of regional groupings. In the 1930s it became clear that the depression which had hung over British industry since 1918 and had brought heavy and prolonged unemployment was predominantly a feature of areas dominated by heavy industry. One means of tackling the problem was thought to be a regional policy, since many of the problems were perceived to be of local rather than national origin. The result was that government attention was drawn to the regions from the time of the Special Areas Act (1934) onwards. Ironically, this was just the point when many of the old constraints which had tended to encourage intra-regional links were beginning to dissolve. The region as a concept for government purposes came to the fore when the conditions which had dictated regional trade and regional links had largely evaporated. It was the ability to diversify on to a national scale which left some areas of the country out in the cold. As we have seen, the East Midlands did not suffer in this development, at least relative to other parts of the country, but this could not have been predicted in 1918.

Regional boundaries supplemented, without replacing the old established local government boundaries, but in the 1970s an attempt was made to reorganize the total structure in the hope of ironing out the anomalies which had occurred since the county lines were drawn in the tenth century or earlier. Reorganization was long overdue. Within counties local government boundaries were an amalgam of divisions created for the Poor Law in 1834, the Urban and Rural Sanitary Districts of 1872, the adjustments made in 1894 when the multi-purpose Urban and Rural Districts were created, and the internal regroupings as a result of legislation in 1929. The administrative county of Lindsey consisted of three municipal boroughs, nine urban districts and nine rural districts. Among the municipal boroughs Scunthorpe (70, 907) was among the largest in this category in England, while Louth (11, 757) was relatively small. Gainsborough and Skegness, both of them urban districts, had populations in excess of Louth's, while Woodhall Spa and Alford urban

350

districts had populations below 2,300. Among county boroughs Grimsby and Lincoln were below the national average for both population and area. In the countryside several rural districts had geographically inappropriate administrative centres, and boundaries between town and country were drawn without much attention to modern development. Grimsby and Cleethorpes, a major continuous urban area, was divided between two authorities. Similar examples were to be found elsewhere, and from time to time alterations to boundaries had taken place. On the other hand other worthwhile changes, such as the merger of Grimsby and Cleethorpes, which was proposed in 1965, came to nothing.

No one seriously doubted that the social changes of the twentieth century had made a necessity of reform, and it was for this purpose that a Royal Commission on Local Government was established in 1966. However, the election of a Conservative government in 1970 produced a new set of proposals for local government reorganization, and considerable disquiet was voiced over the decision to incorporate part of north Lincolnshire into a new area called Humberside. This was unpopular since it was designed to make a county out of two areas which had little affinity with each other, and, until the opening of the Humber bridge in 1979–80, no easy physical link. It also made little sense in terms of the geography of the area (Marriott 1976). Elsewhere in the region Rutland, England's smallest county and a quaint reminder of the unsystematic way in which the old counties emerged 900 years earlier, finally disappeared into an enlarged county of Leicestershire. Other changes included the incorporation of parts of north-west Derbyshire into Greater Manchester, and the movement of Burton on Trent into Leicestershire. The new units of local government came into force on 1 April 1974. What is perhaps surprising is that the government did not introduce a metropolitan region incorporating Nottingham, Derby and Leicester, but the result was that with the major exception of the loss of Rutland and the creation of south Humberside, much of the area stayed as it had been in the past. Not everyone accepted the changes. Signs proclaiming the existence of Rutland can still be seen on the A606 Nottingham to Stamford road, and with the demise of the county a society was established to record its history.

In the 1980s the East Midlands has been relatively less affected by the industrial depression which has brought decline to the neighbouring West Midlands. Nottingham, with a new concert hall to add to its 1960s Playhouse and its refurbished Theatre Royal, is a regional centre for the arts, and Leicester plays a not dissimilar role since the opening of the Haymarket theatre in 1973. Derby, notwithstanding its new Assembly Rooms, has failed to develop a similar image, although it stands at the southern gateway to the immensely popular Peak District. Lincoln's major attraction is still its cathedral. Beyond the main towns Newark (like Loughborough and Ashbourne) remains a bottleneck for traffic, especially on market days, partly because it is one of the few larger towns without a ring road. Scunthorpe and Grimsby have suffered from the loss of staple industrial interests, further condemning Lincolnshire to the role of backwater within the region. Little trade moves through its ports; Gainsborough according to Pevsner,

> is one of the dreariest of the Midland red brick towns. The factories are all red brick, and those in the centre cannot for a long time have been proud of the appearance of their buildings. Neither the manufacturers

---

Plate 11.3 Nottingham Forest F.C. players Peter Shilton and Kenny Burns celebrating victory in the European Champions Cup Final, 31 May 1979.

Forest, or 'the reds' as they are known, could only be described as a moderately successful provincial football league team from the club's foundation in 1865 until the mid-1970s. Admitted to the Football League in 1892, Forest won the F.A. Cup in 1898, but spent most of the period 1911–57 in the second and third divisions. Returning to Division One in 1957 they won the F.A. Cup in 1959 and were runners-up in the league in 1967. Hard times returned when the club was relegated in 1972.

Forest's fortunes changed following the managerial appointments of Brian Clough in 1975, and Peter Taylor the following year. In 1977 the team gained promotion to the first division, and a year later they won both the League Cup (an achievement repeated in 1979), and, for the first time in the club's history, the first division championship. As a result, Forest progressed into European football, winning the prestigious European Champions Cup in 1979 and again the following year.

nor the council seem capable of thinking of their town in post-Victorian terms.

(Pevsner and Harris 1964: 240–1)

Grantham has been voted the most boring town in England, but like Stamford and Newark, it is now bypassed by the Great North Road which runs past, but no longer through, the region's towns. Visitors to the county today come either for the seaside or to see Lincoln itself.

Today's visitors will see a prosperous region, with the town slums gone, and most local people in work and relatively well off. They will see a region which has enjoyed sporting success, particularly for Nottinghamshire's cricket team, once sustained by framework knitters and miners but more recently by internationals from South Africa and New Zealand. Perhaps more significantly they will discover a region which has been put on the wider map of Europe by Nottingham Forest's victories in the European Cup, the important water-sports centre at Holme Pierrepont near Nottingham, and the racing circuit at Donington Park. Most visitors still come as a result of the lure of Robin Hood and Nottingham Castle, Lord Byron and D. H. Lawrence, but even those passing north without leaving the motorway can still see much of the urban-industrial complex in the distance as they drive through the Erewash valley and on towards the industrial belt of south Yorkshire. They might pass over the Trent with hardly a moment's thought about its illustrious past, although even now plans are afoot to improve the river in order to attract oil and other goods back onto the waterways. Travellers might also ignore the rural tranquillity which is still to be found in parts of Lincolnshire. In doing so they will miss seeing places where – by contrast with the western part of the region – little seems to have changed; the wolds and marshes of south Lincolnshire, for example, where a few farmers, apparently bypassed by the agricultural changes of the twentieth century, still make a living from holdings of little more than 50 acres. On the other hand, by disregarding Lincolnshire the modern traveller will accurately reflect the changes of a thousand years. A visitor to the East Midlands in medieval times would have made for Lincoln (particularly if he was a pilgrim) and, if he was a businessman, for the prosperous wool-producing areas of Lincolnshire and eastern Leicestershire. The hand of time has taken much less toll of these areas, but it has also meant that progress has largely passed by unnoticed; since the year 1000 the whole focus of the region has changed, and finally since 1900 even the remaining communications and locational barriers which helped to tie the region together have fallen away.

Appendix

Population in the East Midlands, 1086–1981

1. The Counties

Year	Derbyshire	Leicestershire	Lincolnshire	, Nottinghamshire	Rutland
1086	9–13,000*	25–30,000	120,000	20,230	2,992
1340	38,000	60,000	400,000	60,500	12,500
1377	32,000	47,595	200,000	43,328	8,991
1545	47,400	61,000		56,250	9,000
1563	47–53,000	35–44,000	110,000		
1603		55–69,000	116,000		
1670	70,000	58–72,000	90–95,000	71–89,000	
1701	113,998	79,123	179,095	85,145	15,404
1725				125,000	
1751	100,734	91,649	153,270	85,009	11,742
1781a	132,345	101,613	210,153	107,347	15,444
1781b	134,197	109,573	195,078	105,647	15,708
1801	161,567	130,081	208,625	140,350	16,300
1811	183,349	150,419	235,224	161,600	16,380
1821	213,333	174,571	283,058	186,873	18,487
1831	237,181	197,003	317,288	225,394	19,385
1841	272,202	215,867	362,602	249,910	21,302
1851	296,084	230,308	407,222	270,427	22,983
1861	339,327	237,412	412,246	293,867	21,861
1871	379,394	269,311	436,624	319,758	22,073
1881	461,945	321,258	469,947	391,784	21,434
1891	528,185	373,584	472,907	445,792	20,659
1901	585,837	434,019	498,868	514,628	19,720
1911	683,423	476,553	563,960	604,098	20,346
1921	714,662	494,469	602,202	641,149	18,376
1931	750,211	541,861	624,883	712,731	17,401
1951	826,437	631,077	705,822	841,211	20,537
1961	877,620	682,568	743,596	902,988	23,504
1971	885,131	772,103	809,148	976,413	27,469
1981†	910,173	844,525	550,758	985,283	–

* Where alternative figures are given a multiplier has usually been employed. Unless stated otherwise in the text, the normal multiplier is 4–5 persons per household.

† From 1974 Rutland was incorporated within Leicestershire, and part of north Lincolnshire in the new county of Humberside.

Sources:

Derbyshire	1086–1377	Blanchard 1967: 473
	1545	Dury 1963: 246
	1563	Riden 1978: 64
	1670	Edwards 1982a: xlii
Leicestershire		VCH Leics III 1955
Lincolnshire	1086–1377	Platts 1985: 11
	1563, 1603	Hodgett 1975: 65–66
	1670	Holmes 1980: 18–20
Nottinghamshire	1086–1545	Dury 1963: 246, 252
	1670, 1725	Chambers 1966: xi, 82
Rutland	1086–1545	Dury 1963: 246, 252
All counties	1701–1781	Deane and Cole 1969: 103
	1801–1981	Census Population Tables

2. The County Towns

Year	Derby	Leicester	Lincoln	Nottingham
1086	490	1,287	5–6,000	833
1327		4,800		
1361		3,840		
1377	1,300	3,152		2,170
1450		4,375		3,000
1524	1,300			
1530			1,500–2,000	
1550		3,550	2,000	3,250
1560			2,300	
1563	2,000–2,500			
1600				3,540
1660		5,000		5,220
1674				5,000–6,000
1700		6,000		
1705			3,000	
1709			3,000	
1712		6,450		
1721			4,000	
1739				10,720
1750	6,250	8,000	4,500	12,050
1775	7,750	10,500	5,500	16,510
1779				17,711
1785		12,784		
1801	10,832	16,953	7,205	28,801
1811	13,043	23,146	8,589	34,030
1821	17,423	30,125	9,995	40,190
1831	23,627	39,904	11,217	50,220
1841	32,741	48,167	13,806	52,164
1851	40,609	60,584	17,536	57,407
1861	43,091	68,056	20,995	74,693
1871	49,810	95,220	26,723	86,621

Year	Derby	Leicester	Lincoln	Nottingham
1881	58,568	122,376	37,313	186,575
1891	65,360	174,624	41,491	213,877
1901	69,266	211,579	48,784	239,743
1911	123,410	227,222	57,294	259,901
1921	131,151	234,143	66,042	262,624
1931	142,403	239,169	66,243	268,801
1951	141,267	285,181	70,333	306,008
1961	132,325	273,298	77,077	311,645
1971	219,582	284,208	74,269	300,630
1981	220,681	328,835	81,305	277,203

Sources: Dury 1963: 247; Law 1972; Chambers 1966: 82–3; Blanchard 1967; Riden 1978: 69; Thirsk 1985, I: 89; Hill 1956: 22–3, 88–9; Hill 1966: 146–7: Hill 1974: 306; Census Population Tables

Bibliography

Abbreviations

DAJ Derbyshire Archaeological Journal
EMG East Midlands Geographer
LAH Transactions of the Leicestershire Archaeological and Historical Society
LHA Lincolnshire History and Archaeology
TTS Transactions of the Thoroton Society
VCH Victoria County History

Abrams, P. and Wrigley, E. A. (eds) (1978) *Towns in Societies*. Cambridge University Press.
Acton, R. (1980) Navigations and the mid-Lincolnshire economy, 1790–1830, *LHA*, 15, 47–54.
Acton, R. (1982) The Market Rasen Canal 1801–1980, *LHA*, 17, 59–64.
Aldcroft, D. H. and Freeman, M. J. (1983) *Transport in the Industrial Revolution*. Manchester University Press.
Aley, S. (1985) The Nottinghamshire landowners and their estates, 1660–1840, unpublished Ph.D thesis, University of Nottingham.
Allin, C. E. (1981) *The Medieval Leather Industry in Leicester*. Leicester, Leicestershire Museums, Art Galleries and Records Service, Archaeological Report, no. 3.
Ambler, R. W. (1976) The transformation of harvest celebrations in nineteenth-century Lincolnshire, *Midland History*, 3, 298–306.
Anderson, P. H. (1985) *Forgotten Railways: the East Midlands* (2nd edn). David St John Thomas, Newton Abbot.
Andrews, C. B. (ed) (1935) *The Torrington Diaries*. Eyre and Spottiswoode, London, 4 volumes.
Armstrong, M. E. (ed) (1981) *An Industrial Island: a history of Scunthorpe*. Scunthorpe Borough Museum and Art Gallery.
Ashton, N. D. (1977) *Leicestershire Water-mills*. Sycamore Press, Wymondham.
Aslet C. (1982) *The Last Country Houses*. Yale University Press.
Aspinall, P. J. (1976) Speculative builders and the development of Cleethorpes, 1850–1900, *LHA*, 11, 43–54.
Austin, M. R. (1973) Religion and society in Derbyshire during the Industrial Revolution, *DAJ*, 93, 75–89.

Austin, M. R. (1982) Tithe and benefice incomes in Derbyshire 1772–1832, *DAJ*, CII, 118–24.

Baker, A. R. H. (1963) Open fields in Derbyshire: some reservations about recent arguments, *DAJ*, **83**, 77–85.

Baker, D. (1983) *Coalville: the first seventy-five years.* Leicester, Leicestershire Libraries and Information Service.

Barber, S. (1982) Irish migrant agricultural labourers in nineteenth-century Lincolnshire, *Saothar: Journal of the Irish Labour History Society*, 8, 10–22.

Barker, K. (1985) Thirty years of struggle: entertainment in provincial towns between 1840 and 1870, *Theatre World*, **39** (2), 68–75.

Barley, L. B. and **Barley, M. W.** (1959) Lincolnshire craftsmen in the sixteenth and seventeenth centuries, *Lincolnshire Historian*, 2 (6), 7–22.

Barley, L. B. and **Barley, M. W.** (1962) Lincolnshire shopkeepers in the sixteenth and seventeenth centuries, *Lincolnshire Historian*, 2 (9), 7–21.

Barley, M. W. (1936) Lincolnshire rivers in the Middle Ages, *Lincolnshire Architectural and Archaeological Society Reports and Papers*, 1, 1–22.

Barley, M. W. (1938) The Barrow-on-Humber Town Book, Lincolnshire Architectural and Archaeological Society Reports and Papers, 2, 13–23.

Barley, M. W. (1949) Newark in the sixteenth century, *TTS*, LIII, 15–25.

Barley, M. W. (1953) Plough plays in the East Midlands, *Journal of the English Folk Dance and Song Society*, VIII (2), 68–95.

Barley, M. W. (1957) Cistercian land clearances in Nottinghamshire: three deserted villages and their moated successor, *Nottingham Medieval Studies*, I, 75–89.

Barley, M. W. (1961) *The English Farmhouse and Cottage.* Routledge and Kegan Paul, London.

Barley, M. W. (1972) *Lincolnshire and the Fens.* Republished by EP Publishing, London.

Barley, M. W. (1986) *Houses and History.* Faber, London.

Barley, M. W. and **Straw, I. F.** (1971) Nottingham. In Lobel, M. D. (ed) *Historic Towns*, vol. 1, Lovell Johns, London.

Bateman, J. (1971) *The Great Landowners of Great Britain and Ireland*, (ed) Spring, D. Leicester University Press.

Beastall, T. W. (1978) *The Agricultural Revolution in Lincolnshire.* History of Lincolnshire Committee, Lincoln.

Beats, L. (1978), The East Midland Association, 1642–4, *Midland History*, 4, 160–74.

Beaver, S. H. (1982/3) Ironstone in Rutland 1882–1982, *Rutland Record*, 3, 110–17.

Beckett, J. V. and **Foulds, T.** (1985), Landholding and society in Laxton in 1841, *TTS*, LXXXIX, 108–21.

Beckwith, I. S. (1967a) The river trade of Gainsborough, 1500–1850, *LHA*, 2, 3–20.

Beckwith, I. S. (1967b) Georgian Tuxford, *TTS*, LXXI, 59–69.

Beckwith, I. S. (1968) *The Making of Modern Gainsborough.* Gainsborough Urban District Council.

Beckwith, I. S. (1982) *Land and Community: three studies in 17th century rural history.* Centre for the Study of Rural Society, Lincoln.

Beresford, M. W. (1967) *New Towns of the Middle Ages: town plantation in England, Wales and Gascony.* Lutterworth Press, London.

Beresford, M. W. (1981) English medieval boroughs: a hand-list: revision, 1973–81. *Urban History Yearbook*: 59–65.

Beresford, M. W. and Finberg, H. P. R. (1973) *English Medieval Boroughs*. David and Charles, Newton Abbot.

Beresford, M. W. and Hurst, J. G. (1972) *Deserted Medieval Villages*. Lutterworth Press, Guildford and London.

Beresford, M. W. and St Joseph, J. K. S. (1958) *Medieval England: An Aerial Survey*. Cambridge University Press.

Bestall, J. M. (1974) *History of Chesterfield vol. I*. Borough of Chesterfield, Chesterfield.

Bestall, J. M. and Fowkes, D. V. (1978) *History of Chesterfield vol. III*. Borough of Chesterfield, Chesterfield.

Bestall, J. M. and Fowkes, D. V. (1984) *History of Chesterfield vol. II part 2: Restoration and Georgian Chesterfield*. Borough of Chesterfield, Chesterfield.

Biggs, B. J. (1977) Early Victorian Schools in North Nottinghamshire, *TTS*, LXXXI, 62–77.

Bindoff, S. (ed) (1982) *The House of Commons 1509–58*. Secker and Warburg, London.

Blanchard, I. S. W. (1967) Economic Change in Derbyshire in the Late Middle Ages, 1272–1540, unpublished Ph.D. thesis, University of London.

Blanchard, I. S. W. (1971) Derbyshire lead production, 1195–1505, *DAJ*, 91, 119–40.

Blanchard, I. S. W. (1972) The miner and the agricultural community in late medieval England, *Agricultural History Review*, 20, 93–106.

Blanchard, I. S. W. (1984) Industrial employment and the rural land market 1380–1520. In Smith, R. M. (ed), *Land, Kinship and Life-Cycle*. Cambridge University Press, pp. 227–75.

Boase, S. L. (1980) The Humberstone Gate pleasure fairs in the late nineteenth century, *Leicestershire Historian*, II, 10, 16–25.

Bowden, P. J. (1962) *The Wool Trade of Tudor and Stuart England*. Macmillan, London.

Bowker, M. (1968) *The Secular Clergy in the Diocese of Lincoln 1495–1520*. Cambridge University Press.

Bowker, M. (1972) Lincolnshire 1536: heresy, schism or religious discontent? In *Studies in Church History*, vol. 9, Oxford University Press, pp. 195–212.

Bowker, M. (1981) *The Henrician Reformation: the diocese of Lincoln under John Longland, 1521–1547*. Cambridge University Press.

Bowler, I. R. (1981) Permanent grass in Leicestershire: the decline of a traditional land use and its role in the farming system, *EMG*, 7 (8), 272–8.

Brand, K. (1985) *The Park Estate*. Civic Society, Nottingham.

Bray, W. (ed) (1906) *The Diary and Correspondence of John Evelyn*. London.

Brazier, S., Hammond, R. and Waterman, S. A. (1985) *A New Geography of Nottingham*. Trent Polytechnic.

Brighton, T. (1981) *Royalists and Roundheads in Derbyshire*. Bakewell Historical Society.

Britnell, R. H. (1981) The proliferation of markets in England, 1200–1349, *Economic History Review*, 2nd ser., XXXIV, 209–21.

Brocklebank, J. A. H. (1962) The New Poor Law in Lincolnshire, *Lincolnshire Historian*, 2 (9), 21–33.

Brown, A. E. (ed) (1970) *The Growth of Leicester*. Leicester University Press.

Brown, T. (1794) *General View of the Agriculture of the County of Derby*. London.

Bryson, E. (1974) *Portrait of Nottingham*. Robert Hale, London.

Buckatzsch, E. J. (1950) The geographical distribution of wealth in England, 1086–1843. *Economic History Review*, 2nd ser., III, 180–202.

Burt, R. (1969) Lead production in England and Wales, 1700–70, *Economic History Review*, XXII, 77–85.

Burt, R. and **Atkinson, M.** (1976) The mineral statistics and Derbyshire lead mining, *Bulletin of the Peak District Mines Historical Society*, VI, 164–7.

Burton, I. E. (1977) Buxton's waters, *Derbyshire Miscellany*, VIII (1), 18–26.

Butler, R. M. (1949) The civil war defences of Nottingham, *TTS*, LIII, 26–33.

Buxton, A. S. (1932) *Mansfield One Hundred Years Ago*. Mansfield.

Caird, J. (1852) *English Agriculture in 1850–51*. London.

Cameron, A. (1971) William de Amyas and the community of Nottingham, 1308–50, *TTS*, LXXV, 68–78.

Cameron, A. (1975) Some social consequences of the dissolution of the monasteries in Nottinghamshire, *TTS*, LXXIX, 50–9.

Cameron, A. (1980) Laxton before 1635, *EMG*, 7 (6), 219–26.

Cameron, A. and **O'Brien, C.** (1981) The deserted medieval village of Thorpe-in-the-Glebe, Nottinghamshire, *TTS*, LXXXV, 56–67.

Cameron, K. (1959) *The Place Names of Derbyshire*. Cambridge University Press.

Cameron, K. (1965) *Scandinavian Settlement in the Territory of the Five Boroughs: the Place-Name Evidence*. University of Nottingham.

Cantor, L. M. (1970–71). The medieval parks of Leicestershire, *LAH*, XLVI, 9–24.

Cantor, L. M. and **Matthews, G. F.** (1977) *Loughborough, from College to University*. Loughborough University of Technology.

Caplan, M. (1970) The poor law in Nottinghamshire 1836–71, *TTS*, LXXIV, 82–98.

Caplan, M. (1984) *In the Shadow of the Workhouse*. University of Nottingham, Centre for Local History.

Carr, J. P. (1965) The rise and fall of Peak District lead mining. In Whittow, J. B. and Wood, P. D. (eds) *Essays in Geography for Austin Wood*. University of Reading, pp. 207–24.

Carus-Wilson, E. M. (1962–63) The medieval trades of the ports of the Wash, *Medieval Archaeology*, VI–VII, 182–201.

Chambers, J. D. (1940) Enclosure and the small landowner, *Economic History Review*, X, 118–27.

Chambers, J. D. (1947) Enclosure and the small landowner in Lindsey, *Lincolnshire Historian*, I (i), 15–20.

Chambers, J. D. (1952) *A Century of Nottingham History*. University of Nottingham.

Chambers, J. D. (1957) The Vale of Trent, 1670–1800: a regional study of economic change, *Economic History Review* supplement.

Chambers, J. D. (1960) Population change in a provincial town: Nottingham 1700–1800. In Pressnell, L. S., *Studies in the Industrial Revolution*. Athlone Press, London.

Chambers, J. D. (1966) *Nottinghamshire in the Eighteenth Century*. 2nd edn. Cass, London.

Chambers, J. D. and **Barley, M. W.** (1961) Industrial monuments at Milford and Belper, *Archaeological Journal*, CXVIII, 236–9.

Chambers, J. D. and **Mingay, G. E.** (1967) *The Agricultural Revolution 1750–1880*. Batsford, London.

Chapman, S. D. (1962) The evangelical revival and education in Nottingham, *TTS*, LXVI, 35–66.

Chapman, S. D. (1963) Working-class housing in Nottingham during the industrial revolution, *TTS*, LXVII, 67–92.

Chapman, S. D. (1967) *The Early Factory Masters*. David and Charles, Newton Abbot.

Chapman, S. D. (1972) The genesis of the British hosiery industry 1650–1760, *Textile History*, 3, 7–50.

Chapman, S. D. (1974a) Enterprise and innovation in the British hosiery industry, *Textile History*, 5, 14–37.

Chapman, S. D. (1974b) *Jesse Boot of Boots the Chemist*. Hodder and Stoughton, London.

Chapman, S. D. (1981) *Stanton and Staveley*. Woodhead Faulkner, Cambridge.

Chapman, S. D. (1982) The Arkwright mills: Colquhoun's census of 1788 and archaeological evidence, *Industrial Archaeology Review*, VI, 5–27.

Chartres, J. A. (1977) *Internal Trade in England 1500–1700*. Macmillan, London.

Church, R. A. (1966) *Economic and Social Change in a Midland Town: Victorian Nottingham, 1815–1900*. Cass, London.

Church, R. A. (1986) *The History of the British Coal Industry, vol. 3 1830–1913*. Clarendon, Oxford.

Clark, P. (ed) (1984) *The Transformation of English Provincial Towns 1600–1800*. Hutchinson, London.

Clark, P. and Slack, P. (1976) *English Towns in Transition 1500–1700*. Oxford University Press.

Clark, R. (1980) A 'Good and Sufficient Maintenance': the augmentation of parish livings in Derbyshire 1645–60, *DAJ*, 100, 69–78.

Clark, R. (1983) Why was the re-establishment of the Church of England in 1662 possible? Derbyshire: a provincial perspective, *Midland History*, VIII, 86–105.

Clarke J. A. (1852) On the farming of Lincolnshire, *Journal of the Royal Agricultural Society of England*, 12, 369–71.

Clarke, J. N. (1976) *Education in a Market Town: Horncastle, Lincolnshire*. Phillimore, Chichester.

Clarkson, L. A. (1958) The English leather industry in the late sixteenth and the seventeenth centuries, unpublished Ph.D. thesis, University of Nottingham.

Clemenson, H. A. (1982) *English Country Houses and Landed Estates*. Croom Helm, London.

Clifton-Taylor, A. (1972) *The Pattern of English Building*. Faber, London.

Coates, B. E. (1965) The origin and distribution of markets and fairs in medieval Derbyshire, *DAJ*, 85, 92–111.

Colvin, H. M. (1963) *The History of the King's Works*. Vols 1 and 2. HMSO, London.

Colvin, H. M. (1970) Grimsthorpe Castle: the North Front, in *The Country Seat: Studies in the History of the British Country House*. Allen Lane, London, 91–3.

Coones, F. and Patten, J. (1986) *The Penguin Guide to the Landscape of England and Wales*. Penguin, Harmondsworth.

Coope, R. (1979) Newstead Abbey in the eighteenth century: the building works of the fourth and fifth Lords Byron, *TTS*, LXXXIII, 46–62.

Cooper, A. (1970) Newark in 1830, *TTS*, LXXIV, 38–44.

Cooper, A. (1971) Victorian Newark, *TTS*, LXXV, 103–14.

Cooper, B. (1982) *Transformation of a Valley: the Derbyshire Derwent*. Hutchinson, London.

Copnall, H. H. (1915) *Nottinghamshire County Records*. Saxton, Nottingham.

Corfield, P. J. (1982) *The Impact of English Towns 1700–1800*. Oxford University Press.

Cossons, A. (1934). *The Turnpike Roads of Nottinghamshire*. Historical Association, London.

Cossons, A. (1958) Early enclosures in Beeston, *TTS*, LXII, 1–10.

Countryside Commission (1981) *Fourteenth Annual Report 1980–1*. HMSO, London.

Cox, J. C. (1885) A religious census of Derbyshire 1676, *DAJ*, 7, 31–6.

Cox, J. C. (1908) Derbyshire in 1327–8: being a Lay Subsidy Roll, *DAJ*, 30, 23–96.

Cox, T. (*c.* 1700a) *Topographical, Ecclesiastical and Natural History of Derbyshire*. London.

Cox, T. (*c.* 1700b) *Topographical, Ecclesiastical and Natural History of Lincolnshire*. London.

Cracknell, S. (1984) Nottinghamshire county carriers in the late nineteenth century, *TTS*, LXXXVIII, 76–88.

Cranstone, D. (1985) The iron industry of the Ashby coalfield, *Leicestershire Industrial History Society Bulletin*, 8, 23–31.

Crook, D. (1983) The establishment of the Derbyshire County Court 1256, *DAJ*, 103, 98–106.

Crook, D. (1984) The community of Mansfield from Domesday Book to the reign of Edward III, *TTS*, LXXXVIII, 14–38.

Crook, D. (1985) The community of Mansfield from Domesday Book to the reign of Edward III: Part II, *TTS*, LXXXIX, 16–29.

Cuthbert, N. H. (1960) *The Lace Makers Society*. Amalgamated Society of Operative Lace Makers, Nottingham.

Daff, T. (1973) The establishment of ironmaking at Scunthorpe, 1858–77, *Bulletin of Economic Research*, 25 (2), 104–21.

Daniel, C. (1985) *The Story of Eyam Plague*. The author, Eyam.

Daniel, M. (1977) The Derbyshire miners and 1649, unpublished paper.

Darby, H. C. (1971) *The Domesday Geography of Eastern England*. 3rd edn. Cambridge University Press.

Darby, H. C. (1976) *A New Historical Geography of England before 1600*. Cambridge University Press.

Darby, H. C. (1977) *Domesday England*. Cambridge University Press.

Darby, H. C. (1983) *The Changing Fenland*. Cambridge University Press.

Darby, H. C. and Terrett, I. B. (1971) *The Domesday Geography of Midland England*. Cambridge University Press.

Darby, H. C. and Maxwell, I. S. (1962) *The Domesday Geography of Northern England*. Cambridge University Press.

Davey, B. J. (1983) *Lawless and Immoral: Policing a Country Town 1838–1857*. Leicester University Press.

Davies, E. (1927) The small landowner 1780–1832 in the light of the land tax assessments, *Economic History Review*, I, 87–113.

Davies, J. C. (1964) *Bowden to Harborough*. The author, Market Harborough.

Deane, P. and Cole, W. A. (1969) *British Economic Growth 1688–1959*. 2nd edn. Cambridge University Press.

Deering, C. (1751) *An Historical Account of the Ancient and Present State of the Town of Nottingham.* Ayscough and Willington, Nottingham.

Defoe, D. (1727) *Complete English Tradesman.* London.

Defoe, D. (1971) *A Tour Through the Whole Island of Great Britain.* (Ed) Rogers, P. Penguin, Harmondsworth.

Delves, A. (1981) Popular recreation and social conflict in Derby, 1800–1850. In Yeo, E. and Yeo, S. (eds) *Popular culture and class conflict: 1590–1914.* Harvester, Brighton, pp. 88–127.

Dias, J. R. (1981) Lead, society and politics in Derbyshire before the civil war, *Midland History*, VI, 39–57.

Dibdin, C. (1801) *Observations on a Tour.* London.

Dobson, R. B. (1977) Urban decline in late medieval England, *Transactions of the Royal Historical Society*, 5th ser., **27**, 1–22.

Dodd, J. P. (1980) The agriculture of Leicestershire in the mid-nineteenth century: a study of the 1854 crop returns. In Williams, D. D. (ed) *The Adaptation of Change.* Leicester University Press, pp. 115–35.

Dodgshon, R. A. and **Butlin, R. A.** (eds) (1978) *An Historical Geography of England and Wales.* Academic Press, London.

Dover, P. (1972) *The Early Medieval History of Boston AD 1086–1400* 2nd ed. Richard Kay, Boston.

Durant, D. (1977) *Bess of Hardwick.* Weidenfeld and Nicolson, London.

Durant, D. and **Riden, P.** (eds) (1980) *The Building of Hardwick Hall: Part 1. The Old Hall, 1587–91.* Derbyshire Record Society, vol. IV.

Durant, D. and **Riden, P.** (1984) *The Building of Hardwick Hall: Part 2. The New Hall 1591–98.* Derbyshire Record Society, vol IX.

Dury, G. H. (1963) *The East Midlands and the Peak.* Nelson, London.

Eagle, E. (1950) Some light on the beginnings of the Lincolnshire bulb industry, *Lincolnshire Historian*, **6**, 220–9.

Eardley-Simpson, L. (1933) *Derby and the Forty-Five.* Philip Allan, London.

Eden, Sir F. M. (1797) *State of the Poor.* 3 vols. White, London.

Edwards, D. G. (1982a) Population in Derbyshire in the reign of King Charles II: the use of hearth tax assessments and the Compton census, *DAJ*, CII, 106–17.

Edwards, D. G. (1982b) *Derbyshire Hearth Tax Assessments, 1662–70.* Derbyshire Record Society, vol. VII.

Edwards, K. C. (1944) *Land Utilization Survey of Great Britain, pt. 60, Nottinghamshire.* HMSO, London.

Edwards, K. C. (1948) Soils of the East Midlands. In Marshall, C. E. (ed) *Guide to the Geology of the East Midlands.* University of Nottingham.

Edwards, K. C. (1954) The East Midlands: some general considerations, *EMG*, **1** (1), 3–12.

Edwards, K. C. (1966a) *Nottingham and Its Region.* British Association, Nottingham.

Edwards, K. C. (1966b) The East Midlands urban region, *EMG*, **4** (2), 63–71.

Elliott, M. (1979) *Victorian Leicester.* Phillimore, Chichester.

Elliott, M. (1980–81) Belief and disbelief in Victorian Leicester, *LAH*, LVI, 88–96.

Elliott, S. (1969) The Cecil family and the development of nineteenth-century Stamford, *LHA*, **4**, 23–32.

Ellis, C. D. B. (1976) *History in Leicester 55 BC–1969.* 3rd edn. Leicester.

Emery, A. (1985) Ralph, Lord Cromwell's manor at Wingfield (1439–*c.* 1450): its construction, design and influence, *Archaeological Journal*, **142**, 276–339.

Estall, R. C. (1957) The distribution of coal from the East Midlands division, *EMG* no. 8, 11–21.

Evans, R. H. (1949) Nonconformists in Leicestershire in 1669, *LAH*, XXV, 98–143.

Evans, R. H. (1952) The Quakers in Leicestershire 1660–1714, *LAH*, XXVIII, 63–83.

Everitt, A. M. (1969) *The Local Community and the Great Rebellion*. Historical Association, London.

Everitt, A. M. (1973) Town and country in Victorian Leicestershire: the role of the village carrier. In *Perspectives in English Urban History*. Macmillan, London, pp. 213–40.

Everitt, A. M. (1977) River and wold: reflections on the historical origin of regions and pays, *Journal of Historical Geography*, **3** (1), 1–19.

Everitt, A. M. (1979) Country, county and town: patterns of regional evolution in England, *Transactions of the Royal Historical Society*, 5th ser., **29**, 79–108.

Farey, J. (1811–17) *General View of the Agriculture . . . of Derbyshire*. 3 vols. Nicol, London.

Fawcett, C. B. (1960) The East Midland (or Trent) province. In *Provinces of England: A Study of some Geographical Aspects of Devolution*. Hutchinson, London.

Fiennes, C. (1947) *The Journeys of Celia Fiennes*. (Ed) C. Morris. Cresset Press, London.

Fisher, F. J. (1961) *Essays in the Economic and Social History of Tudor and Stuart England*. Cambridge University Press.

Fisher, J. R. (1981) Issues and influence: two by-elections in south Nottinghamshire in the mid-nineteenth century, *Historical Journal*, **24**, 155–65.

Fleming, D. (1981/2) Faction in civil war Leicestershire, *LAH*, LVII, 26–36.

Fletcher, A. J. (1971) The Hope Valley in 1851, *DAJ*, **91**, 169–82.

Fletcher, A. J. (1973) Petitioning and the outbreak of the civil war in Derbyshire, *DAJ*, **93**, 33–44.

Fletcher, A. J. and **Stevenson, J.** (eds) (1985) *Order and Disorder in Early Modern England*. Cambridge University Press.

Flinn, M. W. (1984) *The History of the British Coal Industry, vol. 2. 1700–1830*. Clarendon, Oxford.

Ford, T. D. and **Rieuwerts, J. H.** (1983) *Lead Mining in the Peak District*. 3rd edn. Peak Park Planning Board, Bakewell.

Foulds, T. (1980) The history of Thurgarton Priory before 1316, *TTS*, LXXXIV, 21–32.

Foulds, T. (1984) Thurgarton priory and its benefactors, unpublished Ph.D. thesis, University of Nottingham.

Fowkes, D. V. (1967) Nottinghamshire parks in the eighteenth and nineteenth centuries, *TTS*, LXXI, 72–89.

Fowkes, D. V. (1971a) The progress of agrarian change in Nottinghamshire, *c.* 1720–1830, unpublished Ph.D. thesis, University of Liverpool.

Fowkes, D. V. (1971b) The development of Ironville, *Derbyshire Miscellany*, **6**, 31–3.

Fowkes, D. V. (1977) The breck system of Sherwood Forest, *TTS*, LXXXI, 55–61.

Fraser, D. (1966) Nottingham and the Corn Laws, *TTS*, LXX, 181–204.

Fraser, D. (1979) *Power and Authority in the Victorian City*. Blackwell, Oxford.

Fraser, S. M. (1980) Leicester and smallpox: the Leicester Method, *Medical History*, 24, 315–32.

Freer, D. (1977–78) The dynasty builders of Victorian Leicester, *LAH*, LIII, 42–54.

Frizelle, E. R. and Martin, J. D. (1972) *The Leicester Royal Infirmary, 1771–1971*. No. 1 Hospital Management Committee, Leicester.

Fuggles, J. F. (1970–71) The parish clergy in the archdeaconry of Leicester, 1520–1540, *LAH*, XLVI, 25–44.

Fuller, G. J. (1954) Geographical aspects of the development of Boston (Lincolnshire) between 1700 and 1900, *EMG*, I (2), 3–12.

Fuller, G. J. (1957) The development of drainage, agriculture and settlement in the fens of south-east Lincolnshire during the 19th century, *EMG*, no. 7, 3–15.

Fuller, G. J. (1965) Lead mining in Derbyshire in the mid-nineteenth century, *EMG*, 3, 373–93.

Fuller, G. J. (1970) Early lead smelting in the Peak District: another look at the evidence. In Osborne, R. H. (ed) *Geographical Essays*. Nottingham.

Fuller, H. A. (1974) Landownership in Lindsey *c.* 1800–1860, unpublished M.A. thesis, University of Hull.

Fussell, G. E. (1951) Four centuries of farming systems in Derbyshire: 1500–1900, *DAJ*, LXXI (n.s. XXIV), 1–37.

Gardiner, J. (1983) Great Hucklow – a lead mining village in the nineteenth century: population and occupations. *Derbyshire Miscellany*, 10 (2), 37–44.

Garlic, S. L. (1982) A visit to Derbyshire – being part of a tour through England made by Thomas Wright and others in 1750, *Derbyshire Miscellany*, IX, 160–1.

Gibson, F. A. (**1922**) *The Coal Mining Industry of the United Kingdom*. Cardiff.

Gilbert, E. W. (1960) The idea of the region, *Geography*, 45, 157–75.

Gillett, E. (1970) *A History of Grimsby*. Oxford University Press.

Girouard, M. (1983) *Robert Smythson and the Elizabethan Country House*. Yale University Press, New Haven.

Glasscock, R. E. (1975) *The Lay Subsidy of 1334*. British Academy, London.

Gomme, G. L. (1896) *Topographical History of Leicestershire, Lincolnshire, Middlesex and Monmouth*. Elliot Stock, London.

Goodacre, J. (1978) Lutterworth in the 17th century, unpublished paper.

Gordon, M. D. (1911) The collection of ship money in the reign of Charles I, *Transactions of the Royal Historical Society*, 3rd ser., 4, 141–62.

Goulding, H. E. (1957) Louth: a north Lincolnshire market town, *EMG*, no. 7, 31–6.

Granville, A. B. (1841) *Spas of England and principal sea-bathing places* vol. 2. London.

Gray, D. (1960) *Nottingham through 500 Years: a short history of town government*. 2nd edn. Nottingham.

Griffin, A. R. (1955) *The Miners of Nottinghamshire: a history of the Nottinghamshire Miners' Association, vol. 1. 1881–1914*. Privately published, Nottingham.

Griffin, A. R. (1971) *Mining in the East Midlands*. Cass, London.

Griffin, A. R. (1981) *The Nottinghamshire Coalfield 1880–1981*. Moorland, Ashbourne.

Griffin, A. R. and Griffin, C. P. (1977) The non-political trade union movement. In Briggs, A. and Saville, J. (eds) *Essays in Labour History 1918–1939*. Croom Helm, London.

Griffin, C. P. (1969) The economic and social development of the Leicestershire and south Derbyshire coalfield, 1550–1914, unpublished Ph.D. thesis, University of Nottingham.

Griffin, C. P. (1974) Chartism and opposition to the new Poor Law in Nottinghamshire, *Midland History*, 2 (4), 244–9.

Griffin, C. P. (1977) Three generations of miners housing at Moira, Leicestershire, 1811–1934, *Industrial Archaeology Review*, I, 276–82.

Griffin, C. P. (1977–78) Transport change and the development of the Leicestershire coalfield in the canal age: a re-interpretation, *Journal of Transport History*, IV, 227–38.

Griffin, C. P. (1978) Technological change in the Leicestershire and south Derbyshire coalfield before *c.*1850, *Industrial Archaeology Review*, 3, 65–74.

Griffin, C. P. (1981) Colliery owners and trade unionism: the case of south Derbyshire in the mid-nineteenth century, *Midland History*, 6, 109–23.

Griffin, C. P. (1984) *Nottinghamshire miners between the wars: the Spencer Union revisited.* University of Nottingham, Centre for Local History.

Griffin, N. (1967–68) Epidemics in Loughborough 1539–1640, *LAH*, XLIII, 24–34.

Grigg, D. B. (1966) *The Agricultural Revolution in South Lincolnshire.* Cambridge University Press.

Gudgin, G. (1978) *Industrial Location Processes and Regional Employment Growth.* Saxon House, London.

Guilford, E. L. (1924) Nottinghamshire in 1676, *TTS*, XXVIII, 106–13.

Gurnham, R. (1972) The creation of Skegness as a resort town by the 9th Earl of Scarbrough, *LHA*, 7, 63–76.

Gurnham, R. I. (1976) *A History of the Trade Union Movement in the Hosiery and Knitwear Industry, 1776–1976.* National Union of Hosiery and Knitwear Workers, Leicester.

Hadfield, C. (1966) *Canals of the East Midlands.* David and Charles, Newton Abbot.

Hall, R. (1974) Occupation and population structure in part of the Derbyshire Peak District in the mid-nineteenth century, *EMG*, 6 (2), 66–78.

Hall, R. (1978) Economy and society in the Derbyshire Peak District, 1861, *DAJ*, 98, 72–82.

Hallam, H. E. (1958) Some thirteenth-century censuses, *Economic History Review*, 2nd ser., X, 340–61.

Hallam, H. E. (1959–60) Salt making in the Lincolnshire fenland during the Middle Ages, *Lincolnshire Architectural and Archaeological Society: Reports and Papers*, 8, 85–112.

Hallam, H. E. (1965) *Settlement and Society: A Study of the Early Agrarian History of South Lincolnshire.* Cambridge University Press.

Hallam, H. E. (1967) The agrarian economy of south Lincolnshire in the mid-fifteenth century, *Nottingham Medieval Studies*, XI, 86–95.

Hallam, H. E. (1981) *Rural England 1066–1348.* Fontana, London.

Hallam, H. E. (1985) Age at first marriage and age at death in the Lincolnshire fenland, 1252–1478, *Population Studies*, XXXIX, 55–69.

Harden, G. (1978) *Medieval Boston and its Archaeological Implications.* South Lincolnshire Archaeological Unit, Heckington.

Hardy, S. M. (1955–56) The development of coal mining in a north Derbyshire village, 1635–1860, *University of Birmingham Historical Journal*, V, 147–66.

Haresign, S. R. (1983) Small farmers and allotments as a cure for rural depopulation on the Lincolnshire fenlands, 1870–1914, *LHA*, **18**, 27–36.

Harris, H. (1968) *The Industrial Archaeology of the Peak District*. David and Charles, Newton Abbot.

Harrison, J. F. C. (1959) Chartism in Leicester. In Briggs, A. (ed) *Chartist Studies*. Macmillan, London.

Harvey, P. D. A. (1973) The English Inflation of 1180–1220, *Past and Present*, **61**, 3–30.

Hatcher, J. (1977) *Plague, Population and the English Economy 1348–1530*. Macmillan, London.

Head, P. (1962) Putting-out in the Leicester hosiery industry in the middle of the nineteenth century, *LAH*, XXXVII, 44–59.

Heape, R. G. (1948) *Buxton under the Dukes of Devonshire*. Hale, London.

Heath, J. E. (1975) Railway excursions in the nineteenth and twentieth centuries, *Derbyshire Miscellany*, 7 (3), 121–3.

Heath, J. E. (1978) Education in Derby between 1870 and 1903, *Derbyshire Miscellany*, 8 (4), 131–9.

Heath, J. E. (1979) The borough of Derby between 1780 and 1810, *Derbyshire Miscellany*, 8 (6), 181–97.

Heath, J. E. (1980) The Derbyshire constabulary – its establishment, *Derbyshire Miscellany*, 9, 19–22.

Heath, J. E. (1982) *The Illustrated History of Derbyshire*. Barracuda, Buckingham.

Heath, J. E. and Christian, R. (1985) *Yesterday's Town: Derby*. Barracuda, Buckingham.

Hensman, E. W. (1923) The East Midlands in the second civil war, *Transactions of the Royal Historical Society*, 4th ser., 6, 126–59.

Henstock, A. (1969) Cheese manufacture and marketing in Derbyshire and north Staffordshire, 1670–1870, *DAJ*, **89**, 32–46.

Henstock, A. (ed) (1980) *The Diary of Abigail Gawthern of Nottingham, 1751–1810*. Thoroton Society Record Series XXXIII.

Henstock, A. (1986) A road traffic census of Nottingham in 1819, *TTS*, XC, 94–100.

Hewson, J. E. (1986) Who were the Skegness pioneers? A study of the people who settled in the new town of Skegness, *LHA*, **21**, 63–5.

Hey, D. (1980) *Packmen, Carriers and Packhorse Roads*. Leicester University Press.

Heydon, S. (1979–80) The provision of medical care for the poor in Leicester in the 1830s, *LAH*, LV, 65–71.

Hill, J. W. F. (1948) *Medieval Lincoln*. Cambridge University Press.

Hill, J. W. F. (1956) *Tudor and Stuart Lincoln*. Cambridge University Press.

Hill, J. W. F. (1966) *Georgian Lincoln*. Cambridge University Press.

Hill, J. W. F. (1974) *Victorian Lincoln*. Cambridge University Press.

Hill, J. W. F. (1979) *A Short History of Lincoln*. Lincoln Civic Trust.

Hill, M. (1972) The geography of 25 market places in Derbyshire and Nottinghamshire from 1861 to 1969, unpublished M.A. thesis, University of Nottingham.

Hillier, K. (1983) *Ashby de la Zouch: the Spa Town*. Ashby.

Hilton, R. H. (1985) Medieval market towns, *Past and Present*, **109**, 3–23.

Hinde, T. (ed) (1985) *The Domesday Book: England's Heritage Then and Now*. Guild Publishing, London.

Hodgett, G. A. J. (1975) *Tudor Lincolnshire*. History of Lincolnshire Committee, Lincoln.

Hodson, J. H. (ed) (1962) *The Wollaton estate and the civil war, 1643–1647*. Thoroton Society Record Series XXI, 3–15.

Holderness, B. A. (1972a) The agricultural activities of the Massingberds of South Ormsby, Lincolnshire, 1638–1750, *Midland History*, 1 (3), 15–25.

Holderness, B. A. (1972b) Rural tradesmen, 1660–1850 – a regional study in Lindsey, *LHA*, 7, 77–83.

Holderness, B. A. (1974) Aspects of inter-regional land use and agriculture in Lincolnshire, 1600–1850, *LHA*, 9, 35–42.

Holderness, B. A. (1979) The land market in the East Midlands, 1670–1820. In Wanklyn, M. D. G. (ed) *Landownership and Power in the Regions*. Wolverhampton Polytechnic.

Holmes, C. (1980) *Seventeenth-Century Lincolnshire*. History of Lincolnshire Committee, Lincoln.

Holmes, W. D. (1958) The Leicestershire and south Derbyshire coalfield (1) the coal mining industry, *EMG*, 10, 16–26.

Holt, J. C. (1982) *Robin Hood*. Thames and Hudson, London.

Honeyman, K. (1982) *Origins of Enterprise: business leadership in the Industrial Revolution*. Manchester University Press.

Hopkins, J. S. (1955) Nottinghamshire farming, *Agriculture*, LXII, 173–6.

Hopkinson, G. G. (1957) The development of the south Yorkshire and north Derbyshire coalfield, 1500–1775, *Transactions of the Hunter Archaeological Society*, VII, 295–321.

Hopkinson, G. G. (1959) The inland navigations of the Derbyshire and Nottinghamshire coalfield, 1777–1856, *DAJ*, 79, 22–41.

Hopkinson, G. G. (1969) Railway projection and construction in south Yorkshire and north Derbyshire, 1830–50. *Transactions of the Hunter Archaeological Society*, 9, 8–26.

Hopkinson, G. G. (1979) Road development in south Yorkshire and north Derbyshire, 1700–1850, *Transactions of the Hunter Archaeological Society*, 10, 14–30.

Horn, P. (1967–70) The Leicester and Leicestershire Agricultural Labourers Union, *Leicestershire Historian*, 1 (5), 152–9.

Horriben, E. (1985) Hucknall collieries: an example of nineteenth century migration and the effect on a village community, *Nottinghamshire Historian*, 34, 7–11.

Hosford, D. H. (1976) *Nottingham, Nobles and the North*. Archon Books, Hamden.

Hosford, W. H. (1960) The Elizabethan serfs of Long Bennington, Lincolnshire, *Nottingham Medieval Studies*, IV, 105–12.

Hosford, W. H. (1968) The manor of Sleaford in the thirteenth century, *Nottingham Medieval Studies*, 12, 21–39.

Hoskins, W. G. (1940–41) The Leicestershire country parson in the sixteenth century, *LAH*, XXI, 89–114.

Hoskins, W. G. (1946) The deserted villages of Leicestershire, *Transactions of the Leicestershire Archaeological Society*, XXII, 241–64.

Hoskins, W. G. (1949) The origin and rise of Market Harborough, *Transactions of the Leicestershire Archaeological Society*, XXV, 56–68.

Hoskins, W. G. (1950) Galby and Frisby. In *Essays in Leicestershire History*. Liverpool University Press.

Hoskins, W. G. (1951) *The East Midlands and the Peak*. Collins, London.

Hoskins, W. G. (1955) An Elizabethan Town: Leicester. In Plumb, J. H. (ed) *Studies in Social History*, Longman, London, pp. 33–67.

Hoskins, W. G. (1957) *The Midland Peasant*. Macmillan, London.

Hoskins, W. G. (1963) English provincial towns in the early sixteenth century. In *Provincial England*. Macmillan, London.

Howard, J. (1777) *The State of the Prisons*. Eyres, Warrington.

Howell, C. (1976) Peasant inheritance customs in the Midlands. In Goody, J., Thirsk, J. and Thompson, E. P. (eds) *Family and Inheritance*. Cambridge University Press, pp. 112–55.

Hunt, H. G. (1957–58) The chronology of parliamentary enclosure in Leicestershire, *Economic History Review*, 2nd ser., **10**, 265–72.

Husain, M. S. (1975) The increase and distribution of new commonwealth immigrants in Greater Nottingham, *EMG*, **6** (3), 105–29.

Inkster, I. (1978) Scientific culture and education in Nottingham, 1800–43, *TTS* LXXXII, 45–50.

Jack, S. (1965–66) Monastic lands in Leicestershire and their administration on the eve of the dissolution, *LAH*, XLI, 9–40.

Jackson, G. (1971) *Grimsby and the Haven Company 1796–1846*. Grimsby Public Libraries.

James, M. E. (1970) Obedience and dissent in Henrician England: the Lincolnshire Rebellion, 1536, *Past and Present*, no. 98, 3–32.

Johnson, A. M. (1980) The reformation clergy of Derbyshire, 1536–59, *DAJ*, **100**, 49–63.

Johnson, J. A. (1979) The family and kin of the Lincolnshire labourer in the eighteenth century, *LHA*, **14**, 47–52.

Johnson, J. A. (1983) 17th Century agricultural practice in six Lincolnshire parishes, *LHA*, **18**, 5–14.

Johnson, M. (1970) *Derbyshire Village Schools in the Nineteenth Century*. David and Charles, Newton Abbot.

Johnson, R. (1953) An ancient Swanwick coal mine, *DAJ*, **73**, 114–20.

Johnson, S. A. (1962) Some aspects of enclosure and changing agricultural landscapes in Lindsey from the sixteenth to the nineteenth century, *Lincolnshire Architectural and Archaeological Society. Reports and Papers*, 9, 134–50.

Johnson, S. A. (1963) Enclosure and changing agricultural landscape in Lindsey, *Agricultural History Review*, **11**, 95–102.

Johnston, W. B. (1955) The East Midlands and the post-war development in manufacturing, *EMG*, no. 4, 3–18.

Jones, E. D. (1977) Some economic dealings of Prior John the Almoner of Spalding, 1253–74, *LHA*, **12**, 41–3.

Jones, E. L., Porter, S. and Turner, M. (1984) *A Gazetteer of English Urban Fire Disasters, 1500–1900*. Historical Geography Research Series, no. 13.

Jones, M. K. (1986) Lady Margaret Beaufort, the Royal Council and an Early Fenland Drainage Scheme, *LHA*, **21**, 11–18.

Jones, R. B. (1954) *The Pattern of Farming in the East Midlands*. University of Nottingham.

Kain, R. J. P. (1986) *An Atlas and Index of the Tithe Files of mid-nineteenth century England and Wales*. Cambridge University Press.

Keeler, M. F. (1954) *The Long Parliament, 1640–1642: a biographical study of its members*. American Philosophical Society, Philadelphia.

Kennedy, M. E. (1983) Charles I and local government: the draining of the East and West Fens, *Albion*, 15, 19–31.

Kerridge, E. (1967) *The Agricultural Revolution*. Allen and Unwin, London.

Kilmurry, K. (1980) *The Pottery Industry of Stamford, Lincolnshire A.D. 850–1250: Its Manufacture, Trade and Relationship with Continental Wares*. British Archaeological Report, British Series 84.

Kirkham, N. (1968) *Derbyshire Lead Mining through the Centuries*. D. Bradford Barton, Truro.

Kirkham, N. (1971–73) Wingfield Manor in the civil war, *Derbyshire Miscellany*, 6, 139–52.

Langdon, J. (1984) Horse hauling: a revolution in vehicle transport in twelfth and thirteenth century England? *Past and Present*, 103, 37–66.

Langton, J. (1984) The industrial revolution and the regional geography of England, *Transactions of the Institute of British Geographers*, n.s. 9, 145–67.

Law, C. M. (1962–65) An outline of the industrial development of Mansfield, *EMG*, 3, 206–15.

Law, C. M. (1972) Some notes on the urban population of England and Wales in the eighteenth century, *Local Historian*, 10 (1), 13–26.

Law, C. M. (1980) *British Regional Development since World War I*. David and Charles, Newton Abbot.

Leave, R. V. (1967) The port of Immingham, *EMG*, 4 (3), 127–42.

Lee, J. M. (1956) The rise and fall of a market town: Castle Donington in the nineteenth century, *LAH*, XXXII, 52–80.

Leland, J. (1907) *The Itinery of John Leland*. (ed) L. T. Smith, London.

Leleux, R. (1984) *A Regional History of the Railways of Great Britain: vol IX the East Midlands* 2nd edn, David and Charles, Newton Abbot.

Levine, D. C. (1977) *Family Formation in an Age of Nascent Capitalism*. Academic Press, New York.

Lewis, M. J. T. and Wright, N. R. (1973) Boston as a port, *Lincolnshire Industrial Archaeology*, 8 (4), Special issue.

Lindley, K. (1982) *Fenland Riots and the English Revolution*. Heinemann, London.

Lindsay, J. (1960) An early industrial community: the Evans cotton mill at Darley Abbey, Derbyshire 1783–1810, *Business History Review*, 34, 277–301.

Lindsay, J. (1965) The Butterley coal and iron works, 1792–1816, *DAJ*, 85, 25–43.

Lindsay, J. (1980) 'Excellent order throughout': Derby workhouse, 1834–44, *DAJ*, 100, 95–102.

Lloyd, I. (1978) *Rolls-Royce*. 3 vols. Macmillan, London.

Lloyd, P. (1980/1) The coroners of Leicestershire in the early fourteenth century, *LAH*, LVI, 18–32.

Lloyd, T. H. (1977) *The English Wool Trade in the Middle Ages*. Cambridge University Press.

Lowe, R. (1798) *General View of the Agriculture of the County of Nottingham*. Nicol, London.

Lucas, M. D. (1985) Popular religious attitudes in the City of Lincoln 1520–1600, unpublished M.A. thesis, University of Nottingham.

Lyth, P. (ed) (1985) *Farms and Fields of Southwell: a study of enclosures*. University of Nottingham, Centre for Local History.

Macaulay, Lord (1913) *The History of England*, vol. 1. Macmillan, London.

McLynn, F. J. (1979) Nottingham and the Jacobite rising of 1745, *TTS*, LXXXIII, 63–9.

McLynn, F. J. (1983) The regional distribution of Jacobite support in England before 1745, *Journal of Regional and Local Studies*, 3 (2), 14–27.

Malcolmson, R. W. (1973) *Popular Recreations in English Society, 1700–1850*. Cambridge University Press.

Marchant, R. A. (1960) *The Puritans and the Church Courts in the Diocese of York, 1560–1642*. Longman, London.

Marriot, A. T. (1976) The reform of local government areas in north Lincolnshire, 1974, *EMG*, 6 (5), 241–55.

Marshall, J. D. (1960) Nottinghamshire labourers in the early nineteenth century, *TTS*, LXIV, 56–73.

Marshall, J. D. (1978a) Local and regional history, or both? a dialogue, *The Local Historian*, 13 (1), 4–7.

Marshall, J. D. (1978b) The study of local and regional 'communities': some problems and possibilities, *Northern History*, XVII, 203–30.

Mastoris, S. N. (1985) A tax assessment of 1504 and the topography of early Tudor Nottingham, *TTS*, LXXXIX, 37–56.

Maude, S. M. (1974) Population, mobility and urban growth: a study of migration in the nineteenth century with particular reference to Nottingham, unpublished M.Phil. thesis, University of Nottingham.

Meller, H. E. (ed) (1971) *Nottingham in the Eighteen Eighties: a study in social change*. University of Nottingham.

Mellows, W. T. (1948) The estates of the monastery of Peterborough in the county of Lincoln, *Lincolnshire Historian*, 3, 100–14.

Metcalf, S. (1984) The idea of a park: the select committees and the first public parks, *Journal of Regional and Local History*, 4 (1), 18–30.

Miller, E. and Hatcher, J. (1978) *Medieval England: Rural Society and Economic Change 1086–1348*. Longman, London.

Mills, D. R. (1980) *Lord and Peasant in Nineteenth-Century Britain*. Croom Helm, London.

Mills, D. R. (1982) Rural industries and social structure: framework knitters in Leicestershire, 1670–1850, *Textile History*, 13 (2), 183–204.

Millward, R. (1985) *A History of Leicestershire and Rutland*. Phillimore, Chichester.

Millward, R. and Robinson, A. (1975) *The Peak District*. Eyre Methuen, London.

Mingay, G. E. (1956) The agricultural depression, 1730–50, *Economic History Review*, 2nd ser., VIII, 323–38.

Moir, E. (1969) *The Justice of the Peace*. Pelican, Harmondsworth.

Molyneux, F. H. (1962–65) Industrial development in Boston, Lincolnshire, *EMG*, 3, 267–81.

Morrill, J. S. (1976) *The Revolt of the Provinces*. Allen and Unwin, London.

Morris, G. M. (1968) Primitive Methodism in Nottinghamshire, 1815–32, *TTS*, LXXII, 81–100.

Mounfield, P. R. (1964–65) The footwear industry of the East Midlands (I), *EMG*, 3, 293–306.

Mounfield, P. R. (1967) The footwear industry of the East Midlands (IV), the modern phase: Northamptonshire and Leicestershire since 1911, *EMG*, 4 (3), 154–75.

Mounfield, P. R., Unwin, D. J. and Guy, K. (1984) Spatial and organizational changes in the East Midlands footwear industry 1957–80, *EMG*, 8 (6), 166–86.

Mullins, S. and Glasson, M. (1985) *Hidden Harborough*. Leicestershire Museums, Leicester.

Nixon, F. (1969) *The Industrial Archaeology of Derbyshire*. David and Charles, Newton Abbot.

Nolan, G. M. (1984) Cast iron houses in Derby, *Journal of Regional and Local Studies*, 4 (1), 54–60.

Obelkevich, J. (1976) *Religion and Rural Society: South Lindsey, 1825–75*. Clarendon Press, Oxford.

Odell, P. R. (1957) Urban spheres of influence in Leicestershire in the mid-nineteenth century, *Geographical Studies*, IV, 30–45.

Oldfield, G. (1984) The Nottingham Lace Market, *Textile History*, 15 (2), 191–208.

Olney, R. J. (1979) *Rural Society and County Government in Nineteenth-Century Lincolnshire*. History of Lincolnshire Committee, Lincoln.

Osborne, R. H. (1954) Population concentrations and conurban tendencies in the middle Trent counties, *EMG*, 1 (2), 30–7.

Osborne, R. H. (1966) *Atlas of Population Change in the East Midland Counties 1951–61*. University of Nottingham.

Owen, C. C. (1968) The early history of the Upper Trent Navigation, *Transport History*, 1, 233–59.

Owen, C. C. (1978) *The Development of Industry in Burton-on-Trent*. Phillimore, Chichester.

Owen, C. C. (1984) *The Leicestershire and South Derbyshire Coalfield 1200–1900*. Moorland, Ashbourne.

Owen, D. M. (1971) *Church and People in Medieval Lincolnshire*. History of Lincolnshire Committee, Lincoln.

Owen, L. V. D. (1945) The borough of Nottingham, 1066–1284, *TTS*, XLIX, 12–27.

Owen, L. V. D. (1946) The borough of Nottingham, 1284–1485, *TTS*, L, 25–35.

Palmer, M. (ed.) (1982) *The Aristocratic Estate: the Hastings in Leicestershire and South Derbyshire*. Loughborough University.

Palmer, M. (1983) *Leicestershire Archaeology: the Present State of Knowledge, no. 3 Industrial Archaeology*. Leicestershire Museums, Leicester.

Palmer, M. (1984) Industrial landscapes of the eighteenth and nineteenth centuries. In Reed, M. (ed) *Discovering Past Landscapes*. Croom Helm, London, pp. 85–131.

Patterson, A. T. (1954) *Radical Leicester, 1780–1850*. University College, Leicester.

Pearson, R. E. (1968) Railways in relation to resort development in east Lincolnshire, *EMG* 4 (5), 281–94.

Peers, C. R. (1975) *Kirby Muxloe Castle near Leicester*. 2nd edn. HMSO, London.

Pelham, R. A. (1951) The provisioning of the Lincoln Parliament of 1301, *University of Birmingham Historical Journal*, 3, 16–32.

Perkins, E. R. (ed) (1979) *Village Life from Wills and Inventories: Clayworth Parish 1670–1710*. University of Nottingham, Centre for Local History.

Perkins, J. A. (1975a) Tenure, tenant right, and agricultural progress in Lindsey, 1780–1850, *Agricultural History Review*, 23 (1), 1–22.

Perkins, J. A. (1975b) Working-class housing in Lindsey, 1780–1870, *LHA*, **10**, 49–55.

Perkins, J. A. (1976) The prosperity of farming in the Lindsey uplands, 1813–37, *Agricultural History Review*, **24** (2), 126–43.

Perkins, J. A. (1977a) *Sheep Farming in Eighteenth and Nineteenth Century Lincolnshire*. Society for Lincolnshire History and Archaeology, occasional paper 4, Sleaford.

Perkins, J. A. (1977b) The parish and the housing of the working class in Lindsey, 1790–1850, *LHA*, **12**, 65–70.

Pevsner, N. and Harris, J. (1964) *The Buildings of England: Lincolnshire*. Penguin, Harmondsworth.

Pevsner, N. and Williamson, E. (1978) *The Buildings of England: Derbyshire*. 2nd edn. Penguin, Harmondsworth.

Pevsner, N. and Williamson, E. (1979) *The Buildings of England: Nottinghamshire*. 2nd edn. Penguin, Harmondsworth.

Pevsner, N. and Williamson, E. (1984) *The Buildings of England: Leicestershire and Rutland*. 2nd edn. Penguin, Harmondsworth.

Phillips, A. D. M. (1979) The landlord and agricultural improvements: underdraining on the Lincolnshire estate of the earls of Scarbrough in the first half of the nineteenth century, *EMG*, **7** (4), 168–77.

Phythian-Adams, C. (1977) Rutland reconsidered. In Dornier, A. (ed) *Mercian Studies*. Croom Helm, London.

Phythian-Adams, C. (1986) *The Norman Conquest of Leicestershire and Rutland: a Regional Introduction to Domesday Book*. Leicestershire Museums, Art Galleries and Records Service.

Pickersgill, A. C. (1979) The Agricultural Revolution in Bassetlaw, Nottinghamshire, 1750–1873, unpublished Ph.D. thesis, University of Nottingham.

Platt, C. (1976) *The English Medieval Town*. Secker and Warburg, London.

Platts, G. (1985) *Land and People in Medieval Lincolnshire*. History of Lincolnshire Committee, Lincoln.

Plumb, J. H. (1955) *Studies in Social History*. Longman, London.

Plumb, J. H. (1972) *The Commercialisation of Leisure in Eighteenth Century England*. University of Reading.

Pocock, D. C. D. (1963) Iron and steel at Scunthorpe, *EMG*, **3**, 124–38.

Pollard, S. (1980) A new estimate of British coal production, 1750–1850. *Economic History Review*, 2nd ser., XXXIII, 212–35.

Postles, D. (1979) Early coal mining at West Hallam, *DAJ*, **99**, 221–2.

Powell, A. G. (1955a) The 1951 census: (2) an analysis of population changes in Leicestershire, *EMG*, **1** (3), 3–15.

Powell, A. G. (1955b) The 1951 census: (3) an analysis of population changes in Nottinghamshire, *EMG*, **1** (4), 29–41.

Priestley, J. B. (1977) *English Journey*. Penguin, Harmondsworth.

Pritchard, R. M. (1976) *Housing and the Spatial Structure of the City: residential mobility and the housing industry in an English city since the Industrial Revolution*. Cambridge University Press.

Pruett, J. H. (1978) *The parish clergy under the later Stuarts: the Leicestershire experience*. University of Illinois Press, Urbana.

Pye, N. (ed) (1972) *Leicester and Its Region*. British Association, Leicester.

Quincey, T. (1775) *A Short Tour in the Midland Counties of England performed in the Summer of 1772 with an account of a similar excursion undertaken September 1774.* The author, London.

Raban, S. (1981) Prayer, property and provocation: the religious in medieval Lincolnshire, *LHA*, **16**, 39–44.

Raistrick, A. (1977) *Two Centuries of Industrial Welfare: the London (Quaker) Lead Company.* Moorland, Ashbourne.

Rake, D. J. (1974a) Spatial changes in industrial activity in the East Midlands since 1945: changes through movement and changes through acquisitions, *EMG*, **6** (1), 1–16.

Rake, D. J. (1974b) Spatial changes in industrial activity in the East Midlands since 1945: the hosiery industry, *EMG*, **6** (2), 51–65.

Rake, D. J. (1975) Spatial changes in industrial activity in the East Midlands since 1945: the footwear industry, *EMG*, **6** (4), 173–84.

Rake, D. J. (1976) Spatial changes in industrial activity in the East Midlands since 1945: the engineering industry, *EMG*, **6** (6), 265–74.

Rawstron, E. W. (1954) Power production and the River Trent, *EMG*, **1** (2), 23–30.

Rawstron, E. M. (1958) Some aspects of the location of hosiery and lace manufacture in Great Britain, *EMG*, **2** (9), 16–28.

Rawstron, E. M. (1964) Industry. In Watson, J. W. and Sissons, J. B. (eds) *The British Isles: a systematic geography.* Nelson, London.

Reed, M. (1981) Pre-parliamentary enclosure in the East Midlands 1550–1750, and its impact upon the landscape, *Landscape History*, III, 58–68.

Renn, D. F.. (1968) *Norman Castles in Britain.* John Baker, Humanities Press, London.

Reynolds, T. (1982) Marketing in nineteenth-century Lincolnshire, unpublished paper.

Richardson, W. A. (1949) *Citizen's Derby.* London University Press.

Riden, P. (1973) *The Butterley Company, 1790–1830: a Derbyshire Ironworks in the Industrial Revolution.* Privately published, Chesterfield.

Riden, P. (1977) The origin of the new market of Chesterfield, *DAJ*. 97, 5–15.

Riden, P. (1978) The population of Derbyshire in 1563, *DAJ*, 98, 61–71.

Riden, P. (1984) *History of Chesterfield, vol. 2. Tudor and Stuart.* Chesterfield Borough Council.

Riden, P. (1985) *George Sitwell's Letterbook, 1662–6.* Derbyshire Record Society, vol. 10.

Rigby, S. H. (1984a) Urban decline in the later middle ages: the reliability of the non-statistical evidence. In *Urban History Yearbook*, 45–60.

Rigby, S. H. (1984b) Boston and Grimsby in the Middle Ages: an administrative contrast, *Journal of Medieval History*, **10**, 51–66.

Rigby, S. H. (1985) 'Sore decay' and 'fair dwellings': Boston and urban decline in the later Middle Ages, *Midland History*, **10**, 47–61.

Rimmington, G. T. (1978) *Education, politics and society in Leicester, 1833–1940.* Lancelot, Hantsport.

Rippon, A. (1980) *The Book of Derby: from Settlement to City.* Barracuda Books, Buckingham.

Robinson, D. N. (1981) *The Book of the Lincolnshire Seaside.* Barracuda Books, Buckingham.

Robinson, E. (1969) The Derby Philosophical Society. In Musson, A. E. and Robinson,

E. (eds) *Science and Technology in the Industrial Revolution*. Manchester University Press, pp. 190–9.

Robinson, G. W. S. (1953) The geographical region: form and function. *Scottish Geographical Magazine*, **69**, 49–58.

Rogers, A. (ed) (1965) *The Making of Stamford*. Leicester University Press.

Rogers, A. (1966) The Lincolnshire county court in the fifteenth century, *LHA*, I, 64–78.

Rogers, A. (1970) *A History of Lincolnshire*. Darwen Finlayson, Henley-on-Thames.

Rogers, A. (1972) The 1851 religious census returns for the city of Nottingham, *TTS*, LXXVI, 74–88.

Rogers, A. (ed) (1979) *Coming into Line: Local Government in Clayworth, 1674–1714*. Centre for Local History, University of Nottingham.

Rogers, A. (1981) Rural industries and social structure: the framework knitting industry of south Nottinghamshire, 1670–1840, *Textile History*, **12**, 7–36.

Rogers, A. and Watts, M. (1978) The Evans list and dissenting congregations in the East Midlands, 1715–29, *Bulletin of Local History: East Midlands Region*, XIII, 14–27.

Royal Commission on Historical Monuments (1964) *Newark on Trent: the civil war siegeworks*. HMSO, London.

Royle, S. A. (1978) The development of Coalville, Leicestershire, in the nineteenth century, *EMG*, 7 (1), 32–42.

Royle, S. A. (1978–79) 'The spiritual destitution is excessive – the poverty overwhelming': Hinckley in the mid-nineteenth century, *LAH*, LIV, 51–60.

Royle, S. A. (1979–80) Aspects of nineteenth-century small-town society: a comparative study from Leicestershire, *Midland History*, 5, 50–62.

Russell, R. C. (1956) *The 'Revolt of the Field' in Lincolnshire: the origin and early history of Farm Workers trade unions*. National Union of Agricultural Workers, Boston.

Russell, R. C. (1960) Government aid to school building in Lincolnshire, 1833–1870, *Lincolnshire Historian*, 2, 16–21.

Russell, R. C. (1965) *A history of schools and education in Lindsey, Lincolnshire, 1800–1902*. Lindsey County Council.

Sainty, J. C. (1970) *Lieutenants of Counties, 1585–1642, Bulletin of the Institute of Historical Research Supplement no. 8*, Athlone Press, London.

Sanders, H. F. (1934) Early puritanism and separatism in Nottingham. *Transactions of the Congregational Historical Society*, 12, 100–11.

Saville, J. (1957) *Rural Depopulation in England and Wales, 1851–1951*. Routledge and Kegan Paul, London.

Seaborne, M. V. J. (1964) Cob cottages in Northamptonshire, *Northamptonshire Past and Present*, 3 (5), 215–28.

Schofield, R. B. (1981) The promotion of the Cromford Canal Act of 1789: a study in canal engineering. *Bulletin of the John Rylands Library*, 64, 246–78.

Schofield, R. S. (1965) The geographical distribution of wealth in England 1334–1649, *Economic History Review*, 2nd ser., XVIII, 483–510.

Scotland, N. A. D. (1977) Methodism and the 'Revolt of the Field' in East Anglia 1872–96, pt. 1, *Proceedings of the Wesley Historical Society*, 41 (1), 2–11.

Scotland, N. A. D. (1981) *Methodism and the revolt of the field: a study of the*

Methodist contribution to agricultural trade unionism in East Anglia 1872–96. The Author, Cheltenham.

Scott, J. (1971–73) Turnpike roads in Derbyshire, *Derbyshire Miscellany*, 6, 198–209.

Seddon, P. R. (1978) The application of Forest Law in Sherwood Forest, *c.* 1630–1680, *TTS*, LXXXII, 37–44.

Seddon, P. R. (1980) Marriage and inheritance in the Clifton family during the seventeenth century, *TTS*, LXXXIV, 33–43.

Seddon, P. R. (1982) The Nottinghamshire militia and the defence of the Restoration, 1660–1670, *TTS*, LXXXVI, 79–88.

Sheail, J. (1972) The distribution of taxable population and wealth in England during the early sixteenth century, *Transactions of the Institute of British Geographers*, LV, 111–26.

Sigsworth, E. M. (ed.) (1980) *Ports and Resorts in the Regions.* Hull College of Higher Education.

Simmons, J. (1974) *Leicester Past and Present.* 2 vols. Eyre Methuen.

Simon, B. (1968) *Education in Leicestershire 1540–1940.* Leicester University Press.

Siviour, G. R. (1974) The changing relationship between railways and the iron and steel industry in the East Midlands, *EMG*, 6 (1), 29–39.

Skelley, J. (ed) (1976) *The General Strike 1926.* Lawrence and Wishart, London.

Slade, C. F. (1956) *The Leicestershire Survey c. AD 1130.* Department of English Local History Occasional Paper no. 7, Leicester.

Smith, D. M. (1959) The employment structure of the counties of Derbyshire, Leicestershire and Nottinghamshire, *EMG*, 2 (12), 26–37.

Smith, D. M. (1960) The Nottingham lace industry, *Northern Universities Geographical Journal*, 1, 5–15.

Smith, D. M. (1962) The cotton industry in the East Midlands, *Geography*, 47, 256–69.

Smith, D. M. (1964) The location of elastic-web manufacturing in England and Wales, *EMG*, 3 (6), 326–36.

Smith, D. M. (1962–5) Changes in the employment structure of the East Midlands, 1951–61, *EMG*, 3, 282–7.

Smith, G. I. (1937) *The Land of Britain: part 69 Lincolnshire (Parts of Holland).* Geographical Publications Ltd, London.

Smith, P. A. (1975) Chartists in Leicester, *Leicestershire Historian*, 2 (6), 27–31.

Smith, R. (1974) The relief of urban poverty outside the Poor Law, 1800–1850: a study of Nottingham, *Midland History*, 2, 215–24.

Smith, R. S. (1957) Huntingdon Beaumont, adventurer in coal mines, *Renaissance and Modern Studies*, I, 115–53.

Smith, R. S. (1962) Glass-making at Wollaton in the early seventeenth century, *TTS*, LXVI, 24–34.

Smith, R. S. (1964) The Willoughbys of Wollaton, 1500–1643 with special reference to early mining in Nottinghamshire, unpublished Ph.D. thesis, University of Nottingham.

Smith, R. S. (1967) Sir Francis Willoughby's iron works, 1570–1610, *Renaissance and Modern Studies*, XI, 90–140.

Spavold, J. (1981) The sanitary pottery industries of south Derbyshire, 1840–1914, *Industrial Archaeology Review*, 5 (2), 143–54.

Stafford, P. (1985) *The East Midlands in the Early Middle Ages*. Leicester University Press.

Standen, J. D. (1958) The social, economic and political development of Derby, 1835–1885, unpublished M.A. thesis, University of Leeds.

Steel, D. I. A. (1979) *A Lincolnshire Village*. Longman, London.

Stenton, D. M. (1965) *English Society in the Early Middle Ages*. Penguin, Harmondsworth.

Stevens, J. (1977) *England's Last Revolution: Pentrich 1817*. Moorland, Ashbourne.

Stevenson, P. (1970) *The Nutbrook Canal: Derbyshire*. David and Charles, Newton Abbot.

Stone, T. (1794) *General View of the Agriculture of the County of Lincoln*. Nicols, London.

Storey, R. L. (1970) Lincolnshire and the Wars of the Roses, *Nottingham Medieval Studies*, XIV, 64–83.

Storey, R. L. (1984) A fifteenth century vicar of Laxton, *TTS*, LXXXVIII, 39–41.

Stovin, J. (1982) *Journals of a Methodist Farmer, 1871–75*. Croom Helm, London.

Strachan, A. J. and Bowler, I. R. (1976) The development of public parks and gardens in the city of Leicester, *EMG*, 6 (6), 275–83.

Sturges, R. W. (1977–78) Context for library history: libraries in 18th century Derby, *Library History*, 4, 44–52.

Sturges, R. W. (1978) Harmony and good company: the emergence of musical performance in 18th century Derby, *Music Review*, XXXIX, 178–95.

Styles, G. T. (1971–73) The formation of the Derby poor law union, *Derbyshire Miscellany*, 6, 55–67.

Swift, R. C. (1982) *Lively People: Methodism in Nottingham 1740–1979*. University of Nottingham, Department of Adult Education.

Swindell, K. (1964–65) The Cromford cotton mills: their site and location, *EMG*, 3, 461–9.

Swinnerton, H. H. (1929) The physiographic sub-divisions of the East Midlands, *Geography*, XV, 215–26.

Taylor, H. M. and Taylor, J. (1965) *Anglo-Saxon Architecture*. 2 vols. Cambridge University Press.

Taylor, S. (1947) Musical life in Derby in the 18th and 19th centuries, *DAJ*, 67, 1–54.

Taylor, S. (1977) The effect of marriage on job possibilities for women, and the ideology of the home: Nottingham 1890–1930, *Oral History*, 5, 46–61.

Thirsk, J. (1957) *English Peasant Farming*. Routledge, London.

Thirsk, J. (1961) Industries in the countryside. In Fisher, F. J. (ed) *Essays in the Economic and Social History of Tudor and Stuart England*. Cambridge University Press, pp. 70–88.

Thirsk, J. (1964) The common fields, *Past and Present*, 29, 3–25.

Thirsk, J. (ed) (1967) *Agrarian History of England and Wales, vol. IV 1500–1640*. Cambridge University Press.

Thirsk, J. (1973a) Field systems of the East Midlands. In Baker, A. R. H. and Butlin, R. A. (eds) *Studies of Field Systems in the British Isles*. Cambridge University Press, pp. 232–80.

Thirsk, J. (1973b) The fantastical folly of fashion: the English stocking knitting industry, 1500–1700. In Harte, N. B. and Ponting, K. G. (eds) *Textile History and Economic History*. Manchester University Press, pp. 50–73.

Thirsk, J. (1974) The disappearance of the English peasantry, unpublished paper.

Thirsk, J. (1978) *Economic Policy and Projects*. Clarendon Press, Oxford.

Thirsk, J. (ed) (1985) *Agrarian History of England and Wales, vol. 5 1640–1750* Parts I and II. Cambridge University Press.

Thirsk, J. and Cooper, J. P. (1972) *Seventeenth-Century Economic Documents*. Clarendon Press, Oxford.

Thomas, M. (1975) The rioting crowd in Derbyshire in the 18th century. *DAJ*, 95, 37–47.

Thomis, M. I. (1968) *Old Nottingham*. David and Charles, Newton Abbot.

Thomis, M. I. (1969) *Politics and Society in Nottingham, 1785–1835*. Blackwell, Oxford.

Thompson, D. M. (1972) The churches and society in nineteenth century England: a rural perspective. *Studies in Church History*, 8, 267–76.

Thompson, D. M. (1979) Church extension in town and countryside in late nineteenth century Leicestershire, *Studies in Church History*, 16, 427–40.

Thompson, K. M. (1980) The building of the Leicester Union workhouse. In Williams, D. D. (ed) *The Adaptation of Change*. Leicester University Press, pp. 59–76.

Tolley, B. H. (1981) Technical education and the University College of Nottingham. In Roderick, G. and Stephens, M. *Where did we go wrong?* Falmer, Lewes.

Tolley, B. H. (1982) The people's scientific university: science education in the East Midlands, 1860–1890, *Midland History*, VII, 116–31.

Tolley, B. H. (1983) Nottingham University: a centenary essay, *Bulletin of Local History: East Midlands Region*, XVIII, 1–7.

Tranter, M. (1981) Landlords, labourers, local preachers: rural nonconformity in Derbyshire, 1772–1851, *DAJ*, CI, 119–38.

Tucker, D. G. (1985) Millstone making in the Peak District of Derbyshire: the quarries and the technology, *Industrial Archaeology Review*, VIII, 42–58.

Turland, G. (1983) Survey of the mobility of framework knitters in four Nottingham-shire framework knitting villages in 1851, unpublished paper.

Turnbull, G. L. (1977) Provincial road carrying in England in the eighteenth century, *Journal of Transport History*, IV, 17–39.

Turner, M. (1980) *English Parliamentary Enclosure*. Dawson, Folkestone.

Turner, P. (1978) Colliery development in the inter-war period – the opening of the Markham collieries, Derbyshire, between 1924 and 1930, *DAJ*, 98, 83–6.

Turnor, E. (1782) *A short view of the proceedings of the several committees and meetings held in consequence of the intended petition to parliament from the county of Lincoln, for the limited exportation of wool*.

Unwin, T. (1981) Rural marketing in medieval Nottinghamshire, *Journal of Historical Geography*, 7, 231–51.

Unwin, T. (1983) Townships and early fields in north Nottinghamshire, *Journal of Historical Geography*, 9, 341–6.

VCH Derbyshire. II (1907).

VCH Leicestershire. II (1954).

VCH Leicestershire. III (1955).

VCH Leicestershire. IV (1958).

VCH Nottinghamshire. II (1910).

VCH Rutland. I (1908).

Vollans, E. C. (1949) Derby: a railway town and regional centre, *Transactions of the Institute of British Geographers*, **15**, 93–112.

Walker, V. W. (1963) Medieval Nottingham: a topographical study, *TTS*, LXVII, 28–45.

Waller, R. J. (1979) A company village in the New Dukeries coalfield: New Ollerton, 1918–39, *TTS*, LXXXIII, 70–9.

Waller, R. J. (1980) 'Between Two Worlds': contemporary reactions to the arrival of mining in the Dukeries, 1913–39, *TTS*, LXXXIV, 73–80.

Waller, R. J. (1983) *The Dukeries Transformed: the social and political development of a twentieth-century coalfield.* Oxford University Press.

Walton, J. K. (1983) *The English Seaside Resort: a social history 1750–1914.* Leicester University Press.

Wardle, D. (1966) Working-class children in Nottingham from the Blue Books, *TTS*, LXX, 105–14.

Wardle, D. (1967) Education in Nottinghamshire in the age of apprenticeship 1500–1800, *TTS*, LXXI, 36–54.

Wardle, D. (1971) *Education and Society in Nineteenth-Century Nottingham.* Cambridge University Press.

Warren, K. (1961) The Derbyshire iron industry, *EMG*, **2**, 17–33.

Watson, A. (1981) The Chesterfield Union workhouse, 1839–47, *Journal of the Bakewell and District Historical Society*, **8**, 10–20.

Watts, M. R. (1978) *The Dissenters: from the Reformation to the French Revolution.* Oxford University Press.

Wedlock, G. H. (1954) Loughborough: an outline urban survey, *EMG*, **1**, 12–19.

Weekley, I. G. (1957) Industry in the small county towns of Lincolnshire, Northamptonshire and Rutland, *EMG*, **7**, 21–30.

Weir, C. (1986) *A Prospect of Nottinghamshire.* Nottinghamshire Local History Association, Nottingham.

Welby, G. (1974) Rulers of the countryside: the justice of the peace in Nottinghamshire 1775–1800, *TTS*, LXXVIII, 75–87.

Weller, J. C. (1957) *Say to the Wind: a study of the revival of religion in Nottingham, 1780–1850.* Privately published, Nottingham.

Wells, F. A. (1968) *Hollins and Viyella: a study in Business History.* David and Charles, Newton Abbot.

Wells, F. A. (1972) *The British Hosiery and Knitwear Trade: its history and organization.* 2nd edn. David and Charles, Newton Abbot.

Wells, R. A. E. (1984) *Riot and Political Disaffection in Nottinghamshire in the Age of Revolutions, 1776–1803.* University of Nottingham, Centre for Local History.

West, F. (1974) Infant mortality in the East Fen parishes of Leake and Wrangle. *Local Population Studies*, **13**, 41–4.

West, F. H. (1956?) *The Great North Road in Nottinghamshire.* Newark.

Wheeler, P. T. (1982) The development of the country park concept, with special reference to Nottinghamshire, *EMG*, **8**, (1), 12–24.

White, A. J. (1984) Medieval fisheries in the Witham and its tributaries, *LHA*, **19**, 29–35.

White, W. (1832, 1844, 1853) *History, Directory and Gazetteer of Nottinghamshire.*

Whiteman, A. (1986) *The Compton Census of 1676.* British Academy, London.

Willan, T. S. (1936) *River Navigation in England 1600–1750.* Oxford University Press.

Williams, J. E. (1955) Paternalism in local government in the nineteenth century, *Public Administration*, 33, 439–46.

Williams, J. E. (1962) *The Derbyshire Miners: a study in industrial and social history.* Allen and Unwin, London.

Willies, L. (1979) Technical development in Derbyshire lead mining, 1700–1850, *Bulletin of the Peak District Mines Historical Society*, 7, (3), 117–51.

Willies, L. (1986) Prosperity and decline in Derbyshire lead mining, *Bulletin of the Peak District Mines Historical Society*, 9, (5), 251–82.

Wilson, L. F. (1970) The state and the housing of the English working class with special reference to Nottingham 1845–1914. Ph.D. thesis, University of California, Berkeley.

Wood, A. C. (1937a) *Nottinghamshire in the Civil War.* Clarendon, Oxford.

Wood, A. C. (1937b) A note on the population of six Nottinghamshire towns in the 17th century, *TTS*, XLI, 18–26.

Wood, A. C. (1940) The revolution of 1688 in the north of England, *TTS*, XLIV, 72–104.

Wood, A. C. (1945) The Duke of Kingston's Regiment of Light Horse, *TTS*, XLIX, 73–83.

Wood, A. C. (1948) *A History of Nottinghamshire.* Thoroton Society, Nottingham.

Wood, A. C. (1950) The history of trade and transport on the River Trent, *TTS*, LIV, 1–44.

Wordie, J. R. (1983) The chronology of English enclosure, 1500–1914, *Economic History Review*, 2nd ser., XXXVI, 483–505.

Wright, N. (1982) *Lincolnshire Towns and Industry, 1700–1914.* History of Lincolnshire Committee, Lincoln.

Wright, S. M. (1983) *The Derbyshire Gentry in the Fifteenth Century.* Derbyshire Record Society, VIII.

Wyncoll, P. (1966) *Nottingham Chartism.* Nottingham Trades Council.

Wyncoll, P. (1985) *The Nottingham Labour Movement 1880–1939.* Lawrence and Wishart, London.

Young, A. (1813) *General View of the Agriculture of the County of Lincoln.* 2nd edn. Nicol, Lincoln.

Index

(N.B. D = Derbyshire, Le = Leicestershire, Li = Lincolnshire,
N = Nottinghamshire, R = Rutland)

Abneys, 180
agriculture, 6, 7, 15, 16, 46–51, 88–9,
        121–30, 194, 200–210, 320–
        6
airports, 331
alabaster, 6, 58, 68, 69, 75, 96, 283
Alford (Li), 263
Alfreton (N), 161, 232, 283, 335, 336,
        337, 338
Allestree Hall, 323
allotments, 209
Alport (D), 95
Ambion (Le), 79
Anabaptists, 167
Ancaster (Li), 37, 40
Ancholme Level, 127, 179, 271
Annesley (N), 277, 278, 312
Anstey (Le), 291
Arch, Joseph, 214
Arkwright, Richard, 195, 287, 288
Armitage, John, 148
Arnold (N), 307, 316, 326, 346
Asfordby (Le), 331, 338
Ashbourne (D), 59, 60, 62, 66, 93, 122,
        148, 182, 183, 184, 219, 239,
        306, 351
Ashby de la Zouch (Le), 5, 60, 64, 83,
        148, 174, 182, 235, 261, 335,
        349
Ashby Puerorum (Li), 213
Ashford (D), 24, 71, 73, 95

Ashover (D), 35, 164, 283
Aske, Robert, 106
assarting, 19, 29
assembly rooms, 228
Aston Hall, 110
Audley, Lord, 87
Averham (N), 111
Awsworth (N), 194, 283
Axholme (Li), 16, 19, 27, 35, 104, 125,
        126, 127, 174, 175, 181
Aylestone (Le), 227, 316, 317
Ayscough of Stallingborough, 108

Bagshawe, William, 181
Bakewell (D), 24, 59, 60, 62, 66, 71, 73,
        93, 146, 239, 306
Bakewell, Robert, 204
Balle family, 24
Barber Walker Company, 279
Bardney (Li), 31
Barley, Levi, 268
Barlings, 32
Barlow (D), 162
Barnack (Li), 40
Barnsdale Hill, 323
barons revolt, 28
Barron, William, 197
Barrow-on-Humber (Li), 119
Barrow-on-Soar (Le), 21, 24, 83, 283,
        304

Barrowden (R), 63
Barton-in-Fabis (N), 35
Barton-upon-Humber (Li), 15, 59, 61,
    143, 237
Barwell (Le), 291, 312, 348, 349
Basford (N), 122, 193, 194, 225, 226,
    246, 252, 290
Basford Incorporation, 217
Baslow (D), 95, 197
Bass, Michael, 249, 250, 259
Baston (Li), 46
Beauchief Abbey, 73
Beaumont, Huntingdon, 160
Beaumont, John, 107
Beaumont, Lord, 83
Beauvale (N), 32, 33, 106, 108
Beckett, John, 197
Bedells, Caleb, 290
Beeley (D), 197
Beeston (N), 122, 129, 225, 233, 290,
    308, 316, 347
Belgrave (Le), 227, 309
bellfounding, 58, 292
Belper (D), 224, 233, 288, 347
Belton House, 63, 64, 111, 122, 173,
    323
Belvoir (Le), 28, 60, 62, 83, 109, 111,
    160, 173, 174, 196
Belvoir, Vale of, 7, 18, 20, 121, 122,
    129, 177, 324, 331
Benington (Li), 67
Benniworths of Toynton, 197
Bestwood (N), 326
Bevercotes (N), 336
bicycles, 292
Bilborough (N), 160, 316
Billesdon (Le), 304
Billingborough (Li), 45
Bilsthorpe (N), 336, 337
Bingham (N), 214, 237, 238
Birmingham, 5
Birstall (Le), 316
Bitteswell (Le), 324
Blaby (Le), 304, 316
Black Death, 9, 16, 18, 20, 53, 61, 77,
    78, 82, 85, 87
Blidworth (N), 336
Blome, Richard, 140

Blount family, 87
Blyth (N), 31, 37, 117, 237
boards of health, 294–5
Bolingbroke (Li), 24, 26, 28, 141, 173
Bolsover (D), 26, 28, 60, 66, 119
Boot, Jesse (Lord Trent), 293, 309, 319
bordars, 22, 34
Borrowash (D), 325
Boston, 8, 15, 43, 52, 53, 56, 58, 59, 60,
    63, 67, 69, 70, 72, 75, 76, 89–
    90, 91, 92, 96, 117, 131, 132,
    133, 139, 144, 150, 151, 172,
    173, 174, 177, 181, 194, 216,
    219, 234, 235, 237, 243, 249,
    250, 253, 254, 264, 290, 293,
    314, 319
Bosworth, Battle of, 85, 98
Bothamsall (N), 344
Bottesford (N), 200
Bourne (Li), 26, 28, 75, 144, 217, 237
Brackenhurst (N), 323
Bradford, William, 167
Bradgate Park, 21, 83
Bradley (Le), 33
Bradmore (N), 197
Braunstone (Le), 316, 318
breck system, 7, 47
Breedon (Le), 33, 283
brewing, 151
Brewster, William, 167
brick, 5, 75, 112, 134, 139
bridges, 146
Brigg (Li), 60, 141, 144, 334
British Celanese (Derby), 311
British Company, The (Loughborough),
    292
Broadholm Nunnery, 106
Brocklesby Hall, 323
Bromley House Subscription Library,
    255
Brownlow, Sir John, 111
Broxholme (Li), 213
Brush (Loughborough), 312, 330, 338
Buckminster (Le), 343
bulb growing, 207, 325
Bullock, William of Norton, 162
Bulwell (N), 193, 194, 214, 225, 316
Bunny (N), 197

Burbidge, Thomas, 241
Burgh, Sir Thomas, 83
Burley (R), 63, 111, 197, 342
Burrough Court, 323
Burton Lazars (Le), 32
Burton on Trent, 5, 18, 30, 33, 46, 62,
        75, 96, 144, 149, 151, 272,
        343, 351
Butlins Holiday Camp (Skegness), 315
Butterley Company, 271, 278, 280, 281,
        339, 342
Buxton, 5, 109, 140, 219, 225, 235,
        236, 283, 344
Byng, Hon. John, 142, 195, 205, 227,
        233, 235, 237, 238, 262, 268,
        269, 273, 283, 286, 288
Byron, Lord, 195, 353

Caird, James, 203, 204, 205
Caistor (Li), 59, 141, 217, 271
Calke (D), 31, 33, 107, 111, 197, 323
Calverton (N), 35, 156, 181, 214, 326,
        336
canals, 9, 190, 262–5
Car Colston (N), 35
Carlton (N), 316
Carlton Castle, 26
Carlton in Lindrick (N), 15
Carrington (N), 225
Carrs of Sleaford, 108
carrying, 148, 195, 268, 272
Castle Bytham (Li), 35, 54, 71
Castle Donington (Le), 54, 60, 70, 177,
        221, 238–9, 324, 331
Castle of the Peak *see* Peveril Castle
castles, 25–8
Castleton (D), 5, 59, 60, 61, 66, 203
Cavendish, Sir Charles, 109
Caythorpe, 323
Chaddesden (D), 317
Chambers, J. D., 208
chantries, 107
Chapel St Leonards (Li), 315
Charley (Le), 33
Charnwood Forest, 6, 15, 20, 24, 41,
        88, 107, 114, 123, 157, 262,
        321, 328

Chartism, 295–6
Chatsworth, 109, 111, 197
cheese, 41, 122, 154, 203, 204, 272
Chellaston (D), 76, 96, 283
Chester, earls of, 26
Chesterfield, 8, 59, 62, 64, 93, 104, 132,
        133, 141, 143, 144, 145, 146,
        162, 173, 182, 183–5, 219,
        225, 233, 239, 251–2, 256,
        289, 304, 312
Chesterfield canal, 280
Chilwell (N), 122, 326
church, 29–33, 37–8, 105–7, 166–77,
        212–15, 256–8
church buildings, 15, 35–7, 85, 167,
        213–14, 257
Church Gresley (D), 31
civil wars, 165, 169–75
Clarke, J. A., 210, 212
clay, 5, 6, 283, 344
Clay Cross (D), 224, 233, 266, 329,
        335, 348
Clay Cross Company, 272, 341, 342
Claypole (Li), 217
Clayton and Shuttleworth, 292
Clayworth (N), 114, 119
Cleethorpes (Li), 140, 239, 268–9,
        314–15, 351
Clifton (N), 35, 85, 276, 316
Clifton family, 85, 175
Clifton Hall, 322
Clinton and Saye, Lord, 108
Clipsham (R), 40, 53
Clipstone (N), 336, 337
Clipstone Park, 20, 51
Clumber (N), 195, 203, 322
cloth (industry and trade), 54, 58, 64,
        66, 78, 90, 91, 94, 138
coal, 5, 9, 68, 73, 95–6, 102, 148, 150,
        151, 160–2, 185, 193, 270–2,
        276–80, 335–41
Coalville, 8, 224, 232, 233, 277, 279,
        292, 335, 338, 346, 348
Cochett, Thomas, 159
Codnor (D), 162, 279, 337
Coke, John, of Melbourne, 180
Coleorton (Le), 160, 161, 162
Coleswain, 25

colleges of education, 319
Colston Bassett (N), 66
Colwick Hall, 241
communications, 67–9, 145–51, 260–
    74, 327–31
Compton survey, 179
Coningsby (Li), 114
constables, 119
Cook, Thomas, 268
Cooper, Thomas, 208
copper, 169, 283
Corby Glen (Li), 199, 217, 320–1, 322
Corn Laws, 204, 205
coroners, 43, 86, 132
Cossall (N), 51, 68, 161
Cotes (Le), 149
Cotgrave (N), 129, 181, 336
cottagers, 44
Cottam (N), 343
cottars, 22
Cottesmore (R), 324
Cotton, Charles, 140
cotton industry, 287–9, 347
country parks, 321–2
county communities, 165–6
court leets, 116
Crich (D), 71, 283
Crick, Thomas, 291
cricket, 229
crime, 215, 240–1
Cromford (D), 163, 224, 233, 283, 287
Cromwell, Lord, 83, 87
Crowland (Li), 30, 31, 33, 85, 107, 174
Crowle (Li), 113
Croxton Abbey, 33
culture, 228–9, 235
Curzon family, 87, 182, 195

Dale Abbey, 31, 33, 106
Dallison family, 176
Danelaw, 3, 13
Darcy family, 28
Darley Abbey, 288
Darley Dale (D), 343
Darlton (N), 20
Darwin, Dr Erasmus, 229
de Aincourt, Walter, 25

de Alselin, Geoffrey, 25
de Busli, Roger, 25, 31
de Ferrers, 24
de Ghent, Gilbert, 26
de Grantmesnil, 24
de Tateshale, Robert, 26
Deeping St James (Li), 19
Deering, Charles, 144, 148, 153
Defoe, Daniel, 114, 122, 132, 134, 135,
    139, 140, 141, 146, 149, 154,
    155, 163
Denby (D), 161, 284
Denison, William, 197
Derby, 3, 5, 8, 26, 43, 53, 54, 56, 59,
    62, 67, 72, 75, 89, 93, 96,
    101–2, 132, 133, 134–5, 142,
    144, 148, 173, 177, 184, 185,
    193, 219, 224, 225, 227–32,
    239, 243, 244, 245–6, 249,
    250, 251, 252, 253, 255, 256,
    261, 274, 284, 286, 290, 292,
    303, 304, 305, 306, 309, 310–
    11, 317, 319, 325, 329, 330,
    346, 347, 351, 355–6
Derby arboretum, 250, 268
Derby silk mill, 159
Derwent, River, 59, 135, 150, 158, 288
deserted villages, 81
Devonshires, earls and dukes, 180, 182,
    184, 197, 198, 235, 237, 283
Deyncourt family, 28
Digby, Sir John, 173
Dishley (Le), 204
dissolution of the monasteries, 108
Domesday Book, 13, 15, 16, 19, 21, 25,
    46, 52, 53, 59, 61, 66, 67, 70,
    71
Donington (Li), 144
Donington Hall and Park, 195, 197, 353
drainage, 205
Dronfield (D), 219
Duffield (D), 21, 24, 26, 145
Dymoke of Scrivelsby, 108

Eakring (N), 344
Earl Shilton (Le), 291, 312, 349
East Bridgford (N), 326

East Leake (N), 193
East Midlands, 3, 5
East Midlands Association, 172
East Retford (N), 59, 60, 66, 68, 117, 133, 144, 151, 184, 219, 239, 258, 283, 306, 319
Easton Hall, 323
Eastell (Le), 342
Eastwood (N), 265, 276, 284, 331, 335
Eaton (Le), 342
Eaton Hall, 323
Ecton Hill, 283
Edensor (D), 197
Ednaston Manor, 323
education, 219–21, 253–6, 318–20
Edwards, K. C., 2
Edwinstowe (N), 35, 54, 336, 337
Egmanton (N), 344
elastic web manufacture, 290, 347–8
electricity industry, 9, 336, 343–4
Elloe (Li), 41
Elvaston Castle, 197, 322
Empingham (R), 63, 148
enclosure, 50, 127–9, 190, 200–2, 210, 221
engineering, 292, 333, 348–9
Epperstone (N), 214
Epworth (Li), 125, 213
Ermine Street, 69
estate villages, 221
Evelyn John, 134, 135
Everitt, Alan, 1, 2
Everton (N), 181
Evesham Abbey, 18
extension lectures, 255
Exton (R), 197, 342
Eyam (D), 104, 209

fairs, 61, 144, 210, 237–8
family structure, 39
Fane family, 176
Farey, John, 211, 237, 262, 274, 276, 282, 293
Farnsfield (N), 201, 214
Felkin, William, 225
fen drainage, 125, 168, 179, 205
fenlands, 6, 16, 24, 124

Fiennes, Celia, 134, 135, 138, 140, 143, 146, 155
fishing, 41, 71, 75, 314
fitz Gilbert, Baldwin, 26, 31
Fitzherbert, R., 24
Fleet (Li), 45
Flintham (N), 181, 196
Folkingham (Li), 26, 28, 83
football, 232, 352, 353
footwear industry, 291, 333, 348
Forest of the High Peak, 18
Foss Dyke, 67, 68, 69, 76, 78, 91, 92, 150, 164, 270
Fosse Way, 69
Foston (Le), 127
Fox, George, 177
framework knitting, 102, 112, 134, 141, 156–8, 164, 185, 199, 284–5, 344–7
freemen, 22, 24, 34, 43
Frieston (Li), 31, 67
Frodingham Iron Company, 282

Gainsborough, 59, 68, 71, 93, 116, 132, 133, 140, 144, 145, 148, 149, 151, 153, 167, 172, 174, 175, 181, 194, 206, 217, 225, 227, 237, 238, 253, 271, 273, 292, 312, 344, 352–3
Gainsborough, Earls of, 198
Gainsborough Old Hall, 83
Galby (Le), 47, 81, 86
gallows, 44
Gant family, 28
Garendon (Le), 32, 33, 197, 323
Gawthern, Abigail, 225, 240
Gedling (N), 276
Gell, Sir John, 173
General Strike (1926), 338
Gibralter Point (Li), 322
Gilbertines, 31
gilds, 56, 58, 59, 98
glass-making, 160
Glossop (D), 219
Goose Fair (Nottingham), 229
Gopsall (Le), 322
Gotham (N), 214, 283, 331, 344

Goxhill (Li), 82
Grace Dieu (Le), 107
granite, 6, 262, 283
Grantham, 18, 24, 43, 53, 56, 59, 63,
        64, 70, 83, 93, 132, 133, 139,
        143, 144, 148, 151, 172, 175,
        177, 206, 219, 235, 243, 263,
        267, 274, 292, 306, 312, 329,
        334, 335, 348, 353
Granville, Dr, 289
gravel working, 344
Great Easton (Le), 199
Great Exhibition (1851), 292
Great Hucklow (D), 199
Great North Road, 64, 93, 139, 147,
        185, 260, 274, 330, 331, 353
Gresley (Le), 161
Grey, Thomas, 83
Grey family, 170
Greys of Codnor, 87
Grimsby, 41, 53, 56, 59, 63, 71, 75, 93,
        131, 132, 133, 139, 140, 219,
        224, 225, 233–4, 235, 243,
        250, 254, 268, 305, 313, 314,
        331, 351
Grimsthorpe Castle, 109, 111, 174, 180,
        206
Grindleford Bridge, 146
Gunby Hall, 111
Gunthorpe (N), 117
gypsum, 5, 283, 331, 344

Hacconby (Li), 45
Halford family, 170
Hallaton (Le), 210
Hammeringham (Li), 213
Hardwick, Bess of, 109
Hardwick Hall, 109, 322
Hargreaves, James, 287
Harlaxton (Li), 197, 221, 322
Harpur-Crewe family, 197
Harshorne (Le), 162
Harston (Le), 343
Hartington (D), 62
Hartington, Lord, 182
Hartopp family, 170
Harworth (N), 336

Hasland (D), 146
Hastings family, 83, 170, 322
Hatfield Chase, 125
Heanor (D), 161, 232, 336, 337, 346
Hearth Tax, 103, 112
Heathcote, John, 290
Heckington (Li), 35
Hemington (Le), 19
Henson, Gravenor, 297
Hinckley, 8, 32, 59, 132, 141, 143, 144,
        148, 151, 156, 157, 185, 224,
        233, 237, 261, 267, 284–6,
        291, 295, 304, 312, 346
Holbeach (Li), 67, 263
Holland (Lincs), 4, 29, 52, 67, 98, 104,
        117, 177, 216, 218
Holm Hall, 110
Holme Pierrepont (N), 322, 353
Holmes, Clive, 165
Holwell (Le), 342
Holywell (Li), 45
Home Brewery Company, 197
Hope (D), 21
Hopton (D), 44
Horncastle, 122, 141, 144, 173, 194,
        238, 240, 254, 263, 271, 304
Hornsbys (Grantham), 292
horses, 122, 229
Horsley (D), 26, 28
hosiery *see* framework knitting
Hoskins, W. G., 111, 112
hospitals, 107, 232, 235
Hougham House, 174
houses, 39–40, 111–15, 210–12, 246–
        9, 288–9, 315–17
Howes of Langar, 180, 322
Hucknall (N), 194, 278, 306, 338
Hudson, George, 265
Humberstone (Le), 79, 227
hunting parks, 20, 21
Huntingdon, Earls of, 107, 118, 180,
        184
Hussey family, 107, 176
Hutchinson, John, 172
Hyson Green (N), 225, 257, 290, 307

Iliffe, William, 156

Ilkeston (D), 44, 217, 219, 223, 225, 232, 240, 249, 254, 276, 281, 284, 312, 335
Immingham (Li), 314, 329
improvement commissions, 241
industrial relations, 208–9, 279, 293–7, 306, 308–15, 327, 338–41, 346–7
industrial revolution, 9
industry, 71–6, 94–6, 154–64, 274–93, 331–49
Ingarsby (Le), 80
Ingoldmells (Li), 44, 67, 315
iron industry, 5, 58, 72, 150, 162, 185, 280–2, 329, 331, 341–3
Ironville (D), 280, 284

Jacobite rising (1745), 181, 182
Jessop, William, 263
Johnson, Richard, 37
justices of the peace, 86, 117, 118, 132, 176, 180, 215

Kedleston Hall, 195, 323
Keighton (N), 81
Kelham Hall, 196
Kesteven (Lincs), 4, 8, 19, 46, 50, 98, 200, 216
Ketsby (Li), 140, 141
Kibworth Beauchamp (Le), 176
Kibworth Harcourt (Le), 28, 40, 87
Kimberley (N), 193, 194, 331
King, Bishop, of Lincoln, 267
Kingston, Duke of, 182, 184, 196
Kingston Hall, 196
Kingston-on-Soar (N), 221
Kirby Bellars (Le), 33
Kirby Muxloe (Le), 40, 83
Kirkby-in-Ashfield (N), 277, 304, 312
Kirkstead (Li), 31
Kneesall (N), 85, 181

lace industry, 193, 290, 347
Lace Market (Nottingham), 290
Lamb, Lizzie, 270

Lambarde, William, 135
Lambley (N), 193, 326
Lancaster, Thomas of, 86
landownership, 25, 108–11, 195–9, 322–3
Langley Mill (D), 276
Langley Priory (Le), 107
Langtoft (Li), 44, 46
Lathkilldale (D), 164
Launde (Le), 32, 33
Lawrence, D. H., 341, 353
Laxton (N), 25, 27, 34–5, 37–8, 47, 48, 50, 54, 85, 112, 119, 201, 209, 320, 321, 325
Lay Subsidy Returns, 52, 67, 98, 101
le Despenser, Philip, 82
lead industry, 5, 7, 42, 49, 52, 59, 71, 73, 93, 95, 102, 150, 151, 154, 163, 185, 282–3, 331, 343
Leake (Li), 67, 104
leather industry, 58, 66, 75, 154, 155
Leavers, John, 290
Lee, Rev. William, 156, 157
Leicester, 3, 5, 8, 26, 32, 45, 53, 54, 56, 57–8, 59, 70, 72, 75, 78, 90, 96, 102, 105, 122, 131, 132, 133, 134, 144, 148, 155, 157, 174, 180, 184, 185, 193, 194, 219, 224, 225, 227–32, 241–2, 243, 244, 245, 246, 247, 249, 250, 253, 254, 255, 257, 258, 261, 284, 286, 289, 290, 291, 292, 295, 296, 302, 303, 305, 309, 316, 317–18, 319, 330, 345, 346, 347, 348, 349, 351, 355–6
Leicester Abbey, 58, 81
Leicester University, 319–20
Leighfield Forest, 15, 88, 123
Leland, John, 131, 133
Lenton (N), 144, 153, 225, 226, 307
Lenton Priory, 31, 33, 56, 58, 75, 81, 106, 108, 160
Leverton (Li), 118
Levinz, William, 182
libraries, 249, 255
limestone, 5, 6, 37, 39, 40, 283, 344
Linby (N), 35

Lincoln, 3, 6, 8, 15, 26, 30, 52, 53, 54,
      56–7, 59, 63, 67, 70, 72, 73,
      75, 76, 78, 89, 90, 96, 102,
      106, 131, 132–3, 135, 148,
      150, 151, 167, 172, 174, 175,
      177, 181, 194, 206, 217, 219,
      224, 225, 228–32, 237, 243,
      244, 246, 247, 249, 250, 252,
      253, 254, 255, 257, 261, 271,
      274–5, 292, 293, 306, 311,
      317, 319, 346, 351, 353, 355–
      6
Lincoln, Battle of, 26
Lincoln, Bishop of, 26, 30, 37, 41, 103
Lincoln Castle, 28, 43
Lincoln Cathedral, 37, 55, 56
Lincoln City F.C., 232
Lincoln Parliament (1301), 63
Lincolnshire Rising, 106
Lindsey (Lincs), 3, 18, 46, 50, 71, 98,
      218
Lindsey, Earls of, 180
Lindsey Survey, 18
Little Bytham (Li), 71
Little Casterton (R), 53
local government, 42–6, 86–8, 115–21,
      132–3, 215–19, 239–50,
      315–20, 350–1
Lockington (Le), 19
Lombe, Thomas, 136, 157, 158, 159
London Lead Company, 164
Long Bennington (Li), 111
Long Eaton (D), 224, 225, 233, 290,
      297, 306, 347
Long Whatton (Le), 19
lord lieutenancy, 116
Loughborough, 64, 103, 141, 142, 143,
      144, 148, 219, 224, 225, 232,
      233, 235, 292, 293, 295, 296,
      302, 304, 312, 318, 319, 335,
      346, 348, 351
Loughborough University, 320
Lount (Le), 161
Louth, 30, 37, 43, 53, 54, 56, 59, 61,
      93, 106, 132, 133, 141, 144,
      148, 172, 184, 194, 210, 212,
      219, 235, 237, 243, 261, 304,
      313, 330

Lowdham (N), 326
Lowe, Robert, 274
Lowe, William, 241
Luddism, 241, 285, 293
Luffenham (R), 324
Lutterworth (Le), 60, 105, 143, 144,
      148, 267, 330

Mablethorpe (Li), 67, 269, 315
Macaulay, Lord, 140
Manners, Earl, 111
manor courts, 43, 44, 133
Mansfield, 6, 8, 24, 64, 66, 117, 122,
      141, 144, 148, 184, 185, 195,
      219, 224, 225, 232, 239, 240,
      242, 252, 256, 258, 277, 286,
      289, 291, 304, 305, 306, 311–
      12, 319, 346, 347
Mansfield Woodhouse, 20, 312
manumission, 24
Manvers, Earl, 198
Market Deeping (Li), 19
market gardening, 325–6
Market Harborough, 60, 61, 64, 142,
      144, 148, 237, 267, 274, 320,
      324, 334, 335, 347
Market Rasen (Li), 235, 239, 263, 304
Market Staunton (Li), 35
markets, 60, 61–3, 93–4, 102, 140–2,
      237–9, 258
marsh, 124
Marshall, J. D., 2
marl, 6, 51
Massingberds of Ormsby, 122, 149,
      198
Matlock, 311, 319, 344
Matlock Bath (D), 235
Matlock Bridge (D), 71
Mattersey (N), 32, 33
mayors, 132
Measham (Le), 151, 161, 162, 279, 280,
      348
mechanics institutes, 255
Melbourne (D), 28, 37, 54, 62, 155,
      221, 325
Melland, Bryan, of Middleton-by-
      Youlgrave, 163

Mellish, William, 203
Melton Mowbray, 61, 62, 64, 79, 141, 144, 148, 184, 235, 237, 273, 281, 306, 320, 329, 334, 335, 338, 346, 348, 349
Messingham (Li), 210
methodism, 211, 213, 214, 256
Mickleover (D), 46
Middle Carlton (Li), 79
Middleton (D), 199
Middleton, Lord, 182, 198
Midland Agricultural College, 319
Milford (D), 288
militia, 177
milk production, 272, 325
mills, 38, 47
millstones, 73, 96, 150, 159, 283
mineral resources, 9
Misterton (N), 146
Moira (Le), 279, 280
Moira, earls of, 279
monastic foundations, 30–3, 56, 85, 106, 107
Monson, Sir John, 127, 179
Monson family, 176
Monyash (D), 35, 49
Morley Park (D), 280
Morris, Herbert (Loughborough), 292, 312, 349
Mountsorrel (Le), 59, 60, 283
Municipal Corporations Act, 243
municipal socialism, 249–50
Muskham (N), 85
Musters, John, 241

Narborough (Le), 261
Nether Haddon (D), 95
New Clipstone (N), 312
New Eagle (Li), 61
New Holland (Li), 213
New Humberstone (Le), 316
New Sleaford (Li), 59
new towns, 60
Newark, 26, 53, 64, 67, 68, 72, 75, 117, 122, 132, 133, 139, 142, 144, 148, 151, 172–4, 181, 182, 184, 195, 219, 224, 249, 256,

258, 268, 273–4, 283, 306, 312, 344, 351, 353
Newbo in Sedgbrook (Li), 31
Newbold (D), 146, 162
Newcastle, earls and dukes of, 111, 172, 173, 175, 182, 184, 198, 203, 226, 241
Newcomen engines, 161, 164, 282
Newhall (Le), 161
Newstead (N), 32, 33, 106, 107, 111, 195, 196
Nicholas, Sir Edward, 172
Noel family, 180
nonconformity, 181
Normanton (N), 201, 214
North Cadeby (Li), 79
North Collingham (N), 181
Northamptonshire, 5
Norwell (N), 114
Norwell Woodhouse (N), 20
Nottingham, 3, 5, 8, 26, 53, 54, 56, 58, 59, 62, 67, 68, 69, 70, 72, 75, 78, 90, 96, 102, 105, 112, 113, 115, 117, 122, 132, 133–4, 148, 157, 158, 173, 180, 181, 182, 184, 185, 193, 194, 216, 219, 224, 225–32, 239, 240–1, 243, 244, 246–9, 250, 251, 252, 253, 254–5, 256–7, 258, 261, 268, 270, 274, 284, 285, 286, 290, 291, 292, 293, 295, 296, 302–3, 304, 305, 306, 316, 318, 319, 325, 329, 330, 345, 347, 351, 355–6
Nottingham Boys High School, 254
Nottingham Castle, 111, 241
Nottingham Forest F.C., 232, 352, 353
Nottingham Girls High School, 255
Nottingham University, 81, 256, 258, 308, 319
Notts County F.C., 232
Nuthall (N), 193, 194

Oadby (Le), 304, 316
Oakham, 54, 62, 148, 224, 334, 335, 346
Oakthorpe (Le), 162

O'Connor, Feargus, 295, 296
oil, 9, 344
Oldcotes Hall, 109
Ollerton (N), 35, 237, 336, 337, 339,
        341, 346
open fields, 5, 47, 128
Ossington (N), 111
Overton (N), 62
Owston (Le), 32
Oxton (N), 214

Pappillon Hall, 323
Papplewick (N), 288
parish government, 119
partible inheritance, 29
Paterton (D), 79
Paxton, Joseph, 197
Paynell, Ralph, 25
Peak District, 321, 344
Peak Forest, 21
Pelhams of Brocklesby, 197
Pentrich Rebellion (1817), 241
Peterborough Abbey, 17, 30
Peveril, William, 25, 26, 58
Peveril Castle, 26, 28, 61
Pilgrimage of Grace, 106, 116
Pilton (R), 342
Pinchbeck (Li), 16, 67, 168
Pindar, George, 133
pipemaking, 3
Pinxton (N), 276, 335
placenames, 8, 20, 44
Plungar (N), 344
Pole, Ralph, 87
police, 218, 243
poor relief, 118, 212, 217, 218,
        250–3
population, 5, 16–18, 78–81, 101,
        103–5, 132, 191–5, 223–5,
        301–4, 354–6
Portland, dukes of, 196, 198, 203
pottery making, 9, 11, 15, 58, 72, 73,
        75, 284
Preston (R), 53
Priestley, J. B., 307, 309, 311, 314,
        345
prisons, 215, 216

public health, 244–6
puritanism, 168, 176

Quakers, 177
quarrying, 96
quarter sessions, 87, 117, 215

Radford (N), 122, 225, 226, 290, 307
railways, 9, 190, 265–7, 329
Ratcliffe-on-Soar (Le), 324, 331, 336,
        343
Ravensdale Park, 21
Rearsby (Le), 324
reformation, 106, 107, 166
religious houses *see* monastic
        foundations
Renishaw (D), 146, 153, 161, 329
Renishaw Company, 342
Repton (D), 15, 31, 33, 62, 67
Repton, Humphry, 197
Revesby (Li), 212
Revolt of the Field, 210, 214
Revolution (1688), 179
ridge and furrow, 49
Ripley (D), 335, 336, 337
Rippingale (Li), 40
Riseholme, 323
roads, 145–9, 260–2, 330–1, 344
Robin Hood, 19, 42, 353
Robinson, G. W. S., 1
Robinson, Sir John, 197
Rolls-Royce, 292, 311, 349
Rowarth, Mayor William, 252
Rowsley (D), 95
Ruddington (N), 35, 193, 326
Rufford (N), 30, 32, 33, 107, 109, 196,
        322, 323, 336
Ruston and Hornsby (Lincoln), 311
Rutland, earls and dukes of, 107, 108,
        173, 180, 197, 200, 204

salt, 71, 75, 78, 95
Saltfleetby (Li), 67
Salvation Army, 258
Sandiacre (N), 94, 290, 331, 347

sandstone, 6
Savile, A. W., 198
Scandinavian settlement, 15
Scarbrough, earls of, 205, 207, 269
Scrivelsby Court, 323
Scrope, Sir Gervase, 175
Scrope family, 176
Scrooby (N), 115, 167
Scunthorpe, 5, 37, 224, 232, 239, 281,
    312, 331, 333, 342, 351
Selston (N), 68, 276, 279
serfs, 22, 111
settlement, 18–22, 81–2
Shardlow (Le), 149, 217, 272, 328
Sheepbridge Company, 312, 329, 342
Sheldon (D), 49
Shelford (N), 85, 111, 173
Shepshed (Le), 19, 199, 295, 335
sheriffs, 42, 117
Sherwood Forest, 6, 7, 15, 16, 19, 75,
    123, 147, 156, 203, 322, 330,
    337
ship money, 167–8
Shipley (D), 284, 322, 336
Shireoaks, 197
shopkeepers, 145
Shore, Samuel, 197
Shrewsbury, earls of, 107, 108, 109,
    116, 153, 162
Sileby (Le), 291, 348, 349
silk industry, 286–7
Sitwell, George, 146, 153, 162
Skegby (N), 193
Skegness, 268, 269–70, 314–15, 334
slaves, 34
Sleaford (Li), 18, 26, 28, 30, 44, 45, 61,
    68, 93, 106, 144, 172, 174,
    180, 194, 238, 263, 304, 314,
    348
Smalley (D), 161
Smith's Bank (Nottingham), 158
Smythson, Robert, 109
Sneinton (N), 225, 226, 290, 307
Soar, River, 149
soils, 6
sokemen, 22, 24, 34
Somercotes (D), 146
Somerton (Li), 26

Sorocold, George, 135, 158, 159
Southwell (N), 151, 174, 217, 224, 237,
    238, 306, 312–13
Southwell Minster, 6, 30
Southwell Peculiar, 116
Spalding, 16, 26, 31, 32, 33, 54, 61, 67,
    70, 82, 117, 139, 141, 143,
    181, 216, 237, 238, 239, 325,
    326
Spencer, George, 339
Spilsby (Li), 141, 144, 237, 314
Spondon (D), 309
sport, 231–2
Spott, Wulfric, 30
Stainby (Li), 16
Stamford, 3, 8, 11, 15, 26, 28, 40, 43,
    44, 53, 54, 56, 58, 59, 63, 64,
    67, 69, 70, 72, 73, 75, 83, 89,
    90, 93, 131, 132, 133, 135,
    138–9, 143, 144, 151, 172,
    174, 177, 200, 219, 224, 235,
    243, 249, 253, 261, 263, 267,
    268, 284, 290, 306, 313, 319,
    334, 335, 353
Stamford, earls of, 180
Stanford (N), 322
Stanford Hall, 111, 323
Stanton (D), 95, 329, 341, 342
Stapleford (N), 331
Stapleford Park, 94, 111
Staunton Harold (Le), 161, 162, 195,
    197
Staveley (D), 161
Staveley Coal and Iron Company, 277,
    281, 312, 329, 335, 341, 342
steel production, 281–2, 342
Steetley (D), 37
Stenson, William, 277
Stephenson, George, 265
Stoke, Battle of, 85
Stoke Rochford, 323
Stone, Thomas, 275
Stoughton (Le), 45
Stovin, Cornelius, 207
Stow (Li), 15, 30, 41, 71
Stow Green, 144
Strelley (N), 160
Strelley family, 151, 160

Stretton (D), 162
Strutt family, 221, 250, 285, 288
Sturge, Joseph, 296
Sudbury (D), 111, 197, 221
Suffolk, Duke of, 108, 116
Sutton Bonington (N), 119
Sutton-in-Ashfield (N), 277, 304, 312,
    319, 346
Swadlincote (D), 161, 348
Swannington (Le), 20, 161, 265, 279
Swineshead, 26
Swing riots, 209
Swithland slate, 283

Taddington (D), 202
Tailbois, Ivo, 26, 31
Tapton (D), 146
Tattershall (Li), 26, 28, 38, 83
temperance movement, 258
Tennyson, Alfred, 269
Tetbury (D), 283
thatching, 114
theatres, 229, 235
Thoresby (N), 111, 195, 196, 197, 337
Thornton (Li), 40, 107
Thorold family, 176, 180
Thorpe in the Glebe (N), 79, 81
Thrumpton (N), 197
Thurgarton (N), 32, 197
Thurgarton Incorporation, 217
Thurlby-by-Bourne (Li), 35
Thurmaston (Le), 316
Tickencote (D), 37
Ticknall (D), 197, 283
Tideswell (D), 35, 148, 209
Tilton (Le), 342
timber, 71
Tirwhitt family, 176
Tissington (D), 217
Tixover (Le), 37
Toki, 26
Tollerton (N), 331
Torksey (Li), 53, 59, 68, 71, 72, 73, 75,
    92, 109, 150, 151
Torksey House, 174
Toton sidings, 329
Towle, James, 293

town clerk, 132
town houses, 102
towns, 53–67, 89–94, 131–45, 223–
    59, 304–15
trade: overseas, 52, 70–1, 233–4, 314;
    inland, 63, 67–9, 148–54,
    270–2
trade unions *see* industrial relations
tram-roads, 265
travel, 69
Trent, River, 8, 53, 67, 68, 69, 76, 102,
    139, 149, 151, 155, 164, 173,
    189, 262, 263, 271, 272, 328,
    343, 353
Trent Navigation Company, 328
Trent Polytechnic, 319, 323
Trowell (N), 161
Tunstead, de, 21
Tunstead, John, 87
Turners of Alfreton, 161
turnpike roads, 147, 159, 260–2
Tutbury Castle, 76, 96, 109
Tuxford (N), 20, 143, 219, 237
Tyrwhit of Kettleby, 108

Ulverscroft (Le), 32, 33
Union of Democratic Mineworkers,
    339, 341
Uppingham (R), 63, 143, 144, 261

Vaughan College (Leicester), 255
Venn, Daniel, 157
Vermuyden, Sir Cornelius, 125, 126,
    127, 163
Verney family, 180
Vernon family, 87
Victoria Dwellings (Nottingham), 247,
    248
villeins, 22, 24, 34, 44

Wainfleet (Li), 59, 141
Wake, Bishop, 146
Walkers of Rotherham, 197
Wallingwells (N), 32, 106
Waltham on the Wolds (Li), 141, 144

Wars of the Roses, 83
Welbeck (N), 32, 33, 107, 109, 111, 173, 195, 196, 322
Welbourne (Li), 26
Welland, River, 68
Wellow (N), 35
Wesley, Charles, 256
Wesley, John, 256
West Bridgford (N), 307, 316, 326
West Burton (N), 343
West Hallam (D), 284
West Stockwith (N), 146
West Wykeham (Li), 79
Whalley, Peniston, 176
Whetstone (Le), 335
Whitwick (Le), 162
Wigston Magna (Le), 24, 41, 47, 79, 81, 103, 105, 111, 112, 157, 199, 200, 304, 316
Wilkes, John, 161, 279
Wilkes, Joseph, 280
Willersley Castle, 195
William the Conqueror, 13, 18, 22, 25, 51, 54
Willingthorpe (Li), 59
Willmore, Tom, 214
Willoughby (N), 174, 181
Willoughbys of Eresby, 82
Willoughbys of Wollaton, 95, 108, 151, 153, 160, 161
Winceby (Li), 173
Wingerworth (D), 162
Wingerworth Company, 281
Wingfield Manor, 83, 109, 175

Winster (D), 217
Wirksworth (D), 5, 54, 59, 62, 66, 71, 83, 93, 132, 141, 283, 284, 306, 344
Witham, River, 68, 150, 263
Wiverton, 111, 173
Woodhall Spa (Li), 235, 237
Wollaton (N), 109, 110, 121, 151, 153, 160, 161
Wollaton Hall, 151, 160, 175, 316, 323
Woodborough (N), 35, 326
woodland, 15, 19
wool (trade and industry), 7, 15, 58, 59, 64, 68, 69, 70, 72, 73, 90, 92, 124, 156, 275
Wordsworth, Bishop, 250, 257
Worksop, 32, 37, 109, 143, 148, 197, 258, 306, 346, 348
Wormhill, de, 21
Worthington (Le), 162
Wragby (Li), 263
Wrangle (Li), 67, 104
Wright, Joseph, 287
Wycliffe, John, 105

Yarborough, earls of, 198
Yatestoop (D), 164
Yaxley, Parson, 176
Youlgreave (D), 73, 209
Young, Arthur, 208, 212, 262, 275, 293

Zouch, Sir John, 162